FILM THEORY:
AN INTRODUCTION

Robert Lapsley
and Michael Westlake

FILM THEORY
AN INTRODUCTION

MANCHESTER
UNIVERSITY PRESS
Manchester and New York

distributed exclusively in the USA by Palgrave

Copyright © Robert Lapsley and Michael Westlake 1998, 2006

The right of Robert Lapsley and Michael Westlake to be identified as the authors of this work has been asserted by them in accordance with the Copyright, Designs and Patents Act 1988.

First edition published 1988 by Manchester University Press

This edition published 2006 by
Manchester University Press
Oxford Road, Manchester M13 9NR, UK
and Room 400, 175 Fifth Avenue, New York, NY 10010, USA
www.manchesteruniversitypress.co.uk

Distributed exclusively in the USA by
Palgrave, 175 Fifth Avenue, New York, NY 10010, USA

Distributed exclusively in Canada by
UBC Press, University of British Columbia, 2029 West Mall,
Vancouver, BC, Canada V6T 1Z2

British Library Cataloguing-in-Publication Data
A catalogue record for this book is available from the British Library

Library of Congress Cataloging-in-Publication Data applied for

ISBN 0 7190 7375 8 *paperback*
EAN 978 0 7190 7375 5

First published 2006

14 13 12 11 10 09 08 07   10 9 8 7 6 5 4 3 2

Typeset in Gilliard
by Koinonia, Manchester
Printed in Great Britain
by Bell & Bain Ltd, Glasgow

CONTENTS

Foreword to the First Edition

'Film needs theory' said Alan Parker, 'like it needs a scratch on the negative.'[1] The supposition is not an uncommon one: directors, calling on inspiration and imagination, don't need it, and neither do audiences, who have only to watch and respond. Bring in theory, the assumption goes, and you can say goodbye to the magic of the movies.

For some twenty years serious writing on film has operated on the diametrically opposite principle that theory is inescapable, that far from being an intruder it is always already there. In watching a film the spectator is not merely a passive receptacle imbibing its meaning, but is engaged in a succession of interpretations which depend on a whole set of background beliefs and without which the film would not make sense. On the basis of such beliefs – or theories, whether formalised or not – the spectator sees faces, telephones, desert landscapes rather than patches of colour; ascribes motives to characters; judges certain actions as good and others as bad; decides that this film is realistic and that one is not; distinguishes the happy from the unhappy ending; and so on. The apparently simple act of spectating thus involves theories of representation, of human nature, of morality, of the nature of reality, of the conditions for human happiness, etc. Similarly, for the filmmaker, however self-consciously intuitive the approach, there is inevitably a comparable set of theories underlying the production of a film. For the critic, or for anyone engaged in a discussion of cinema, judgements also involve theories. For example, the suggestion that the increase in muggings can be traced to the increased incidence of violence in films involves at least a theory of signification (how meaning is produced), and one of subjectivity (how spectators are affected by texts).

Given this inescapability, film theorists have argued that the underlying assumptions and beliefs of audiences, filmmakers and critics should be rendered explicit rather than left implicit and uncriticised. Indeed, those claiming to stand outside theory are simply unaware of the theory they are using; they imagine that what is in fact but one way of thinking about cinema is the only way, thus blinding themselves to alternatives. Recent theorists have seen the social institution of cinema as too important to allow the presuppositions underlying its production and consumption to be left unexamined. Cinema has effects, and they are not always happy ones. In the words of Frank Lentricchia: 'Art is [an instrument], one of the powers that create us as sociopolitical beings'.[2] From the perspective of the politics of 1968 and after, cinema contributed to the maintenance of capitalism; from a more recent feminist perspective, it performs the same service for patriarchy. Either way, there was a need for transformation. But in order to change cinema there had first to be an understanding of it, and this is the task theorists have set themselves since the late 1960s. Not only was it necessary to demystify commonsense thinking about cinema, it was also essential to develop new, more adequate theories.

For the opponents of theory, such an endeavour was unprecedented: the uninvited guest spoiling the movie-making, movie-going party. In reality, however, there was more continuity than is sometimes supposed. Long before 1968 there was a tradition of explicit theories of film, notably those of Eisenstein, Bazin and Kracauer (though they were generally marginalised as esoteric figures, with most writers on film adopting a commonsensical aesthetic based on personal expression, realism and humanism). Nor was there anything new about a desire to analyse the social functioning of cinema, as this had been one of the two main preoccupations of writing on cinema since its beginnings. (The other was the validation of cinema as art, which, having dominated criticism up until the arrival of post-1968 theory, made an emphasis on film's social effects seem novel.) What was new was the fact that theory no longer sought accommodation with the existing criticism and aesthetics, and was not presented as an improvement or refinement of current critical practice, but was avowedly bent on its overthrow. Not evolution but revolution was on the agenda; the allegiance of the new theory was to a radical Left politics totally opposed to existing regimes, both social and intellectual. Existing critical modes were condemned as complicit with an exploitative and oppressive social order. What was also new was that theory now derived from a revolutionary set of ideas that came to be known as structuralism, and that challenged the conventional notions of history, society, signification and human subjectivity on which the prevailing criticism was based. In sweeping it aside, theory, it was anticipated, would produce knowledge where there had previously been opinion, science where there had been only ideology.

The response of the critical establishment to the arrival of theory was, not surprisingly, hostile and has largely remained so. Abuse, ridicule and summary dismissal rather than reasoned argument characterised its general tenor, a consequence in part of its issuing from the quarters under attack, but also of the seemingly formidable difficulty of the new theory, which drew on conceptual fields start-lingly unfamiliar to critics with a liberal arts background. The idea that the theory is difficult persists, even among those sympathetic to its political project. However, it is our contention that film theory is not so much difficult in itself, in the way that, say, high energy physics or the later philosophy of Wittgenstein is, but difficult because it presupposes knowledge that people encountering it do not possess. We have written this book in the light of this supposition. We have attempted, as far as the limited compass at our disposal allows, to elucidate the main conceptual precursors of contemporary film theory, to show how these were taken up and developed in order to solve a series of problems around the institution of cinema, and to sketch some of the more important arguments and debates within film studies during the past two decades.

FOREWORD TO THE SECOND EDITION

The first edition of this book was designed to provide a clear and easily accessible account of the intellectual background and some of the main themes and debates arising in a particular moment in film theory, a period which began in France in the late 1960s and then developed in Britain and the United States. Even at the time of the book's publication, the seemingly overarching synthesis that Theory – as it came to be known – had attempted to produce was already beginning to be challenged from various quarters (developments that we signalled in the Afterword to the original edition). By and large, *Film Theory* partook of the intellectual and cultural moment in film studies that it described.

Two features of this moment stand out in particular. One of these was the paramount importance of politics. In contrast to the period preceding it, what mattered was not the aesthetic quality of films but their political effectivity, and the task of the theorist was to analyse this and alert readers to it. The other dominant feature was the role of the theoretical itself: new theories were emerging which seemed to provide the resources required for political analysis. The combination of these two produced a sense of excitement and exhilaration that is hard to convey to those who did not experience it.

There were three related reasons for this heightened sense of the possibilities ahead for theorists. Firstly, a succession of dramatic new (and, as it later transpired, not so new) ideas had emerged, which seemed to turn existing thinking upside down and to herald a new dawn in which all established notions and world-views were called into question. Not least among their revolutionary implications was a new interdisciplinarity that broke down traditional boundaries between subjects and indeed brought into play new areas of thought that had either been marginalised by academic discourse (e.g. psychoanalysis) or had hitherto barely existed (e.g. semiotics).

Secondly, the new ideas appeared to have a claim on the attention of the larger public. Writing on film – leaving aside traditional popular, promotional and star-centred discourses – was no longer an arcane intellectual activity of peripheral concern to the rest of society, but became part of a larger project of social and political critique in the interests of emancipation. Film, in a word, mattered; and it mattered so much that for a time it appeared that nobody seriously concerned with cinema could ignore developments which seemed to possess both a compelling force and an unquestionable authority. Work on cinema was envisaged as having a political impact far beyond the then relatively undeveloped world of university film studies.

Finally, there was a common project, based on a recognition that Theory was incomplete and faced certain unresolved problems. Among these, one of the most pressing was that of the subject: how were subjects in the form of directors, actors or spectators to be theorised in the light of the new thinking? For if the aim was to establish how films produced their political impact, then it was necessary to have an understanding of the subjectivities on which they impacted. In general, however, there was a confidence that through a common project and community of purpose this and other problems could be resolved.

Broadly, the project aimed to provide an account of textual functioning, to explain how texts operated to produce particular ideological effects. Here the focus was less on the 'text in itself' than on the exchange between the text and spectator; art was process rather than product. While this emphasis was not entirely new, it did seem, however, that the advent of new theories could unlock doors that had previously remained shut.

In *Finnegan's Wake* Joyce writes that in stories the 'self is othered'. From a very different angle, Theory came to a similar conclusion: while watching a film, spectators are changed and hence come to perceive the world differently. What mattered, in other words, was not so much the content of the film, but the way spectators become involved in it. The theoretical aim was to explicate the terms of involvement – by, for example, considering spectators' identifications (with hero or heroine, say, or the love object, or the charismatic villain) and desires (for certain outcomes, such as the punishment of the guilty, the success of the deserving, or the union of the couple). In such ways the spectator becomes 'othered', transformed, to the extent that he or she can be said to be constituted differently or indeed reconstituted; and above all constituted so as to accept certain ideological perspectives as the truth.

The initial inspiration for this approach came from structuralism, the intellectual movement that became à la mode in France in the late 1950s and 1960s. Its impact derived in large part from its critique of the preceding intellectual fashion, existentialism. Broadly speaking, existentialism held that human beings are fundamentally free to determine what they will become. Faced with choices, we make decisions that define our being, just as the heroes and heroines of countless Hollywood films confronted by a crisis have to decide on a course of action and are defined by their decisions. Structuralism, in contrast, emphasised the importance of structures in shaping individuals. Kinship structures shape our personality; linguistic structures set limits to what we can think; ideological structures determine our political outlook; and so on. The subject for structuralism is more constituted than constituting, no longer the self-determining individual of existentialism but the effect of that into which he or she is born and lives.

Such thinking was of enormous influence for Theory, especially its early phase. Texts were perceived as pre-existing structures that shaped and constituted the spectator to believe this or that; and the task of Theory was to explain the interplay between relatively unfree spectators and relatively dominant structures. In the course of this book, we outline the various theoretical enterprises undertaken to this end and indicate something of the project's eventual fate.

Put at its simplest, Theory had two conditions of possibility: the existence of a radical emancipatory alternative and the apparent availability of a theoretical framework explaining why people subscribed to ideologies inimical to their interests. With the passage of time, it became clear that neither of these conditions obtained, and the project consequently foundered.

Let us consider these two factors in more detail. First, the politics of emancipation proved to be more complex than imagined, which led to a dissolution of the sense of a communal enterprise and robbed Theory of much of its authority. Not only did the socialism in whose name Theory had made its first advances go into a crisis from which it has yet to re-emerge, but other radical political movements also became increasingly fractured, as group after group emerged from the silencing attendant on their marginalisation to challenge existing forms of thought. Thus feminism, to cite an obvious example, though never entirely homogeneous, became less consensual by the day. Even in those areas where there was consensus, for instance in matters relating to manifest injustices, such as those pertaining to living and working conditions, the assumed leadership role for intellectuals became increasingly irrelevant. Those engaged in such struggles no longer needed, if ever they did, a theoretically formed intelligentsia to point out inequities and direct political action.

In other more contentious areas, such as those relating to the creation and formation of new modes of subjectivity or new forms of sexual relationship, theorists again had to abandon any pretensions to a leadership role as the disparate nature of the individuals in their supposed constituencies became ever more apparent. In a conjuncture where the singularity of each social group and the uniqueness of each individual was increasingly proclaimed, it became less and less plausible for theorists or intellectuals to claim to be speaking in the name of any significant social group.

This conjunction of the growing disrepute of socialist ideals and the fragmentation of feminism and other radical movements problematised Theory's commitment to critique. If there were no obviously viable radical social and political alternatives to neo-liberalism and global capitalism, on what grounds could ideological critique proceed? If no viable counter-imaginary could be envisaged, how could the existing imaginary of, say, Hollywood be criticised?

By and large most of the radical political movements became happy to seek to advance their cause within the framework of the liberal democratic state, and to make use of the ideological resources of the system, such as the notions of equity, human rights and inalienable freedoms. Faced by the supposed 'end of history' and the apparent triumph of capitalism, proponents of critique were reduced to putting the existing order in question by revealing its historical contingency in order to keep things open for an as yet unknown future, emphasising its dependence on particular conceptual approaches and the possibility of thinking otherwise. In contrast to the apparently firm grounds for critique available in the 1970s, it became a matter of arguing not on the basis of clearly established political goals but in the name of as yet unspecified forms of freedom.

In a climate where the notion of an elite vanguard group of intellectuals seeking mastery came to be seen as both impossible and undesirable, Theory's authority could only decline. What was needed was not direction from and legislation by an elite supposedly in the know, but radical democracy in which every voice could be heard in its difference.

As well as problems stemming from shifting conceptions of the political, there was the added difficulty that Theory's attempt to provide a systematic and coherent account of textual functioning largely failed. (Indeed, as its explanatory system proved to have less efficacy than imagined, it became apparent that much of what had seemed dramatically new was no more than a revisiting of Nietzsche, Heidegger and Sartre.)

Just as difference came to be foregrounded in relation to politics, so too did it register in terms of the spectatorial experience. Rather than spectators being unilaterally positioned by the text, various ethnographic studies of actual audiences were making it increasingly evident that people from different backgrounds, cultures and histories saw and interpreted films very differently. Any attempt at generalisation came to seem naïve and misguided.

Furthermore, the explanatory reach of theory fell far short of what its proponents had anticipated, in that the exchange between spectator and text proved more complex than envisaged. Two aspects of this theoretical impasse can be briefly touched upon here.

The first of these was that structuralism as a resource for explaining textual functioning was at best one-dimensional. For it proved to be impossible to develop a plausible account of the exchange between spectator and text which did not ascribe a greater degree of agency to the spectator than structuralism, with its talk of the subject as the effect of pre-existent structures, allowed. The recognition that spectators are active, deploying competences, knowledges and skills in responding to films, effectively finished off structuralism – today the term is never heard – and ushered in post-structuralism. For structuralism, if art was more process than product, it was a process constrained and controlled by the structures that pre-existed the subject. For post-structuralism, the process exceeded any structures that were in place. The emphasis in conceptualising the exchange between text and spectator consequently shifted: it was no longer seen as the effect but as an event in an open-ended process.

This shift to post-structuralism brought significant benefits. Whereas with structuralism there had always been the problem of how subjects were to escape the structure – in Theory it was held that the only exit from the textual structures of mainstream cinema was via the radical textual structures of avant-garde practice – post-structuralism suggested that no structures were stable. The subject was in process everywhere and not just while reading avant-garde texts. Change was possible because change was always already happening. No structure was finally closed or fully determinant.

Such a change of emphasis, although politically attractive, was at the same time the ruin of Theory's ambitions to formulate an all-encompassing theory of textual functioning. For if the subject is active, then she brings into play innumerable other factors drawn from her historical, social and cultural background. In consequence the inputs into the event of art become so numerous and complex that any specification of the political effectivity of a text becomes tentative in the extreme. Because the spectator is active and every spectator is different, the experience of film will in every case be singular.

This leads on to the second point, namely that certain dimensions of the spectatorial experience seemed to defeat Theory. Since Theory tended to conceive of texts as ideological operations and since what mattered were the ideological constructions thereby entailed, attention to ideology was a constant in both the Marxist and feminist moments of Theory (as indeed it has continued to be in later theoretical engagements around post-colonialism and the on-going concerns with gender and sexuality). From this perspective other aspects of the text, especially its affective component – the emotional experience of watching a film – were important only insofar as they helped enforce the ideology or, in some cases, subvert it. While it is true that in many contexts identification, analysis and contestation of that ideology is of overriding importance, there are other contexts in which all that is excluded by such ideological analyses is of greater consequence. In other words, artworks are more than mere vehicles for ideology, and Theory's commitment to the study of film as a 'specific signifying practice' missed much of what was specific to film. An obvious example would be the aesthetic dimension. Possibly one reason Theory avoided the aesthetics of film was the difficulty of discussing it. Moreover, in every text there is something other than the aesthetic, something that is inimical to systematic elaboration. Freud, for instance, had written in *The Interpretation of Dreams* of the navel of the dream, a kernel that resisted interpretation. And as Heidegger pointed out there is strife within any work between the intelligible and the unintelligible, the outcome of which is something that resists comprehension and remains inscrutable.

In his *Encyclopaedia* Hegel famously proclaimed 'the death of art'. By this, he did not mean to deny that further artworks would be produced nor that some at least of these works would be new in character. He meant rather that the self-understanding previously achieved through art had been superseded by the altogether profounder and more encompassing self-understanding possible in philosophy. Thought, for Hegel, had a deeper understanding of reality than art; it could capture both what was important in art and what art tried and failed to understand. This dream of a knowledge of art that went beyond what art itself knew was revived by Theory. Theory dreamed it would shortly know all that art knew and more besides. But as increasingly it became evident that texts resist enclosure in a single reading or theoretical model and that their workings can never be rendered entirely transparent, the prospect of a complete explanation of textual functioning faded.

So what followed from the impasse of Theory? It is this question we address in the Retrospect in this new edition of *Film Theory*. In it we try to map something of subsequent developments, outline some of the debates between conflicting and competing outlooks and indicate some directions for future work. In view of the much more extensive corpus of writing on film studies arising from the widespread establishment of film and media departments in universities, we have been obliged to adopt a more general account of Theory's legacy than we were able to provide in relation to the relatively limited corpus available at the time of the first edition. However, although necessarily less detailed, the Retrospect will, we hope, serve a similar purpose as previously in giving students a compass or map with which to chart the varied terrain of contemporary thinking about cinema.

Finally, a word on our own position. It will be evident from the Retrospect that we hesitate between approaches, not least because different contexts and moments involve different priorities and so call for different approaches and strategies. If ever there was a moment when *Screen* seemed to offer the only path, it is long gone. No single way to approach film studies exists. Indeed, given the plurality of practices that is postmodernity it is hard to see how anyone could now plausibly advance claims for the universal validity of a particular orientation while delegitimising all others.

That said, we have no truck with the notion that theory is now terminally exhausted and should be abandoned, since such a position risks forgetting one of the central arguments advanced by the proponents of Theory, namely that there is nowhere outside of theory. Like it or not, no-one can escape the requirement to theorise. For reality dictates neither the terms of its representation nor those of its conceptualisation, yet at the same time it demands that we both represent and conceptualise.

Of necessity, subjects represent themselves to themselves and to others, just as we necessarily represent external reality, including other people. Such representations are not reflections, but constructs, contingent responses. And while they may claim to represent reality truthfully and completely they never do; it is always possible to represent differently. As Slavoj Žižek emphasises, there is always an irreducible gap between the real and any form of symbolisation. Representations do not render things in themselves, any more, and more importantly, than they render others in themselves – which is why we keep on representing, talking, making films.

Equally, subjects inescapably conceptualise, in that we always try to make sense of representations, whether this be what someone is saying to us or the latest film by Wong Kar Wai. But here too the terms of intelligibility are not given: there is always a gap between what we seek to conceptualise and our conceptualisation. As with the 'aesthetic dimension' in our analysis above of works of art, the task is interminable because something always exceeds the grasp of theorising.

The idea that no theory can capture the full complexity of what is happening is summed up by Lacan's 'There is no metalanguage'. As stated, it is obvious that the aphorism is self-contradictory, since it is itself metalinguistic. But this was Lacan's point: although there is no metalanguage, we cannot but search for one. Or as Žižek puts it, human beings are destined to ask themselves questions which they cannot answer, recurrent questions about self-identity, the desire of the other, the historical contingency of each individual conscious-ness, and so on.

The challenge for theory today can be likened to what Lacan was proposing when he said that ideally psychoanalysis should be rein-vented in each session (because each analysand is unique and each session is different). The task is twofold: on the one hand to be prepared to revise and reject existing theories whose inadequacies have been demonstrated, on the other to develop new theories more appropriate to the conjuncture and forms of subjectivity currently emerging. While such new theories will never prove to be the final word, they can still be improvements on their rivals. In any case, the interminability of the generation of knowledge is no reason for defeatism or quietism. To end on a personal note, if we got into Theory because it seemed to have the answers, we remain in it because it did not.

Politics

Contemporary film theory has been indelibly marked by the political upheaval in France during 1968. Whatever the longer term consequences in other respects, recent thinking about cinema has in no small measure been formed by *les événements*. Two emphases stemmed from that moment: one, that film must be thought of in political terms; two, that theory was indispensable to the political task. The alliance of cinema and politics was by no means novel – the surrealist movement and post-war Italian realism are two earlier examples – but the resolute commitment to theory marked the post-1968 alliance as distinctive. Coming after a period associated with a belief in 'the end of ideology', when film criticism had been largely concerned with aesthetic questions, film theory now declared that all criticism was inescapably political. Critics and filmmakers, as indeed all other artists and intellectuals, could no longer, it was asserted, take refuge in an art-for-art's-sake aestheticism, but must submit their practices to the political challenge of whether they furthered or obstructed progressive social change. There was no place outside or above politics; all texts, whatever their claims to neutrality, had their ideological slant.

An early manifestation of the politicisation of film was the formation in Paris during 1968 of the significantly named Estates General of Cinema. Comprising filmmakers, technicians and critics, it provided an institutional platform for the articulation of two questions that would dominate film theory thereafter, and that would call on very considerable conceptual resources for their answers. The questions were, firstly, how does mainstream cinema contribute to maintaining the existing social structure (i.e., what is its characteristic ideological operation and what are its mechanisms?)? And secondly, what is the appropriate form for an oppositional cinema that will break the ideological hold of the mainstream and transform film from commodity to instrument of social change?

The change of direction of the then highly influential film journal *Cahiers du Cinéma* exemplifies the impact of the historical moment. From being an existentialist-cum-Catholic purveyor of American cinema, committed to a romantic theory of the artist, it suddenly became dedicated to a political analysis of its own critical activity. Its editorial group concluded that, although there was no possibility of escaping the capitalist system, they could at least refuse the role they had previously adopted and begin to subvert the system from within. Accordingly, they abandoned their existing evaluative approach as being hopelessly complicit with the dominant ideological order, turning instead to a scientific analysis of the production, distribution and reception of film. The immediate task was to establish a theoretical base on which could be assembled a body of knowledge that would challenge and ultimately change the dominant ideology. The sole criterion for judging films was the extent to which they offered resistance to the unhampered reproduction of that dominant ideology.

As with *Cahiers*, so with other film-related journals in France and elsewhere, among them, outstandingly, the British journal *Screen*, which came to dominate English-language theoretical film culture during the 1970s. Throughout there was an insistence on the indispensibility of theory, wedded to politics, for the analysis of cinema's role in the perpetuation of the social formation. To establish how cinema functioned ideologically, how meaning was produced, and how it involved the spectator, was a project that would draw on an unprecendented combination of Marxism, semiotics and psychoanalysis. At the outset of the project the single greatest influence was the Marxist philosopher Louis Althusser.

Since its beginnings, Marxism had been troubled by three problem areas that had occasioned debate among Marxists and rendered it suspect to non-Marxists. The first of these was the question of Marxism's epistemological status. Was it a science, as its founders proposed, giving objective knowledge of social reality? Or was it, as some of its adherents and most of its detractors claimed, just another ideology, conferring no special epistemological advantage, offering at best a unifying political and economic perspective?

Secondly, there was the problem of base and superstructure. In the 1859 preface to *A Contribution to the Critique of Political Economy*, Marx wrote: 'The sum total of these relations of production constitutes the economic structure of society, the real foundation on which arises a legal and political superstructure and to which correspond definite forms of social consciousness. The mode of production of material life conditions the social, political and intellectual life process in general.'[1] On a 'vulgar Marxist' or 'economist' reading this meant that everything in the superstructure was uniquely and mechanically determined by the economic base. The trouble with such an account was that superstructural diversity was either ignored or reduced to the economic, which in both cases made the explanation unsatisfactory. If, on the other hand, the superstructure was allowed a measure of autonomy, the problem then became one of deciding what, if any, determining role was left to the economic base.

Thirdly, Marxism had been constantly embarrassed by the equivocal question of ideology. Two basic, and contradictory, ways of conceiving ideology run through Marxist writings and form the background for many a theoretical, political and aesthetic dispute. The first of these, in maintaining that social being determines consciousness, promotes the position that in any social formation different classes have different and opposed ideologies. The conflict between ideologies thus reflects the material conditions and circumstances of mutually opposed classes; typically, within a capitalist formation, those of bourgeoisie and proletariat. The other, the so-called 'dominant ideology thesis', takes up Marx's suggestion in *The German Ideology* that 'the ideas of the ruling class are in every epoch the ruling ideas,' and proposes that the dominant class succeeds in instilling its ideology into all other classes.[2] Under this conception, the ideology of the subordinate class or classes, far from reflecting their social being, coincides with that of the ruling class and therefore runs counter to their own interests. By and large Western Marxists, faced by capitalism's continued survival and the failure of the proletariat to adopt revolutionary politics, had inclined to the latter conception. However, it did little to explain how petit-bourgeois intellectuals, but not the masses, could be immune to ruling class ideology.

For a while, from the mid-60s to mid-70s, the theoretical intervention of Louis Althusser appeared to have decisively settled these three problem areas. We shall examine each of his resolutions in turn.

When Althusser joined the French Communist Party after World

War II he found that politics and political considerations were crudely dominant. Political practice dictated political theory, which was held to be no more than the expression of a specifically proletarian viewpoint in opposition to bourgeois ideology. For Althusser, who saw this state of affairs as theoretically embarrassing and politically retrograde, it became a matter of winning a degree of autonomy for theory by establishing its scientific status. He proceeded not by appealing to a traditional notion of scientific knowledge as corresponding to reality, but followed Gaston Bachelard in arguing that such views rested on a naive faith in experience as a guide to truth. On the contrary, Althusser said, experience is opaque and can become knowledge only when worked on, transformed by and sited within a conceptual system. Termed 'problematics', such conceptual systems determine what questions can be asked and what problems posed, and therefore determine what answers and solutions can be given. All belief is produced within problematics. As long as a problematic is dominated by the 'practico-social' it remains ideological. Knowledge is produced only within scientific problematics, and it is guaranteed not by what lies outside of it, reality, but by its own theoretical practice. In effect, Althusser adopted a Spinozan position – that truth is its own measure. The conceptual objects produced within the problematic, while distinct from their referents, the real objects in the real world, are congruent or adequate to them, though there is no way of verifying this independently: 'Theoretical practice is. . . its own criterion and contains in itself definite protocols with which to validate the quality of its product, i.e., the criteria of scientificity of the products of scientific practice.'[3]

Marxism, said Althusser, is just such a scientific problematic, and became so following what he termed the epistemological break in Marx's writing, around 1845, when ideological notions such as alienation and human essence were replaced by concepts not given in experience, such as relations of production. The humanism of the early Marx belonged therefore to a pre-scientific problematic. Only when it took those discourses and transformed them could the break with ideology be achieved. In rejecting essentialism and humanism Marxism became a science, with its own distinct object of knowledge defined theoretically by its conceptual system.

In relation, next, to base and superstructure, Althusser considered that any straightforward economic determinism was woefully inadequate, as was borne out by the persistence of archaic superstruc-

tural formations in countries where the economic base had been transformed (most obviously the Soviet Union). What was needed was
a model of society possessing a much greater degree of what Vincent
Descombes has referred to as 'play'.[4] To this end Althusser urged a
complete break with Marxism's Hegelian heritage, which conceived
of society as a totality whose every aspect expressed a single principle
or essence. Two tendencies towards Hegelian essentialism could be
identified within contemporary Marxism. One was economism,
which held that changes in the superstructure directly mapped
changes at the level of the economic base. The other was humanism,
by which developments at every social level were seen to be expressive
of a pre-given human nature. Althusser's anti-economist, anti-
humanist Marxism broke with both.

In opposition to essentialism and the concomitant notion of expressive totality Althusser conceived of the social formation as decentred,
that is, having neither a genetic point of origin nor a teleological
point of arrival. The social formation consists of three practices or
instances, the economic, the political, and the ideological, each of
which transforms a determinate raw material by determinate means
into a determinate product. Because each has its own specificity and
effectivity, this conception represented a break with the crude base/
superstructure model. The way was therefore open for an analysis
of 'the relative autonomy of the superstructure with respect to the
base. . . [and] the reciprocal action of the superstructure on the base'.[5]
The pertinent concept here was that of society as a 'decentred structure in dominance': 'decentred', in that the economy was no longer
all-determining and allowed scope for differential developments
among the practices; 'structure', in that society, through the reciprocal
interaction of the distinct instances, was more than a composite of
events, factors or forces; and 'in dominance', in that the instances
were hierarchised, with the economic determining which of the three
should be dominant in a given mode of production (the ideological
in feudalism, the economic in capitalism) or particular historical conjuncture.

The reconciliation so effected between base and superstructure
retained an appropriate emphasis on the economic through determination in the last instance, at the same time as it did justice to the
complexity of the social formation: '. . . on the one hand determination in the last instance by the (economic) mode of production; on
the other the relative autonomy of the superstructures and their

specific autonomy.[6] However, 'from the first moment to the last, the lonely hour of the last instance never comes.'[7] Thus Althusser stopped short, but only just, of allowing full autonomy to the various instances and of sanctioning a thoroughgoing plurality of determinations.

In this view the central contradiction between capital and labour, which under capitalism took the characteristic form of class struggle ('the motor of history'), became operative only when implicated with developments within the other instances. Marx had recognised this, according to Althusser, but had lacked the conceptual apparatus to think it through. In particular he had lacked a notion of causality that could delineate the determination of the elements within the social structure by that structure, which, while present in its effects, was absent as a totality.[8] According to Althusser, neither a linear, mechanistic causality nor a Hegelian, expressive causality were adequate to the task. Some other form of causal relation was required.

In the first of his two bids to conceptualise a social structure whose elements are reciprocally determining, Althusser borrowed the concept of overdetermination from psychoanalysis. As used by Freud, this had two rather different senses, each of which Althusser took up. It signified both that a mental phenomenon, say a symptom, could be attributed to several determinations, and that it was the symbolic representation of conflicting forces, typically incompatible wishes. Hence, within the social formation any given historical moment would be overdetermined by the instances of the economic, the ideological and the political, at the same time as it represented a compromise between various social contradictions.

The stress on representation is more pronounced in Althusser's important second attempt to think the problem through by means of structural causality. Developed from Spinoza's conception of God as both creator and creation, structural causality specifies that the elements of the whole are determined by the structure of the whole. Like the Spinozan God, the structure does not stand outside its effects but is immanent within them. From the radical anti-humanism implicit in this position, it follows that history is a process without a subject. Men are no longer agents actively shaping history, either as individuals or classes, but rather are supports of the process within the structure. A clear precedent for such a view is given in the preface to the first edition of *Capital*: '. . . individuals are dealt with here in so far as they are the personifications of economic categories, the bearers [*Träger*] of particular class-relations and interests.⁹ As the bearers of positions, individuals, for Marx and Althusser, cannot be held responsible for the relations in which they are caught up. Instead they are constituted as the effects of such relations; or, as Marx put it in the *Grundrisse*, 'production not only creates an object for the subject but a subject for the object', a statement that in many ways anticipates structuralism (of which more later).¹⁰ The question of the adequacy of a conception of the subject as the bearer of a position, and more specifically whether this needs to be supplemented by some notion of agency, is something we shall return to a number of times in the course of this book when discussing the relations of the spectator to film.

As for the third problem, that of ideology, Althusser could apparently more than meet the objections raised against the dominant ideology version. The question of how Marxists themselves escaped the dominant ideology was answered by saying that historical materialism was a scientific, and therefore non-ideological, problematic, guaranteeing the quality of its knowledge. And the further question as to why the oppressed were unable to perceive their true political and economic interests was answered in terms of an elaborate and powerful account of the workings of the dominant ideology that dispenses entirely with the notion of false consciousness central to the Hegelian tradition in Marxism.

The first move was to provide a new, expanded definition of ideology as 'the imaginary relation of individuals to their real conditions of existence'.¹¹ Instead of being the generally accepted propaganda of the ruling class ideology became virtually synonymous with lived experience – less a set of representations than a relationship to the world. As 'an omni-historical reality' ideology could have no history, in that such a lived relationship would exist in all societies,¹² indispensable to social cohesion, 'an organic part of every social totality'.¹³ But it would not function in all societies to maintain the rule of the exploiters over the exploited. Under this conception, ideology did not merely reflect or represent the economic interests of the ruling class but was endowed with its own effectivity and materiality.

Drawing on the psychoanalytic theories of Jacques Lacan (to which we shall return later), Althusser explained how ideology functioned by saying that the lived relationship to the world consisted principally in the process whereby the individual was constituted as a subject. Whilst engaged in social practices each individual is addressed or

'interpellated' in various terms that confer a social identity: 'All ideology hails or interpellates concrete individuals as subjects.'[14] Individuals are addressed and constituted as subjects by pre-existing structures
and practices, though the terms of address and hence subjectivity
vary according to the social role occupied at any particular moment.
Because an individual subject always exceeds the identities assigned,
acceptance of them involves misrecognition; despite this, however,
individuals acquiesce in these identities and are precisely subjected
by them. Ideology obtains from individuals the recognition that they
really do occupy the place it designates as theirs So constituted, the
individual perceives the perspectives of ideology as self-evident truths
and experiences a world where ideology is constantly affirmed and
confirmed. Interpellation occurs primarily through ideological state
apparatuses, as Althusser called them – church, family, educational
system, trade unions, media etc. – and it is these rather than the
repressive state apparatus of police and courts that play the major
role in securing the reproduction of social relations. Through them
people gain both their sense of identity and their understanding of
reality.

In answering the critics of Marxism, Althusser's theoretical intervention had the effect of enhancing its credibility. It could now be
seen as offering, firstly, scientific knowledge; secondly, a non-reduc-
tive account of the functioning of social formation; and lastly, a theory
of ideology that acknowledged its materiality and determining force.
Althusser's advances in these three areas evoked confidence among
film theorists that at least the first of the questions posed by the
Estates General could now be answered. To begin with, there was
the prospect of a scientific understanding of the workings of cinema
that would break with the ideologically complicit, impressionistic
criticism of the past. Next, by means of relative autonomy, texts could
be related to their historical determinants. And finally, through the
notion of interpellation, the political effectivity of texts could be
explained. Cinema could thus be related to the larger historical process at the same time as it acquired a legitimacy hitherto denied it,
as a form of ideological struggle.

The film journals *Cahiers du Cinéma* and *Cinéthique* both adopted
an Althusserian Marxist perspective in the aftermath of 1968. They
were in agreement that the ideological operation of mainstream
cinema contributed to the reproduction of the capitalist system, and

that its success in so doing was a function less of content than of form. The two journals were also in agreement in calling for a revolutionary cinema that would break with the dominant ideology in respect of both form and content, and would establish a quite different relationship with its audience. But beyond this common terrain they were frequently at odds, with three areas of disagreement being of relevance to our concerns.

They differed first of all in the extent of their condemnation of the mainstream. For *Cinéthique* virtually the whole of commercial cinema did no more than offer mere pseudo-pleasures as compensation for the alienation engendered by capitalism. Under the guise of innocence, it presented the ideological perspective of the ruling class as the truth, and therefore should be condemned in its entirety. *Cahiers*, on the other hand, was inclined to take a more qualified view, which it supported with a sevenfold classification of films, only one category of which – admittedly the bulk of commercial and arthouse cinema – it condemned outright. In these category A films the dominant ideology is reproduced 'in pure and unadulterated form'.[15] They are films in which 'ideology is talking to itself', in which spectator and text are bound together in a closed circuit of illusion.[16] The remaining six categories (of which two concerning *cinéma vérité* may be subsumed within categories B and D) were to varying degrees a challenge to or disruptive of the dominant ideology. Films belonging to category B were the most highly regarded, since they attacked the dominant ideology on two fronts: form as well as content. Almost as satisfactory were films in category C, which, though not expressly political in content, achieved an effectiveness through their formal atypicality and experimentation. Category D, comprising films with an expressly oppositional political content but that made use of conventional narrative forms (such as the films of Costa-Gavras), was regarded as altogether less of a challenge to the dominant ideology. Finally, category E contained 'films which at first sight seem to belong firmly within the ideology and to be completely under its sway, but which turn out to be so only in an ambiguous manner'.[17] Though overtly reactionary in standpoint they are subject to 'an internal criticism. . . which cracks the film apart at the seams', and are therefore open to readings that will expose their inconsistencies and fissures.[18] As examples of category E, *Cahiers* cited the work of Dreyer, Rossellini and Ford, and proceeded in subsequent issues to subject a number of such films to detailed analysis, the best known example of which is John Ford's *Young Mr Lincoln* (to which we shall return in chapter 4).

A second area of dispute was over the means of relating film to the social formation. Here, *Cahiers* accused *Cinéthique* of reductionism, as exemplified by Gérard Leblanc's equation, 'Welles + Randolph Hearst + RKO = Citizen Kane = Nazism = Bazin' (Bazin was *Cahiers*' founding father), with its absence of any conception of the relative autonomy of practices as expounded by Althusser.[19]

Finally, *Cahiers* was sceptical about *Cinéthique*'s call for a thoroughgoing anti-illusionist 'materialist' cinema of opposition, to be the cinematic equivalent of Althusser's theoretical practice, providing scientific knowledge of cinema. Their proposal, *Cahiers* said, was a theoretical and practical impossibility, based equally on a misreading of Althusser and a misunderstanding of ideology. Cinema was necessarily an ideological product, and while currently an instrument of the capitalist ruling class it could in principle promote socialist ideas and values. What was at stake was who controlled it and which ideology it reproduced, not changing its epistemological status.

In reprinting the debate between *Cahiers* and *Cinéthique* the British film journal *Screen* was not merely following in the tracks of the French journals. It would, over the next few years, take up the project initiated by the questions of the Estates General and develop its own comprehensive answers to them. *Screen*'s ambitious attempt to think through the relatons of ideology, signification and the subject, drawing on semiotics and psychoanalysis as well as Althusserian Marxism, would make it 'the most important theoretical journal concerned with aesthetic discourse in Britain'.[20] In the first phase of its development *Screen*'s project was conceived in terms provided by the philosophical and methodological movement known as structuralism, which, though already utilised by *Cahiers* and *Cinéthique*, was taken considerably further by *Screen*.

The task of defining structuralism is complicated by the fact that most structuralists repudiated the label when it was applied to them. Nevertheless, a whole array of theorists in a wide variety of hitherto unrelated fields were in agreement on its basic tenets, among them that the study of humanity could be put onto a scientific footing. Although this aspect of it was short-lived, a more general structuralist orientation has persisted, and can be summed up in the single notion that the human subject is constituted by pre-given structures. In this it may be seen as the diametrical opposite of the postwar orthodoxy it replaced, namely, existentialism. Whereas for the existentialist human beings shape themselves and their lives through a series of conscious and free decisions, for the structuralist subjectivity is determined by structures such as language, family relations, cultural conventions and other social forces. The existentialist conceives of the subject as self-constituting, the structuralist conceives of the subject as constituted: the 'I think' of the one is the 'I am thought' of the other (as when Lacan writes, 'I am not a poet, but a poem. A poem that is being written, even if it looks like a subject.').[21]

Apart from Althusser, two structuralist thinkers were of prime importance for film theory: Ferdinand de Saussure, the founder of structural linguistics, and Jacques Lacan, whose contribution to psychoanalytic theory is second only to Freud's. Since we shall be returning to each of these at length in subsequent chapters, we shall here only indicate how they both emphasised the role of structures anterior to the individual subject. For Saussure, the meaning of any utterance is produced only in relation to a pre-existing system of linguistic rules (termed *langue*) that precede the individual speaking subject, who must submit to them in order to become a member of society. Lacan spelled out the way in which submission to these rules implies considerably more than simply learning and obeying the laws of grammar. Rather, it involves the very constitution of subjectivity, for it is through language that society articulates the permissible roles and identities available to the subject (and specifies others as transgressive or insane).

To the post-1968 film theorists there seemed to be a profound consonance between structuralism and Marxism. Marx's fundamental premise that the material conditions of social being determine consciousness could with little difficulty be recast in structuralist terms by substituting 'structures' for 'conditions' and 'subjectivity' for 'consciousness'. Both Marxism and structuralism rest on a conception of society as a configuration of structures and on a conception of subjectivity as constituted by being positioned by these structures. In this sense Marx could be seen as a proto-structuralist . Althusser too had an explicit debt to structuralist thinking in his adoption of Lacan for his theory of interpellation – as he was later to admit, 'the young pup called structuralism slipped between my legs'.[22] It seemed to film theorists that semiotics and psychoanalysis would remedy the deficiencies in Marxism by supplying it with a theory of language and of the construction of the subject. The investigation of film's ideological operation required knowledge both of its signifying system and its affective dimension. Saussure would provide the first, Lacan the second, and historical materialism would then be the keystone in the theoretical arch by relating signification and subjectivity to history.

The structuralist moment in film studies was centred on Althusser's notion of interpellation as a way of explaining the political functioning of the filmic text. As a pre-existing structure, the text interpellates the spectator, so constituting him or her as a subject. The idea that the subject is constituted by the text – is precisely an effect of the text – was the emergent orthodoxy in this period of film studies. Thus conceived, cinema's power lay in its ability to so position the subject that its representations were taken to be reality. But while Althusser was central to the structuralist moment, *Screen* sought to advance beyond him (just how far was to become clear only in retrospect). Like *Cahiers* before it, *Screen* invoked Saussure to provide a theory of meaning production. If, as Saussure had proposed, meaning was produced only within structures of signification, then language was constitutive, productive, had its own materiality. The materiality of language could then be related, by means of the notion of relative autonomy, to the materiality of ideology. At the same time *Screen* turned towards Lacan, already present through Althusser, as providing the potential to explain not only the structures of misrecognition attendant on interpellation, but also the all-important affective dimension of cinema: the question of pleasure.

By the late 1970s it was becoming clear that *Screen's* project for a unified theory of signification, ideology and subjectivity was unachievable, the reasons for which were both political and theoretical.

Politically, the most important developments were the eclipse of Marxism and the associated emergence of 'the new politics'. Since the reasons for the loss of faith in Marxism have been widely discussed elsewhere, we shall simply signal the contributory elements as being a growing appreciation of the failings of actually existing socialisms, a concomitant sense that socialism had yet to be invented, and a growing pessimism about whether it ever could be, given the new class configurations in advanced industrial economies.[23] In the face of these developments many on the Left felt that the traditional language of socialism had collapsed. The grand revolutionary schema of traditional class politics seemed in any case to bear little relation to the needs of those whose oppression was in the process of being articulated through 'the new politics'. The relevance of the notion of class to the struggles of, variously, women, blacks, third world liberation movements, the ecological movement and so on, was at the very least tenuous. Instead, such groups have tended to concentrate on the particularity of their own political activities, with a pragmatic emphasis on single issues and specified aims. In rejecting the revolutionary/reformist dichotomy of Marxism, they have sought to redefine the political in terms both of new strategies for struggle and new notions of what an alternative social order might be.

The loss of faith in Marxist politics had its counterpart at the theoretical level, where Althusser's rereading of Marx was coming to be seen as generating as many problems as it solved. Within film studies the waning of Althusser's influence can be attributed to the damaging effect of specific criticisms directed towards the three areas in which he had supposedly made major advances.

In respect of the first of these, epistemology, Althusser's claim to scientificity was attacked from all quarters.[24] The basic charges were that he had done little more than assert the scientificity of Marxism, and that his reasoning was in any case circular. In response to this criticism Althusser himself came to acknowledge that his attempt to establish a rigorous separation of science and ideology had been a failure. Given this admission, it was a short step to conclude, as many did, that there was only ideology, only a variety of perspectives. Thus Althusser's failure to establish the scientific credentials of Marxism helped usher in the relativism that was to be a pronounced feature of post-structuralism.

Next, the rethought base/superstructure model, which had purportedly solved the problems attendant on more primitive conceptions, was held by Althusser's critics to have failed to do so. For Levine, structural causality, the underpinning of the reconceived relations among the parts and the whole, was 'programmatic and unsubstantiated. . . a place holder rather than a developed concept', and was a means of evading the question of the hierarchy of instances in determination and its mechanism.[25] For Paul Hirst, the very notion of relative autonomy was 'inherently unstable', implying either that the political and ideological reflect the economic, in which case one is back with economism, or that there is a degree of autonomous action on the part of the former in relation to the latter, in which case there is what Hirst calls a necessary non-correspondence between base and superstructure.[26] Along with his co-authors in *Marx's 'Capital' and Capitalism Today* he designated relative autonomy, therefore, as a merely 'gestural concept' that attempted to establish an impossible position in affirming both the primacy of the economic and the irreducibility of the other instances to it.[27] Whatever acted on the economy as a determining element could not, their argument went, at the same time be wholly determined by the economy. Such criticisms were given weight by the fact that nobody – certainly nobody in film studies – successfully made use of the concepts of relative autonomy and determination in the last instance to theorise the relations between the levels of the social formation.[28]

The third aspect of Althusser's reworking of Marxism, namely, his theory of ideology, also came in for extensive criticism. Paul Hirst argued that Althusser, for all his polemic against the notion of ideology as false consciousness, had in fact failed to break with it. Ideology's representations were still at root misrepresentations obscuring the reality of capitalist exploitation. Even more damaging was the criticism he levelled at Althusser's notion of interpellation. His argument may be simply expressed: if ideology functions by constituting individuals as subjects through interpellation, which involves misrecognition, then it can only do so by virtue of there being a pre-existing subject who can misrecognise him or herself. In short, the notion of interpellation assumes what it aims to explain.[29]

Althusser's own retraction of many of his central ideas, including the autonomy of theory, the epistemological break, and the ISAs (ideological state apparatuses) hypothesis, in response to these criticisms only contributed to the waning of his influence. But for the *Screen* project, the single most damaging element of Hirst's critique, one that would prove to have far-reaching implications for film theory, was his attack on the notion of interpellation. In effect, it was to dislodge the foundation stone of the theoretical edifice *Screen* was attempting to construct. For Hirst's argument pointed to a dimension of Althusser's work that the first generation of Althusserians (not least those working in film theory) had tended to ignore, namely, its reliance on a notion of agency.

The central anti-humanist tone of Althusser's work represented an attempt to eliminate the humanist notion of the subject as a self-conscious, autonomous being whose actions could be explained in terms of beliefs, intentions, preferences and the rest. Dismissing all such 'philosophical twaddle about man' he proposed instead that subjects are the supports of their functions and places in the social formation.[30] Under this conception the subject's beliefs, intentions, and so forth, are the effect, not the cause, of social practices. However, as effects, they are nonetheless needed to explain, among other things, the working of ideology, since the mechanism whereby subjects are constituted as the effects of pre-given structures – interpellation – requires that subjects possess certain skills and capacities. Foremost among these attributes of agency is the capacity to understand, judge and, above all, interpret. But if this is the case, then the possibility must be allowed that contradictions within the social formation may be such that the individual can resist the process of interpellation, either through desires and preferences weighing against it, or through beliefs that may enable the subject to reflect on the process and reject it. Endowed with skills and capacities, then, subjects are able variously to reject the identitites assigned, perceive supposed truths as fallacious, and formulate alternatives. These very real possibilities of resistance – as history frequently testifies – show that ISAs are effective only in varying degrees and not, as the thrust of Althusser's account might suggest, invariably successful.[31]

As has been suggested in a recent re-evaluation of Althusser's Marxism, he was himself very much alive to these issues, recognising both that there were oppositional ideologies present within the social formation and that such oppositional forces determined the nature and effectiveness of the ISAs, which were therefore never conflict-free, but, rather, a site of struggle.[32] However, those taking up Althusser's conception of ideology within film theory were slow to appreciate these aspects of his work, a failure that resulted in fatal flaws in early attempts to theorise the relation of the spectator to film. By bringing together interpellation with a Saussurean concept of language as possessing its own productivity, film theory assessed the ideological effectivity of texts on the basis of their internal structure alone. The text itself was invested with causal powers, univocally determining the response of the spectator. But once it was allowed that the subject could be agent as well as effect, and that the subject's response could be determined by forces elsewhere in the social formation, then it followed that the text was not the sole determinant of the mode of its reception. (We shall return to this all-important topic at various points throughout the book).

The theoretical critique of Marxism was not confined to Althusser's formulations, but extended to the classic doctrines of Marx himself. The attack on Marxism by Paul Hirst and his collaborator Barry Hindess came from the unlikely direction of epistemology. Their argument derived from two sources within structuralism: Althusser's concept of the problematic on the one hand, and the post-Saussurean idea of discourse as constitutive on the other. (The first was by far the more important.) For Althusser, it will be recalled, knowledge is not given by experience but is produced within discourses organised by a scientific problematic. These discourses produce conceptual objects that are logically distinct from any real object in the world, and are validated by criteria internal to theoretical practice. Where Hindess and Hirst parted company with Althusser was over his contention that these conceptual objects are 'adequate to' objects in the real world. For them, since all meaning and hence all conceptual objects are produced within discourse, the 'objects of discourse exist only in and through the forms of discourse in which they are specified'.[33] While there was no denial of the actual existence of an extra-discursive realm, there was, however, no question of a discourse being validated by its correspondence to the real since the only specification of the real was within discourse.

Called into question by this turn of thinking is that most central of modern philosophy's projects, epistemology, with its concern to provide general principles for the validation and invalidation of propositions and discourses. According to Hindess and Hirst, epistemology typically proceeds by positing that there is at once a distinction and a correlation between the two realms of discourse and of external reality. These realms are distinct in that objects exist prior to and independently of discourse; and they are correlated in that certain forms of discourse are held to correspond to objective reality. The question as to whether or not a particular discourse is to be judged as accurately representing or reflecting reality is answered by reference to a certain privileged discourse, whose special status allows it to specify the terms for access to or accurate representation of the real. Such a privileged discourse, which in one form or other is common to all epistemologies, thus functions as the standard against which all other claims to truth are to be tested. For empiricism, it is a discourse designating experience and its givens – sense data, observations, fact. For rationalism, it is a discourse in which certain privileged concepts give the essence of the real. In both cases truth is a matter of compatibility and falsehood a matter of incompatibility with the privileging discourse. But in both cases, Hindess and Hirst argued, epistemology's privileging of one discourse or another is grounded in nothing beyond dogmatism. Since the only access to the real is through discourse, then no one discourse can be privileged by establishing its correspondence to the real, and hence no act of privileging on such grounds is warranted. Rationalism, for example, has no grounds for granting certain concepts immunity from further criticism and questioning.

It was here that the target shifted from epistemology to Marxism, in that it rested on a rationalist privileging of certain concepts, among them that of society as 'a totality with a necessary structure, composed of certain "instances" in definite relationships' and that of the economy as determining in the last instance.[34] Because of the unwarranted privileging of such concepts, Marxism had come to obstruct rather than assist in the analysis of society. Hindess and Hirst proposed abandoning each of the above-mentioned dogmas, and argued that the analysis of particular social practices and institutions would be better conducted in terms of their conditions of existence. While every social practice has its conditions of existence within the social formation, it neither secures those conditions through its own action nor determines the form they take. From this it follows that they cannot be specified in advance by a general theory (unless the claim of rationalism to give the essence of the real is conceded). Each political, cultural and ideological practice, though related to other practices, has its own conditions of existence and its own autonomy. In particular the economic is relieved of the determining primacy it has within Marxism.

While the arguments of Hindess and Hirst were not universally accepted – Terry Lovell within film theory, and Terry Eagleton and Fredric Jameson in areas related to it, all retained an explicit allegiance to Marxism – their critique was welcomed by many of those active within 'the new politics', who saw it as clearing the ground for and legitimating a theorisation of modes of oppression neglected by historical materialism. Its influence on film theory was pervasive (viz. Paul Abbott in *Screen* in 1979: 'The difficulty for the conceptualisation of politics is that a politics cannot be provided by a *general* theory. . .') if not always acknowledged.[35]

There was a similarly warm reception amongst the proponents of the new politics for the parallel intellectual developments in France, where structuralism had been superseded by post-structuralism. However, there were differences between British and French post-structuralism, of which the most important was the far greater eclipse of Marxism in France, associated with the rise of the *nouvelles philosophes* – to the extent that Paris could reasonably be designated 'the capital of intellectual reaction'.[36] Behind the much publicised pronouncements of the new philosophers on the gulag and the indissociablity of 'terror' from any totalising theory, especially Marxism, there stood, however, a far more substantial body of thought associated with Foucault, Derrida and Lyotard, which has subsequently come to be known as 'post-structuralism'. These three very different thinkers were united in their distrust of projects like Althusser's, which attempted to provide a totalising metalanguage yielding the truth. Indeed, if post-structuralism can be reduced to a phrase, it is that there can never be a metalanguage encompassing and explaining all other discourses. This theme will be expanded in later chapters, where we shall consider the work of Derrida and Lyotard; for the moment we shall concentrate on Michel Foucault, a figure who in the last decade has provided the political underpinning of film theory as decisively as Althusser did in the aftermath of 1968.

If Marx was a precursor of structuralism, the same may be said of Nietzsche in relation to post-structuralism. His ideas certainly bear on, and are a good way of approaching, the work of Foucault. Nietzsche was a complex, not to say contradictory, thinker, opposed to all forms of systematisation. He conceived of reality as having neither end nor purpose, being but a directionless play of opposed forces, a flux of events – the product of what he termed 'the will to power'. This primordial, yet divided and conflictual striving underlies the transient configurations of society. Because the world is in a constant state of change, of becoming, there can be no truths, but only perspectives: each individual, constituted by the multiplicity of forces, interprets reality from the standpoint of his or her own needs or interests. Facts are always interpretations; the search for truth is an endless succession of changing interpretations; truth is what it is advantageous or useful to believe; and there are as many truths as there are perspectives. Since 'we cannot see around our corner' we are inevitably caught up in a prison-house of language.[37] We have no choice but to think in language, 'a mobile army of metaphors, metonymies, anthropomorphisms. . . [which] come to be thought of. . . as fixed, binding and canonical'.[38]

Foucault's thinking, like Nietzsche's, is perpectivist; even more so in that it does not offer an ontology. So although, in a Nietzschean vein, he wrote of society as 'a multiple and mobile field of force relations, wherein far-reaching but never completely stable effects of domination are achieved' and placed the emphasis on events rather than things, Foucault nonetheless did not offer a global theory of society.[39] Indeed, for Foucault no such totalising theory is possible, for there are as many conceptions of society as there are perspectives on it. Thus when, contra Marxism, he argued that society has no centre or determining principle, but is instead a dispersed plurality of practices, and that history has no single motor such as the class struggle, but is, rather, an ensemble of power relations producing a succession of different forms of subjugation and domination, he was not counterposing the truth to falsehood, but simply offering one perspective in preference to another. As with Nietzsche, there are no facts, only interpretations, and there is no interpretation that is not part of the social process. There is, therefore, no vantage point outside or above the play of power. Every perspective, Foucault maintained, is embodied in a discourse, and each discourse produces a different version of reality, specifying equally what is defined as objectively the case and what is to count as true and false. As with Nietzsche and Saussure, language does not reflect reality but is constitutive of it; or rather it produces realities, since for Foucault there is no single reality.

For our purposes three features of discourse are of prime importance. Firstly, discourses are historically contingent. Much of Foucault's endeavour has been to show that what appears to be self-evidently the case is constructed within historically specific discourses (he gave emphasis to the approach by adopting the Nietzschean term 'genealogy': hence his dictum that 'man is a recent invention.')[40] Secondly, discourses are involved in relations of power. Any relation of domination entails a correlated field of knowledge, and vice versa; hence discourse itself becomes 'the thing for which and by which there is struggle'.[41] For example, madness and sexuality are not givens, but are constructed within discourses whose manner of construction produces effects of domination and subjection. It was as a consequence of a particular discourse concerning madness that asylums were established, and of a discourse on sexuality that certain prohibitions were instituted. Any one discourse is counterposed to and silences others. Thirdly, it is not only the realm of objects that is constituted within discourse, but so too is the subject. By defining, classifying and categorising, different discourses institute different modes of subjection: 'The individual' Foucault wrote, 'is not the *vis à vis* of power; it is, I believe, one of its prime effects.'[42]

Though superficially Foucault's work on madness, prisons, sexuality and medicine had little bearing on cinema, it proved attractive to many film theorists, since film as 'an instance of discursive practice' was necessarily implicated in power relations.[43] The questions of the Estates General were still on the agenda, and Foucault's concern with signification, subjectivity and power could be assimilated to the continuing analysis of films in terms of their political effectivity. (Whose interest do they serve? What relations of domination do they help maintain?) Moreover, such analyses could still be conducted in terms that respected the specific materiality of cinema. For although Foucault was critical of both semiotics and psychoanalysis, his work shared certain points of emphasis with each of them. Like the Saussureans he saw representations as productive of meaning, and so could be taken up in order to elaborate the post-1968 commonplace that a film's political effectivity resided less in what it represented than in how it did so. Thus from Foucauldian standpoint, Teresa de Lauretis wrote of cinema as 'a set of regulated procedures, mechanisms and techniques of reality control'.[44] Analysis would then call into question the reality so constructed, showing that its representations were historically contingent and that the mode of representation had effects of domination and subjection through its implication in power relations. Like Lacan too, Foucault conceived of the subject as a social construction, not an anthropological given. Thus cinema as discourse assigns identities and particular modes of subjection; it is a strategy 'operating a kind of policing of places and identifications available to the subject'.[45] More specifically, it was possible to apply Foucault's idea of sexuality as produced by discourse to cinema, which could be seen as exemplifying 'the deployment of sexuality by its endless investigations and confessions, its revealing and concealing. . . its mechanisms of capture and seduction, confrontation and mutual reinforcement.'[46] Here, as with other varieties of subjection through discourse, the analysis of the discursive operations as arbitrary and historically contingent would open up the alternative of other discursive forms, ones offering different perspectives and different modes of subjectivity.

While much of this evidently recapitulated the earlier Althusserian concern with ideological demystification – the two approaches were equally opposed to essentialism and in agreement that subjectivity was constituted – there were also divergences stemming from the perception that Foucault had avoided the pitfalls of Althusser. Foucault never claimed scientific status for his work, thinking of it instead solely as one strategy conceived from within relations of power. Rather in the manner of those who saw 1968 as 'la prise de la parole', Foucault's remark that 'the intellectual discovered that the masses no longer need[ed] him to gain knowledge', could not have been in greater contrast to the Althusserian understanding of les événements as evidence of the need for a theoretical vanguard.[47] Further-more, his genealogical approach made no attempt to account for the historical determinations of discourses or to systematise their mutual relations, thereby effectively bypassing the problems attendant on base and superstructure. Nor did he need to explain, as did Althusser, how subjects came to be duped by ideology about the nature of reality, since reality as much as the subject was constituted within discourse.

Further aspects of his work recommended themselves to those com-mitted to the new politics. According to the Marxist conception, power was located in the state, and therefore always negative and repressive. By contrast, Foucault conceived of it as multiple, omnipre-sent and enabling, the result of the plural relations of the social field. He drew attention to modes of repression other than those associated with state repression and the 'extraction of surplus value'. Such think-ing was of particular relevance to modes of oppression that turned on subjection, for instance, through a demand to conform to a stereotype, something that had obvious bearing on film, where the practice of representation plays an important role in assigning iden-tities through norms. The other side of Foucault's conception of power, its positive aspect, is the ever-present possibility of resistance ('We're never trapped by power: it's always possible to modify its hold.'), which recommended itself to those in the new politics who felt that the dominant ideology thesis had ruled out resistance.[48]

Despite these perceived merits, there were a number of problems associated with Foucault, especially as regards his applicability to film. Indeed, his successful avoidance of many of the difficulties encoun-tered by Althusser was purchased at a price. The general absence of explanation as to how discourses and regimes of power came about could be seen as a serious deficiency, especially for those schooled in the Marxist belief that understanding is a precondition for actively producing change. More specifically, while his analyses of discourse had obvious relevance to discourses around cinema (notably those about authorship and realism, in which contexts he will recur in later chapters), the relation of his thought to the cinematic experience was less clear. Because cinema is not a single discourse like those on sexuality or madness, but is, rather, a site for discursive conflict, it is neither institutionalised as knowledge nor is its relation to other discourses easily specifiable. Furthermore, while Foucault's work established that conceptions of the subject were produced within discourse and that these conceptions functioned to constitute the subject, he gave no account of that process of constitution. There was nothing in his work comparable to Althusser's theory of interpellation, and therefore it could not be used, as Althusser's had been, to give an account of the exchange between spectator and film.

The absence of anything analogous to interpellation occasioned a divide within post-structuralist film theory. There were, on the one hand, those deeming necessary the development of a theory specifying the mechanism of the constitution of the subject, if any account of film's political functioning was to be given. They turned to psychoanalysis. On the other hand there were those who saw psychoanalysis as problematic (not least because of Foucault's criticisms) and believed that the all-important political tasks of analysing and evaluating film had no need for any mechanism relating spectator to text. Their refusal aligned them with Foucault, in whose work they saw an explanation of the existing distribution of power and forms of subjection and as opening up the possibility of transforming them. For them, nothing more was needed.

The broad shift of film theory from structuralism to post-structuralism occasioned fewer differences and discontinuities than might be supposed. Despite the shift in conceptual terminology, the emphasis remained theoretical; and despite the eclipse of Marxism and the rise of the new politics, there was a continued commitment to oppositional politics. What did change was the attitude towards 'grand theory', which was now held to be inappropriate to the strategic requirements of the new politics. But by and large the questions remained centred on signification, subjectivity and history. The stress was still on representations: how they are related to the moments of their production and reception, how they bear on political and cultural struggles, how they are constructed within systems of signification, and how they function to constitute subjectivity. If the aspirations of theory were more modest and its bearing on politics expressed in more pragmatic terms, there was also a greater confidence in the possibility of achieving political goals, albeit not those of classically conceived revolution. Emblematic and in the vanguard of the new politics was the women's movement.

During the past decade the politics of gender has effectively displaced the politics of class within film theory. The impetus for this shift came from the resurgence of the women's movement in the late 1960s, when, in addition to such longer-standing concerns as women's economic exploitation, political exclusion and cultural disadvantaging, questions of feminine identity and of the representation of women were perceived to be of central importance. As a consequence, cinema, concerned as it is with representation and identity, has been seen as playing a vital role in maintaining the oppression of women. As the first editorial of *Camera Obscura* put it: 'Women are oppressed not only economically and politically, but also in the very forms of reasoning, signifying and symbolical exchange of our culture. The cinema is a privileged place for an examination of this kind in its unique conjuncture of political, economic and cultural modes.'[49] More specifically, cinema was important because 'it has been at the level of the image that the violence of sexism and capitalism has been experienced.'[50]

The early 1970s saw a number of developments around women's engagement with cinema that heralded the coming hegemony of feminism within film studies. In 1973 two books were published denouncing sexist representations of women in films: Molly Haskell's *From Reverence to Rape* and Marjorie Rosen's *Popcorn Venus*.[51] Around the same time the first feminist film journals appeared, including the influential *Camera Obscura*, and in the already existing journals an increasing proportion of articles were concerned with the representation of women. At the other end of the cinematic spectrum, women filmmakers working outside the established framework of production and distribution had their films exhibited and acclaimed, often at conferences and festivals on women and film, which were also beginning during this period. At all points, then, within the institution of cinema – production, consumption, criticism – women's voices were beginning to be heard.

At this stage the emphasis was on consciousness-raising: increasing women's awareness of what was at stake in cinema. The overall aim was to expose the misrepresentations of dominant cinema and to prepare the way for an alternative, distinctively feminist film culture. There were a number of different, yet related aspects of this consciousness-raising stage.

It included, first of all, a denunciation of the greater part of Hollywood's output (of all the media, Hollywood earned the greatest opprobrium) as mystificatory and manipulative in relation to women. As Claire Johnston commented, 'despite the enormous emphasis placed upon woman as spectacle in the cinema, woman as woman is largely absent.'[52] Or as Sharon Smith put it, in the first issue of *Women and Film*, 'women in any fully human form have almost completely been left out of film'.[53] That is, women appeared only as objects of the male voyeuristic gaze or as patriarchally defined stereotypes.

While the bulk of Hollywood was thereby damned, there was a small proportion of its films that had women as protagonists, in particular those such as *Klute, Julia, Girlfriends, An Unmarried Woman* and *Alice Doesn't Live Here Any More*, made to some extent in response to women's criticisms of the mainstream. The debate around these films, then, was a second aspect of this stage, and it turned on whether they broke with existing stereotypes and contributed to a redefinition of femininity. While some argued that they contained genuinely progressive elements, others saw them as merely part of a process of recuperating the gains of the women's movement so as to perpetuate the status quo.

A third aspect of this period was the recovery of a lost history of women's filmmaking in various capacities – as writers, editors and above all as directors. This was paralleled by a condemnation of the industry for its near-total domination by men in these crucial productive sectors. As well as bearing on demands for a greater involvement of women in cultural production, this disinterment of an ignored dimension of cinema was a way of restoring a history and an image of which women had been deprived by male domination. In general, the results of such research, despite the recovery of women directors (in Hollywood, Dorothy Arzner and Ida Lupino) and of neglected feminist classics like Germaine Dulac's *The Smiling Mme Beudet* (1933) and Leontine Sagan's *Maedchen in Uniform* (1931), presented however 'a particularly depressing picture of discrimination and marginalisation'.[54] There was, finally, in order to counteract the prevailing misrepresentation and exclusion, a call for a cinema which would break with received notions of femininity and depict women truthfully. By expressing the hitherto invisible reality of women's experience and by representing the true desires of women, such a cinema would 'create a discourse, a voice, a place for [women] as subject'.[55] Films of this kind (of which *The Life and Times of Rosie the Rivetter* was one of the most lauded) giving positive, undistorted images of women to displace the existing stereotypes, were then used in the context of women's groups as a contribution to the active struggle against oppression.

The impact of this first consciousness-raising stage was extensive, and its value is affirmed by the continuance of its various aspects up to the present. Nevertheless, by the mid-1970s, in the light of the film theory developments associated with structuralism, many women felt a growing dissatisfaction with the assumptions on which much of feminist film theory proceeded. The most fundamental reproach was that it proceeded either explicitly or implicitly on the basis of a presumed feminine essence that had been repressed under patriarchy and that it was the task of the women's movement to emancipate from its state of alienation. This essentialist tendency was most marked in the assumption that women possessed an inbuilt knowledge of true femininity with which to judge the authenticity of filmic representations of women, and in its corollary that any film made by a woman was ipso facto feminist. If, as structuralists argued, subjects were constituted by pre-existing social and signifying structures, these assumptions were untenable. Nor indeed did they seem desirable, for the idea of a fixed, immutable essence could be all too easily assimilated to a vision of a fixed – and patriarchal – natural order. Much more useful was a conception of femininity as a construct, one that theory could enable women to understand and hence change. Principal among the sites for this social construction of female identity was cinema itself; change this, and you would produce new modes of subjectivity.

More specifically, structuralism opened the way to a more theoretically informed analysis of film's ideological operation. Thus Claire Johnston: 'Women's cinema should not only concern itself with substituting positive female protagonists, focussing on women's problems, etc.: it has to go much further than this if it is to impinge on consciousness. It requires a revolutionary strategy which can only be based on an analysis of how film operates as a medium within a specific cultural system.'[56] Changing consciousness, in other words, was possible only on an understanding of what consciousness was and how it was formed. Accordingly, the same structuralist amalgam of historical materialism, semiotics and psychoanalysis that had been developed by predominantly male theorists within a Marxist perspective was now redeployed by feminists.

So, while some feminists continued to place their trust in experience, there were others who, drawing upon Althusser, argued that experience was complicit with ideology and provided no reliable guidance either in criticising mainstream cinema or in developing an alternative. A radical, theoretical break was needed, they said, in order to found a feminist cinema. Furthermore, Althusser's notion of relative autonomy offered a way, it seemed, of locating patriarchal ideology in a determinate social and historical context, thereby improving on the sometimes simplistic reflectionist formulations that were current (e.g. 'That there are fewer films about strong and independent women today than there were in the 1940s is attributable in the US to a capitalism in decline'.[57]) As well as supporting the view that film is embedded in society in a complex and mediated way, Althusser's retheorisation of the social formation with its emphasis on the effectivity of ideology was in any case welcome to those women socialists who had remained unconvinced that their oppression was explicable or their emancipation attainable at a strictly economic level. From Saussure, the idea that meaning was produced only within signifying systems gave support to a new insistence that film was not the mere transmitter of existing ideology but was in itself productive of it. And lastly, a conception of the spectator, drawn from Althusser and Lacan, as constituted as a subject in watching a film seemed a more satisfactory explanation of the reproduction of patriarchal ideology than that of false consciousness, with its implication that Hollywood had successfully duped women audiences. It had been obvious enough that the ideological operation of cinema depended on its affective dimension, on the relation established between film and spectator at the level of pleasure and desire. After all, for Hollywood the women's film was precisely the 'weepie', moving women to tears.[58] Many women now believed that psychoanalysis provided a way of accounting more precisely and insightfully for the modes of subjectivity produced by cinema.

The adoption of these theories transformed the study of film by women. The questions of the Estates General – that of dominant cinema's ideological operation and that of the appropriate form of an oppositional cinema – were recast in terms of the dominance of patriarchy and feminist opposition, and answered by means of the concepts of structuralism. In relation to the first question, Hollywood's ideological operation had to be seen not as the simple misrepresentation of women but as the production of particular meanings. Films could no longer be evaluated solely on the basis of their 'truth' about women, since form as well as content determined their effectivity. Instead, attention had to be paid, firstly, to the mode of production of meaning (because of the absence of meaning prior to signification), and, secondly, to the ways in which modes of signification implicated the subject in the text. There was, thereby, a displacement of concern 'from "images of" to the axis of vision itself – to the modes of organising vision and hearing which result in the production of that "image"'.[59] In this women were using a theory of cinema's ideological functioning comparable to that conceived by *Screen*: i.e., cinema's system of representation 'tries to fix the spectator in a specific closed relationship to the film';[60] and 'the subject of cinema is actually formed with the processes of language and representation'.[61]

A representative instance of this approach was Elizabeth Cowie's reading of *Coma*.[62] The film's central figure, Susan Wheeler, had been seen by some critics as exactly the sort of heroine demanded by feminists: an independent woman with a career (as a surgeon), who is active in the narrative: initiating actions, discovering the truth and resourcefully overcoming dangers. Such a reading, said Cowie, ignored the cinematic codes at work in the film, in particular in relation to the genres on which it drew: the detective film and the suspense film. In respect of the former, the film contradicts the conventions of the genre in that, unlike the male heroes of classic Hollywood, Susan as detective is not always the bearer of knowledge. Susan's position is better understood within the conventions of the suspense film, where the protagonist is perceived as a victim, beset by dangers of which she remains unaware and of which the audience has knowledge. Given these narrative structures, it becomes more difficult, Cowie argued, to maintain that the film is a progressive text.

The theoretical approach also made it evident that the Hollywood product was more differentiated than had been previously allowed. By means of 'the active reading' appropriate to *Cahiers*' category E, both individual films and complete genres could be reread as progressive and/or subversive. One such reading 'against the grain' was that offered by Claire Johnston of *Dance Girl Dance*, directed by

Dorothy Arzner. The film traces the career of aspiring ballet dancer Judy O'Brien, who is forced to enter a vaudeville act where she is spectacle rather than artist. At first sight the film would appear to belong unproblematically to a familiar subgenre in which the showbiz background is a pretext for the display of women as spectacle. But it performs an act of internal self-criticism, 'cracking open the entire fabric of the film and exposing the workings of ideology in the construction of the stereotype of woman.'[63] One night Judy turns in fury on her male audience and for once returns their gaze as she tells them how she sees them, thus shattering the sense of mastery and security they have enjoyed. The moment is as much one of attack on the audience in the cinema watching the film as it is on the audience within the diegesis (the 'world' of the fiction). Though the break is immediately recuperated by having the diegetic audience break into enthusiastic applause, thus putting the disruptive female discourse once again into the arena of spectacle, the moment is nonetheless one in which, albeit briefly, the ideology of patriarchy has been discomforted and put in crisis. Through it the supposedly happy ending of Judy swooningly accepting the offer of marriage from the man who has just addressed her as 'silly child' is rendered deeply ironic. Patriarchy's victory is at best hollow. The ending exposes the anomalies inherent in her position, notably the contradiction 'between women's desire for self-expression. . . and the cultural processes which articulate a place for woman as spectacle'.[64]

Among genres, melodrama, which had hitherto been vilified as trading in the most demeaning stereotypes of women, could now be perceived as subversive. Its characteristic inability to contain the various contradictions it sought to manage resulted in incoherent and fissured texts, thereby exposing rather than concealing the oppression of patriarchy. Similarly, film noir could be seen in terms of a return of the repressed: 'Despite the ritual punishment of acts of transgression, the vitality with which these acts are endowed produces an excess of meaning which cannot finally be contained.'[65] Attempts such as these to reclaim lost genres did not pass unquestioned, however. Janet Bergstrom commented on classical cinema's capacity to efface the traces of disruption: its powers of containment should not be underestimated.[66] Judith Mayne doubted that the supposed contradictions of these genres could be clearly differentiated from the tensions inherent in any narrative form – rather than exceptions to the rules of classical cinema, they were the enactment of them.[67] In relation specifically to melodrama, Laura Mulvey suspected that its contradictions were not discernible only through an active reading, but comprised its overt content. The genre functioned to rechannel the energies associated with those contradictions, thereby acting as 'a safety valve for ideological contradictions centred on sex and the family'.[68] In its favour, Mulvey allowed that even the simple fact of acknowledging the explosive potential sexual difference within the family was of considerable aesthetic importance.

The second consequence of the impact of structuralism on feminist thinking was in relation to oppositional cinema. It resulted here in the advocacy of avant-garde filmic practice: a truly progressive cinema would need to break with all existing modes of representation. Such an approach was in contrast to the style adopted during the conscious-ness-raising stage, when it had been assumed that 'the camera by its very nature and the good intentions of its operator [could] grasp essential truths and by registering typical shared experiences [could] create political unity through the process of identification'.[69] Under the influence of Saussurean ideas, it was now argued that an alterna-tive cinema had above all to be, not an unproblematic realist mode of representation, but self-reflexive, so as to draw attention to the work of the film and the relation between it and the spectator. The existing cinematic language was indelibly complicit with the domin-ant ideology; the camera was not innocent; film could never be trans-parent; there could be no successful challenge to the patriarchal order couched in the prevailing structures of thought and representation. As Laura Mulvey asked: 'If you're engaged in cultural struggle out of oppression, where cultural marginality has been one hallmark of that oppression and the language of high culture seems riddled with male domination, how can you – given all this – speak?'[70] The answer was, through a radical avant-garde cinema, exemplified by the work of, among others, Chantal Akerman, Yvonne Rainer, Marguerite Duras, and Sally Potter.

The first, structuralist theoretical moment in feminist film criticism has more recently been superseded, as it became apparent that the promise of overarching theory – what we have termed the *Screen* project – was unfulfillable. The influence of Althusser, in particular, was short-lived. Althusserian theory had never enjoyed the authority in the women's movement that it had elsewhere. The movement was far from monolithic, and many women remained unconvinced of the necessity of theory at all, let alone that which was the preserve of an intellectual élite. The fact that advances had been made without it, and that there was nothing in the women's movement comparable to the Leninism that was a feature of the post-1968 theoretical moment, inclined women to be sceptical about the political indispensability of Althusser's 'theoretical practice'. Furthermore, Marxism's neglect of the social consequences of sexual division was well established, and therefore, when the Althusserian project encountered the problems we have discussed earlier in the chapter, women were quick to abandon it. Put schematically, gender and class appeared to be two quite different axes of exploitation and oppression, with the former no less important than the latter. With regard to psychoanalysis, there was in some quarters an even greater suspicion, since its practice was designated as coercive in the direction of a passive femininity, and its theory, centring on castration and the phallus, as implacably sexist.

For those women more sympathetic to theory, the collapse of the Althusserian project has eventuated in a diverging of the ways. Some women have inclined towards a post-structuralist stance, accepting that there is no possibility of a final word, no encompassing meta-discourse, and have tended to use theory in a pragmatic, eclectic fashion, predominantly in devising new modes of thought and hence of social being. In embracing the open-endedness of post-structuralism there was frequent recourse to the thinking of Derrida, Lyotard and especially Foucault, with his concern for the relations among discourse, power and sexuality, and his emphasis on the possibility of resistance. Thus, for example, Kaplan wrote: 'Discourses cannot simply control/ contain all within their compass, so that gaps open up through which change can take place. The gaps, that is, permit points of resistance which enable new articulations, which, in turn, begin to work on and to alter the dominant discourse.'[71]

More generally there was a refusal to repeat the totalising tendency of the post-1968 political moment. Instead there was a stress on heterogeneity against the homogeneity of theoretical totalisation, on difference against sameness. It was in fact in rethinking and re-evaluating the concept of difference, specifically sexual difference, that the post-structuralist disposition was most evident. Whereas an earlier generation of feminists had perceived sexual difference as sustaining male dominance, and had therefore sought to annul it and the discursive categories associated with it, there was now a call for the 'delineation and specification of difference as liberating, as offering the only

possibility of radical change.[72] Under a patriarchal regime of difference women had been conceived as absence, lack, negativity; but
from a post-structuralist perspective such terms only stigmatised
within a context of Western, phallocentric discourse that valorised
identity, unity and presence. In a deconstructive move, feminists
could seize and re-evaluate the tokens of the feminine 'as the under-
side, the repressed of a classical or rational/conceptual discourse. . .
[as] aligned with the heterogeneity which always threatens to disrupt
systems of signification'.[73] Indeed the feminine could be identified
with difference itself, keeping everything on the move and preventing
the ossification into fixed categories of traditionally conceived
masculine and feminine.

Other women have, on the contrary, seen the present situation as
something of an impasse, and have attributed this to the anti-essentialism common to both structuralism and post-structuralism. The
problem with the anti-essentialist position is that if femininity is not
given but constructed within signification and cultural processes then
there can be no place outside from which to pass judgement on them.
Condemned therefore to a Nietzschean perspectivism, women can
offer an indictment or critique of patriarchy only on the grounds of
some kind of aesthetic preference. Thus Christine Gledhill, writing
in 1984: 'We seem trapped. However we try to cast our potential
feminine identifications, all available positions are already constructed
from the place of the potential other so as to repress our "real" difference. Thus the unspoken remains unknown, and the speakable
reproduces what we know, patriarchal reality.'[74] And Aimee Rankin,
in 1987 writes: 'How can one challenge terms of representation from
within its very practice? How can alternative or oppositional meanings be articulated, except through existing discourses, which already
embody in their structuring principles the ideological reproduction
of the culture they serve?'[75]

Given this situation many women have concluded that 'the risk
of essence' is one they are prepared to take.[76] However, since the
debate between essentialism and anti-essentialism turns on the problem of psychoanalysis, we shall postpone further discussion of it until
chapter 3.

CHAPTER 2

Semiotics

Of the several components of post-1968 film studies, it was semiotics, or what was presumed to be semiotics, that most provoked the film criticism establishment. Semiotics and semioticians were denounced in the pages of quality dailies and weeklies: semiotics was 'a procrustean enterprise', comparable to 'painting by numbers', at once 'unwittingly absurd' and 'insidiously political', practised by 'possessed sectarians', 'pod-people', and 'overdressed ladies bedecked in bangles and baubles', whose general demeanour had 'the poised vigilance of a lobotomised ferret'.[1] The outcry seems inappropriate to Saussure's original proposal for a theory of signs:

A science that studies the life of signs within society is therefore conceivable. . . I shall call it semiology (from the Greek *semeion*, sign). Semiology would show what constitutes signs, what laws govern them. Since the science does not yet exist, no one can say what it would be; but it has a right to existence, a place staked out in advance.[2]

Thus stated, semiology, or semiotics, as it became more generally called, is hardly very threatening. What rattled the critics were the claims made on behalf of a semiotics of cinema, which amounted, if they were to be believed, to a notice of redundancy for those engaged in conventional criticism.

A semiotics so conceived heralded the end of all traditional aesthetics. Ideas of art as organic unity, as revelation, as the communication of inspired vision, were discarded and replaced by the supposition that all meanings and aesthetic effects were explicable in terms of determining structures and mechanisms. Art, in a word, was open to scientific analysis. In providing 'a scientific basis for aesthetic judgements in the cinema', semiotics, it was argued, would mark the end of critical impressionism.[3] No longer would notes jotted down during a single screening, worked up in a literary style and larded with cultural references, suffice as criticism. Moreover, it was believed that the semiotic project would contribute to the political cause of demystification, of denaturalising representations and exposing them as constructed precisely of signs. The very fact of trying to forge a scientific semiotics would, Metz proposed, 'bring with it a great capacity for demystification, an irreversible break with impressionistic and idealist discourses and all claims for the ineffable'.[4] Although there is no reason to suppose that Saussure himself had anything so radical in mind, his proposal for a science of signs could manifestly be given such an interpretation, and to this extent the rancour of the critical establishment was not misdirected.

Despite his call for a semiotics, Saussure's actual achievement pertained to the more limited field of natural language, the science of which – linguistics – he is commonly held to be the founder. Even so, he committed none of his discoveries to paper, leaving it to his students to reconstruct his theories from lecture notes after his death. Such, however, has been the impact of his thought, it can be said 'we are all Saussureans now'.[5]

In view of the many admirable summaries of Saussure's work we shall limit our account to the broadest of outlines. The first important point to make is that Saussure broke with previous approaches to the study of language in asking not how it developed but how it works. Philology had been content to trace the evolution of a word or sound over the centuries; Saussure sought to explain how that word, that sound produced meaning. The essence of the explanation he gave – and this is the second crucial piont – is that meaning exists only within a system. In contrast to the naive view that language acquires its meaning by reference to a world of things anterior to, or independent of, signification, Saussure argued that meaning derives solely from the system within which particular utterances are articulated. The system, known as *langue*, and actual or potential utterances, *parole*, may be compared to the rule system of chess and to the set of moves that may be actually or potentially played. *Langue* defines both what are permissible or impermissible utterances (as do the rules of chess in relation to moves) and what their significance is (again, as in chess).

In explicating the functioning of language as a system Saussure distinguished between the signifier and the signified, which together comprise the linguistic sign (typically a word). The signifier is the actual sound (or if written, the appearance) of the word; the signified is the concept or meaning attached to it. The relationship between the two is arbitrary, since there is nothing in the nature of things to dictate that a signified should have a particular signifier – the same signified has different signifiers in different languages. But more than that, Saussure claimed, the value of a signifier is given not by its relation to a pre-given signified but by its relation to other signifiers, a concept perhaps best explained once again by analogy with chess. If the meaning of a signifier is analogous to the value of a piece on a chessboard, then it becomes evident that meaning will change according to context in the same way that the value of, say, a pawn will depend on what stage of the game has been reached, where it is in relation to other pawns, how many pieces are left on the board, and so on. In other words meaning is produced by a system of differences. Such differences may be specified in relation to two basic axes, the paradigmatic (or axis of selection) and the syntagmatic (or axis of combination). The former pertains to potential substitutes for any element in the signifying chain: the substitution of 'h' for 'c' in the word 'cat', or the substitution of 'television' for 'mat' in the sentence 'The cat sat on the mat'. The latter axis, the syntagmatic, runs as it were horizontally from one signifying element to the next, and pertains to the way meaning is established by the combination of any given element with other elements in the signifying chain. The meaning of an element is therefore determined by its relation both to the present set of elements it is in combination with and to the absent set of elements that could be substituted for it. The essential point is, as Saussure put it, 'in language there are only differences'.[6] This so-called 'diacritical' theory of meaning was to prove the single most influential idea operative within film semiotics.

Other approaches to semiotics in addition to Saussure's were taken up as being of possibly greater relevance to film studies, the principal among which was that developed by the American philosopher C. S. Peirce around the turn of the century. It was his philosophical rather than linguistic investigations that took him in the direction of what he called 'semiotic', specifically through a concern with symbols, which he saw as the 'woof and warp' of all thought and scientific research.

The Peircean sign points in two directions: on the one hand towards the person to whom it is addressed and in whose mind it creates an idea or secondary sign, called the interpretant, and on the other towards that which it stands for, called the object. A sign thus mediates between object and interpretant, entities that would otherwise be unrelated. Very roughly the object is equivalent to what another discourse terms the referent, the thing in the real world that the sign stands for, except that in Peirce, as has been pointed out by Silverman, the status of the real is unclear.[7] Though at times Peirce maintains that there is direct experience of reality, elsewhere he argues that it can be known only through representations, so that objects are simply representations whose validity is consensually established. This latter position tends towards a Nietzschean perspectivism, as when Peirce writes 'My language is the sum total of myself; for the man is the thought.'[8] In any case, the interpretant is the idea produced in the mind of the intepreter by the sign, and is not dissimilar to Saussure's signified. Yet for Peirce this too is a sign, with its own interpretant, which in turn is a sign with its interpretant, and so on – opening up a prospect of what post-structuralists would call unlimited semiosis.

Depending on whether they are considered from the standpoint of the mediating sign, or that of the object, or that of the interpretant, signs can be classified into different trichotomies, only the second of which has been taken up by film theory and therefore need concern us here. The relevant classification, then, based on the relationship of signs to their object, is that of icon, index and symbol.

For a sign to be an icon it must have some physical quality or configuration of qualities that it shares with the object. As Peirce puts it, 'Anything whatever, be it a quality, existent individual or law, is an icon of anything, insofar as it is like that thing and is used as a sign of it'.[9] Resemblance, then, is the basis of iconicity. Examples of icons would be representational paintings, diagrams, statues, photographs and onomatopoeic words. Next, an index is a sign that becomes so 'by virtue of a character which it could not have if its object did not exist', irrespective of whether it is interpreted as a sign.[10] Another way of putting it is to say there is necessarily a causal relationship between object and index, so the sign is the effect of the object. Just about any calibrated instrument, such as a barometer, thermometer, speedometer or ammeter, functions as an index of what it is measuring; as also does smoke of fire, a weathercock of wind direction, a knock on the door of a visitor or pain of physical damage. Indeed, it is through a continual reading off of indexical meanings that one is able to make sense of the world at all. Lastly, a symbol is arbitrarily linked to its object 'by means of an association of ideas or habitual connection'.[11] With neither resemblance nor causal relation between sign and object, the basis for signification must be convention, and therefore most natural language and languages parasitic on it, like morse code, as well as the codes of gesture (to some extent) and dress, consist of symbols. It should also be noted that a sign may fall into more than one category. The photograph, for instance, as was pointed out by Peirce, is both icon, in that it is similar to its object, and index, in that it is an effect on photographic emulsion of light interacting with the object.

At various times during the last two decades Peirce's ideas have been taken up by film theorists, though they have never been as influential as Saussure's. The best known adoption of Peirce was by Peter Wollen in his widely read and cited *Signs and Meanings in the Cinema*, in which he pointed out that cinema operates with all three categories of sign: index (by virtue of being the effect of the photographed real), icon (through sound and image) and symbol (in that it uses speech and writing). He berated other theorists, for example Metz, for having concentrated on only one of these dimensions to the exclusion of the others. More recently, Kaja Silverman has shown that Peirce enables distinctions to be made that are unavailable to Saussure, notably that whereas the relation of linguistic signifiers to their signifieds is preponderantly symbolic, the specific components of film, such as photography, editing, lighting and so on, are weighted equally towards the iconic and the indexical.[12] Because of cinema's typically greater involvement with these latter, it has been argued elsewhere, there is less of an apparent gap between the sign and its object than there is with symbols, which explains cinema's capacity to naturalise the most blatant stereotypes.[13] Peirce's ideas have also recently been taken up by Gilles Deleuze and Teresa de Lauretis, and in view of this renewed interest they may play a more prominent role for film studies in the future.[14]

By and large, however, the film semiotics of the late 1960s and early 1970s was derived from Saussure. One reason for this dominance is almost certainly to be found in the line from film theory's political underpinning to the thesis that stressed language's status as cultural production and thence to any position, such as Saussure's, in which language was dependent on societal convention. Such a position was at least consistent with the claim – requirement, even – that language did not mirror but constructed the work, and was therefore inevitably complicit with ideology. Both the notion that meaning is produced within a signifying system and that the relationship between signifier and signified is arbitrary could be squared with the idea of a language as social product. This conception of language as a cultural system interposed between human beings and the real world was to receive further powerful support from the work of Lacan.

Two aspects of Lacan's thinking on language were to be crucial for film theory. The first of these was a Nietzschean conception of language as constitutive: 'the world of words. . . creates the world of things';[15] 'things only signify within the symbolic order'; 'nothing makes sense until you put a sign on it'.[16] The idea that neither words nor images transmitted neutrally a pre-given reality, but offered a perspective through which reality was constituted, is readily traceable to Nietzsche. According to Nietzsche, language coerces us into thinking in particular ways through categories that remain largely unconscious. Language, as he famously expressed it, secretes a mythology. By substituting 'ideology' for 'mythology' one gets exactly what film theorists took up from Lacan's reading of Saussure; that film is a language appearing to render the real transparently but actually secreting an ideology. The task therefore was to create a new language, enabling men and women to think what had previously been unthinkable.

The second aspect was Lacan's conception of meaning as produced in the exchange between subject and a set of signifiers. Here Lacan modified Saussure's idea of the linguistic sign by giving primacy to the signifier and by introducing a bar between signifier and signified (thus, $\frac{S}{s}$, where S is the signifier and s the signified), implying that there is a continual sliding of signifieds under signifiers as these enter into new relationships. In other words, meaning is not at all the stable relationship between signifier and signified presumed by Saussure. What stops the slide and momentarily fixes meaning is the punctuation of the signifying chain by the action of the subject, expressed by Lacan in the graph below.[17] In this illustration the vector SS' represents the signifying chain and the vector $\triangle S$ represents the retroactive construction of meaning by the subject. Meaning is always

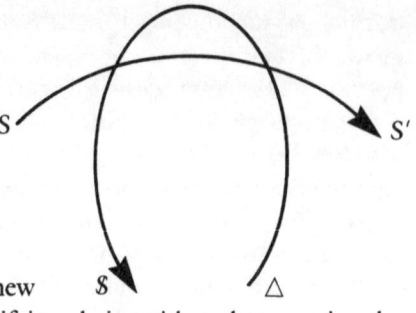

provisional and changes as new
elements are added to the signifying chain, with each successive element setting up expectations as to what will follow and retroactively
changing the meaning of what precedes it. Thus meaning is produced
by the subject in this process of punctuation; but, equally, the subject
is produced by the meanings available in the signifying chain, for
the subject is such by virtue of a self-conception that is only available
within discourse. The desire of the subject engenders varying
interpretations of the unfolding text; the text offers in return the
condition of subjectivity. For Lacan there is, therefore, an unceasing
dialectic of the subject and meaning, an idea that would recur in
various guises within film theory.

The overriding question for any semiotics of cinema was first and
foremost, is cinema a language? It was generally agreed that the answer to this hinged on whether cinema directly imitated, or was
analogous to, or was, in a Bazinian sense, an extension of reality; or
whether it was a form of writing, dependent on an arbitrary and
conventional sign system.

   The question was answered by the pioneering film semiotician
Christian Metz with an equivocal 'yes and no'. Yes, it was a language,
but no, it was a language without a *langue*, where *langue* is understood in a Saussurean sense as 'a system of signs intended for inter-
communication'.[18] Like Saussure in relation to natural language, Metz
wanted to achieve an understanding of how films are understood,
but he recognised fundamental differences between language and
cinema that prevented the wholesale importation of Saussure's concepts. The concept of *langue* was inapplicable to cinema for three
basic reasons. The first of these was that cinema is not available for
inter-communication; if it is communication at all (rather than
expression), it is one-way communication. Next, the filmic image is
quite unlike the Saussurean sign, with its arbitrary relation between

signifier and signified, and instead, in its reproduction of the conditions of perception, can be termed 'a block of reality': 'The cinema
has as its primary material a body of fragments of the real world,
mediated through their mechanical duplication.'[19] Whereas a verbal
signifier acquires its significance from its place within a system, that
of an image derives from what it duplicates. Moreover, as well as
resemblance there is a material link between the image and its object,
making it index as well as icon, and therefore motivated. However,
there were qualifications even in Metz's early work, as when he
acknowledged that an image necessarily involves distortion and deformation. Later, this idea was developed through the identification of
codes at work in the image. Despite such qualifications, the general
tenor of the argument was that cinema duplicated rather than articulated reality.

The third reason for refusing cinema the status of *langue* was that
it lacks the double articulation that, according to André Martinet
and other linguisticians, is the hallmark of natural language. The
characteristic economy of language, through which an infinity of
utterances can be generated by means of a very small number of basic
units, is achieved through this double articulation. At the level of
the first articulation a limited number of words (more properly morphemes, the lexicon of any language) are combined in different orders
to provide a limitless number of utterances. But a still greater
economy is permitted through a second articulation, by which morphemes are made up of a very much smaller number of phonemes,
these being the smallest distinctive units of a language. These are
without meaning in themselves, but systematised on the basis of
phonological properties to produce consequential differences – in
English that, say, between 'l' and 'r'. Cinema lacks this second articulation; it has nothing corresponding to phonemes. The most obvious
candidate would be the shot, except that, unlike the phoneme, which
by itself is without meaning, the shot possesses a meaning. But nor,
contended Metz, is the shot the equivalent of the single word. A
number of reasons are offered for this contention: shots, like statements but unlike words, are infinite in number; they do not pre-exist
in a lexicon, but are to an extent the invention of the filmmaker (as
statements are of the speaker). Moreover, the shot is a unit of discourse ('The image of a house does not signify "House" but "Here
is a house".') and its meaning is not given by a system of paradigmatic
contrasts, i.e., it is not determined by the absent units that could

take its place.[20] Metz concluded that the shot is more like a statement than a word, but even here the resemblance is limited in that a statement is reducible to discrete elements, the morphemes and phonemes, in a way that the shot is not.

If cinema is not *langue*, it is nonetheless language, at least 'to the extent that it orders signifying elements within ordered arrangements different from those of spoken idioms – and to the extent that these elements are not traced on the perceptual configuration of reality itself (which does not tell stories)'.[21] Cinema transforms the world into discourse, and is not therefore simple duplication. But a semiotics of the cinema cannot work at the level of the image, since each image is unique, novel and analogous to reality, with its meaning produced not by its place within a system but by what it duplicates. There is no process of selection from a lexicon of images in cinema as there is from the verbal lexicon of a natural language.

It was because of this paradigmatic poverty that Metz was led to explore the semiotics of cinema in terms of syntagmatic relations. Combination, not selection, was to be the key to its understanding. While the image might not be coded the narrative certainly was, and since cinema consisted predominantly of narrative, and indeed, since its historical development had produced a number of recognisable narrative forms and structures, it was appropriate that a semiotics of cinema should concentrate on the spatio-temporal logic of narrative. Metz's so-called *grande syntagmatique* was an attempt to provide an exhaustive classification of the segmentation of cinematic narratives.[22] Arranged in a hierarchy from the autonomous shot, the smallest segment, to the sequence, the largest segment, the system of classification would permit any film's narrative syntax to be formalised. The decisive element of the classification is the so-called autonomous segment, of which the most obvious example would be the temporally continuous scene. Thus hierarchisation in terms of length and complexity is what constitutes the classification. In all there are eight levels within the hierarchy, and Metz approached their arrangement through a series of either/or disjunctions. For instance: did the segment consist of one or more than one shot? If more than one, was the segment chronological or achronological? If chronological, was it simultaneous or sequential? – and so on. The resultant hierarchy of autonomous segments runs as follows:

1) the autonomous shot, which is of two kinds, either the sequence shot, where a whole scene is contained within a single shot, or the insert, for instance a subjective image within a larger segment

2) the parallel syntagm, as occurs when two motifs are interwoven in a montage in which their temporal or spatial relationship is unspecified

3) the bracketing syntagm, a montage of brief shots representative of, say, a situation or way of life

4) the descriptive syntagm, in which a series of shots comprise a composite description of a single moment

5) the alternating syntagm, which runs together two sequences in alternate shots, each with its own temporal development yet as a whole implying simultaneity, as in just about any chase sequence with shots of pursuers and pursued

6) the scene, in which a succession of shots implies temporal continuity

7) the episodic sequence, where there is an organised discontinuity of shots

8) the ordinary sequence, where the discontinuity is simply the omission of moments judged unimportant.

By way of illustration of its categories and to show the application of the method Metz proceeded to analyse the film *Adieu Philippine*, which remains the *locus classicus* of the *grande syntagmatique*.[23]

While the rigour of the *grande syntagmatique* still commands respect – David Bordwell having recently termed it 'the outstanding achievement' in the study of cinematic narrative structure – film theorists by and large have found little application for it.[24] One case study that did make use of it was John Ellis's analysis of Ealing, in which he showed that some two thirds of *Passport to Pimlico* consists of segments respecting a unity of time and place (scenes, ordinary sequences, and autonomous shots), a syntactic arrangement that contributed to the film's realism. Even Ellis, however, found there were inadequacies in Metz's classificatory scheme, a feeling that was echoed by other commentators. It was found, for example, that certain of the categories, such as that of the autonomous shot, were so broad as to include such a diversity of cinematic forms that they were of little demarcatory use. Another difficulty was deciding in which particular category any given segment should be located – a scene and an ordinary sequence are often hard to distinguish. There was also the more general question as to what is to count as an autonomous segment, something that in practice can often only be settled on the basis of a reading of the film, thereby introducing a semantic element into what was conceived as a purely syntactic exercise. It was further found that many films, especially those out of the run of the mainstream, contained passages that did not fit neatly into any of Metz's categories. Consequently there was a tendency among theorists when analysing films to segment them in terms other than those given through the *grande syntagmatique*, viz. the textual readings performed by Heath and by Bellour. Even without these various difficulties there existed a still more serious charge against the *grande syntagmatique*, namely, that it pointed towards an arid formalism that could neither account for film's specific production of meaning nor satisfy the political demand that its mechanisms for the reproduction of ideology be exposed.

Metz's revised semiotics was at once more complex and more flexible than this early model.[25] While retaining the concept of cinema as a language he abandoned the attempt to locate a specific set of rules underlying the articulation of each cinematic text. Instead he came to treat cinema and the cinematic text as fields of signification in which a heterogeneity of codes, some specific to the cinema and others not, interacted with one another in ways that were specific, systematic and determinate at certain specified levels of cinematic discourse (individual films, particular genres) and hence at certain specified levels of analysis. Among specifically cinematic codes he distinguished codes of editing and framing, of lighting, of colour versus black and white, of the articulation of sound and movement, of composition, and so on. Non-cinematic codes included costume, gesture, dialogue, characterisation and facial expression. A further important distinction was made between cinematic codes and cinematic sub-codes, where the former organise elements potentially or actually common to all films, say lighting, and the latter refer to specific choices made within a particular code, say that of low-key in preference to high-key lighting. Codes, therefore, do not conflict, whereas sub-codes do, it being a matter of one choice rather than another. Different codes and their sub-codes are in a syntagmatic relation of combination; sub-codes from the same code are in a paradigmatic relation of substitution. The codes of genre and authorship are additive, as in the Westerns of Ford or the comedies of Hawks; but the sub-codes Ford and Hawks within the code of authorship, and the sub-codes Western and comedy within the code of genre, are (generally speaking) only commutable. A cinematic code is often defined predominantly by the meanings of its sub-codes, a weighting that contrasts with the codic stability of natural language. Cinematic codes may be seen as consisting of signifiers awaiting the signifieds that come from their mobilisation in sub-codes. For example, the general significance of the code of authorship cannot be grasped outside of the specific operation of the sub-codes Ford, Hawks and the rest.

The film semiotics propounded by the novelist and film director Pier Paolo Pasolini was utterly different in inspiration and conception from that of Metz, being the theoretical corollary of the uncompromisingly anti-bourgeois realism of his films. While he agreed with Metz that cinema has no *langue*, it was for a very different reason. For Pasolini 'the cinema is a language which expresses reality with reality. So the question is: what is the difference between the cinema and reality? Practically none.' In addition to this, he stated: 'When I make a film. . . there is no symbolic or conventional filter between me and reality, as there is in literature.'[26]

Where Pasolini parted company with Metz was in his contention that cinema is a language with a double articulation, albeit one quite distinct from that of natural language. Cinema's smallest units, corresponding to phonemes, are, according to Pasolini, objects, actions or events that are unaltered by being reproduced on film. Termed 'cinemes', these possess their own meaning, one that is natural rather than conventional, and are combined into larger units – shots – that are the basic significant units of cinema and correspond to morphemes in natural language. It is through this second articulation, the selection and combination of objects and events from the real world (the so-called 'profilmic – that which is in front of the camera), that the cinema is able to articulate reality. As distinct from phonemes, however, cinemes are both infinite, or at least countless, and have the feature that they are, as it were, compulsory: 'we cannot but choose from among the cinemes that are there, that is to say, the objects, forms and events of reality which we can grasp with our senses'.[27]

Yet another approach to cine-semiotics was offered by Umberto Eco, who was critical of both Pasolini and Metz. Pasolini came in for criticism on a number of grounds, among them his conception of reality and his thesis that the objects and events of the real world, quite outside any cultural code, provide the primary constituents of cinematic discourse. Far from being presented with reality in the cinema, Eco argued, we are presented with signifiers subject to cultural codes through which they are read as signifieds. Where Pasolini perceived nature, Eco detected culture. Events, actions, objects, forms of human interaction such as gesture, far from having the supposed extra-cultural rawness Pasolini imagined, are inextricably imbricated with convention, code, system and, by extension, ideology. Pasolini's error was in effect to conflate signifier, signified and referent under the rubric of reality. A second criticism was that the analogy between cinemes and phonemes did not stand up, because phonemes only have meaning in combination, not in themselves, whereas cinemes, in being recognisable objects, do have meaning in themselves. And the further supposed equivalence between the shot and the morpheme was also open to question. Like Metz, Eco suggested that the shot was much closer to an utterance than to a single word. A shot of Sylvester Stallone naked to the waist firing a rocket launcher does not signify 'Rambo', but rather 'Here is Rambo', or more probably 'Here is Rambo single-handedly defeating the Evil Empire'.

Eco also criticised Metz along similar lines. He, too, had failed to appreciate the extent to which images were not mere simulacra or duplicates of reality, and therefore non-arbitrary and motivated, but were indeed the habitat of codes. Metz's assumption of this irreducible primacy of the image, analogous to reality, had supported his conception of cinema as a language without a *langue* and had led to a concentration on how images are combined in syntagmatic structures. Eco contended that, far from inhabiting a domain below the level of codic organisation, images owe their very existence to the workings of cultural codes, of which no fewer than ten are potentially operative in the communication of the image: codes of perception, codes of transmission, codes of recognition, tonal codes, iconic codes, iconographic codes, codes of taste and sensibility, rhetorical codes, stylistic codes and codes of the unconscious.

Eco's contention can be illustrated by considering just one theme, that of the cultural training necessary in order to perceive a similarity between a physical object and an iconic representation of it. Because the physical properties of the two are very different, and therefore give rise to different perceptual experiences, similarity can only be perceived as a result of a cultural background that both includes a knowledge of the conventions of, say, painting and has specified what should be regarded as pertinent in determining similarity. For instance, a single line image of a horse's profile relies on a cultural decision that it shall count as an image and as such requires a trained eye to see it as a horse's profile. In other words, 'similitude is produced and must be learned'.[28] Indeed, the history of the visual arts abounds with examples of works that to us seem self-evidently realistic but confounded their contemporaries because they transgressed the conventions of the time. Even (and from the standpoint of a cine-semiotics, especially) the photographic image, seemingly so analogous to reality, requires training to be recognised.

From the above it will have become apparent that Eco's principal quarrel with both Pasolini and Metz was their too narrow delimitation of the bounds of the cultural. In fact Eco's declared aim was to explain every case of signification 'in terms of underlying systems of elements mutually correlated by one or more codes'.[29] His stress on the importance of convention and culture is taken over into his conception of the sign, which he defines as everything that, on the grounds of a previously established social convention, can be taken as something standing for something else. Convention, therefore, is the necessary condition for signification. Such conventionality, as we have seen, extends even to iconic signs, which seem at first sight to elude it. Their apparent indubitable motivation yields to an appreciation of the codes that make them possible as signs. On the other hand, Eco does allow that iconic signs are not completely arbitrary and that they reproduce some but only some of the conditions of normal perception of an object. Those features that are held in common between image and object, for example the stripes on a drawing of a zebra, are still subject to the normal perceptual code through which we perceive the object, in this case, as striped.

In developing his argument apropos cinema, Eco registered his disagreement with both Metz's contention that it had a single articulation and Pasolini's that it had a double articulation, and claimed for it instead a triple articulation. At the first level of articulation the total image can be broken down into meaningful units, recognisable in themselves, known as 'semes'. For example, 'man in bizarre blue outfit with cape' and 'New York skyline' are semes that combine to form a shot of Superman flying over New York. Semes can in turn be analysed into smaller iconic signs, such as 'clenched fist' or 'determined jawline', which are only recognisable in the context of the seme since they are part of a graphic continuum and appear as non-discrete. This is the second articulation. Then, finally, iconic signs can be analysed as comprising a third articulation of the conditions of perception, that is things such as angles, curves, textures, effects of light and shade, and so on. These in themselves have no meaning, and in this respect are analogous to phonemes, being defined simply in differential and oppositional terms. But they are essential to the construction of meaning in that their progressive alteration will at a certain point articulate a different iconic sign. The overall effect of this unique triple articulation of the cinematic code is to permit a far greater degree of realism than any other form of representation. 'Confronted with a conventionalisation so much richer, and hence a formalisation so much subtler than anything else, we are shocked into believing we stand before a language which restores reality to us'.[30]

Like Metz, Eco was to subject his early thinking to an auto-critique and to move away from what became seen as a static conception towards one with a greater degree of flexibility. Instead of thinking of signs in terms of elementary units with fixed values (the basis of the triple articulation), which was rejected as emphasising structure at the expense of process, Eco now argued that signs are better thought of as sign-functions correlating a unit of expression with a unit of content in a temporary encoding: 'Signs are the provisional result of coding rules which establish transitory correlations of elements, each of these elements being entitled to enter – under given coded circumstances – into another correlation and thus form a new sign.'[31] It is context that determines what is and what is not to count as an element of a sign. Signs are therefore sensitive to context.

As a consequence of this new emphasis, semiotic analysis is no longer a matter of identifying a fixed number of articulations in fixed interrelationships because, depending on context and point of view, 'an element of first articulation can become an element of second articulation and vice versa'.[32] As de Lauretis puts it:

Even if in a given iconic continuum, an image, one can isolate pertinent discrete units or figurae, as soon as they are detected, they seem to dissolve again. In other words, these 'pseudo-features' cannot be organised into a system of rigid differences, and their positional as well as semantic values vary according to the coding rules instituted each time by the context.[33]

Signs, or rather sign functions, are to be seen as texts whose elementary units can be identified only within a signifying process. The various codes then become purely temporal devices posited in order to explain a certain message rather than a secure ground to meaning.

Under such a conception, 'the classical notion of "sign" dissolves itself into a highly complex network of changing relationships' and meaning becomes an effect of a continual process of codic readjustment without any final referent or closure.[34] Eco's revised semiotics can be seen as consistent with post-structuralism and its denial of all fixity of meaning, something we shall come to later in this chapter.

The effect of semiotics, or more particularly its central thesis that meaning is produced by a system of differences, was to call into question existing modes of thinking about cinema. The insistence that cinema is production ran against its innocent reception 'as natural, as life, as beauty' unfolding before the spectator.[35] More particularly, it challenged conventional modes of thinking, dependent as they were on such notions as 'source', 'origin', 'centre', 'expression', 'representation', 'full subject' and so on. If meaning was produced through, and only through, signification, it could not have a source or origin elsewhere that needed merely to be expressed in language or film. Similarly, there was no longer any question of signification representing that which already existed. For anything to exist as an object it had to be encoded as such, and therefore it was a matter of one sign for, or against, another. Such a refusal of pre-significant or extra-discursive objects extended to the human subject, who was also denied the satisfaction of apparent self-sufficiency outside of language. For if the subject's self-conception (an essential constituent of its being) could be formed only in signification it could no longer be the 'full subject' of humanist ideology.

According to Stephen Heath there were two traditions in thinking about the relationship of language and cinema prior to semiotics. The first of these was a cinematic purism that saw in language, 'that dangerous supplement', with its power to misrepresent as well as represent, something that clouded the direct truth of the image.[36] The aesthetic correlative to this epistemological apartheid between word and image was realism. The second tradition held that cinema was, precisely, a language, and it was because of this that it was entitled to claim parity with the other arts. With resources as extensive or more so than those of literature or painting, film could become the means of expression of the artist's vision. The camera was not merely the mechanical device for recording pre-existing reality but the pen, the brush, of the creative cineaste. Here, in other words, was an aesthetic of authorship.

Since authorship and realism are considered at length in chapters 4 and 6, here we shall simply signal the effect semiotics was to have on thinking about each of them. As far as realism was concerned, the central challenge was to its assumption of transparency. Far from being a window on the world, which for some theorists was its unique capacity and true vocation, cinema is, according to the semioticians, a work of construction, always within signification. The seeming reality it constructs is only accepted as such because it coheres with the prevailing ideology's version of reality. The reality effect is no more than a set of codes subservient to ideology. Film is not reproduction and representation of a pre-existent reality but the production and construction of an imaginary one. Semiotics similarly intervened against traditional ideas of the author as the origin of the meaning of the text. Because meanings do not pre-exist the text, there can be no question of expression of authorial intent or communication of meaning. Any ascription of authorship can only be in terms of a construction from the codes functioning within a text or corpus of texts. Whatever the intentions, conscious or unconscious, of a John Ford, the distinctive Fordian structure is to be found in the films he directed and not elsewhere. For both realism and authorship, then, the impact of semiotics was to render the conventional position untenable.

It was indeed the work of Stephen Heath that was to give the decisive orientation to the study of semiotics in film. In relation to the debates among the previously mentioned film semioticians, Heath sided with Eco against the early Metz and Pasolini, who, he maintained, in supposing that the image duplicated reality, ignored the specific activity of cinema. Underlying the apparent naturalness of the image, there are, as Eco had shown, processes of codification and conventionalisation. Nevertheless, for Heath it was Metz who had to be the focus of attention, since in his revised semiotics he succeeded in bringing out the social basis of cinema through codes and conventions that were normally invisible. Heath's concern with the relation between spectator and film was, more than anything else, what moved film semiotics in a new direction. Here he parted company with Eco, who had turned away from any such project, and instead followed Julia Kristeva in her call for a theory of the speaking subject consituted within language. This would entail, she said, leaving behind the study of formalised meaning systems as the instrument of transcendental subjects, and entering a phase under the sign of psychoanalysis in which signification was seen as involved in the construction of subjectivity.[37] Heath's deliberations on the implications of this shift from the structures of the text to the process of reading marked him out as considerably more than an astute commentator on continental semiotics.

The development of these ideas occurred in two distinct phases, with Althusser and Lacan respectively as the predominant influences. In the remainder of this chapter we shall be concerned with detailed elaboration of each phase and with some of the debates to which they gave rise.

In the first phase the institution of cinema was held to constitute individuals as subjects, in a manner analogous to ideological state apparatuses. Addressed by the text, the spectator accepts the identity assigned and is thereby *fixed* in a position where a particular mode of perception and consciousness appears natural. He or she is locked into a structure of misrecognition, into an imaginary relationship to the real conditions of his or her social existence. The ideological perspective imposed by the text makes it, according to this conception, seem like a window on reality. During this phase, therefore, there was an attempt to relate the materiality of ideology to that of signification, where ideology was understood not as a system of ideas but as a practice of representation producing 'the subject as the place where a specific meaning is realised'.[38] In a word, the reader was interpellated by the text, the spectator by the film.

One inflection of the theory was towards a typology of texts and drew upon the work of Emile Benveniste. His central contention was that linguistics, and in particular the analysis of discourse, could no longer afford to ignore the role of the subject within signification, for the very good reason that language is so deeply marked by subjectivity. One aspect of this is the role played by personal pronouns, which, unlike common nouns with their relatively fixed meanings and referents, signify entirely according to context. Pronouns and other so-called shifters like 'here', 'now' and 'this' lack a stable, continuous significance, but are nonetheless integral and indispensable to language. Without the possibility of each speaker being established as a subject through the use of shifters, notably the first person pronoun, language might even cease to function at all. Because of the entrenchment of subjectivity in language, Benveniste urged linguisticians to turn their attention from the abstract system of *langue* to the operation of discourse within specific social contexts.

To this end he proposed a distinction to supplement that between *langue* and *parole*, namely, between enunciation (*énonciation*), the act of speaking, and the enounced (*énoncé*), what is spoken. This then allows a further distinction between the subject of the enunciation, the subject who speaks, and the subject of the enounced, who is represented within the utterance. In most social exchanges there is no need to distinguish between the two subjects and they are taken as coinciding. But there are evidently occasions when the two do appear as distinct, as when a speaker utters a self-referring lie, a pointed instance of which is the liar paradox, the statement 'I am lying'. If the subject of the enunciation is telling the truth then the subject of the enounced is lying, and vice versa; they cannot both be telling the truth, therefore they are necessarily distinguished.

Benveniste's distinction between the two subjects and his example of the liar paradox were taken up by Lacan as support for his contention that personal identity necessarily involves an element of misrecognition. For Lacan, the subject of the enunciation and the subject of the enounced were disjunct not only in such special cases but were so in principle. Whenever the subject utters the word 'I' and identifies with the 'I' so represented there is always a discrepancy between the two, because what is and must be absent is that which alone could close the gap, namely, the unconscious.

The idea that the representation in discourse of the subject was thereby a misrepresentation was, according to the film theorists who adopted it, exactly applicable to what happened in certain forms of cinema. The argument ran as follows. Though all discourse has a subject of enunciation who produces meaning, this subject is not, as might be supposed, necessarily the author of the text. It is rather the individual who occupies the place of the subject of enunciation in what Benveniste terms 'the unceasing present of enunciation'.[39] While this position may be occupied by the author writing or director directing the text, it is also occupied by each reader or spectator in making sense of the text. With certain texts the so-constituted subject of the enunciation misrecognises his or her situation because, though both text and positioning by it are produced, the text does not permit an awareness of such production on the part of the spectator. Unlike other texts, which avow their origins in contingency and acknowledge their viewpoint as perspectival, texts of this kind do not appear to have been produced by an act of enunciation at all. Rather, they present themselves as unenounced, as writing themselves, and so the

spectator, unaware of his or her positioning, accepts their representations as reality.

Such thinking issued in the crucial distinction between those texts
that effaced the marks of their own production and of their construction of spectators and those, usually self-reflexive avant-garde texts,
in which this did not happen. The categorisation rested on two further
opposed terms borrowed from Benveniste: *histoire*, a mode of enunciation where the pronouns 'I' and 'you' only occur in reported speech
and all marks of subjectivity are suppressed; and *discours*, in which
such shifters are present, and which exhibits 'the imprint of the process of enunication in the utterance'.[40] Impersonal and atemporal in
address, *histoire* is the typical mode of enunciation of written history
and of novels adopting this historical form, with events narrated in
an indefinite past tense by an absent narrator. It would include a
novelist such as Balzac, a passage from whom Benveniste cited as an
example, in which 'no one speaks here; the events seem to narrate
themselves'.[41] *Discours*, on the other hand, is typified by conversation,
letters, speeches and those forms of writing in which the narrator is
in the foreground addressing the reader, such as the epistolary novel.

A large proportion of all narrative films falls within the category
of *histoire*, and indeed it could be put forward as the defining feature
of traditional cinema that it effaces all traces of its enunciation, presenting stories 'from nowhere, told by nobody, but received by someone (without which it would not exist)'.[42] What that someone cannot
do is recognise that in ocupying the position of invisible enunciator
he or she is constituted by the film. Instead the spectator experiences
him or herself as a pure subject, empty and absent, a pure capacity
for seeing what appears to be simply there. All 'content' is seemingly
on the side of the film, elsewhere, anywhere but inscribed as subjectivity. Of course *discours* is not entirely absent from narrative cinema.
It exists both as characters' dialogue and as characters' point of view
shots, but such explicit instances of enunciation are contained within
a supervening narrative that specifies who is speaking and looking,
and also establishes that their words and vision are partial. The narrative itself, locating the enunciations of the characters, is always at
pains to present itself not as *discours* but as *histoire*, unfolding before
the spectator as completed, comprehended, resolved and impartial.
The representations on screen appear not as one point of view but
as reality itself. The narrative closes around a world as it would appear
to the all-seeing eye of God – a privileged position that the spectatorial

'I' is only too pleased to occupy.

To sum up this first phase of thinking about the relation between text and subject, the central emphasis throughout was on the text's power to determine the subject's response. Watching a film necessarily entailed adopting the spectator position that was inscribed in the text; to comprehend was to be positioned. In the second phase a far more complex and sophisticated theory was elaborated, once again pioneered by Stephen Heath, who revised his earlier opinions as he came to appreciate the limitations of Althusser's theory of ideology.

In appropriating Lacan to help explain how ideology functions, Althusser had concentrated on the mirror phase, in which the child perceives and identifies with an idealised self-image, and from this had derived his notion of interpellation, in which the individual is called to an image of him or herself, is caught up in a structure of misrecognition and thereby becomes constituted as a subject within ideology. For Althusser, Heath wrote, 'the subject is thus the individual always held in the identity – the identification – of interpellation'.[43] This entails, first of all, that people are fixed in positions of subjection through their self-conceptions operating within a system of representation; and secondly, that they are locked into illusion. Determined and deluded, they 'go all by themselves, like so many automata'.[44]

There were in this account, Heath argued, insurmountable problems that went beyond those recognised by Hirst in his critique. Hirst's perception that interpellation involved a pre-given subject pointed to a fundamental incompatibility between Althusser's and Lacan's views on subjectivity. Because of Lacan's emphasis on the primacy of the signifier there can be no individual prior to the processes of language to become the support for the identification. But further, not only is the subject not pre-given, it is always necessarily in process, being constituted through the process that is language. These criticisms were given expression in an influential article in the *Edinburgh Magazine* of 1976, where Heath wrote:

There is no subject outside of a social formation, outside of social processes which include and define positions of meaning, which specify ideological places.

There is a concrete history of the construction of the individual as subject and that history is also the social construction of the subject; it is not in other words that there is first of all the construction of a subject for social/

ideological formations and then the placing of that constructed subject-support in those formations, it is that the two processes are one in a kind of necessary simultaneity – like the recto and verso of a piece of paper.

The individual is always entering, emerging, as subject in language.[45]

In underlining the importance of process Heath drew attention to two related aspects of the constitution of the subject. The first was that the subject is as much constituting as constituted because, according to Lacan, the subject halts the slide of the signifier, thereby becoming the producer as well as the product of meaning. There was therefore, Heath said, a 'dialectic of the subject',[46] in which language is not the sole determination but is rather 'an area of determinations. . . the condition-and-effect of social practice'.[47] Although the subject is always implicated in discursive practices, this is not to say that the effects of meaning and subjectivity are produced by the organisation of discourse alone. Signifying practices should rather be thought of as 'subject productions', a phrase which implies productions both by and of the subject.[48] Meaning and subjectivity come into being together, each engendering the other in a process of endless dialectic.

This complex idea of the dialectic of the subject, which will recur frequently in the course of this book, is perhaps best explained by reference to concrete examples. In each case there is an exchange between the subject and the other – whether that other be an aspect of the world, a person, or a film – involving an act of interpretation. For instance, different people confronted by the same stretch of open moorland will respond differently: for the walker it is an enticing prospect for vigorous exercise, for the agoraphobic a terror-inducing void. In each case the subect is constitutive in that the interpretation is not inherent in the object – the landowner interprets it differently again; but at the same time the subject is constituted by the object, in that, according to the interpretation, he or she is to a lesser or greater extent transformed by it. The subject is at once the producer and the product of the meaning. Two further examples would be the condition of the lover in the erotic relation and that of the analysand in the analytic situation. In the former instance, the lover constitutes the beloved as the idealised object of desire, while being constituted in the condition of infatuation by this interpretation of the independently existing object. Similarly, in the analytic situation, the (mistaken) presumption that the analyst is the one who knows the meaning of the analysand's discourse engenders a mode of subjectivity in which the analysand can discover something of what he or she wants. When applied to the relations between spectator and film this conception entails that both make their contribution, what Heath called 'give-and-take'.[49] Without this, the subject can only be thought of as either inescapably determined by the text or as voluntaristically creating meanings (which, though politically more hopeful than immobility, leaves little or nothing to be achieved in the realm of the textual). In each case political intervention becomes a redundancy, in the one because meanings are unalterably fixed, in the other because they are already fluid. Instead the relation of subject and text is a movement of exchange: 'the subject makes the meanings the film makes for it, is the turn of the film as discourse'.[50]

The other aspect of the stress on process was that the subject's constitution within language is a moment of division. Entry into language is the condition for subjectivity and identity, but also for the unconscious, which functions to invalidate any attempt to capture the subject's reality. Not unity but division, not identity but non-identity, these are the terms for the constitution of the subject. Nothing of this, however, pervades Althusser's account of subjectivity. For him the pre-given individual is constituted as a subject by a pre-given representation; the self-image presented through interpellation is the subject's identity. What vanishes in this is the distinction between subject and representation, for they are one and the same. Psychoanalysis, by contrast, insists on the interminable elusiveness of the subject, the impossibility of ever fully defining it, by virtue of the unbridgeable gulf between the subject of the enunciation, who speaks, and the subject of the enounced, who is spoken of. Thus the subject is never completely positioned or captured by its representations. Although existing in society and in ideological formations, the subject always exceeds any representations of such formations, and the attempt to limit and unify it belongs to the fictive realm of the imaginary. Since the individual is not one but is process, heterogeneity, multiplicity and unfinished, there is no possibility of ideological apparatuses simply constructing subjectivity. *Therefore the cinema as institution does not position but contains.* Its attempt to achieve a complete closure that will hold the subject in position never absolutely succeeds. Its representations can never fully represent, its bids to fix in place must finally fail. So although a film may adopt and construct forms of interpellation the notion of interpellation is inadequate as an account of the relations of film and spectator. Instead, these should be thought of as 'signifying practice, as so many relations of subjectivity, relations which are not the simple "property" of the film nor that of the individual-spectator but which are those of a subject production in which film and individual have their specific historical and social reality as such'.[51]

Heath's intervention concluded with a call to shift the analysis away from text as system towards text as process, away from 'the object cinema' towards 'the operation cinema'. In its fixation on the formal attributes of texts, semiotics risked blocking the understanding of how cinema is related to other practices as well as the more general relations among signification, ideology and history. Semiotics was in danger of becoming an obstacle rather than the royal road to the analysis of the text's political functioning. To circumvent this danger Heath elaborated a conception of film (proposed originally by Jean-Louis Comolli) as a 'specific signifying practice'. Each term in the formulation was explicated as follows: 'Signifying indicates the recognition of film as system or series of systems of meaning, film as articulation'; 'specific is the necessity for analysis to understand film in the particularity of the work it engages, the differences it sustains with other signifying practices', which requires a semiotic analysis that attends to the the heterogeneity present in particular textual systems and to the range of codes at work. [52] Practice, the crucial term, was conceived in Althusserian terms as the processes of transformation of a determinate, given raw material into a determinate product. The term 'practice' entailed that film was not some neutral medium transmitting a pre-given ideology, but was the active production of meaning, with its own materiality and effectivity. As such, it broke with reductionist accounts that conceived films as mere reflections of pre-existing social forces or as having political effectivity only in so far as they communicated explicitly political messages. The term also carried the further implication that since film is the work of production of meanings, the question of the positioning of the spectator enters into the analysis of film. In this way the classical, and by now obscurantist, opposition between form and content could be bypassed in favour of the operations of film and the relations of subjectivity so entailed. As specific signifying practice film was to be studied in terms not of *langue* and *parole* but of discourse, thereby implicating a subject (to be theorised by psychoanalysis). Under such a conception cinema is one of a number of 'machines' generating ideology, specifically in that through its mechanism 'the spectator is moved, and related as subject in the process and images of that movement'.[53] Or in the words of Teresa de Lauretis, cinema is 'a work of semiosis: a work that produces effects of meaning and perception, self-images and subject positions for all those involved, makers and viewers.'[54] The work of Lacan was to figure centrally in thinking through the complexities of this second phase. Although Heath was not entirely uncritical of Lacan (his occlusion of history being one cause for concern), he was on the whole confident that Lacanian psychoanalysis could overcome any difficulties. Others, however, as we shall see, were somewhat less confident.

In the mid-1980s the semiotics concerned with formal systems (as opposed to semiotics relating to the subject) survives within film theory only in the form of specific detailed studies around narrative, point of view, editing and so on. Although such work is admirably rigorous it no longer occupies the position of centrality that semiotics briefly enjoyed in the aftermath of 1968, when its apparent scientific status threatened to displace all other filmic discourses and to become the necessary precondition for advance in any area of film study.

Of the various reasons for the eclipse of semiotics, the most important for film theory was the failure to integrate it with historical materialism. Initially it had seemed a relatively straightforward matter to bring together Althusser's notion of the materiality of ideology with Saussure's of the materiality of signification. After all, each could only apparently gain from the other: historical materialism lacked an adequate theory of signification (this lack was especially felt with the growing emphasis on ideology and its existence as representations), and semiotics lacked the theoretical means of relating signification to its social context. Semiotics would fill the lack in historical materialism, and vice versa. Furthermore, the rigour of semiotics chimed nicely with the Althusserian promise of scientificity. The outline of such an integrated theory would at once figure how a text produced an ideological representation of the world and how it constituted the individual as subject for that representation.

But as the enterprise proceeded it became evident that relating the signifying process to history and the social formation was more difficult than had been anticipated. It became apparent that Saussure's theory of meaning was less of a foundation stone than a stumbling block, the problem being that the logic of the model was at odds with the intention behind its deployment. Instead of allowing the exchange between spectator and text to be related to history, the model had the effect of evacuating history from that exchange. The exit to social reality was blocked both via the text and via the subject: if meaning was produced by a system of differences then the process of signification became autonomous and therefore difficult to relate to other social practices; the spectator as constituted by the text was difficult to relate to the subject as constituted elsewhere. It was these issues that underlay two important debates in the late 1970s: between Ros Coward and the Centre for Contemporary Cultural Studies (CCCS); and between Paul Willemen and Colin MacCabe.[55]

The broad project of CCCS was not dissimilar to *Screen's*, in that they were using Marxist theories of ideology, pre-eminently Althusser's theory of relative autonomy and ideological state apparatuses, to analyse various cultural phenomena such as the press and television. Coward's basic contention was that in studying representation they disregarded Saussure, in that they took representations to be both expressive of pre-given meanings and determined by the class interests of their source. What this omitted was firstly that signification produces meaning rather than simply expresses pre-given meaning, and secondly that it has its own specificity and is irreducible to any other practice. Coward did not argue that signifying processes are fully autonomous, and indeed insisted that they are not. It was rather that although the means of representation has its conditions of existence, these are not expressed or represented by it. Institutions like cinema or television are clearly shaped by social forces, but because of the determining action of the means of representation such institutions do not necessarily represent the economic interests in which they are constructed. Nor is there any easy way to relate signification to such forces.

In reply, CCCS denied that their position was as reductionist as Coward had suggested, giving various reasons to show they respected the *relative* autonomy of signifying practice. Coward's position, they said, despite her gestural attempts to reconcile specific signifying practice and the social formation, effectively gave *complete* autonomy to signification. The question then arose as to whether she was still working in any sense within a Marxist framework; for their part they would continue the immensely difficult task of relating culture to the class society in which it existed, a task that required the development of a general social theory based on the work of Gramsci and

Althusser. Coward, for her part, remained unphased by the suggestion that she had ceased to be a Marxist since, like Hindess and Hirst,
she saw Marxism as having unduly privileged certain concepts that
blocked the way towards necessary political analyses, not least among
them those pertaining to the oppression of women. Rather than continue to rely on the incoherent concept of relative autonomy, the
new politics was better served by thinking of the social formation
in terms of conditions of existence rather than determination (especially determination by the economic in the last instance) and by concentrating on the specificity of signification. In women's struggles,
for instance, a prime concern must be to combat and transform existing systems of representation. The role of theory was therefore not
to provide totalisations of society but to intervene in particular struggles as a tactical instrument. As usual in such debates matters were
not finally resolved, but of the two positions it was Coward's that
was to be the more influential. For our purpose the importance of
the debate was in the indication it gave of the unravelling of the
theoretical fabric holding together Althusser, Saussure and Lacan,
further evidence of which was apparent in the debate between
Willemen and MacCabe.

The debate turned on the vexed question of subject position, a
concept we have already seen developed through two phases, one
based on interpellation, the other on the dialectic of the subject. Willemen perceived that for all the sophistication of the second phase,
there was a major problem with it in that if the subject was already
in place, produced by other social practices and able to work on the
text, it became impossible to specify a text's effectivity on the basis
of its structure. Because of this problem there was a tendency to fall
back on the earlier phase, whereby the text unilaterally determined
the spectator's reading. Here, though, the spectator was a mere function of the text, locked into position by the unalterable chain of signifiers. It was this formalism, with its implications of 'subjugation. . .
not to say terrorism', that Willemen wanted to challenge.[56] His
immediate target was a paper by Edward Branigan contrasting two
films by Fellini and Oshima. It exemplified that formalist criticism
which identified and described the structural codes present in films,
such as point of view, spatial organisation and editing, which were
in themselves supposedly of determinate effect on spectators. Analyses
of this kind, Willemen argued, became immanent, hypostatising the
text and hence the reader, with both frozen into immobility. Their

effect was to evacuate ideology, the social formation and history, and to block 'the theorisation of the construction of subjectivity in social practices'.[57] Because the text inscribes a reader, irrespective of his or her social and historical placement, in an inevitable fixity, there is no room for the workings of ideology except through this monolithic determination. Formalism ignored the outside of the text, 'an outside consisting of discourses in struggle, discursive formations cohering into conjunctures of ideologies'.[58] In other words, it ignored the multiplicity of social forces and practices at play, at work, in the reading of any text. Against formalism's hypostatisation, Willemen contended that texts were open to a multiplicity of readings. Meaning is a product not simply of the text, but of historically and socially constructed subjects engaging with the text. Whereas for the formalists the text is a unified structure with determinate effects, for Willemen it is unstable, offering only provisional coherences that vary according to context and reader. Any code functions within an ideological configuration that not only gives it meaning but also specifies its place within ideological practice. Instead of being determined once and for all by the codes of the text, the political effectivity of the text is a function of the mode of reading. Under the pressure of diverse and variable readings, texts may be transposed into more or less any ideological space, may be commandeered for even quite contradictory critical ends. The best any purely textual analysis can do is open up problematic areas of that ideological space by activating the repressions, contradictions and latencies within it. In making these claims for the real plurality of readers and readings Willemen's views coincided to a large extent with those of Umberto Eco mentioned earlier.

Like Eco, Willemen saw the formalist identification of the textually constructed reader with the real reader as being of no value in the analysis of the text's political functioning. No such analysis was possible unless it took the historically formed subject into account as well. Not only are the textually constructed reader and the real reader radically divergent, but the constructed reader is itself a multiplicity formed through the various subject positions offered by the text – as too is the historically formed real subject. Thinking through the relations between them was, Willemen appreciated, a formidable task, but he was confident that relative autonomy provided the framework with which to do so. Ultimately the organisation of the ideological and discursive formations in which the subject was situated was a function of 'the real', and this in turn was to be identified with the relations of production. It is the place occupied within the relations of production that determines which institutions and discursive regimes will be encountered. Each individual reads texts in terms of his or her 'concrete experience', that is, in terms of the ideologies and discourses he or she has encountered.

Willemen was concerned that this traditional, even commonsensical, viewpoint should neither fall back into a mechanistic determinism nor detract from the effectivity and productivity of signifying practice. He insisted that both the subject and reality are constituted in discourse. The relations among the real (which is logically prior to discourse), reality (which exists for a subject), subject and discourse are to be thought of in terms of a dialectic, whereby the real determines the encounter with discourses, which produce reality and affect the subject's passage through the real. Subjects work both on and in discourses: their positionality in the real and in reality must be distinguished yet 'thought together in a dialectical movement of mutual determination'.[59]

This analysis led him to the conclusion that ideological struggle would involve two simultaneous components. One, by challenging and displacing existing discourses, would alter the balance of forces within institutions; the other, in parallel, would replace the existing discourses with new ones, so providing alternative subject positions within ideology. Analysis and politics, theory and practice, were inextricably bound together.

Despite Willemen's insistence that he nowhere lost sight of the effectivity of signification or the dialectic of the subject, Colin MacCabe was unconvinced. For MacCabe detected what had troubled Coward in the work of CCCS, namely, the presumption that cinema stands in a representational relation to the ideological, the political and the economic. As a practice with its own specific effectivity, cinema can be neither the representation nor the expression of anything pre-given, but must be understood in terms of discourse and the production of subject positions. This does not lead back to formalism, because textual structures do not of themselves determine readings but are, as MacCabe put it, always imbricated with the ideological. This adherence to the notion of the dialectic of the subject entailed that the text neither preceded ideology, nor the reverse; the imbrication of the two meant that reading is a function both of the text's formal organisation and of ideology, which itself can only exist within a discursive formation. Willemen, said MacCabe, failed to think of the relation of text and ideology in terms of imbrication, but in maintaining a general theory of discourse and politics held fast to a belief in the separate fields of the textual and the extra-textual. The one comprised the formal articulation of the text, its codes and structures, operating to produce effects in the reader; the other was an historically given ideological and political space outside of cinema determining how any film would be read. The separation of these two, according to MacCabe, resulted in a syphoning-off of determinacy from the textual to the extra-textual, ultimately allowing no determining reality for the discursive as against 'the real'. Rather than thinking in terms of inside (cinema) and outside (ideology), the concept of discourse enabled one 'to think the operations by which cinema is constantly transforming the outside inside, and that inside a further element in the outside'.[60] Classic narrative cinema is perpetually referring to an outside which is 'pulled into place, into space' in the film's address to the spectator, thereby becoming an inside that confirms the outside.[61]

As an illustration of this process MacCabe cited *Nashville*, a film that has as its theme the respective realities behind the country music scene and populist politicking. While the music of the performers, the speeches of the politicians and the diegetic television reportage of both tell little of, indeed conceal, what is really going on, the picture track renders this invisible visible for the spectator. Taken behind the rhetoric of pork-barrel politics, and the clichés and stereotypes of the televison reporter, the spectator is offered a comprehensive and omniscient vision, a position of knowledge. Now although the address to the spectator comes from the articulation of shot and narrative, it is not solely the work of the codes scrutinised by formalist analyses, but rather relies on an audience already subscribing to a belief in the 'falsity and idiocy of Middle America'.[62] *Nashville* thus pulls its public 'into the place that it already occupies'.[63] The spectator is shown what she or he already believes, namely that all political activity is a futile charade incapable of changing social reality, and therefore succumbs to the political apathy that the film promotes as its ideological project. Truth and transformation are represented as mutually exclusive; showing it like it is is to show that nothing can be done about it; knowledge is impotence.

MacCabe's article bears testimony to the increasing and finally insoluble difficulties facing the post-1968 project of determining the political effectivity of the text. In proposing such effectivity as a function, firstly, of subject position, and secondly and more sophisticatedly, of the constituted-constituting subject, the model had confronted many problems (some of which we have already discussed, others to be taken up later), but the one on which the enterprise foundered was that to which it had returned time and again, namely the subject. If the dialectic of the subject was a reality, if the subject was as much producer as produced, then the political effectivity of the text could not be determined by an analysis of the text alone. That is, immanent analyses of its structures, organisation, strategies and codes would not permit the final determination of the relations of subjectivity it would constitute. The exchange, therefore, between text and society, between discourse and history, became so complex as to preclude anything beyond the most provisional and gestural of generalities.

In coming to appreciate these difficulties MacCabe, in his most recent writings (*Theoretical Essays*), has in certain respects moved closer to Willemen's position, but more importantly towards one that could be called postmodernist (a topic we shall return to in chapter 7). With the possibility of the single revelatory analysis of the text foreclosed, there can only be readings for readers, different models of its *modus operandi* for different theoretical approaches adopted. Both text and reader take their form from 'a dizzyingly vast series of determinations'.[64] There is no longer any question of ascertaining the unique meaning of the text, any more than there is of establishing the single subject position constituted by it or the sole political effect of its textual operations. 'The spectre of endless difference [can]not be dispelled theoretically (for every reader a different meaning, for every reading a different meaning).'[65] In which case, it may be wondered, is all possibility of analysis thereby precluded? To this MacCabe answered no: though analysis could no longer claim to be final or unique, there was a more limited, provisional and modest option based on what he has called shared questions. In practice, MacCabe writes, we share questions about sexuality and power, education and the national language. In our professional, academic or other shared practices, such questions find their validity, as do, by implication, their answers.

On the strength of the debates outlined above, it became evident that the semiotic enterprise as originally conceived was in need of re-evaluation. While still available for admirably rigorous close textual reading, it could no longer be seen as the way forward in the understanding of the political functioning of cinema. Developments within post-structuralism powerfully reinforced this trend. We shall here limit our elucidation to certain pertinent aspects of the work of Jacques Derrida, leaving to one side both the bulk of his critique of Western metaphysics, and other post-structuralists (notably Foucault and Lyotard, who are treated elsewhere in this book).

Our starting point will be Derrida's when he writes: 'This is my starting point: no meaning can be determined out of context, but no context permits saturation.'[66] It is fundamental to any signifier, word or text that it can be repeated; indeed signification precisely depends on this condition of repeatability, or iterability. But what determines the meaning is the context in which the signifier, word or text occurs; and since this is variable and boundless, the meaning of successive iterations are equally so. Just as no one person or institution can finally control the contexts in which a text will be situated, no one person or institution can specify the limits of meaning accruing to the text. Readers constantly relate any given text to others, so producing new meanings, new interpretations. The possibility of 'the text overrun[ning] all the limits assigned to it' entails that meaning is always potentially both different and deferred (Derrida's term *différance* has this dual sense as well as designating that spatio-temporal difference is the condition of meaning).[67] The absence of any fixed or final meaning, the constant entering into new textual relationships, which Derrida refers to as 'nonmasterable dissemination', is what decisively distinguishes Derrida's account of language from that of Saussure.[68] In effect, Saussure had been blind to the radical implications of his conception of the sign, appreciating that signification is an effect of a system of differences but failing to conclude (in large measure because of his privileging of speech over writing, with the implication of a meaning-intending presence behind speech) that there could therefore be only endless difference.

Derrida also took issue with Lacan, who, while in principle recognising the implications of the primacy of the signifier, did not (said Derrida) do so in practice. The focus of Derrida's disagreement was Lacan's reading of a short story by Edgar Allan Poe, 'The Purloined Letter'. In the story, a letter (whose content is never revealed) has been sent to the Queen, who, in order that it may not be discovered by the King, hides it by pretending there is nothing to hide, laying it openly on the table when the King enters while she is reading it. The King sees nothing, but the Minister realises what is going on and steals it by gathering it up with his other papers, thereby gaining power over the Queen. The Minister in turn hides it by placing it where it can be seen in a card rack on his mantelpiece, a ploy that fools the secret police the Queen has ordered to retrieve it, but not, subsequently, the detective Dupin. Correctly identifying the crumpled piece of paper as the purloined letter, Dupin returns the following day, distracts the Minister's attention and takes the letter, substituting for it a facsimile on which he has inscribed a pointed quotation, thereby settling an old score with the Minister. For Lacan, the story functions almost as an allegory for a number of psychoanalytic truths, summed up by the formulation 'a letter always arrives at its destination'.[69] While Lacan meant several things by this, among them that the subject is caught up in the compulsion to repeat, that the unconscious is never silent, and that the role of the analyst is to ensure that the messages sent by the analysand are delivered to their true addressee, for our purposes the important theme is the one discussed in this chapter, that of the role of the symbolic in the constitution of the subject. In the same way that the subject is not master of the signifier but is rather subjected by it, so are the characters in the story defined by their relation to the letter, changing as this relation changes. Thus in respect of the two triadic scenes of King, Queen, Minister and police, Minister, Dupin, the positions instituted by the letter are the same but are occupied by different characters – in the first scene the Minister is the robber, the Queen is the dispossessed, and the King notices nothing; in the second these positions are taken up by Dupin, the Minister and the police respectively. As their positions change, so do not only their actions but also their characteristics – when Dupin occupies the third place he becomes the aggressor, while the hitherto aggressive Minister takes on the feminised role previously enacted by the Queen. In short, then, the tale illustrates the centrality of the signifying chain in the constitution of subjectivity. It is, of course, this notion on which so much of 1970s film theory turned.

Although Derrida did not directly challenge Lacan's psychoanalytic theses, he did question this reading of Poe on the grounds that Lacan found in the text only what he wanted to find there. By treating the text as a mere representation of pre-given psychoanalytic truths Lacan was violating his own Saussurean precept that the signified continually slides beneath the signifier, a point that he made in the course of the analysis itself. Instead, however, of following the logic of his position and allowing that it is impossible to pronounce the final word on a text, Lacan did the reverse, deciphering the hidden meaning of the story. At one point in the analysis, for example, Lacan likened the letter to the phallus; but this, claimed Derrida, was a classsic piece of Freudian reductionism, in which the phallus is accorded the status of a transcendental signified, a meaning given prior to signification. Rather than acknowledging the dissemination of meaning, Lacan sought to master the text using the phallus as the key. In so doing he failed to perceive the possibility that 'a letter can always not arrive at its destination' – though equally, of course, it may arrive.[70] Meanings, in other words, can never be safeguarded against the vagaries of interpretation; they can always go astray.

Within film theory Derrida is perhaps best conceived of as a structuring absence. Although initially cited by the post-1968 theorists as support for the materiality of language, references to his work became subsequently less frequent. In the structuralist phase there was obviously a serious incompatibility between the requirement that texts determine readers' responses (through interpellation) and Derrida's project. Once it is allowed that the human subject has a degree of agency in the reading of a text (and in the last chapter we showed that it must be), then the notion of dissemination renders any positioning by the text untenable. For if interpellation can only operate through an act of interpretation on the part of the reader, then there is no guarantee that a text will always interpellate in the same way. After Derrida there can be no question of specifying the text's effectivity independently of the context of reception: readings differ; a letter does not always reach its destination. Structuralists, therefore, could only lose by co-opting him. For post-structuralists, on the other hand, committed as they were to a plurality of readings of texts, the grounds for maintaining a distance were less evident, but may be traced to a general preference for a Lacanian perspective.

Even when it entered its post-structuralist phase film theory was concerned above all else with the text's political effectivity, and was therefore disinclined to indulge in the flamboyant propagation of meanings associated with many Derrideans engaging with literature. For film theorists the important thing was that film, as Frank Lentricchia said of literature, 'makes something happen'.[71] While accepting that there is no final meaning to the text, no limiting its meaning to the demands of any one institutional framework (of relevance, among other things, in challenging the established protocols of teaching texts), they were insistent that in any given, historically defined instance the text is read in a particular way and that this has an effect upon the reader. Just as the open stretch of moorland that induces terror in the agoraphobic has a very different meaning for and effect on the rambler, the landowner or the birdwatcher, so too with any text: openness of meaning, yet determinacy of effect. Derrida's concern was not with how meanings are produced, but rather with how they can miscarry; for film theorists, however, the dominant concern was to study the determinations at work in particular historical moments giving rise to particular meanings, and they needed therefore a model of signification that would take account of what Derrida termed 'external constraints'. This need was seemingly met by Lacan's conception of the dialectic of the subject: that in the act of enunciation subject and meaning come into being together.

To recall Lacan's graph reproduced earlier in this chapter, the signified slides beneath the signifying chain, which the subject punctuates retroactively to produce meaning. Thus, in so far as film theory was concerned with accounting for the effectivity of signification, it tended to look more to Lacan than Derrida. However, as we shall show in the following chapter, there were serious problems attaching to Lacan.

CHAPTER 3

Psychoanalysis

The application of psychoanalysis to cinema is by no means new. In particular, the productions of Hollywood (the 'dream factory') were amenable to psychoanalytic interpretation, displaying, as they did, the familiar repertoire of Freudian motifs. Such readings, however, tended towards reductionism in that the ostensible meaning of the film (comparable to the manifest content of the dream) was displaced by the hidden, Freudian meaning (equivalent to the dream's latent content), which tended towards a certain sameness. The loss of particularity and difference effectively discredited psychoanalysis as a critical method. However, its reintroduction into film studies was on the very different grounds of the need for a theory of the relations of the subject to discourse, which is exactly what Jacques Lacan's reworking of Freud appeared to offer. Although we shall show at the end of this chapter that a reading of Lacan as making good a deficiency in Marxism and semiotics was more problematic than was assumed, we shall for the moment simply sketch those aspects of his work that were taken up during the 1970s, most notably his account of the development of the subject.

The child is born into the experience of lack, what Lacan terms the *manque à être* (the 'want to be'); and the subject's subsequent history consists of a series of attempts to figure and overcome this lack, a project that is doomed to failure. Though the form and experience of lack may alter, the basic reality of its persists and defies representation. In retrospect – and for Lacan this history, like all histories of the subject, his own theory included, can only be retrospective – the child interprets the prior union with the mother as anterior to lack, a condition where it was everything and lacked nothing.

Throughout its life the child will attempt to recapture this imagined entirety in a search for that which will overcome the lack, the missing component Lacan terms *l'objet petit a* and whose most obvious prototype is the breast. This stands as a representation, no more than that, of what is ultimately unrepresentable, in that the object that could overcome the lack is non-existent. As compensation for the continual failure to re-establish unity, the child will console itself with imaginary solutions, notably in idealised images of itself as complete.

In Lacan's account of the child's development there are three determining moments: the mirror phase (the acquisition of a sense of self), the *fort-da* game (the accession to language), and the Oedipus complex (the submission to the laws of society). We shall summarise each of these in turn.

The mirror phase occurs between the ages of six and eighteen months and is the child's primary means of establishing the difference between itself and the world. On seeing itself in a mirror, or more complexly through identification with the body of another, usually the mother, the child responds jubilantly to this image whose completeness and unity contrast with its own experienced disunity and lack of motor control, and assumes 'that's me'.

In certain respects the child gains from the assumption. It facilitates an awareness of the body as localised and separate from the environment, which is a prerequisite for coordinated physical activity; and on the basis of this newly acquired awareness of boundaries the child is then able to develop a sense of its own separate identity, without which there can be no social interaction. However, these gains are offset by losses, in essence those of misrecognition, alienation and division. Because the self-image represents a state of maturation not yet achieved and a degree of completeness and perfection never to be attained, the image is a narcissistic self-idealisation or, as Lacan puts it, 'a mirage', designed to parry the lack in being and 'to preserve the subject's precarious pleasure from an impossible and non-compliant real'.[1] As well as misrecognition the identification involves alienation, in that it is typically sanctioned from another, from elsewhere. The announcement 'That's me' (though not yet in so many words) is verified by an adult, again, usually the mother, holding the child up before the mirror. The child thus identifies with her perception of it (or more accurately what it imagines she wants it to be). In saying 'That's me' it is saying 'I am another'. As Juliet Mitchell points out, Lacan considers that the subject 'can only conceptualise itself when it is mirrored back to itself from the position of another's desire'.[2] That is, the child is divided from the moment it forms a self-conception. In finding compensation for the *manque à être* in the fictive unity offered by the mirror, it encounters yet further division, which overlays and complicates the original lack, an irreducible gap between the reality of the child's being and the idealised image it assumes as its own.

The mirror phase is usually conceived as emblematic, or indeed the founding moment, of the so-called imaginary, one of the three constitutive orders of subjectivity, of which the other two are the symbolic and the real. Our reading of Lacan, however, would draw all three into the domain of the mirror phase, as indeed into the other formative phases of the subject. The *imaginary* comprises the repertoire of images that the subject invokes to annul the originary gap, and is present in the mirror phase as the image of the other with which the child identifies and which masks its division. The *symbolic*, it will be recalled, comprises the Other of laws, rules, codes and prohibitions, to which the child must submit in order to enter society, and is present in the mirror phase because the identity available to the child comes from elsewhere, from another subject – in the above example, the mother – whose desire is always already conditioned by it. The Other is present here as it is everywhere, assigning the child a place even before it is born. Finally, the *real* is defined negatively as that which the imaginary seeks to image and the symbolic seeks to symbolise. But it necessarily eludes all such attempts, remaining outside imagination and symbolisation, while retaining an effectivity. An example given by Lacan is the trauma of the separation from the mother, which is present in the mirror phase both as the *manque à être* prompting the narcissistic idealisation of self and as the gap between this idealised image and the subject. The interpenetration of the three orders is worth stressing because they have sometimes been thought of as separable, a misunderstanding that has had adverse consequences for the attempt to theorise the relation between film and spectator.

Like the mirror phase, the *fort-da* game brings the child both gains and losses. It was originally named and described by Freud in 1915, having watched his grandson Ernst throw a cotton reel out of sight then retrieve it by means of an attached thread, while accompanying the two actions with the sounds 'o' and 'a' respectively. Freud hypothesised that the reel symbolised the child's mother and that the game was a way of coming to terms with her absence. In throwing the reel away the child moved from a state of helplessness (I am abandoned by my mother) to one of agency or even mastery (I abandon my mother). Lacan's subsequent reading of the game de-emphasised the supposed bid for mastery and instead proposed that it represented the child's accession to language. The emphasis came to be placed on the child's invocation of a symbol to stand in for what was missing and through which the mother's comings and goings could be represented. It was her absence that prompted the adoption of the reel as signifier, which stood in a metaphoric relation to mother and child, present only by virtue of the absence of what it represented. Like Hegel, Lacan conceived of the word as the mur-derer of the thing: no representation is ever adequate to what it claims to represent. As we shall see, this is crucially the case with the subject's self-representation. The *fort-da* game is a language system in micro-cosm, in that the signifiers 'fort' and 'da' are defined relationally, each by what it is not. The subject, therefore, is caught up in a pre-existing language whose terms are organised diacritically and not by any relation to the real.

The gains for the child are those of entry into society, with all the concomitant possibilities for cooperation and communication. But these gains exact a toll of yet further division and experience of lack. For instance, although the child can now articulate its needs as demands, like calling for 'juice' to assuage its thirst, there is always a surplus in demand that amounts to a request to the Other, here usually the mother, to make good the *manque à être*. Typically figured as the demand for unconditional love, it is bound to remain unsatis-fied because no such love exists – hence Lacan's comment that loving is giving what one does not have. The discrepancy between the satis-faction of the need and the unsatisfied demand for love is the condi-tion for desire, the unfulfillable search for the eternally lost object (*objet petit a*). The entry into language and the discovery of lack in the Other therefore precipitates the child into the constitutionally unsatisfiable state of desire.

In a further sense, too, the entry into language is the birth of desire. Because the laws of society are inscribed within language, entry into the symbolic order entails that the child submits to its pre-given place and role, while that which is not consonant with such a social identity is consigned to the unconscious. When the child accepts this identity, as it must, its desires and the terms in which they are figured are determined by the Other, by the laws of society. Desire is always destined to pass through 'the defile of the signifier'; that is, 'man's desire is the desire of the Other'.[3] Henceforth the subject's relationships are, at their simplest, triangular: not subject and object, but subject, Other and object (where the terms of both subject and object are given by the Other). 'Everything emerges from the structure of the signifier'.[4]

The relationship of subject, Other and object is perhaps best approached from the side of the subject, and since this aspect of Lacan's theory has been a major focus of attention by film theorists we shall look at it in some detail. As will have become apparent already, Lacan's subject is nothing except by and through language. The subject is such only by virtue of a self-conception, but this necessarily involves misrecognition. The subject's self-representation occurs either by a name or by the first person singular pronoun, in both cases by a signifier taking its meaning from other signifiers. As with the mirror phase, this necessarily involves alienation and division, because here too there is an acceptance of an identity determined elsewhere, in this case from within the Other, the symbolic order, language. That is, the subject can only appear if represented in the Other, while simultaneously and consequently all that is repressed as heterogeneous to the identity given through any signifier means that representation is always inadequate to the subject's being. As Stephen Heath put it, the subject is at once 'represented and excluded, becoming some one by its constitution as less-than-one'.[5] The unconscious is the field of exclusion entailed by representation. Therefore in representing itself by a signifier the subject appears only to disappear. Because of the inescapable coexistence of the unconscious with language, the subject is as inescapably destined to division in its attempts at self-representation.

The necessary division of the subject can be articulated as the difference between the subject of the enunciation and the subject of the enounced. The 'I' who speaks is always in excess of the 'I' who is spoken of. In other words, the first person singular pronoun 'designates the subject of the enunciation, but it does not signify it'.[6] That is, by virtue of the unconscious and the fact of being in process, the subject eludes all attempts to pin it down in language: 'when the subject appears somewhere as meaning, he is manifested elsewhere as "fading", as disappearance'.[7]

Lacan proposed that the 'no win' situation of the subject could be explicated by the so-called 'vel of alienation'. He likened the 'or' to that offered by the highwayman to his victim in the phrase 'Your money or your life': choose money and you lose both, choose life and you lose your money, ending up with a life deprived of something. Lacan's version of a Venn diagram similarly offers a choice between meaning and being.

Choose being, and the subject disappears into non-meaning; choose meaning and 'meaning is only left curtailed of the part of the non-meaning which is, strictly speaking, what constitutes, in the realisation of the subject, the unconscious'.[8] The general implication is that there is no way you are going to keep everything, and the attempt to do so will result in your losing both. Better, as Roger Thornhill was advised by his mother in *North by Northwest*, to 'just pay the two dollars'.

Thus the subject comes into being at the cost of division, only to experience a renewed sense of lack, of *manque à être*; this it seeks to fend off with an idealised self-image as a unity, which however is always subverted by the process of the subject in the symbolic, by the challenge of the unconscious to any identity.

The third major constitutive moment of infancy is in the Oedipus complex, when the child encounters sexual difference. As we have seen, the human infant is entirely helpless and dependent on the mother, a potentially terrifying state. To ameliorate its condition the child takes refuge in the fiction that it is as indispensable to the mother as she is to it. The child imagines itself to be what she lacks, and therefore desires: what Lacan terms the phallus. 'The phallus signifies what the mother on her own has not got. It indicates lack . . . [and] at the same time it stands for what makes up that lack.'[9] It is precisely and only a signifier, not an existing object, that represents the necessarily absent object of desire. Lacan insisted that it was not to be equated with the penis (for neither men nor women possess it). Through identification with the phallus the child imagines it will complete the mother and be itself completed, recovering the lost unity it has come to believe preceded its own lack and which, if regained, will annul it. Such a state of union with the mother is figured as an Edenic condition of plenitude and the absence of all lack. However, the child's solution to its problem is exposed as illusory when it discovers that it is not and cannot be the phallus. For there is a third person, the father, whom the mother desires and who the child presumes possesses the phallus. The Oedipal scenario turns on this intervention of the father, the moment of castration when the Law of the Father ('Thou shalt not desire what was my desire') places an interdiction on the child's desire to be what the mother desires.

The father, then, is the third term, breaking the mother-child dyad and rupturing its imaginary wholeness. Henceforth the child must exchange its earlier identification with the phallus for the identity assigned by the Name of the Father, and the phallus now figures the fact of sexual difference, with the father perceived as having it and the mother as lacking it. Given this sexual division between those representing lack and those having what would seemingly make it up, the child has to come down on one side or the other: it cannot be both, it cannot be neither, and it has no choice which one it is.

Confronted by this divide the boy assumes the masculine identity assigned to him by the symbolic. But as we have seen in our discussion of the accession to language, entry into the symbolic always produces a renewed sense of lack, recapitulating the original *manque à être*. In an attempt to compensate for this the boy indentifies with an idealised figure, namely the father as the supposed possessor of the phallus. This move, though, is ultimately doomed to failure, as in taking his place within the symbolic the boy comes to understand 'that there is desire, or lack, in the place of the Other, that there is no ultimate certainty or truth, and that the status of the phallus is a fraud.'[10] Thus castration is the moment when the Other (O) is recognised as the barred Other (Ø). Whereas in the mother-child dyad the Other had been fantasised as the place where demands are met, it is now revealed that there is nowhere demand can be fulfilled and desire satisfied. Rather than a secure destination the child has reached only a precarious sexual identity, one always liable to challenge from the unconscious, constantly fading, decentred and divided.

The girl's Oedipal trajectory is harder to specify, its difficulty compounded by what Jane Gallop has referred to as 'the contagion. . . from subject matter to theoretical description.'[11] Freud's own problems here are well known, with his talk of 'the dark continent of female sexuality' and the notable absences in his account of its development. His basic conception was that the girl's trajectory is the same as the boy's until the discovery of the mother's castration, when she is faced by three options: either to give up on sexuality altogether because she cannot compete, or to seek to acquire the phallus herself, or to take her father as love object. Only through the last of these options does she enter the female Oedipus. Though the father apparently has the phallus, under the pressure of social taboos the girl must renounce him and seek substitute love objects who also appear to have the phallus, at the same time as identifying with her mother who has not got it. However, this identification with the supposedly castrated mother has proved difficult to explain. The Lacanian psychoanalyst Catherine Millot has put the problem thus: for the girl 'there is no ideal feminine identification possible other than the phallic woman; but this is precisely a pre-Oedipal identification.'[12] Hence, 'the recognition of castration. . . leaves no possibility. . . of a straightforward post-Oedipal identification with the woman.'[13]

Nor are matters any easier in Lacan's version. The broad outline of his account, at least as expounded by Jacqueline Rose in her introduction to *Feminine Sexuality*, is clear. The subjectivity of women, like that of men, is constituted within language and the symbolic; their sexual identity is enjoined on them by the law, is therefore not pre-given but legislated; this identity, as for men, is taken up with reference to the phallus, in this case a matter of not possessing it. It is also clear that the woman's relation to this assigned identity is even more troubled than is the man's to his assigned identity in that she is constituted as a subject within a symbolic order where women are treated as objects. Not the least aspect of this objectification is the role women play in the fantasies of men who, divided in the symbolic, use them to represent their own problems in relation to desire, to *object petit a*. Women figure both as the representation of lack, in that the 'lack inherent in being human. . . is projected onto women', and as that which can make good the lack, as *the* woman (though of course, as Lacan insists, *the* woman does not exist).[14] On the one hand she is constituted as what men are not, as lacking, as 'not-all', and on the other as the terminus to desire, the site of *jouis-sance*, the everything.

Lacan argued that the woman's difficulties in the symbolic are such that she is excluded, which has been on occasion interpreted as meaning that women lack a voice. For example, Ann Rosalind Jones has written: 'Lacanian theory reserves the "I" position for men. Women. . . occupy a negative position in language.'[15] But such readings have been contested. Thus Millot reiterates Lacan's argument that there is nothing missing in the real. It is not a question of women being denied access to the symbolic, of being deprived of speech, but of a lack arising from the symbolic itself, of which they are a part. Jacqueline Rose too stresses that women's exclusion is *by* not *from* language. The 'not' of the 'not-all' derives from women being defined against men, as the exception to the phallic rule. What is unclear in either interpretation is why women take up their assigned identities and the consequences this process has for their sexuality. The absence within psychoanalysis of a satisfactory explanation of feminine sexuality was, as we shall see, severely to restrict its value in understanding the exchange between film and women spectators.

The critical question emerging from this selective account of the construction of the subject is how the relations of the subject to his or her discourse are to be conceived. The particular problem Lacan faced was how to represent the situation of a subject that is at once constituted and constituting. Lacan wished to say both that the signifier is anterior to the subject (or that the subject is an effect of language) and that the subject is anterior to the signifier (so that language represents the subject). The problem lay in overcoming the explicit contradiction of maintaining both. The answer was the *graphe complet*, Lacan's figuration of the subject in process.[16]

For our purposes a full explication of the graph is unnecessary, it being sufficient to note that it is organised around two vectors: the vector of speech, which is the subject's signifying chain; and the vector of the drive, which is the search for satisfaction. Both of them pass through the Other (the symbolic), and the graph illustrates the effect of that passage on the constitution of the subject.

The vector of speech, the lower of the two left-to-right arrows, is a different version of the graph already discussed in the previous chapter. The vector passes through the Other (A/*l'Autre*), language's synchronic dimension, the place where every signifier is stored and where the subject is constituted. But for there to be meaning, the signifying chain must be punctuated by the barred subject $ (barred because the subject is never fully represented in speech, i.e., there is always the unconscious), who is thereby constitutive as well as constituted. The subject calls a momentary halt to the slide of the signifiers at the punctuation point $s(A)$. Belonging to the diachronic not to the synchronic, this is the moment when meaning emerges in the retroactive contextualising of signifiers and the anticipatory construction of those to come. In this moment something of what the subject desires is at once expressed and repressed. The barred subject $ is represented at the point $s(A)$, but only inadequately. The subject's appearance in the field of the Other occurs only through a stand-in, a representative, and therefore at the cost of division. The subject is thus 'constituted only by subtracting himself', because by punctuating his or her discourse to give it sense s/he can only appear after the fact, by which time s/he is in the process of becoming something else.[17] The appropriate tense for this situation is 'the future anterior of what I shall have been for what I am in the process of becoming'.[18] This fading of the subject at $s(A)$ prompts him or her to seek compensation in an idealised image, $i(a)$, which will fend off the lack. Such a specular image, whose prototype is the image in the mirror, produces a misrecognition of the self, *m*, the *moi*, thereby effecting the junction of the imaginary and the symbolic, otherwise known as suture.

The upper part of the graph duplicates the lower, with the arrow here representing the vector of the drive. In seeking satisfaction, the drive addresses a demand to the Other, one that is made at the site ($ ◊ D), which like A below it is also a place. It is where the subject seeks to overcome the lack in being by demanding unconditional love, and because in so doing s/he discovers the impossibility of what s/he demands it is therefore the site of castration. The various symbols of the formula expand as follows. $, again, is the barred subject, eclipsed and fading, and D is the demand. The lozenge, ◊, has two meanings, each dependent on an interpretation of its graphemic origins. If read as the conjunction of the mathematical symbols < (less than) and > (greater than), it signifies the impossibility of the demand being granted. If, on the other hand, it is taken as the symbol used by silversmiths to guarantee authenticity, then it stands for the uniqueness of each particular individual's demand. The correspondence between upper and lower parts of the graph continues with S(A), which like s(A) is a moment, not a place. It occurs when the subject enters the symbolic and discovers that the Other is lacking. Finally, castration gives rises to desire, d, on the upper right of the graph, which loops over the top in the direction of fantasy, ($S \lozenge a$), where S is the barred subject, a is the *objet petit a*, and $\lozenge$ is the screen onto which the subject projects his or her own uniquely fantasised *objet petit a*.

Broadly speaking, two phases may be distinguished in the use made of psychoanalysis, each of which emphasised one aspect of the Lacanian model. In the first, structuralist, phase, centred on the work of Baudry, Metz and Mulvey, the emphasis was on the constitution of the ego in the mirror stage (on the *graphe complet*, the portion

$$m | \underline{\qquad \longleftarrow \qquad} | i(a)).$$

In the second, post-structuralist, phase, associated for instance with the work of Cowie and Rose, the emphasis was on desire and fantasy on the graph

$$(S \lozenge a \ | \underline{\qquad \longleftarrow \qquad} | d).$$

Another way of distinguishing the two phases would be to say that the first was concerned with sameness and the second with difference.

In her article 'Visual Pleasure and Narrative Cinema', Laura Mulvey concentrated on the more classically Freudian features of Lacan's theory, notably identification, voyeurism and fetishism. In view of its impact, especially among feminist writers on cinema, we shall follow her argument through in some detail.

The argument opens with the suggestion that the pleasure offered by mainstream Hollywood-type cinema, its 'fascination', depends on pre-existing psychological patterns at work within the spectator. Such pleasure is indissociable from dominant cinema's capacity to articulate patriarchal ideology around sexual difference, or more precisely, its capacity to negotiate the contradictions inherent in this ideology. By offering a kind of satisfaction to the alienated subject of patriarchy, cinema ensures its own commercial success. Principal among pleasures offered are those of identification, where the spectator narcissistically identifies with an idealised figure on screen, typically a male hero whose actions determine the narrative, in a process that recapitulates the discovery of the image of oneself in the mirror phase; and scopophilia, or pleasure in looking, through which the spectator indulges in a more socially acceptable form of peeping tom-ism whereby the other, typically a woman, is turned into an object of fantasy, so giving the voyeur a position of control and mastery. In respect of this latter pleasure, however, the security and mastery of the spectator seated in the solitary intimacy of darkness is in fact deeply problematic. For the image of the woman also brings with it what the spectator's look would disavow, the fact of sexual difference itself and the concomitant threat of castration. In order to allay the anxiety so engendered, the Hollywood film tends to respond with two basic strategies. One of these is to deepen the already present voyeuristic aspect of cinema, coupling it with sadism, so that the difference figured by women is investigated by the constant re-enactment of the discovery of the lack. Such texts, of which *films noirs* are outstanding examples, attempt to master the anxiety both through their typical investigation of the woman and by their narrative punishment of her. The other strategy is to turn the woman into a fetish object, thereby containing the threat of difference through disavowal. Instead of lacking, women are represented as being complete and perfect. Here, parts or the whole of the female body are endowed with a value that compensates for the lack elsewhere, typified by the overinvestment in Monroe's breasts, Grable's legs, Hayworth's shoulders. Though this fetishisation is found throughout Hollywood, and is indeed an integral part of the star system, it finds its apotheosis in the films of von Sternberg, where the female body is no longer relayed through the looks of the male characters in the fiction but is offered directly to the spectator as a highly stylised and fragmented perfect product.

The avowed purpose of Mulvey's analysis was destruction. By examining dominant cinema's pleasures and exposing their phallocentrism she hoped to create the space for an alternative cinema speaking 'a new language of desire', involving a totally different regime of spectating.[19] There is, towards the end of the article, a shift in approach that brings it close to the Althusserian orthodoxy of interpellation. Implicit in her discussion of voyeurism and fetishism, the conception of the spectator being positioned by the text in such a way as to be blind to other perspectives becomes explicit around the organisation of looks within cinema. (Since we shall return to this topic in chapter 5, we shall do no more here than note its presence in Mulvey's article.) Interpellation, in providing an identity and a perspective on reality, bears on that aspect of the *graphe complet* which involves the identifications of the mirror phase. And this aspect, as we shall see, proved to be central to the theories of the apparatus associated with Jean-Louis Baudry and Christian Metz.

In developing their ideas the theorists of the apparatus were indebted to earlier studies of perspective in Renaissance and post-Renaissance painting. Such studies, for the most part from within a Marxist framework, had emphasised the importance of form over content in determining the ideological effectivity of art. It was not simply that the paintings of the Renaissance began to speak the language of bourgeois ideology through their adoption of greater realism, more secular subject matter and an increasingly marked individualism of style, but also, and more importantly, the system of perspective based on a convergence towards a vanishing point in the picture indicated that there was a single, unique point in the imaginary space outside it from which its content was perceived. In other words, perspective gave the spectator an omniscient unitary place from which to view what was depicted, thus reinforcing the bourgeois notion of the subject as a free unique individual.

Jean-Louis Baudry's article 'Ideological Effects of the Basic Cinematographical Apparatus' was an early attempt to think through the implications of perspective for cinema. Because the camera lens is modelled on the same optical principles that underlie the perspectival system of Renaissance painting, cinema ensures that the spectator is established as the active centre and producer of meaning. The events, people, landscapes and objects of the film, its fictional reality, are always and necessarily seen from a fixed point in its imaginary space, one that is occupied by the spectator. Thus visually positioned, the spectator is blinded to the work of the film, its frame-by-frame construction of what passes for reality. And just as the succession of those frames is effaced in favour of a continuous vision, so too is the film's ideological operation. Far from disrupting the unitary, perspectivally-defined position of the spectator's vision, thereby revealing both their and the spectator's contingency, the succession of images in fact augments the spectator's imaginary dominance. The movements of the camera, the reframing of the shots, the cuts from one image to another are indeed comparable to the operations of an eye 'no longer fettered by the body, by the laws of matter and time' and are not, as might have been expected, a threat to that transcendental supremacy.[20] The movability of the camera, with the resulting multiplicity of perspectives, in fact provides the most favourable circumstances for 'the manifestation of the transcendental subject'.[21] Further, the various cinematic devices of framing, movement and editing are perceived by the spectator as acts of synthesis and constitution, and hence serve as evidence for the existence of a synthesising, constitutive, that is, transcendental, subject. Those very textual operations that would appear to put in question the spectator's self-identification as transcendental actually work to confirm this misrecognition. Although the subject's (mis)recognitions and (mis)perceptions are in reality a function of the text, the textual strategies in play convince him or her of the opposite. In sum, Baudry argued, the spectator is constituted by the meanings of the text but believes him or herself to be their author. This is precisely an account of the process of interpellation, where the subject appears to be the source of the meanings of which he or she is an effect.

In a later article, 'The Apparatus' (1975), Baudry moved away from a reliance on the Lacan of the mirror phase towards a more classically Freudian model to explain the ideological effects of the cinematic apparatus and in particular the impression of reality it created. Once again he challenged the view that this was a consequence of cinema's uniquely mimetic power, arguing here that this was less significant than its capacity to institute a mode of subjectivity analogous to the state of dreaming. At once enabled by and enabling of sleep, the dream, according to Freud, involves a state of regression comparable to the beginning of psychic life, where perception and representation are not differentiated. Thoughts are transformed into images, word presentations are transposed into thing presentations, repressed desires find expression and satisfaction in hallucinated images. That is, the fantasies of the dream wish appear as reality, indeed as 'more that real', for unlike waking perceptions the representations of the dream impose themselves on and submerge the subject. The desire to recreate this state of regression is, Baudry maintained, 'inherent in our psychical structure' and has in the course of history given rise to a number of art forms, like painting and opera, although these are mere 'dry runs' for cinema, failed attempts to achieve its unique capacity to correspond to the dream state.[22] Nowhere is this more effectively brought about than in the darkness of the auditorium with the spectator immobile and passive, gazing at moving images. The apparatus, projecting images onto a screen, mimes a form of archaic satisfaction, returning the spectator to a time when the separation between the subject's body and the world was ill-defined. It is this archaic identification rather than those secondary ones of the mirror phase that is fundamental to the desire for cinema and that explains the spectator's attachment to the images. The peculiar impression of reality engendered by cinema derives from the subjectivity constructed by it rather than the content or formal organisation of the film texts themselves. Only by acknowledging the force of the unconscious in the subject was it possible to account both for the desire for cinema and its reality effect.

Despite Baudry's second thoughts it was the first of these articles that exercised the greater influence, not least on Christian Metz. In his seminal article 'The Imaginary Signifier', Metz returned the Lacanian concept of the mirror phase to the centre of the theoretical stage as he addressed the question of what, in the light of psychoanalysis, can be understood of cinema's specific characteristics in relation to the spectating subject. At the outset, he distinguished two 'machines' operating within the cinematic institution: one being cinema as industry, making commodities whose sale as tickets provides the return on the original investment; the other being the spectators' psyches, experiencing film as the pleasurable 'good object' and hence wanting more of the same. The economy of the former, the circulation of money, is interdependent with the economy of the latter, the circulation of pleasure. Metz's major theoretical concern was with the second of these two machines.

His analysis opens with a definition of the cinematic signifier as distinctively different from those of the other major art forms. In the first place, cinema operates over a much wider perceptual range than most other arts, bringing in sound, vision and the perception of movement in an ordered time sequence. And secondly, in comparison with those arts, such as theatre, opera and other spectacles, that do involve as rich a perceptual register, cinema does not offer perceptions belonging to the same time and space as the audience but images and recordings of what is absent. Instead of the presence of real players, sets and props, the screen presents its audience with a world that is physically absent, 'in effigy . . . in a primordial elsewhere'.[23] Whether or not what is perceived is functional, the actual unfolding of it on screen is – which is why Metz can write, 'every film is a fiction film'. The distinctive feature of cinema, therefore, is this necessarily imaginary, absent quality, quite apart from whatever imaginary world it may happen to represent. The cinematic signifier is itself imaginary. Hence cinema uniquely involves its audience in a play of absence and presence, whose prototype is the imaginary completeness of the absent image of the child in the mirror. Screen images are 'made present in the mode of absence', and it is this combination of the presence of a rich perceptual field and the absence of what it conveys that essentially defines cinema.[24]

fantasy

With this much established, the analysis then proceeds to enquire what modes of subjectivity are implied by the characteristic play of absence and presence. Paralleling Mulvey, but differing in certain crucial respects, Metz maintained that three basic processes were operating: identification, voyeurism, and the related phenomena of disavowal and fetishism. Of these three, his proposals around identification proved to be the most influential.

In order to function at all in social life, Metz argued, people must have a sense of identity; hence the process of identification must accompany all social practices. The question then is, 'With what. . . does the spectator identify during the projection of the film?'[25] Given that cinema has already been established as a technique of the imaginary and in so far as the screen bears a certain resemblance to a mirror, the obvious answer would be that the spectator identifies with an image of him or herself in a manner analogous to the mirror phase. This, however, is ruled out on two grounds. One is that the screen, unlike the mirror, does not image the spectator's body. And the other is that films only make sense to subjects who have passed through the mirror phase, entered language and accepted the laws of the symbolic. In other words, the imaginary of cinema presupposes the symbolic. (It is here, incidentally, that Metz claims he departs most markedly from Baudry.)[26] An alternative answer to the question would be that the spectator identifies with a fictional character or with a star (the answer given by Laura Mulvey). While accepting that such identification does exist and provides one of the pleasures of cinema, Metz argued that it is in fact secondary, requiring an act of recognition by an already constituted identity for it to occur. If this is so, it is necessary to discover the source of this prior, primary identification that enables the spectator to recognise his like on screen.[27]

The answer to this further question is that 'the spectator identifies with himself, with himself as a pure act of perception'.[28] The reasoning runs as follows: conscious always that he is in the cinema, in the presence of something only imaginary and hence, regardless of what happens on screen, unthreatening, the spectator is aware, firstly of himself as absent from the screen, placed outside it in a position of all-seeing mastery; and secondly, of the condition of films being perceived, namely that he exists there in the auditorium as the seeing, hearing subject without which the film would have no point or even existence. This dual knowledge on the part of the spectator permits him to identify with his own act of seeing and hearing, as a pure instance of perception, 'as a kind of transcendental subject anterior to every there is'.[29] The point has been made by subsequent commentators in possibly more accessible terms. Thus, Stephen Heath writes that the apparatus of look and identification institutes the spectator in 'the totalising security of looking at looking'.[30] And John Ellis states that identification with the cinematic apparatus 'involves the fantasy of self as a pure perceiving being.'[31]

Such identification is powerfully reinforced – and here Metz's debt to Baudry becomes more pronounced – through the spectator's concomitant identification with the camera, whose monocular perspectival regime inscribes the place from which vision acquires a godlike omniscience. The spectator is the camera at once actively training its gaze upon objects and passively receiving the imprint of its perceptions. The homology between apparatus and spectator extends to the cone of projection of light onto the screen, which parallels an ideology of vision as just such a searchlight beam illuminating the field of the subject's intentionality. So profound is the homology between apparatus and the activity of perception that the two are taken as identical and indissociable – on the side of activity: camera eye, the projector, the cone of visual intention; on the side of passivity: sensitised emulsion, screen, retina. Yet for all the omniscience and omni-vision deriving from the identification, indeed because of them, the subject is nonetheless caught up in alienation and misrecognition, both 'transcendental yet radically deluded'.[32]

In his discussion of voyeurism and fetishism Metz covered some of the same ground as Mulvey, but with a very different theoretical concern. Whereas Mulvey had seen them as the basis for understanding the relationship between the spectatorial gaze and representations of women, Metz was concerned to show that their structures dupli-

cated the cinematic machine of spectating, and hence are deeply implicated in it. To oversimplify, one might say that Mulvey's concern
was with the cinematic signified and Metz's was with the cinematic
signifier.

The two sexual drives on which cinema relies are scopophilia, the
desire to see, and what Lacan referred to as the invocatory drive, the
desire to hear. What distinguishes these drives from others is their
even greater dependence on lack, not only in that they foster a fruitless
search for the lost object that can never be recaptured, but also in
that they must maintain a necessary distance from their respective
objects. While the drives associated with orality and anality seek a
degree of fusion between their source and their aim, those of vision
and hearing require the maintenance of the gap between the body
and the object. This holding at a distance is indeed a diagnostic feature
of the major arts such as painting, sculpture, music, and theatre, but
what further distinguishes cinema in respect of the scopic drive is
not so much the distance as the absence of the object. In theatre and
opera the co-presence of the spectator and performer ensures that
there is a presumed complicity between the two, so that the spectator's
voyeurism is matched by the performer's exhibitionism, making them
'the two protagonists of an authentic perverse couple'.[33] In cinema,
on the other hand, the performer is present when the spectator is
not (during shooting) and the spectator is present when the performer
is not (during projection). The reciprocating acknowledgement of
the existence of the other is far less pronounced, even absent, as, for
example, in the convention of the actor never looking directly at
camera and so confronting the spectator with his own voyeuristic
gaze. This shame-faced, unacknowledged, non-consensual looking
of the cinema spectator at that which 'lets itself be seen without presenting itself to be seen' places cinema in a direct line of descent
from the primal scene, the unwitnessed witnessing of the parents'
copulation.[34] Various features of the cinematic institution contribute
to this affinity. The spectator sits in darkness before a lit screen,
making for an 'inevitable keyhole effect'; then, though a member of
an audience, he nonetheless remains essentially solitary; the actors
necessarily remain in ignorance of the spectator; and finally, the film
unfolds in a place that is simultaneously close and yet definitely in-
accessible, all of which makes the experience of voyeurism in the
cinema one of transgression.[35]

The pertinence of psychoanalytic concepts to the elucidation of the relation between subjectivity and the cinematic signifier is most marked, according to Metz, in disavowal and fetishism. Like the cinematic signifier itself, these turn on the play of absence and presence, and, while not going as far as to posit a simple equation between the cinematic situation and fetishism, Metz points to their shared features. The structure of disavowal can be conceived in terms of discrepant knowledge and belief. The child's discovery of sexual difference institutes an anxiety in the face of the threat emanating from the lack in the Other, figured as the absent maternal phallus. To ward off the threat the child disavows difference and the lack in the mother, resulting in the characteristic formula encompassing the contradiction: 'I know very well but all the same. . .' If, subsequently, some object is elected to mask the lack disavowed, an object that simultaneously denies that anything is absent but whose presence acknowledges that it is, then disavowal has taken the specific form of fetishism.

Metz argued that something very comparable to this takes place around the cinematic institution. The spectator knows very well that what he is watching is a fiction, but all the same he maintains the belief, indeed his pleasure is dependent on the belief, that it is not. Cinema is thus founded on a regime of spectating at once knowing one thing and believing its opposite, which, as we have seen, is precisely the structure of disavowal. Indeed, with its rich sensorial presence and objective absence, the cinematic image 're-plays the game of castration: "to be or not to be", death, anxiety'.[36] Like the fetish, which 'disavows a lack and in doing affirms it without wishing to'[37] the cinematic apparatus itself is 'a kind of substitute for the penis'.[38] Or rather, 'it is not exactly a substitute for the penis, but for the *absence* of the penis', both affirming the presence of what is absent and emphasising the fact of that absence.[39] Cinema's technical achievement is to make what is absent so forcefully present that the spectator almost, but never completely, forgets that it is absent. Unless this awareness of absence is sustained there cannot be an appreciation of what is made present. The spectator's enchantment depends, as in classical fetishism, on a simultaneous awareness of what is present and what is absent. Just as the fetish completes the female body and disguises its lack, so the technical accomplishment of the cinematic apparatus perfects the imaginary signifier and masks the absence on which it turns. The fetishist gains pleasure from the object that stands both for the woman's lack and her lack of lack;

the cinephile gains pleasure from the never-quite-closed gap between imaginary presence and real absence. So for Metz there are effectively two levels of fetishism: one where the apparatus is the fetish, the other where the image and its meaning (as for Mulvey) become the fetish.

Thus Metz answered his original questions: How does cinema perpetuate itself? How does cinema produce pleasure and the desire to return for more? Cinema is the imaginary signifier, that is, it involves a process of signification turning on an absence that it seeks to fill but never finally does. In the gap between presence and absence a lack constantly reappears, and it is this lack that renews desire, so guaranteeing the perpetuation of cinema as institution. Although his solutions were not received without some dissent – John Ellis, for example doubted the transgressive quality of film spectating pointing to the authorisation conferred on voyeurism by the present of others in the cinema – and despite an undeniable current of phallocentrism running through his analyses (to which we shall return), Metz's work had a tremendous impact on film studies.

Central to the thinking of both Baudry and Metz was the theme of the misrecognition devolving on cinematic signification, a theme that was taken up again in the debate around suture. This very complex concept refers both to the relation of the subject to his or her discourse, and to the junction of the imaginary and symbolic thereby entailed. In speaking, or in enunciating a text, the subject is divided, but defends itself against this division by a pseudo-identification in which it imagines itself a unity. As a concomitant of every act of signification, suture in some form or other accompanies all linguistic and social practices. However, when the concept was taken up by film theory it was considerably simplified. With film theory's early emphasis on cinema as a discourse organised around absence and lack, subsequently inflected through an Althusserian terminology, the moment of pseudo-identification was understood as an instance of misrecognition. Suture, therefore, was held to be an effect only of certain texts, or rather of certain textual practices, which (along the lines of the post-1968 typology around political functioning) were those that alienated and deceived. It was only in the latter stages of the debate that the complexities of the concept were duly acknowledged.

The first important theorist of suture was Jean Pierre Oudart, who advanced a description of its operation within cinema in a series of articles in *Cahiers*. He proposed that Lacan's notion of the subject suturing the lack opened up by enunciation with an imaginary entirety fitted the logic of cinema spectating well. His argument ran as follows. The spectator's initial response to the cinematic image is one of jubilation, not unlike that of the child in front of the mirror. The image offers an imaginary plenitude, 'a pure expanse of *jouissance*', in which the spectator is caught up in a fascination with the unreal.[40] Such dyadic bliss is ill-founded and short-lived, for in the cinema, as elsewhere, there is no imaginary without the symbolic. The first intimation of crisis is the discovery of the frame, the terminus of the image that reveals the absent space out of frame and induces anxious questions in the spectator's mind. The image is no longer innocently there; it is there for someone. From this certain questions arise (Who is this missing spectator whose point of view this is? And who is ordering and framing the image?), questions that threaten to expose film as signifying practice, as a constructed and enunciated operation. What annuls the threat is the system of shot/reverse shot, by which a second shot shows the first to have been the field of vision of a character within the fiction. In this way the Absent One turns out to be a particular character whose point of view is disclosed, and the threatening absence is reappropriated within the film. By introducing a character to take the place of the Absent One, the system of shot/reverse shot sutures the rupture in the initial relation of image to spectator and envelops cinematic discourse within the imaginary.

As conceived by Oudart, suture is the tragedy inherent in cinematic discourse, entailing as it does the loss of the totality of the image and hence of spectatorial pleasure. Such a conception is oriented towards an evaluation of films according to whether they expose the specifically tragic nature of cinematic language, with Oudart citing *The Trial of Joan of Arc* as an example of a film that does do so and *Au Hasard, Balthazar* as an example of one that does not. In the case of films that do expose their discursive processes, that do move from the imaginary towards the symbolic, the spectator is no longer positioned in an illusory relation to the text but is actively involved in a process of reading that reveals the film's textuality. In this way the truth of cinema is allowed to unfold and reveal itself.

With Daniel Dayan, the emphasis shifted from suture as the tragedy inherent in cinematic discourse to the *ideological* operation of a particular mode of discourse.[41] In taking up the concept from an Althusserian standpoint he represented the play of absence and presence in ideological terms, as a particular mode of interpellation or filmic address constituting the individual as subject. Along with other post-1968 thèorists, he held that a film's ideological functioning was less a partisan depiction of the world than a mode of enunciation that masked the ideological origin of its discourse. Like Baudry and Oudart, Dayan understood the cinematic image as the equivalent of classical painting organised by perspective, with the spectator constituted as a subject in a position of imaginary dominance by the specular effect of the image's spatial organisation. Unaware of the codes positioning him or her, the thus-constituted subject is denied the knowledge that the representations of the film are the product of a semiotic system. What is threatened by the potential exposure of this, through framing and so on, is the film's successful ideological operation. In order to sustain it, various strategies have been developed, primarily the shot/reverse shot system, which, by locating the origin of the image in the diegesis rather than in the process of representation, is able to render the working of the film's codes invisible. Consequently 'the spectator. . . absorbs an ideological effect without being aware of it.'[42]

Dayan's account of suture has been criticised on various grounds. Barry Salt, whose exhaustive analyses of the textual procedures of classic cinema have overturned many received ideas, has demonstrated that shot/reverse shot comprises only some thirty to forty per cent of the total cuts in Hollywood narrative from the 1930s onwards.[43] Contra Dayan, who maintained that other forms of shot were unusual, Salt pointed out that for most films the majority of shots were not within the shot/reverse shot format, and moreover that films such as *Birth of a Nation*, in which only three out of over 2000 cuts employ the reverse angle, work powerfully on their audiences. And if the device was so effective why, Salt demanded, was it not pushed to extremes (say, seventy percent or more of the cuts) in all commercial films rather than just a few.

William Rothman questioned the dominance of the two-shot sequence (shot/reverse shot) and suggested instead that for Hollywood the norm is a three-shot sequence: first the character looking, then what is seen, then the character again.[44] For example in the Bodega Bay scene of *The Birds* an initial shot of Melanie looking prompts the question, what is she looking at? This is answered by shot two, showing what she is looking at, namely, the Brenner house. Then follows shot three, showing Melanie's reaction to what she has seen. The significant point of this is that the Absent One has no role here at all: the question 'Whose point of view is this?' simply does not arise. Spectators know a point of view shot when they see one, and indeed know that all shots are produced by the cinematic apparatus. The capacity to read a film and to pass judgement on the veracity of the representations is not therefore determined by the suppression of codes at all – if it were, cinema would be an ahistorical institution endowed with the power to deceive in all conjunctures. Hence the process as described by Dayan, functioning on behalf of ideology, is itself a fiction.

A further contribution to the debate was made by Stephen Heath, who, while accepting many of the criticisms made by Salt and Rothman, still held the concept of suture to be important for an understanding of cinema as discourse producing a subject address. In contrast to linguisitic utterances, film images bear few, if any, of the marks of their enunciation, instanced by the relative difficulty of contradicting them. Images make it much harder to quarrel with the ideological representations they offer. The concept of suture is therefore valuable in its emphasis on the cinematic image as an utterance and in making it clear that the apparent completeness of the image is only illusory, that it requires for its completion a subject of enunciation. But at the same time that subject is never finally and fully represented there, because the subject is always fading. This play of incompleteness and completeness is what suture can help to specify: meaning and subjectivity come into being together in the endless process that is the subject's emergence into the symbolic.

But in arguing for the concept's pertinence Heath was not uncritical of his predecessors in the debate. He took issue with the emphasis on shot/reverse shot, pointing out that, as the juncture between the imaginary and the symbolic, suture is present in every enunciation: all texts suture, though they do so differently. In Chantal Akerman's film *News from Home* there is no instance of shot/reverse shot, so according to the Oudart and Dayan conception it should therefore be unsutured, but the spectator is nevertheless 'included and moved. . . in a structure and a rhythm of lack and absence'.[45] More generally he criticised Oudart and Dayan for their transformation of a purely descriptive concept into a means of evaluation, hence into the basis for a typology of films. Their mistake was to suppose that certain films were less implicated in the imaginary than others – for

Oudart, the work of Godard and Bresson, for example. Since the imaginary and the symbolic are always co-present, this shift blocks thinking about the relation of spectator to film. Dayan's linkage of suture with interpellation also came in for criticism. As with all Althusserian readings, Heath said, there was a tendency to emphasise the imaginary at the expense of the symbolic and unity at the expense of division. Moreover, whereas interpellation conceives of the subject as produced, psychoanalysis makes it at once production and product: film does not position the subject but performs it, just as there is a 'permanent performance of the subject in language itself.'[46]

The most important theoretical work of the 1970s deriving from Lacan centred on what Metz termed 'the social regulation of the spectator's metapsychology'.[47] In conceiving of cinema as an institution with both technological and psychological components, the theory offered explanations of how, variously, the subject acquired an imaginary unity, an impression of reality was created, and the institution reproduced itself in promoting the desire to return for more. The strength of the 'hegemonic and totalising model' of the cinematic apparatus developed by Baudry and by Metz was, however, also a source of potential weakness, as two main lines of criticism made apparent.[48]

In the first place, because the substantive features of cinema discussed by Baudry and Metz are found, if not in every film, at least in certain broad categories, the variability of spectator response remains unaccounted for. The fact that different cinema goers react differently to the same film implies that some essential determinants of a film's reception are being neglected by the theory. Secondly, the theory in effect foreclosed on the possibility of transforming cinema, as was argued by Constance Penley. She pointed out that if the effects of the apparatus were total and irresistible then there could be no form of cinema that could subvert its power.[49] Since such forms of oppositional cinema were held by many theorists, notably by feminist critics and filmmakers, to be not only desirable but possible, then there must be some places where the control of the cinematic institution was not total. Both lines of criticism were to lead towards the psychoanalytic concept of fantasy.

It is, of course, something of a commonplace that a parallel may be drawn between the condition of the spectator in watching a film and the condition of the dreamer, daydreamer or fantasist. As John Ellis puts it, 'Images and sounds are received in a state where the normal judging functions of the ego are suspended to some degree (near to sleep), so that what is seen is not subject to the usual expectations of plausibility that we apply to everyday life.'[50] There is, moreover, further similarity between filmic form and content and fantasy itself, so much so that, for instance, Laplanche and Pontalis can describe fantasy in terms of a cinematic metaphor when they write of it as 'the mise-en-scène of desire.'[51] After all, what is Hollywood, with its stars, its happy endings, its interminable elaboration of Eros and Thanatos, but fantasy? However, with this acknowledged, there is the risk of simply repeating the reductionist interpretations offered by the earliest application of psychoanalysis to cinema, the invariably successful hunt for sexual symbolism in apparently innocent texts. The reintroduction of the notion of fantasy might, in other words, turn out to be a limited and regressive move.

That such was not the case may be attributed to two significant differences between its more recent and its earlier application. The first of these was that fantasy was conceived not as originating in the mind of the director but as operating in the exchange between the film and the spectator. The concept, then, was not intended to replace the imbrication of text and spectator with a content analysis, but was a means, precisely a means, of elaborating the relationship between text and spectater. In enunciating a fantasy that drew support from the text, the spectator was at once constituting and constituted.

The second major difference was that instead of fantasy being considered as straightforward wish-fulfilment, it was acknowledged to be a more complex compromise formation in which the repressed ideas were given expression, but only in a distorted form, dictated by the repressing agency. As with the classic symptom, then, enunciated fantasy contained both the unconscious wish and the defence against it. As defined by Laplanche and Pontalis, fantasy is an 'imaginary scene in which the subject is a protagonist, representing the fulfilment of a wish (in the last analysis, an unconscious wish) in a manner that is distorted to a greater or lesser extent by defensive processes'.[52] Fantasy never articulates desire alone but always desire and the law. And even more complexly, it may express conflicting desire and the law in a single ensemble.

An example of fantasy as compromise formation in the analysis of a film is Elizabeth Cowie's reading of *Now Voyager*. In it the fantasy played out is that of the phallic mother. Having displaced her own mother, Charlotte becomes a surrogate mother to her lover's child by taking her in and caring for her, while at the same time denying herself sexual relations with him and leaving his unhappy marriage intact. In this way her initial transgressions, her enactment of homosexual and aggressive impulses, are indirectly punished and thereby legitimated by the film. By not marrying her lover and yet retaining a part of him in his daughter she at once becomes the phallic mother and abides by patriarchal law. Desire and its prohibition are thereby both articulated through the film. Cowie's analysis is not that of Charlotte as analysand, which would merely have a sophisti-cated yet still reductive content analysis, but is instead one of the film itself. The fantasy is the film's, not Charlotte's; it is an effect of its narration and therefore available to the spectator alone, the 'place in which all the terms of the fantasy come to rest'.[53]

Thus the concept of fantasy at once continued and developed the earlier application of psychoanalysis to film. The continuation lay in the attention to the spectator as the subject of the enunciation, the development in the greater complexity accorded to this subject. For in fantasy the spectator engages in multiple identifications, and in its filmic scenarios may identify with several figures simultaneously, women and men, winners and losers, heroes and villains, the active and the passive. This conception of the subject as occupying con-tradictory positions and thus articulating conflict within the psyche, is distinctly different both from traditional notions of identification with the star of the same gender and from the Althusserian model in which the spectator is fixed in position by an assumption of a unified self-image.

The psychoanalytic text most frequently referred to here is Freud's paper 'A child is being beaten', concerning a masturbatory fantasy reported by some of his patients. The fantasy had three phases, which differed according to the gender of the patient. In the first phase, the child being beaten was not the patient and the beater was an adult of indeterminate identity. Freud interpreted this adult as being the father and surmised that the fantasy demonstrated the father's wished-for love by having him beat a rival sibling. In the second phase it is the fantasist who is being beaten by the father. For the female patient this represents a compromise between her desire for the father and her guilt about that desire, the sadism of the first phase thus being transformed into masochism. For the male it re-presents both a masochistic attitude towards the father and an iden-tification with the feminine position, thereby expressing a wish to take the father as love object. The third phase, though resembling the first, continues to act as the agency of the second phase, that of the passive desire for the father. But the male represses his homosexual desire by identifying with the beating adult not the beaten child, so adopting the active masculine position; and simultaneously he adopts a passive position towards the desired phallic mother through the variation 'I am being beaten by my mother'.[54] The female also seeks to avoid incestuous attachment to the father in this phase, but does so by replacing the father with some other adult such as a teacher and by adopting the position of an onlooker, 'a spectator of the event which takes the place of the sexual act'.[55]

Freud's analysis clearly demonstrates that fantasy entails multiple points of identification and places of enunication. An example of the way such complexity can bear on filmic reading is given by Laura Mulvey's study of the Western, where, she proposes, narrative closure typically takes one of two forms, either a marriage, resolving the Oedipus complex and integrating the hero into the symbolic order, or non-marriage, 'a nostalgic celebration of phallic, narcissistic omnipotence'.[56] The tension implicit in this alternative often results in there being two heroes, as in *The Man Who Shot Liberty Valance*, in which Tom (John Wayne) embodies primitive phallic power, but whose defeat of Vallance goes unrecognised and who loses the woman, and in which Ranse (James Stewart), 'the upholder of the law as a symbolic system', is misrecognised as the victor and marries the woman.[57] With this fantasy scenario the spectator is able to identify simultaneously with Tom and Ranse, with Ranse mourning Tom, and with the woman marrying Ranse but loving Tom. Thus the spectator's desire in all its complexity is given expression and becomes 'pleasured'. But the pleasure so gained is not to be conceived in terms of the traditonal wish-fulfilment model.

This last point was something particularly stressed by those most influenced by Lacan, for whom fantasies involve not satisfiable needs but unsatisfiable desires. Because, for Lacan, desire is in pursuit of an eternally lost object, it is more accurate to say that fantasy sustains rather than satisfies desire, that it is the staging or mise en scène of desire rather than its fulfilment. As Lacan put it, 'the fantasy is the support of desire, it is not the object that is the support of the desire';[58] and Cowie, 'the fantasy depends not on particular objects, but on their setting out; and the pleasure of fantasy lies in the setting out, not in the having of the objects'.[59] Desire is therefore perpetuated through ever more elaborate signifying ensembles, one of which is of course narrative, where the spectator both desires and does not desire resolution. When resolution occurs the lost object figured by the narrative will be achieved only to fall once again into loss by the very fact of that achievement. So long as the narrative delays the desired moment, leaving open the question of how and when it will occur, while leading inexorably up to it, then pleasure is the outcome.

An example given by Elizabeth Cowie is the film *Reckless Moment* in which the central characters Lucia and Donnelly circulate through a number of positions.[60] Lucia is variously Donnelly's lover and mother and, in the absence of her husband, father of the household; Donnelly, for his part, is variously lover, son, father and mother. At the end of the film the tensions produced by this sliding between positions are not resolved, only halted; in any case what matters is not so much any would-be resolution, but the succession of figures, equivalences and exchanges put into play by the narrative. Similarly Elisabeth Lyon's analysis of *India Song* as fantasy establishes that the spectator is variously and simultaneously 'the 'I/ego of the camera – the beggarwoman – Ann-Marie Stretter – the Vice-consul – death'.[61] Taking up Lacan's formula $\$ \lozenge a$ (where $\$$ is the barred subject, a the *objet petit a*), she describes fantasy as the relationship of the subject to the non-existent object of desire, figured in the film by the key image of the naked breast of Ann-Marie Stretter. The lozenge in the formula stands for the third element, the Other, which always separates subject and object, and here represents the interchangeability of positions inside and outside the fantasy, the positions of participant and observer. As in *Reckless Moment* there is a circulation that never reaches a resolution: fantasy as the staging of desire can never provide an answer to the question of desire, but can only re-pose it.

More generally, the formula $\$ \lozenge a$ conveniently summarises the several ways in which the concept of fantasy has reoriented the application of psychoanalysis to film. The emphasis is now on *objet petit a*, desire and the symbolic rather than on the imaginary, concomitantly acknowledging that for the subject there is nowhere outside the symbolic order and no Other of the Other. Whereas, then, the earlier metapsychologists argued for the sameness of the effects of the apparatus on spectators, the concept of fantasy entails difference, not simply pertaining to a male/female dichotomy, but in recognition of the uniquely determined complexity of the psychic economy of each spectator. Fantasy means diversity of response to the same film, with each spectator enunciating their own economy of desire through it. Finally, if among the earlier theorists there was a tendency to invoke the unconscious only to ignore it, fantasy insists on it. Fantasy's subject is barred, mobile, fading, present only 'in a de-subjectivised form . . . in the very syntax of the sequence in question'.[62]

Psychoanalysis was introduced into film theory as a supplement to historical materialism and semiotics. The fact that it has not only remained but has moved to a position of centrality might perhaps seem surprising given the problems attendant on it. However, as we have already shown, psychoanalysis in its Lacanian mode proved to be remarkably consonant with post-structuralism, whose underlying precepts came to dominate film theory after the mid-1970s. Nevertheless, despite this alliance, there were a number of outstanding unresolved problems, which we shall discuss in the remainder of this chapter.

The first of these concerned the specific ways in which psychoanalysis had been applied to the study of film. The objection that the use of psychoanalysis in film studies ran counter both to the classic theory and to the more recent Lacanian reworking of it was not simply a matter of defending doctrinal purity. Rather, it intended to signal that any improper use of psychoanalysis would inevitably store up problems for whatever theoretical project it was informing.

Metz's proposition that cinema, more than any other art, involves its audience in the imaginary was challenged along such lines by a number of critics, including most notably Jacqueline Rose and Constance Penley. His claim that the cinematic image places it within the register of the imaginary is, they pointed out, fundamentally at odds with Lacan's thought, for no image has meaning in itself, given directly through vision, but only acquires it within a particular cultural order. Just as for the child the idealised self-image of the mirror phase is given by the mother's look, that is, by the Other, so too is the imaginary always informed by the symbolic. This failure to acknowledge the importance of the Other has significant repercussions for Metz's central thesis, that of the spectator's identification with his own act of perception, leading to a delusory omniscience. According to Constance Penley, Metz's line of argument that the apparatus always installs the spectator as an all-perceiving subject, confuses its aim with its effects, which is particularly apparent when one considers the subject in relation to vision and desire. For in looking, as in speaking, the subject is divided: 'vision always takes place in the field of the Other's vision and desire'.[63] In treating the imaginary as a state of plenitude antecedent to accession to the symbolic, a state to which the spectator as an effect of the cinematic image regresses, Metz misses the workings of desire in the exchange between spectator and film. What is necessarily a triangular relationship is misconceived as dual. A number of consequences accrue to Penley's avowedly Lacanian respecification of these scopic relations. In the first place, the subject of vision is itself an object of representation, because what determines the subject is a look that is outside – for Lacan, in the field of the visible: 'I am looked at, that is to say, I am a picture'.[64] Secondly, there is no such thing as a purely perceptual look, it is always a matter of it being conditioned by the desire of the Other. Because of the structure of desire there can be no question of the look achieving the satisfaction of seeing what it wants to see, but only perpetual deferral down the metonymies of narrative. Finally, the place the subject occupies, more seen than seeing, is itself, by virtue of its implication with the unconscious, unstable and dispersed. All in all, these consequences conspire to thwart the apparatus's aim of constructing a transcendental and secure subject identifying with itself in an act of pure perception. Faced with these criticisms Metz had no defence but to confess 'I am not a Lacanian'.[65]

The second problem, that of the supposed ahistoricality of psychoanalysis, may be dealt with quite briefly. Lovell's objection that psychoanalysis is an 'a-historical theory of the constitution of the subject and its entry into language and culture' can hardly be sustained when one considers that each individual is formed within a unique family configuration that is itself an effect of a wider historical matrix.[66] Psychoanalysis does not, and does not need to, offer a theory of social and familial change; its concern is to chart their effects through the oral histories recounted on the couch. Where Lovell, however, does have a point is that it has proved difficult to theorise the two together, to find a means of integrating psychoanalysis and theories of social change, whether Marxist or otherwise. These difficulties emerged in concrete form, as we have seen already in chapter 2, when attempts to theorise the historicality of the subject in relation to reading texts remained largely unsuccessful.

The third problem, that of feminine sexuality, is by far the most pressing of psychoanalysis's lacunae. Freud's difficulties here are well known, not just in relation to his contentious privileging of the penis in the concept of penis envy, for his failure satisfactorily to theorise the female Oedipus leaves us with no overall explanation of the construction of female subjectivity. While modern feminist advocates of psychoanalysis have tended to turn to Lacanian theory as the place of resolution of these difficulties, it is still far from settled that Lacan has made any significant advance on Freud. At its simplest, the problem is that if in patriarchal culture women are seen as lacking why should anyone assume a feminine identity.

For some feminists any problems here are outweighed by Lacan's central emphasis on the symbolic in the construction of subjectivity, which disposes equally of reductionist notions of biological determinism and of mystical notions of feminine essence. For such as Juliet Mitchell, Jacqueline Rose, and Ellie Ragland-Sullivan, Lacan's theories offer an explanation both for the construction of subjectivity under patriarchy and resistance to it. Their value lies in their 'exposure of the inevitable alliance between "feminine essence" and the natural, the given, or precisely what is outside the range of political action and thus not amenable to change'. [67] The insistence that the 'subject is not constructed from sexuality, [but] sexuality is constructed in the history of the subject' marks therefore a complete break with any idea that anatomy has to be destiny.[68]

Or does it? Is there not one almost axiomatic concept through which anatomy, despite all protestations to the contrary, returns? The phallus, according to Lacan, is not the penis. Possessed by neither men nor women, belonging to the symbolic order and not nature, taking its value like all signifiers from its relation to other signifiers, the phallus signifies the lack indissociable from entry into culture. As such, it permits sexuality to be conceived 'as an arbitrary identity that is imposed on the subject, as a law. . . legislated rather than autonomously assumed', hence provisional, often inappropriate, and potentially open to change.[69] Not everyone, though, is convinced of the phallus's radically non-biological status. For example, Jane Gallop, in many respects sympathetic to Lacan, has detected in his and his followers' work an 'endless repetition of failed efforts to distinguish phallus and penis clearly'.[70] Whatever else it means, the phallus also always stands for the penis, a confusion that is symptomatic of the impossibility of conceiving a non-phallic masculinity at this historical moment.

This problem, along with the more general one around the construction of female subjectivity, was reflected in the uneven development of psychoanalytically informed film theory. Although by the end of the 1970s psychoanalysis had contributed to a persuasive account of the exchange between a film and the male spectator, no comparable account existed for the female spectator. According to Laura Mulvey's widely accepted analysis of the voyeuristic and fetishistic structures organising the male gaze, the woman was what was looked at, not the one who looked. The place of enunciation, ·the place of the look was for the majority of films that of the male. As Mary Ann Doane has noted, 'historically there has always been a certain imbrication of the cinematic image and the representation of the woman'[71] and cinema has 'articulated its stories through a conflation of its central axis of seeing/being seen with the opposition male/female'.[72] Debarred, except as objects, from the characteristically masculine scopic regime of voyeurism and fetishism, women have a very different relation to the image from that of men. The reason for this difference, Doane proposed, is 'the overwhelming presence to itself of the female body', a theme of self-proximity that has been elaborated by Luce Irigaray, Hélène Cixious and Michèle Montrelay.[73] As a consequence woman are unable to establish the distance from the image that is the condition for voyeuristic pleasure and control, narrativising the Other as female image, and instead remain in a relation to it of identificatory narcissism. Women are similarly barred from fetishistic structures. As Doane has written elsewhere, what can fetishism 'have to do with the female spectator for whom castration cannot pose a threat since she has nothing to lose?'[74] In its place the woman's relation to the image is one of 'over-identification', one that is founded on the absence of a distance between seeing and knowing. Such a position is finally untenable precisely because it fails to confer on the spectator the distance needed to read the image adequately.

It follows from the above that female spectators have two principal options: either the assumption of a masculine position; or the assumption of a passive or masochistic position through identification with a female character. We shall consider each of these in turn.

The principal theorist of the masculinisation of the female gaze has been Laura Mulvey, who returned to and expanded on her earlier position in response to criticisms. According to D. N. Rodowick the only place in Mulvey's scenario for the female subject was as a negativity defining castration.[75] Linda Williams similarly objected that the concentration on the male look at the woman left no place for women's own pleasure in looking.[76] Mulvey responded by arguing that Hollywood masculinised its female spectators in offering them male points of view and male identifications. Indeed, there was nothing specific to cinema in this, for across a whole range of folk and mass culture the grammar of narrative 'places the reader, listener or spectator *with* the hero'.[77] Through such identifications women can enjoy the freedom and control typically given to the hero by narratives. The hypothesis could be supported by Freud's own later writings on women, which propose that, because feminity is gained through repressing the masculine tendencies of the phallic phase, neurosis in women is often to be explained in terms of the irruption of this repressed material. What Hollywood offers the female spectator is a socially sanctioned access route to her repressed masculinity. And there is a reinforcement of this process of masculinisation through the parallel, already noted by Freud, between the ego and the hero of any narrative. The phrase 'Nothing can happen to me', so succinctly expressive of the ego's sense of superiority and invulnerability, finds its narrative correlate in the typical hero's passage through the text. In identifying with such a figure and confirming the ego's fantasies, the female spectator is habituated to transsexual identifications. Though the gain is that of the reactivation of the fantasy of 'action', which a proper femininity represses, it is at the cost of a certain uneasiness at violating patriarchal precepts.

Mulvey's version of the female spectator, however, commanded less widespread assent than her theorisation of the male spectator. One alternative version was that provided by Mary Ann Doane, at least over the scopic field sustained by so-called women's films. In analysing a corpus of films addressed to women (e.g. *Rebecca, Suspicion, Gaslight, The Two Mrs Carrolls, Caught, Possessed, Secret Beyond the Door* – titles that in themselves are revealing), she found that the spectatorial options were not limited to either a narcissistic identification with the woman as spectacle or a transsexual identification with the male hero. Instead, these films summoned up an interactive process between text and spectator that could best be comprehended in terms of the third stage of the fantasy 'A child is being beaten', where the woman/girl no longer figures as a participant in the scenario but as a spectator. Such films turn on 'masochistic fantasy instead of sexuality'.[78] In them women are de-eroticised, functioning not as spectacle to be looked at but as protagonists in masochistic scenarios.

Of the two forms these tend to take, one has the woman as the agent of the gaze investigating a secret whose solution entails an act of aggression against her (paradigmatically, the locked room where her husband is planning to murder her), as if 'the woman's exercise of an active investigating gaze can only be simultaneous with her own victimisation'.[79] In the other the woman is afflicted by an illness, the object of the medical rather than the erotic gaze, and constituted within a medical discourse that seeks to tell her story through interpretation of her symptoms. Often blind or mute, she must wait for a man to disclose her truth through medical or psychological discourse. In both kinds of scenario the effect is to desexualise the woman's body, and concomitantly to address the female spectator in such a way that she 'loses not only her sexual identity in the context of the scenario but her very access to sexuality', so recapitulating the de-eroticised, specular stage of the female version of 'A child is being beaten'.[80]

These considerations, however, were part of a larger debate around the work of the theorists of the apparatus, notably Baudry and Metz. While it was generally agreed that they had performed a valuable service in shifting the emphasis from the reproduction of objects to the production of subjects, serious doubts existed about the implication of their work for the female spectator. So inseparable was the machinery of image reproduction and projection from the psycho-perceptual machinery of scopophilia, identification and fetishism, that the place of women in such a system must be deeply problematic. In their account there were two levels of exclusion: from representation and from spectating. Both of these conspired to make 'the very idea of a feminist filmmaking practice seem an impossibility' because 'the simple gesture of directing a camera towards a woman has become the equivalent to a terrorist act'.[81] Given this situation, one strategy, exemplified by the films of Peter Gidal, has been systematically to exclude all images of woman on the grounds that they could only partake of the dominant system of meanings. Yet the very fact that this strategy compounds the exclusion of women makes all the more evident the impasse film theory had reached.

In consequence women theorists became increasingly critical of the concept of the cinematic machine. Drawing on Freud's remark that all complicated machinery and apparatus occurring in dreams stands for the male genitals, Constance Penley suggested that the apparatus as conceived by Baudry and Metz was a 'bachelor machine' with a characteristic 'bacheloresque emphasis on homogeneity and closure'.[82] Their very mode of theorising effectively closed off questions of sexual difference. For Joan Copjec, the apparatus thus conceived was a machine to defend against the alienation and division experienced in the symbolic and hence was a denial of the sexual difference inscribed in the symbolic. Any conception of the apparatus that meets the spectator's demand and fixes him in a secure and unified identity runs counter to the whole drift of Lacan's thinking, and therefore represses those aspects of it most important for women. The only role for women, given the existing theories, was to adopt strategies of subversion: Mary Ann Doane proposed one such strategy at the level of representation: the masquerade. In flaunting herself, in producing herself as an excess of femininity, the woman can reveal that 'it is femininity itself which is constructed as a mask – as the decorative layer which conceals a non-identity', thus challenging the iconographic patterns that function as a support for the male gaze.[83] At the same time, by opening up a distance from the female image the masquerade allows it to become controllable, readable, producible by the woman.

More promising, by and large, than subversion was the prospect of finding an alternative theory of the institution of cinema. What was needed was a mode of theorising that would retain the radical implications of Lacan's notion of the complex constitution of both subject and object through discourse, but would avoid the phallocentrism implicit in Lacan's thinking. Just such an ideologically acceptable, de-phallicised recasting of the relation of subjectivity and discourse was to be found in the work of Foucault.

By adopting Foucault's conception of power, whereby discourses produce domains of objects and modes of subjection, Copjec and Doane advanced a theory of femininity as constructed within discursive practices. Thus, Doane writes: 'Femininity is produced very precisely as a position within a network of power relations.'[84] And Copjec: 'Patriarchy can only be an effect of a particular arrangement of competing discourse, not an expressive totality which guarantees its own self-interest.'[85] For Doane, referring back to her discussion of fetishism and voyeurism, the distinctive closeness and 'presence-to-itself' of femininity is not, as some have supposed, an expression of some essence but is rather the outcome of the place women are culturally assigned. And for Copjec the consequent need was for an analysis of how the multiformity of sexual difference and subject position is related to particular discursive formations and practices.

The work of Foucault was also to provide support for those who believed that psychoanalysis, despite various attempts to feminise it, was indissociably complicit with phallocentrism. Like any other discourse, Foucault said, psychoanalysis was grounded in nothing beyond historical contingency, and therefore could not be judged in terms of any supposed truth, but must stand or fall on the basis of its effects. Its theory and practice amounted to a discourse on sex that was necessarily implicated in power relations. As to whether it had done anything to question or redefine power, his conclusion was that it had not. But there were possibilities for resistance to the subjecting alliance of discourse and power, and in his less guarded moments he suggested that any theorisation of this must start from the body. The suggestion was taken up by feminist film theorists, who sought to re-theorise the relation of the body and discourse in such a way as to do justice to feminine specificity while avoiding essentialism. A conception of the body was necessary, said Doane, 'in order to formulate the woman's different relation to speech, to language'.

One aspect of this reassertion of the feminine body, indeed of the reintroduction of a concept of the body into psychoanalysis, was the adoption by Doane and Copjec of the notion of anaclisis. This term had been used by Freud to designate the way the infant's sexual drives trench on its ego or self-preservation instincts, an obvious example being provided by the oral phase, when the erotic pleasure of sucking the breast is associated with satisfaction of the need for nourishment. Only later does the detachment of sexuality from the bodily function occur, after the child has come to want the secondary pleasure independently of the original somatic need. Taking up this idea, Copjec suggested that the deviation of the drive from the instinct was caused by the introjection of 'a scene of satisfaction into the subject'.[87] Although the body is not the cause of the psyche it nonetheless has a role in structuring it. Likewise Doane argued for the irreducibility of sexuality to bodily function, but also for the latter acting as a support for the former.

Copjec and Doane also both referred to ideas elaborated by women working within or proximate to a Lacanian framework that had been treated with suspicion by the anti-essentialists. Julia Kristeva's linking of discourse with its pre-linquistic somatic precursors (this and other aspects of Kristeva's work are discussed in chapter 7) and, of greater immediate relevance, Luce Irigaray's respecification of the feminine were called on by Doane in support of her position. For Irigaray, because of the phallomorphic tendencies of all existing theories of subjectivity, there was the need for a break with them, but in a non-essentialist direction. Starting from the specificity of the female body, in particular the multiplicity of its erotogenic zones and the nature of female genitals, whose lips constitute a constant and unforbiddable source of mutual embrace and self-touch, Irigaray proposed that female sexuality was plural, non-unifiable and could not 'be subsumed under the concept of subject'.[88] And mirroring this sexuality was an equally non-masculine relation to language, at once polyvalent, plural and free of the restrictive insistence on identity of patriarchal law.

While many feminists considered Irigaray to have lapsed into the very essentialism she sought to avoid, Doane maintained this was altogether too dismissive. It was possible, she held, by using the notion of the body as a support or 'prop', to rethink the relationship between the female body and signifying processes in such a way as 'to define or construct a feminine specificity (not essence)' and 'to provide the woman with an autonomous symbolic representation'.[89] There could be no question of some natural feminine body directly finding expression in a transparent medium. For one thing, the ideological complicity of 'the natural' was such as to rule it out; for another, the body was always written, coded, a function of discourse, with its sexuality implicated in language. Through these qualifications to Irigaray's position the hope was that a middle course could be steered, avoiding equally a reductive essentialism and an anti-essentialism where the body either vanished or was simply a derivative of discourse.

Doubts about this strategy were expressed by Constance Penley. It was, she felt, bound to reproduce the difficulties associated with the essentialist position, where identity and difference are established before they can be adequately questioned. In particular she doubted the value of the concept of anaclisis for these purposes, in that any attempt, however indirect, to derive gendered sexuality from the body endangered the uncompromising insistence of psychoanalysis that sexuality is an arbitrary identity imposed by convention. The law of sexual division requires that everyone take up a position in relation to the phallus, a non-biological entity. Hence, the concept of anaclisis effaced 'the *difficulty* of femininity as a sexual position or category in relation to the symbolic'.[90] A far more effective counter to the maleness of the cinematic apparatus than the reintroduction of the female body was through the concept of fantasy, which offered a way of preserving and accounting for sexual difference without pre-determining what any given individual's sexual identity should be. How any one spectator relates to a filmic narrative depends on their unique pattern of desire, with the only fixity coming from the formal masculine and feminine positions as defined by the fantasy. By giving an explanation variously of the spectator's desire of the image, the fantasmatic relation to that image, including a belief in its reality, and his or her multiple and changing identifications, the theory of fantasy could retain a notion of the cinematic institution while 'con-structively dismantling the bachelor machines of film theory'.[91]

There is, finally, the most fundamental problem of all: the fact that psychoanalysis is founded on the discovery of the unconscious. Since the implications of this are so far-reaching we shall leave discuss-ion of it until our concluding remarks, when its significance for the entire film theoretical project will be easier to gauge.

Authorship

Nothing in recent film theory has excited more controversy than its rulings on authorship. To say, as it has, that the author is meaningful only as a construct of the spectator, to forbid any discussion of texts in terms of authorial intention, and – most notoriously – to announce the death of the author as a fact was, and remains, a scandal to the critical establishment and a violation of common sense to the wider public. This hostility can be traced to the historical modes of thinking about cinema. In our introduction we suggested that serious writing on film has been dominated by two concerns, one of them to establish the status of cinema as art, the other to comprehend its social functioning, and that since 1968 the latter has acceded to the erstwhile hegemonic position of the former. The displaced orthodoxy can be encapsulated by the single word 'auteurism': the belief that cinema was an art of personal expression, and that its great directors were as much to be esteemed as the authors of their work as any writer, composer or painter. The very obviousness of the position was also its strength, for auteurism grounded itself in the commonplaces of the romantic notion of the artist, thereby gaining film entry to the hallowed canon of Art. Because authorship was the basis for cinema's belated acceptance as an art form, the critics who had fought for this recognition were appalled when the existing concept of authorship was dismissed as obscurantist. The particular bitterness expressed towards the new theories by such critics can be understood as the reaction of those who had fought a long battle only to see the terrain they had won being voluntarily abandoned.

In view of the many existing accounts of auteurism we shall do no more than trace the broad outlines of its development. *La politique des auteurs*, first formulated in two articles in the pages of *Cahiers*, was itself a challenge to an existing criticism based on social and political concerns. Alexandre Astruc, writing in 1948, compared the camera with a pen ('la caméra stylo') through which the creative director could express his thought and sensibility; François Truffaut, some six years later, used the term *auteurs* to describe such 'men of the cinema' contrasting their individually creative style with that of the *metteurs-en-scène*, which was effaced in remaining faithful to a film's literary precursor. In being taken up by other critics Truffaut's distinction was given a more stridently evaluative tone, with directors being divided into the elect and the damned according to which category they were assigned. In practice, as has been pointed out by John Hess, those singled out as auteurs tended to concentrate on the themes of spiritual insight and personal salvation favoured by the auteurist critics.[1] The artists, in other words, were those whose films reflected the critics' own ideology.

Auteurism took a more controversial turn when it was applied to the American cinema. Not only was it asserted that a creative artist could work within the constraints of Hollywood, but also that run-of-the-mill commercial products could in fact be works of art. *Cahiers'* championship of directors like Lang, Hawks and Ray, a tactic designed to validate the cinema of those from whom the would-be filmmakers among *Cahiers* critics felt they had most to learn, was taken up with even greater fervour by auteurists in the United States. Of these, the most zealous was Andrew Sarris, who in renaming *la politique* 'the auteur theory' imputed to it a consistency and rigour rarely apparent in any of its manifestations, least of all his own. Whatever else it may have been, auteurism was never a theory. What it *did* become, through Sarris, was an extraordinary plea for the superiority of American cinema over that of the rest of the world, specifically through the agency of a hierarchy of directors from 'the Pantheon' downwards.

In Britain, as in France, auteurism displaced a dominant criticism concerned with the social effects of cinema, by which films were judged according to how well they conveyed 'a certain social, ethical or philosophical content'.[2] For the auteurists such criticism offered only an impoverished textual utilitarianism to the detriment of the aesthetic appreciation of film. Like their French and American counterparts, the auteurist critics associated with the journal *Movie* looked to a cinema 'which had style, imagination, personality and, because of these, meaning'.[3] The *Movie* critics also made their own distinctive contributions. In response to criticisms that it discussed films in primarily thematic terms, *Cahiers* had already begun to concentrate on the mise-en-scène, which, lying between the script and the cutting room, is the characteristic domain of directorial choice: lighting, camera, sets, acting and so on. By taking a script written by someone else and by imposing his directorial style, an auteur makes the film his own, they argued. Sarris too had referred to auteurism's new emphasis on the 'how' of film in contrast to the sociological 'what'. But it was *Movie* that put this programme into practice in a series of close textual readings of films, concentrating above all on the details of mise-en-scène. Such analyses, notably those of Robin Wood and Victor Perkins, were very different in their attention to textuality from anything that had preceded them and would not be surpassed for seriousness in relation to their objects of study until the shot-by-shot semiotic analyses of the post-1968 structuralists.

Despite its aesthetic orthodoxy auteurism provoked opposition even among those committed to a romantic notion of the artist. While it was acceptable that a director such as Bergman, with control throughout the production process, should be deemed comparable to artists working in other fields, it was far from clear why directors inside the studio system should be. In reply, the auteurists invoked the names of Mozart and Michaelangelo, whose work had also been subject to institutional constraints, and pointed out that there were undeniably directors working within Hollywood whose films displayed a discernible consistency and identity of style. Given that they often had to contend with a variety of scriptwriters, studios, actors and genres, the only possible source of this unity was the director himself. Again, in response to the objection that formulaic plots and stereotyped characterisation amounted to an artistic straitjacket, the auteurists argued that the conventions of genre, far from foreclosing on new meanings, in fact enabled their generation. Because any system of rules brings with it the possibility of transgression, genre can be seen as providing a field for variation and elaboration of meaning; hence genre is not something that imprisons a director but precisely allows him a freedom.

In retrospect, the auteurist phase can be applauded for having opened up popular culture to serious study (hitherto confined to the writings of the then little read Frankfurt School), although it did so in order to elevate one small section of it to the status of high art.

Additionally, its attention to mise-en-scène was important in laying the groundwork for subsequent analysis of cinematic specificity, although once again a qualification must be added to the effect that the most impressive studies of this type (the work of David Bordwell, for example) seem to owe more to semiotics and Russian and Czech formalism than they do to auteurism. But from the politicised perspective of its immediate aftermath, much of auteurism seemed irredeemably trivial, exemplifying that aesthetic of consumption that Althusser condemned as being 'no more than a branch of taste, i.e. of gastronomy'.[4] Worse, it appeared to represent a withdrawal from what Habermas has termed 'the public sphere', that realm of wider, extra-academic debate where critical and theoretical issues engage with concrete social issues. With few exceptions, most notably Robin Wood, auteurist critics appeared to have backed off from social reality in favour of arcane and indulgent bickerings among cognoscenti about who was or was not to be admitted to the Pantheon (Sarris) or the Great (*Movie*).

Auteurism's initial response to the criticisms coming from this seemingly unimpeachable intellectual quarter was to adopt the colouration of the enemy. However, in opting for structuralism as a defensive tactic, the auteurists could hardly have made a worse choice, as subsequent debates would soon show. But for a time it seemed that the resultant auteur-structuralism, based on the classic structuralism of Claude Lévi-Strauss, had given auteurism sufficient intellectual credibility to survive.

Lévi-Strauss's structural anthropology was directly inspired by Saussurean linguistics, in particular the work of Roman Jakobson in phonology. Jakobson proposed that underlying the immense variety of sounds in natural languages is a small number of binary phonological oppositions. This universal binarism, the organising principle of all phonemic systems, was taken by Lévi-Strauss as strong evidence for supposing that there is a comparably universal structure within the human mind, functioning irrespective of time and place. Not only language but all human culture, said Lévi-Strauss, is governed by a system of mental constraints operating according to binary oppositional features, a system he termed 'the unconscious'. Hence the anthropologist confronted by the diversity of totemism, kinship systems and myths should proceed in a similar way to the linguistician faced by the heterogeneity of natural languages, aiming to disclose the basic unconscious structure underlying the phenomenal diversity. In studying any of these cultural phenomena, it is essential that a large number of instances be considered, so that the systematic relationships of transformations, homologies and inversions become visible. The procedure must also take cognisance of the fact that the elements of the structure assume their significance in relation to other elements and hence cannot be assigned a fixed meaning in themselves. As with language, it is the selection and combination of elements that produces meaning. A final feature of structuralism that finds clear expression in Lévi-Stauss is its polemical anti-humanism: if language, culture, thought and meaning are the products of an unconscious system, then 'man' and consciousness can no longer be held to be their source. Structural anthropology shows 'not how men think in myths, but how myths operate in men's minds without their being aware of the fact'.[5]

The hope was that auteurism's perceived under-theorisation could be redressed by adopting a Lévi-Straussian structuralism, enabling it to become 'a more scientific form of criticism'.[6] Just as Lévi-Strauss had revealed a unifying structure underlying the diversity of myth and kinship rules, so auteur-structuralism would 'uncover behind the superficial contrasts of subject and treatment a structural hard core of basic and often recondite motifs';[7] these motifs 'united in various combinations constitute[d] the true specificity of an author's work'.[8]

The principal advocate of this 'scientific' approach was Peter Wollen. Having written, under the pseudonym Lee Russell, a number of influential pieces on such auteurs as Ford, Hitchcock and Fuller, he now repudiated existing auteurism as the transplantation of the romantic theory of the artist to Hollywood. Instead of the personal vision of the creative artist the new methodology would reveal in any given oeuvre an objective structure that generated its characteristic meanings, patterns and intensities. Only by studying the whole oeuvre – in the manner of Lévi-Strauss – could the underlying structure be discerned, comprised as it was of elements whose meanings would be determined by other elements within the global structure. With each film the various elements would enter into new relationships and would therefore signify something different. The method, Wollen cautioned, could not be content with simply identifying the diagnostic features that all the films of a given director had in common, it must also discover what distinguishes each film from the others. As well as repetition there must also be an awareness of difference, as well as universality, singularity. The work of an auteur was – consistently with structuralism's taste for binaries – typically organised around one such opposition, or 'master antinomy'[9] In the case of Hawks, the difference between the dramas and the comedies derived from the opposition between the masterful triumphant heroes of the former and the victimised humiliated anti-heroes of the latter. In the case of Ford the master antinomy was that between nature and culture. But the master antinomy manifested itself with even greater complexity in that with each film this varies according to how it is played out across a further set of binary oppositions: garden/wilderness, ploughshare/sabre, settler/nomad, European/Indian, civilised/savage, book/gun, married/unmarried, East/West. Moreover, each opposition has its own specificity and cannot be simply mapped onto any other; the elements within each opposition do not possess a fixed value but are determined relationally in every case. So, for example, the element 'Indian' in the opposition European/Indian may be aligned with the element 'savage' in one film and with the element 'civilised' in another. Its meaning alters with context and in so doing alters the meanings of all other elements it relates to. The method thus permits the identification of a specifically Fordian system while respecting the singularity of each text.

Although *Signs and Meaning* was widely read, providing a popular introduction to novel ideas, its central auteur- structuralism was soon to be abandoned, not least by Wollen himself. The generally anti-auteurist sentiments of post-1968 film culture were antithetical to any residual romantic notions of the artist, even when allied to a supposedly scientific structuralism. But when the rights of alliance and the credentials of its source of salvation were called into question, as they soon were, the discourse around authorship was forced in a quite different direction. The specific objection that auteur-structuralism had failed to found its work theoretically was made by Brian Henderson, who pointed to its failure to address the fundamental questions of the comparability of myths to films and the appropriateness of the structural method to analyse film.[10] Henderson's contention was that a body of myths and a film director's oeuvre are so different as to render the method utterly inapplicable. The fact that myths have no authorial centre, do not originate in a subject, indeed rely on interchangeability of subjects for their perpetuation through constant retelling, makes them strictly non-comparable with a corpus of films whose distinctive signature is that of the author.

Wollen himself was not unaware of such difficulties, as is revealed
by the modifications in the second edition of *Signs and Meaning*. In
the first edition it was the structuring activity of the director, conscious or unconscious, that generated the distinctive character of the
work, hence permitting Wollen to engage in traditional evaluations,
say, of Ford as 'a great artist, beyond being simply an undoubted
auteur'.[11] By 1972, however, Wollen was concerned to distance himself from such traditionalism, the emphasis now being placed not on
expression of the artistic vision, but on 'the unconscious, unintended
meaning [that] can be decoded in the film, usually to the surprise
of the individual involved'.[12] Ford, the director of genius, becomes
'Ford', a structure traced within a set of texts, of which Ford himself
knows nothing. The characteristic structure 'Ford' may be empirically
assigned to a certain filmmaker, whose role is undeniably substantial,
but the two 'should not be methodologically confused'.[13] As Henderson pointed out, the shift between the two editions is that the director
has become the necessarily unconscious catalyst to the materials he
works with rather than having the script act as catalyst to his own
creative imagination, consciously or unconsciously. This opposition,
we would suggest, is not quite as straightforward as it might seem.
The notions of author as unconscious producer of meaning and of
author as catalyst in the production of meaning may or may not be
identical, but any hesitation in equating them can be conceived as
interference from a much more charged opposition, which Wollen
may be seen as attempting to articulate. Indeed, the postscript to
the second edition of *Signs and Meaning* may be read more produc-
tively not as a resolution of the problem of synthesing auteurism
and structuralism, but as a transitional text from a pre-structuralist
concept of the author as creator of meaning to a post-structuralist
concept of the author as a construct of the reader. For the fundamental
tension implicit in the postcript is between thinking of the text as
produced by the author and thinking of the author as produced by
the act of reading. It is here, we would suggest, that the historical
importance of auteur-structuralism resides: as a first step towards
distinguishing the empirical author from the author constructed by
(because desired by) the reader; between John Ford, who sometimes
enjoyed making fun of Lindsay Anderson, and 'John Ford', the structure identified by Peter Wollen in a body of Hollywood films.

In further relation to the demise of auteur-structuralism were growing doubts about the validity of Lévi-Strauss's methodology. First

of all, its supposedly secure foundation in the work of Jakobson was undermined when the adequacy of his claims for a universal phonemic structure in all languages came to be questioned.[14] Moreover, Lévi-Strauss's central concept of a collective unconscious came to be seen as only weakly explanatory once the scientific pretensions of his work were challenged. Even more damning than its lack of scientificity were its ahistoricality and its idealism ('Kantianism without a trans-cendental subject', Paul Ricoeur called it[15]), implying that there could be no real human history, only 'the same song in different keys plus occasional improvisations, over and over again.'[16] Ahistorical idealism was not at all what the historical materialists of the coming generation of film theorists wanted to hear, and thereafter the name of Lévi-Strauss was rarely invoked.

Auteurism's next encounter was with historical materialism, which, in contrast to structuralism, posed a threat to its whole conceptual project. Historical materialism directed attention to two constella-tions of production: one of film as a commodity and the various technical, economic, political and ideological determinants of this; the other the production by the film of meanings with ideological and political effectivity. The conceptualisation of each of these entailed rethinking the notion of the author, which in both cases resulted in a decentring of the authorial role.

From the standpoint of commodity production, films were no longer conceivable as the creations of directors of genius, standing above or outside history; rather, they were the effect of a whole array of determinations making up any particular conjuncture. Under such a conception the director can be awarded no special privilege as either the autonomous or the punctual source of meaning, since he neces-sarily works within the terms provided by the existing conventions of film language and within the institutional framework of film pro-duction. These objections to auteurism were not, in fact, entirely new. A generation previously André Bazin, the then editor of *Cahiers*, had chided 'the young firebrands' of the *politique* for ignoring 'the social determinism, the historical combination of circumstances and the technical background' by which any authorial talent was largely determined.[17] What was new was the impetus given by the post-1968 political climate and by the resurgence of Marxism to the study of both the immediate production context and the larger social framework in which it took place.

As far as the immediate production context was concerned the auteurists had maintained that this was of negligible importance (despite occasional gestures to the contrary, e.g. Sarris: 'All directors, and not just in Hollywood, are imprisoned by the conditions of their craft and culture') in comparison with the authorial presence.[18] But now a series of studies showed how specific conditions of production were inscribed in the text. One early study was that by Ed Buscombe of Raoul Walsh's period of directing films for Warner Brothers.

Buscombe showed that from 1939-51, when Walsh made over twenty films for Warners, he experienced a relative lack of freedom in comparison with the conditions under which his earlier work was produced. At this time Warners were committed to a New Deal ethos, and Walsh accordingly made films displaying 'a feeling of unease about the condition of society and a desire for change'.[19] In both *Public Enemy* and *High Sierra*, for instance, the cause of crime is identified as social deprivation and hardship, a position differing markedly from that inscribed in the gangster films of the 1940s and 1950s, where crime is an effect of individual psychopathology. Similarly, Warners' commitment to the war effort is reflected in Walsh's war films starring Errol Flynn. In general, then, his films of the late 1930s fit in with the studio's social commitment, as do his subsequent films with the studio's changed general policy. They are, in fact, 'typical of the studio for which they were made.'[20] But the ideological preferences of the studio heads were not the only constraints operating on Walsh, for these preferences translated into 'a self-reinforcing system' of production. Having found that their gangster films made money, Warners placed under contract stars such as Bogart, Cagney and Raft, who were associated with gangster roles, which in turn required the production of more gangster films to justify their being on the payroll. Directors working for Warners, therefore, found their assignments dictated by these circumstances. This was not to say, Buscombe concluded, that Walsh brought nothing to his films, but that in working for a studio such as Warners, with its own distinctive policy, he could no longer be simply treated as an auteur dictating the style and content of his films.

Buscombe's attempt to relate the work of the individual director to its historical context came in for criticism, from Colin MacCabe, on the grounds that it was still working with a view of the individual as autonomous and whole, liable only to contingent constraints.[21] The criticism was based on the then dominant belief in the viability

of Althusser's anti-humanist conception of the subject as the support
or effect of a pre-given structure, but, as we have already explained
in chapter 1, such confidence was soon to diminish as it became
apparent that the Althusserian model lacked sufficient explanatory
power. This inadequacy became evident in two subsequent attempts
to theorise the relationship of directors to the production context:
John Ellis's study of Ealing and that by Bordwell, Staiger and
Thompson of Hollywood. In each case it was to prove impossible
to provide a satisfactory account of the relationship without recourse
to a notion of the subject as agent, as constituting as well as constituted.

Ellis proposed that films are the product of three determinants
whose complicated interplay is inscribed in the form of the text. These
three are, first, the existing technology of cinema, which is itself the
effect of the entire history of the cinematic institution, including production, distribution and exhibition; second, the organisation of production itself, in its various stages from inception to completion,
and the forms of control by different groups over these stages and
over exhibition and distribution; and third, the aesthetic and other
beliefs of those controlling production. In articulating the relationship between these determinants, Ellis advanced a sophisticated
dialectic of agency and structure. He showed that although the Ealing
films were made by 'a creative elite' of directors, producers, writers,
etc. enjoying considerable freedom, the conventional notion of auteur
was inadequate to explain the relation of these individuals to their
films.[22] The institutional framework within which they were working,
typically requiring the production of some five ninety-minute films
a year, imposed its own rhythms and patterns of work. Further, the
ideology articulated in the Ealing films did not originate with the
studio's creative elite, but emerged from the contradictory social position they occupied. Their populist political sentiments could, as a
consequence, only find expression in a notion of 'the people' derived
from their own petit bourgeois backgrounds, the stratum of small
shopkeepers and clerks, while the industrial proletariat remained
unfigurable. Ellis's study did more, though, than expose a system of
constraints or direct ideological determinations operating on the
filmmaker; it showed that there was a dialectical relationship between
the filmmaker and the institution. One aspect of this relationship
concerned decision-making: investing in particular forms of technology in the studio, organising production along particular lines,

developing specific technical skills, all required filmmakers to make certain decisions based on a set of economic, technological and ideological considerations; but the result of such decisions was to alter the structure within which further ones would be made, thus enabling certain future modes of filmmaking and foreclosing on others. The distinctive preference for short takes and static camera and the relative absence of location shooting in Ealing films was to be attributed to this complex dialectic rather than to any supposed freely chosen style.

Similarly, Bordwell, Staiger and Thompson presented a model of agents in dialectical interaction with their economic, technological and ideological context. In their version of Hollywood, individuals are not simply bearers of positions, but function in terms of belief, desire and intention. The distinction between, for example, Ford and 'Ford' does not imply the denial of the existence of Ford as an agent in the production process. While the spectator constructs an image of the author on the basis of texts, this in no way rules out the necessity of returning to the concept of the empirical author for any analysis of the production of the film as commodity. Indeed, this was made explicit in the paradigm of Hollywood as a set of norms that the director could choose to follow, or, within certain bounds, transgress. The anti-structuralist tone of the study is given succinct expression in the conclusion, 'Hollywood films constitute a fairly coherent aesthetic tradition *which sustains individual creation*' (our italics).

Studies of the relation of text and author to the larger societal framework proved more problematic than those pertaining to the immediate production context. It was generally agreed that earlier Marxist attempts to theorise this relation were inadequate, tending as they did to rely on one variant or another of the reflection thesis. More promising was the approach suggested by the Althusserian notion of relative autonomy, which would allow both the specificity of a distinctive authorial signifying practice and that of the social formation to be respected, but this too was put into question by Althusser's critics, notably Hindess and Hirst, who argued that the notion of relative autonomy was unstable, either collapsing back into economic determinism or giving rise to a model of society where the various levels were fully autonomous. Such contentions were borne out by the attempts to theorise texts as the products of particular conjunctures. The resulting analyses were either reductionist or failed to establish the relationship. The best known example of such a conjunctural study is the reading of *Young Mr Lincoln* by the editors of *Cahiers*.

Their awareness of the need to avoid reductionism was explicitly stated: 'an artistic product cannot be linked to its socio-historical context according to a linear, expressive, direct causality', since any such relationship is necessarily 'complex, mediated and decentred'.[23] In practice, however, the analysis fell short of such high Althusserian ideals, discovering instead *Young Mr Lincoln* to be the rather unmediated expression of the studio boss's Republican sentiments. By the late 1930s, the argument runs, the major studios were totally controlled by bankers and financiers. The merger of Fox and 20th Century Productions had resulted in 20th Century Fox, which was managed by the staunch Republican Darryl F. Zanuch and was financed by the Chase National Bank. The studio therefore sided with big business against Roosevelt's New Deal, a struggle that intensified in 1937 with another downturn in the economy. In order to avoid further damage to their interests, it became imperative for big business to remove Roosevelt from the White House in the 1940 presidential election. The film *Young Mr Lincoln* was, *Cahiers* proposed, Zanuck's contribution to the campaign. Produced in 1939, on the eve of the election, the film takes as its subject Abraham Lincoln, who was both the most famous Republican president and, because of his origins, character and legendary aspect, the only one ever to have attracted mass support. Through Lincoln, therefore, the Republican Party could be given an aura of moral legitimacy at the same time as capitalism could be validated as 'a univeral Good'.[24]

Cahiers tried to advance beyond the limitations of this obviously somewhat mechanical Marxism by incorporating textual and, derivatively, psychoanalytic considerations into the analysis, but the attempt to bring these different levels together was largely gestural. Despite the insistence that the text is overdetermined and that aesthetic practice is relatively autonomous, neither of these were satisfactorily specified in relation to *Young Mr Lincoln*, the analysis of which called equally on a straightforward economic determinism and a conception of textual aesthetics as fully autonomous. No doubt much of the unevenness and opacity of this as well as other writings of the period were due to the inherent difficulty of learning and theorising simultaneously, but *Cahiers'* analysis was marked by an exceptional discrepancy between its ambition and its accomplishment. Its most notable uncertainty is between a notion of the text as producing meaning and that of it as expressing and repressing pre-given meanings, something that may be seen as representative of the more general problem of how to relate the various levels of practice within the Althusserian model to each other. Indeed, just how the various levels interrelate in practice has eluded all subsequent attempts to resolve the problem.

The most ambitious such study to date has been that by Bordwell, Staiger and Thompson of Hollywood film practice from 1917-60, a period characterised by a distinct and homogeneous cinematic style (which they termed 'the classical style') whose main features were narrative unity, realism and invisible narration. The explicit aim of the study was 'to establish the conditions of existence of this film practice, the relations among the conditions, and an explanation for their changes'.[25] Rejecting any notion of an autonomous practice shaped by immaterial forces, the authors of the study insisted that the explanation must be in terms of material determinants – economic, technological and ideological. Equally, however, they eschewed any crude base/superstructure model, following Ellis in arguing that production and stylistic practices within the industry could not be reduced to mere reflections of economic or political practices beyond it. The various determinations are irreducible to one another and interact mutually. While economic factors undeniably contributed to technological innovation and change as a way of improving efficiency or differentiating the product, it was, they proposed, stylistic factors that made the greatest contribution to the specificity of Hollywood during this period. It was the demand for one particular narrative style among many earlier styles that proved decisive for the organisation of production. Given that technical practices and changes had in the long term to be economically beneficial, the actual deployment of cameras, sound recording, lighting, colour, screen ratio and so on was dependent on stylistic considerations. 'A mode of film practice, then, consists of a set of widely held stylistic norms sustained by and sustaining an integral mode of film production'.[26]

Although the study is clearly indebted to Althusser, it falls short of integrating Hollywood into the larger social formation, and in this fails to validate the potential of the notions of structural causality, relative autonomy and overdetermination in analysing a particular historical moment. While acknowledging the possible determination in the last instance of the economic, there is no final synthesis relating the various practices within Hollywood either to one another or to those external to Hollywood. Rather, the analysis confines itself firstly to particular instances of local determination, and secondly to the conditions of existence of particular practices. Hence, despite their invocation of Althusser, Bordwell, Staiger and Thompson were in practice closer to the approach advocated by Hindess and Hirst, that of specifying the conditions of existence of contingent practices rather than elaborating a global causal model.

The other main focus of attention for historical materialism was on film as a producer of ideology. Designated as the perpetrator par excellence of a pernicious, mystificatory mass culture, Hollywood, from the renewed political perspective, was once more back where it had been before its auteurist celebration, 'a pejorative catchword for vulgar illusionism', except now the animus was directed not against its vulgarity but its mendacity.[27] Just two forms of commercial cinema escaped the prevailing condemnation: films made by those directors who came to be termed 'progressive' auteurs and films within *Cahiers*' category E (see Chapter 1, p. 9).[28]

Principal among the progressive auteurs was the exiled German film director Douglas Sirk, who worked within the Hollywood system during the 1940s and 1950s. During the latter part of this period he was at Universal, where his films, largely aimed at female audiences, would subsequently become the object of particular critical attention. Sirk had convincing political and aesthetic credentials: his thinking had been shaped by the debates on the Left about art and politics during the interwar years, and before becoming a filmmaker he had been active in experimental theatre with an explicitly social commitment. Such activity included staging Brecht's *The Threepenny Opera* in 1929. It was held by those who now championed his Hollywood work that when he fled to America to escape the Nazis he brought with him both a reasoned critique of capitalism and the aesthetic means to pursue it within the studio system. Paul Willemen summed up the situation as one in which he was attempting to criticise the system that gave him the means to make films, but only in so far as they were successful at the box office. Constrained not only by commercial necessity but by content and stories given to him by the studio, he nonetheless was able to make 'frequent use of the techniques Brecht had pioneered'.[29] One such was the device called 'the boomerang image' by the critic Bernard Dort: the staging of the most exotic and desirable images of life, but in such a way that they return to the spectator as an exposure of the realities of an existence that gives rise to such fantasies. In Dort's words: 'What the spectator discovers in the unreality of such an image is himself.'[30] The fulfillment of the wish is also its critique. According to Willemen, Sirk at one and the same time 'mercilessly implicates the audience' through techniques designed to have the maximum emotional impact – there was no finer practitioner of 'the weepie' – and succeeds in creating a measure of distanciation.[31] There are a variety of ways in which this distancing effect occurs. One is to exaggerate the tear-jerking potential of the text through the use of cliché to the point where it begins to break down, as in *All That Heaven Allows*. Here Rock Hudson's resurrection is symbolised by his leg rising beneath the blanket and a deer coming to his window against a backdrop of Christmas-card implausibility. Instead of breaking the rules of the genre Sirk intensified them. Another technique is to use the mise-en-scène to undercut the narrative, as for example through 'baroque colour schemes' or the use of camera angles inappropriate to the meaning of the image.[32] Or again, Sirk's camera is almost continually in motion, but it is usually at some distance from the characters, with medium and long shots predominating, so that there is a resultant effect of simultaneous involvement and detachment. The net effect of these techniques is to expose the 'contradiction between fascination and its critique', so permitting the thematisation of other contradictions in such a way that prevailing ideology stands out in relief.[33]

It might appear that readings such as this simply replaced the reactionary auteur with the progressive one, but matters were complicated by a measure of dissent and equivocation on the question of authorial intention. In discussing Sirk, Willemen at times suggests that he developed his filmic system precisely in order to mount a critique of society – a form of conscious subversion from with – whereas at other times the implication is that Sirk's dialectic of involvement and distanciation was the unconscious dramatisation of the contradictions of Eisenhower's America. From this latter standpoint the picture that emerges of a society whose surface health contrasts with its underlying neurosis could not be equated with Sirk's own personal vision. As in earlier discussions by the critics concerned with aesthetic rather than political questions, the opposition is between the author as conscious originator of the text and the author as its structural effect. Moreover, even if Sirk is allowed the traditional authorial privilege of knowing what he was doing, doubt has recently been cast on his credentials as a critic of postwar American society in that the films over which he had greatest control were also the most conformist.[34] In the words of Pam Cook, 'Sirk would appear to have been less in tension with his material, producing a hidden, underlying criticism, than at one with it; any criticism of the prevailing ideology to be found in his work could therefore be seen as overt, and, moreover, sanctioned by that ideology' – sanctioned, because the unity and homogeneity valorised by traditional auteurism is, from an Althusserian perspective emphasising the fissured text, an overriding aim of ideology.[35]

Thus discussion of progressive auteurs, while stemming from a very different conception of cinema, in certain ways followed the traditional auteurist path. However, the situation with respect to Category E films was more problematic.

The existence of the category followed from *Cahiers'* belief (in contrast to that of, say, *Cinéthique*) that simply because a film is a product of the capitalist system it is not thereby destined only to reflect it. The uniqueness and difference of texts is lost through a blanket condemnation, *Cahiers* argued. What was needed was analysis of the precise articulations of films and the ideology they produced, aspects of which could indeed run counter to the dominant ideological formations. *Young Mr Lincoln* was just such a film: despite its overt ideological mission of validating Republicanism through the figure of Abraham Lincoln, its project fell apart under the internal stresses of the text. We shall follow through the analysis in some detail.

Cahiers specified the film's project as the 'reformulation of the historical figure of Lincoln on the level of the myth and the eternal'.[36] In order for it to succeed there had to be repression of politics and of sexuality; but since the repressed always returns, these would be inscribed in the text in a similar way to the repressed in a patient's psychoanalytic discourse, namely in the silences, dislocations and hesitations. By applying a process of 'active reading' the text could be made to yield up what it left unsaid: those 'constituent lacks' and 'structured absences' that are at once the condition of the text's production of meaning and the disruption of that production.[37] The unsaid is both the condition of the said and a criticism of it; it is what the text does not wish to say but has to.

More specifically, the film's project is to condemn politics in the name of morality. Although Lincoln is presented as a member of the Republican party, and indeed his first words in the film favour the Republican policies of protectionism and a national bank, he is also presented as the embodiment of a morality beside which politics appears trivial. He is not just another politician acting on behalf of a sectional interest, rather he stands for the end of politics, offering the remedy for corruption and self-interested conflict. His relation to the Law and to truth is so intimate that he seems to exercise authority by divine or natural right, which becomes, through a metonymy, equally the right of the Republican party to govern. In this repression of politics Lincoln's later political struggles are passed over, notably his struggle against slavery, which is given only one brief allusion in the film. Such exclusion allows Lincoln to be represented as one who unites rather than divides, who brings harmony not discord: when he is faced in the film with a series of choices that apparently require him to take sides, he manages on each occasion either to reconcile the conflicting parties or to assume an Olympian detachment. Nor is this simply a matter of content, for the form of the film is itself organised around the question of what course Lincoln's life will take, the answer to which the spectator already knows. Hence the formal structure of the film 'effects a naturalisation of the Lincolnian myth'.[38] As Ben Brewster noted in a subsequent comment on the *Cahiers* article, the film falls within the genre of 'the early life of the great man'; the hero's later actions 'are already present in him ab initio and can be revealed in anticipation in apparently trivial incidents.'[39] Lincoln thereby becomes not a politician pursuing a career but someone fulfilling his appointed destiny – a rewriting that not only converts his life into myth but also helps to naturalise capitalism (and by derivation, its representative the Republican party) through a teleological view of history in which the end is predestined.

The repression of politics by establishing Lincoln as the embodiment of the Law is possible only through the further repression of sexuality, only by making him into a figure of 'ascetic rigour' for whom desire is forever postponed. His resistance to the advances of women makes him the more vigilant against the threats to social order of which the narrative makes him the guardian. When Mary Todd (who will in fact become his wife, though not within the time span of this film) invites him out onto a balcony at a dance, he fails to respond to the romantic implications of the situation and instead withdraws into solitary contemplation of the river, the symbol of his destiny. Only as a figure exhibiting 'the external signs of the very puritan sense of election' can Lincoln function as 'the restorer of

Ideal Law'.[40]

Yet the figure so constructed is a highly unstable one. Lincoln is identified with the mother, who in the Fordian oeuvre 'incarnates the idealised figure of Ideal Law' and whose function is to deflect or forbid desire and its associated social disruption.[41] In the film an equation between Law, woman and nature is established by having Lincoln read a law book in the company of Ann Rutledge, *the* woman in his life, on the bank of a river; when, subsequently, he chooses at her graveside to follow a career in law he is accepting the destiny marked out by these three. As a metaphor for the mother, Ann Rutledge has sanctioned his choice; and significantly it is from a mother that he first receives a law book (in payment of services rendered). However, this identification with the mother as the Ideal Law confuses the maternal and paternal roles in the Oedipal triad and makes Lincoln into both castrated and castrator. At some points in the film he is the castrating father, as when he quells a lynch mob or threatens violence to two litigants, while at other points he becomes the castrated inversion of this, as in the dance sequence when Mary Todd complains about his coldness. The argument is further complicated by *Cahiers*' claim that Lincoln is also the phallus, e.g. in the balcony scene, and elsewhere, as the agent of castration, is in possession of the phallus. That is, his role varies between the father and the son (who would be what the mother wants); he is at once in the contradictory positions of being and having the phallus. An obvious reading of this textual configuration would be to see it in terms of a fantasy offering the spectator a number of positions and to attribute the pleasure provided by the film to the economy it instantiates. But *Cahiers*' approach is to conceive of the combination of these incompatible functions in the figure of Lincoln as setting up tensions within the text 'which oppose the order of Ford's world'.[42] So, in the dance sequence, normally in Ford's work the moment of supreme social harmony, Lincoln, whom the film wishes to establish as the bringer of harmony, acts in such a way as to disrupt it. Instead, then, of the mythic figure the film intends, Lincoln is by turns comic, marked in the dance sequence by his social awkwardness and physical ungainliness, and monstrous, as when, during the cross-examination in the trial, his potential for 'castrating power' becomes so evident as to make visible his 'truly repressive dimension'.[43] This violence renders inoperative what could otherwise have been hagiographic, so that when, at the end of the film, he leaves the realm of the social to the accompaniment of thunder and lightning and the 'Battle Hymn of Republic' on the soundtrack, he has become '(like Nosferatu) . . . an intolerable figure'.[44] The film's ideological project founders on the rocks of its own textual inscription.

Where in all of this is the author Ford? Does it make any sense to attribute to authorial intent what runs counter to the film's ostensible aim? It is here that the problem of reconciling the historical materialist concern with determination (or overdetermination) and the post-structuralist concern with the productivity of discourse becomes most marked. There is, in *Cahiers'* analysis, an evident tension between two trends. On the one hand the film is discussed in traditional auteurist terms, with its ideological project attributed to Ford and repeated references to the Fordian oeuvre, all of which is necessary in order to establish Ford as the link between the text and the conjuncture of its production. On the other hand the 'active reading' does 'not hesitate to force the text, even to rewrite it, insofar as the film only constitutes itself as a text by integration of the reader's knowledge'; it assumes that language is productive not expressive of meaning, and Ford therefore is a construct and cannot serve to link film and history.[45] In retrospect it can be seen that the analysis was, like Wollen's *Signs and Meaning,* a transitional text, bridging one organising conception based on authorial intention and another based on textual productivity.

As has already been established in chapter 2, Saussure's theory of signification, with its emphasis on the purely differential nature of signifier and signified, was seen to have profound implications for the notion of language as communication. By extension, its implications for authorship were equally far-reaching. According to the communication model of language, the meaning of an utterance exists first of all in the consciousness of the sender, who then transmits it through the neutral medium of language to the receiver, who thereby becomes acquainted with the meaning intended. The traditional notion of authorship was simply the translation of this to the realm of aesthetics: the author's imagination is the source of the work's meaning, which, transmitted through the chosen expressive medium, provides access for the reader (spectator, listener) to the originating mind. But if meaning is produced within and only within systems of signification, then the conception of the author is radically called into question. Rather 'it is language which speaks, not the author', as Barthes succinctly phrased it.[46] Meaning can no longer be thought of as originating in the mind of the author, and emerges only in the act of reading. Language, says Barthes, 'ceaselessly calls into question all origins'.[47]

The principal proponent of this view within film theory was Stephen Heath, who used it to attack any attempts to improve traditional auteurism. According to Heath, the notion of authorship was an ideological construction that blocked thinking about film's political functioning. For as long as it was retained, language would be seen as instrumental, the means by which the author expressed what was already present within consciousness, and therefore as something to be potentially stripped away to reveal the authorial presence beneath. Furthermore, no theory of the subject within ideology and signifying practice would be possible, because '"man" and "author" go hand in hand, the latter a particular instance of the former.'[48] Only if this conception of an imaginary unity and punctual source of meaning were discarded could there be any materialist theory of the subject, the possibility of which, argued Heath in 1973, had been indicated by Althusser's reworking of Marxism. Consistently with such anti-humanism Heath refused any conception of the subject as a given rather than as constructed, or as a unified being present to itself through its consciousness rather than as divided and opaque. Authorship was incompatible with the investigation of particular modes of subjectivity, whether from an Althusserian standpoint in terms of how positions were imposed on the subject, or from a Lacanian one in terms of texts as 'the space of the process of sense and subject'.[49] Heath's thinking owed much here to Barthes, who wrote:

There is no other time than that of the enunciation and every text is eternally written here and now.[50]

The reader is the space on which all the quotations that make up a writing are inscribed without any of them being lost; a text's unity lies not in its origin but in its destination.[51]

For Heath, therefore, the author was not 'a subject of expression' but 'an effect of the text'.[52]

This line of thought also owed a considerable debt to Jacques Derrida. Although Derrida did not deny the possibility of communication, it was equally the case that in all forms of signification the intentions of the sender of a message might not be realised, a letter might not reach its destination. An author can no more determine how his or her text is read than can the sender of a message control its reception. For Barthes this stage of affairs was a cause for celebration: the 'death of the author' was 'the birth of the reader'.[53] He could declaim that writing was the space where 'all identity is lost', where the paternal lineage of authorial father to textual child breaks down, where a writer can be no longer held to precede or exceed what is written.[54] With the author abolished the restrictive limitation on the textual signified vanishes too, that which refers back to the sanction or validation from its supposed source. Instead 'writing ceaselessly posits meaning ceaselessly to evaporate it': the text is 'a multi-dimensional space in which a variety of writings, none of them original, blend and clash'.[55] Ultimately, Barthes enthused, the refusal of a fixed or final meaning to the text could be equated with a revolutionary refusal of 'God and his hypostases – reason, science, law'.[56]

The prospect of such liberation in reading texts was of less appeal to those working within film theory than it was to those in other arts, notably literature. Rather than exercise the newly sanctioned freedom, the concern here was, as before, to analyse the political effectivity of texts. For this reason Barthes was of less interest than Foucault, whose concern was with the effects of the institution of authorship.

Foucault's work on authorship arose directly from his concern with the relations among discourses, subjects and power. Having asked the general question as to the formation of the concept of 'man', he addressed the specific mode of subjectivity that is the author. Like Barthes, Foucault accepted that the author as God was dead, this being the concomitant of the philosophical move away from 'the theme of an originating subject'.[57] Whereas orthodox criticism continued to use the text as the route back to the author's thought and experience, for Foucault the day of such biographical and psychological criticism was over, along with any notion of the subject as originary or creative. But the suspension by decree of the myth of the free subject endowing the world with meaning was insufficient; more was required than mere sloganising about the common death of man, God and the author. Rather, a new agenda was called for to address the following questions: under what conditions and with what effects does the individual come to fulfill the function of author? For while the author as creative source does not exist the institution of authorship undeniably does. Produced within discourse, organis-

ing and regulating other discourses, the author-function has its effectivity. The meaning attached to the name of an author is not modified
by empirical data pertaining to the actual person (as with other proper
names), but only by reference to the corpus of texts attributable to
the author. If we found that Shakespeare had not written the sonnets
then the author-function would be different, but it would be
unchanged by his not having lived in Stratford. The name of the
author is thereby involved in relations of power. It functions as a
means of classification, grouping together texts and differentiating
them from others; it 'establishes different forms of relationships
among texts. . . of homogeneity, filiation, reciprocal exploration,
authentification or of common utilisation'; it confers a certain status
on texts and guarantees a certain mode of reception distinct from
that accorded to non-authored texts.[58] These functions should be
studied in order that the largely unreflexive employment of the concept of authorship be open to re-examination. For example, those
engaged in the publication of an author's complete works implement
rules of inclusion and exclusion that are neither explicitly formulated
nor theorised. Where should the line be drawn? What goes in? Jot-
tings? Personal memoranda? Notes to the milkman? Once questions
of this kind are raised, the supposed unity of an author's oeuvre is
immediately problematised.

More generally, such questioning and exposure of the author-function
allows an understanding that authorship is but one way, not the way, of
regulating the circulation of texts. It is not the spontaneous attribution of discourses to individuals that it may seem to be, but is rather
the product of a complex operation 'whose purpose is to construct
the rational entity we call an author'.[59] Nor indeed is the author a
constant or invariable function applicable to all texts – some texts,
like railway timetables or advertising copy are unauthored, others,
like episodes of Dallas, are marginally less so, while the films of John
Ford enjoy full authorial status. Moreover authorship is something
that is historically variable. Today scientific texts are anonymous in
that their validity is established in relation to the science itself rather
than the authority of the writer, which was not the case in the Middle
Ages. Conversely, literary texts are now authored, whereas they once
were anonymous, accepted without any requirement of authorship,
with their supposed antiquity the guarantee of their authenticity.

Although Foucault's work was a first step in the historical analysis
of different modes of discourse (and as taken up within film theory

had the effect of developing just such analyses), it offered little in the way of explanation for the existence of the author-function, of why anonymity needed to be avoided. That question is a very real one for film theory, for despite the sustained and theoretically decisive critique of auteurism, mainstream discussion of cinema is still dominated by the quest for the author, its main critical concerns being to distinguish authors from the anonymous mass of directors, to establish their identity by reference to their most characteristic work and distinguishing style or thematic focus, and to pass judgement as to their respective merits. A persistent authorial discourse runs through from publicity ('the new Francis Ford Coppola'), to critical reception in print and on television ('an interesting additon to the Coppola oeuvre'), even to academic discussion ('Coppola's debt to Heidegger'), where it is nominally barred. The question as to *why* authorship is so persistent is, given the character of authorial debate (the endless questions, the never finalised anwers), perhaps best approached through psychoanalysis.

It will be recalled that the subject emerges in the symbolic only at the cost of division, only to fade, and it therefore never achieves the fixed identity it seeks. Confronted by such questions as 'Who am I? What is the desire of the Other', and (most crucial to the psychoanalytic situation), 'Who is speaking and to whom?', the subject has no final answers, but the questions still have an inescapable urgency. At the centre of authorial discourse there is equally a search for an identity, one that is to be achieved through establishing the identity of the author, which, as Foucault has pointed out, has been a principle of unity since the Middle Ages. If an author does not have the requisite coherence – expressed in the complaint that he or she has not found their voice – there is no available point of identification, the satisfaction of finding out who is speaking (and therefore to whom) is denied. But the establishment of an author's identity is in itself not enough, since the subject no more wants to be just anyone than he or she wants to have just anyone. For the subject to be taken by an author there must be a consonance with the subject's psychic economy. While every encounter with a text is unique, since a different economy is instantiated in each encounter with an author, something of the structures in play can be suggested. At its simplest, what is at issue in a reader's concern with an author is the identification of the author as the same as or different from him or herself: there is either an alignment with a positively defined author (I, like Bresson, am a saint), or an oppositional identification against one negatively defined (I, unlike Hitchcock, am not a sadist).

The process is, however, likely to be complicated in various ways. First of all, rather than identifying with the empirical author (on the basis of interviews, biographies and the like), the spectator may do so with an idealised image of the author constructed from a reading of the work, with the figure whose unity is attested by the unity of his or her vision. The identification would thus be not with Fassbinder who behaved badly to his friends, but with Fassbinder whose compassionate vision of damaged lives represents an indictment of late capitalism. In this way the spectator can enjoy a double mastery, on the one hand that deriving from the unifying vision of the idealised Fassbinder, on the other that of placing the empirical Fassbinder within the framework of a judgemental metalanguage. A second modification may be akin to the fetishist's 'I know very well, but . . .' in that the spectator knows that even the idealised Duras does not encompass the world within her vision, but likes to believe she does, thereby fixing world, Duras and spectator in an imaginary unity. Again there is a double mastery, both through identification with Duras's mastering vision and through the possession of a meta-language that subordinates her vision to the spectator's own, which is thereby shown to be more all-encompassing. Finally, as in the fantasy 'A child is being beaten', the spectator may identify with several figures at once, so that, to return to the Fassbinder example, there is identification with both beaters and beaten in his films: with Fassbinder as the observer of the scene, with Fassbinder as at once the beater and beaten, and with oneself as omniscient observer of the all-too-human Fassbinder.

Nevertheless, whatever economy of identifications applies, none is ultimately satisfactory, since the unity invoked to fend off the lack experienced within the symbolic necessarily fails. For this reason there is the constant search for the new and original author, who holds out the promise of an Other that is not lacking, an Other that is One. Though such an Other can never exist, the desire for it is unabated and the quest goes on. Authorship is one way, but not the only way, of finding answers to the question, 'Who is speaking and to whom?' Its survival may be explained by this provision, but it is not guaranteed.

CHAPTER 5

Narrative

To write about narrative is also to chance writing a narrative, for as Barthes has demonstrated, our culture is saturated in narrative: myths, legends, fables, tales, short stories, epics, history, tragedy, drama, pantomime, painting, stained glass windows, films, news, conversation, even dispassionate exposition. Not only does narrative emerge in a wide variety of forms in our own culture, but it is also a cultural universal, present from the beginning of human history in all cultures at all times. As such it has always appeared to be as natural as 'life' itself.

It was this apparent naturalness that film theorists in particular were concerned to contest. By the time of film theory's politicisation a number of studies of narrative had accumulated, mostly within literature and to a lesser extent within film. Among these, structuralist analyses predominated, for instance, the work of Genette, Bremond, Barthes, Todorov, and, within film theory, the Metz of the *grande syntagmatique*. Just as Saussure and Lévi-Strauss had found common structures underlying the diversity of, respectively, language and myth, so structuralist narratology looked for a common structure beneath the diversity of narratives. In order to do this a grammar of narrative was needed, involving the establishment of the minimal units of narrative and the laws governing their selection and combination to produce meaning. The method would give the narratologist faced with an unlimited number of different stories 'a clarifying principle and a central vantage point'.[1]

In taking up the body of work produced, film theorists were partly motivated by the desire for scientific rigour as opposed to the prevailing impressionism, but more importantly by a political impulse to challenge naturalism. Given the project of analysing mainstream commercial cinema and given the fact that such cinema was overwhelmingly narrative in form ('A film is a world which organises itself in terms of a story'),[2] it was an obvious step to turn to this work on narrative structure in order to show, firstly, that texts produced meaning only through procedures and structures that were historically and culturally specific, and secondly, that such procedures and structures were not innocent but were ideologically complicit. What stories relate does not pre-exist them, but comes into being only through them; yet once constructed it has the ideological force conferred by its apparent representation of reality.

The main source of texts for study were the classic Hollywood narratives of the 1930s, 1940s and 1950s, characterised as they were by a set of conventions that have been termed by Noël Burch 'the institutional mode of representation' and that came to be thought of by both filmmakers and audiences as the only way to make films. But as the researches of Noël Burch,[3] and of David Bordwell and his collaborators Janet Staiger and Kristin Thompson have revealed, quite different conventions of mise-en-scène, lighting, camera work, spatial organisation and editing were in operation during the early years of narrative cinema (what Bordwell calls 'primitive cinema').[4] In these films, in places now virtually unreadable, there was often little by way of the centring associated with Western painting and theatre. Actions might take place anywhere within the frame, including the edges and corners; events of narrative significance might occur simultaneously in different parts of the frame. The centred images of the institutional mode of representation (classical cinema, in Bordwell's terminology) evolved only gradually, through such strategies as darkening the periphery of the frame to eliminate secondary elements. In early cinema the role of the camera was also very different, since it chiefly recorded actions taking place at some distance in front of it. Similarly the organisation of space was quite different, with an empty foreground between the camera and the action. Nor was there any taboo on actors looking directly at camera, a taboo that Burch has suggested is a defining feature of the institutional mode of representation. The function of lighting, Thompson has pointed out, was to enable audiences to see what was occurring rather than, as it later became, to guide an understanding of the action. The overall effect of this research has been to show that the classic narrative is a historically contingent form, one road out of several that could have been taken. It became, therefore, a matter of asking what the consequences of this historical development were. More specifically, two questions were put. Firstly, which possibilities for the production of meaning were opened up and which foreclosed? And secondly, what relations with spectators were instantiated by these narrative forms? Of various studies in narratology called on in answering the first of these questions, one of the earliest and most important was the work of Vladimir Propp, which showed that it was possible to analyse the production of meaning at a macro level, independently of the text's relationship with the reader.

Just as Saussure had set aside questions of origin, derivation and reference in studying language, so Propp in *The Morphology of the Folktale* (1928) bracketed out the historical and ethnographic origins of the fairy tales he analysed and instead concentrated on attempting to discover a common structure underlying their diversity. Whereas Propp's predecessors had failed to find any such common basis because of their emphasis on thematic elements, he was able to show that there were certain fundamental components irrespective of variations in setting, character and plot. The first of these components were termed functions, each of which was, or derived from, an action of a character, and was defined in terms of its significance for – precisely its function within – the narrative. Propp identified thirty-one functions, examples being 'a difficult task', 'struggle', 'despatch' and 'a lack'. While any function might or might not occur within a given story, any that did so appeared in a fixed sequence. Further, certain functions always occurred at the same juncture in the narrative – the functions 'absentation' and 'interdiction', for instance, occurred at the beginning of what was termed 'the preparatory action'. Functions also tended to occur in pairs, e.g. 'interdiction'/'violation'. In considering how these functions were distributed among characters Propp found that certain of them clustered together to form what he called 'spheres of action' – the second of the basic structural components. The seven spheres of action were 'the villain', 'the donor', 'the helper', 'a princess and her father', 'the dispatcher', 'the hero' and 'the false hero', each of which might, but did not have to, correspond to particular characters on a one-to-one basis. At the end of his study Propp speculated that the approach might in the future be extended to all narratives, a suggestion that was to be taken up by film theorists. Of the various Proppian analyses of films (among them, *Sunset Boulevard* and *Kiss Me Deadly*) the best known is Peter Wollen's of

North by Northwest.

In this 1976 study Wollen showed that the overall structure of Hitchcock's film conformed to the Proppian model, in that it opens with the introduction of the hero (Thornhill's name is given by the elevator operator) and the establishment of a lack (Thornhill is unmarried) and concludes with the lack made good by the thirty-first of the narrative functions, a wedding ('Come on, Mrs Thornhill', as he lifts his bride onto the top bunk of the train). The structure further conforms to Propp's schema in that the hero sets off to remedy one lack only to become concerned by another, and it is the liquidation of the second lack that concludes the story – a pattern that Propp frequently discovered in his study. Here, Thornhill's unconcern with his marital status changes to concern after falling in love with Eve, who only enters the film a third of the way through.

In more detail, Wollen then analysed the succession of scenes from the film's beginning to its conclusion in terms of Propp's functions and spheres of action. The first function, absentation, typically of one of the members of a family from home, can be applied to Thornhill's losing contact with his mother. The second and third functions, interdiction and violation, frequently operate as a pair, and they do so here: Thornhill's mother has forbidden him to drink, but he goes to a hotel bar and orders a martini. According to Propp the violation of an interdiction is usually followed by the entry of the villain, whose role it is to disturb the peace of the family. The fourth function is then 'the villain makes an attempt at a reconnaissance'. In *North by Northwest* two heavies enter the hotel lobby in search of one Kaplan and have him paged to discover his identity. The fifth function, delivery, in which 'the villain receives information about his victim', corresponds to Thornhill rising to his feet as Kaplan is being paged, causing the heavies to mistake him for their target. The film now jumps on to the eighth function, villainy, in which 'the villain causes harm or injury to a member of a family', an exceptionally important function, says Propp, in that 'by means of it the actual movement of the tale is created'.[5] The preceding seven functions merely prepare the way for this moment. And this, argued Wollen, is precisely what happens in *North by Northwest*. Absentation has taken Thornhill away from his office milieu and rendered him vulnerable; violation of an interdiction anticipates his punishment by the act of villainy; and it is this, the kidnapping of Thornhill by the two heavies, that sets the story in motion.

There is no need to pursue the analysis any further to appreciate why Wollen saw Propp's method as surprisingly easily applicable to a very different kind of narrative from Russian folktales. Both in terms of its detailed development and overall structure the film can be analysed in terms of Propp's categories. Nevertheless, the results of Wollen's experiment remained inconclusive. This was not only because of the difficulty in applying the method to certain episodes in the narrative, as when Thornhill confronts Eve after the crop-dusting sequence, which Wollen admitted requires Eve 'to play the contradictory roles of villain and princess, antagonist and object of desire'.[6] There was also the problem that while the analysis had the effect of highlighting some aspects of the film it neglected others. In certain respects the analysis was a reading against the grain.

Beyond this are larger questions concerning the value of Propp for the understanding of cinematic narrative. It is arguable, for instance, that the typical film develops not along a single narrative axis, but rather more like an orchestral score, with a number of stories at once separate and interrelated. In this case it could be said that Propp's importance lies in exposing the differences rather than the similarities between the folktale and cinema. Again, a number of commentators, influenced by Lévi-Strauss, have argued that the linear sequence of events is merely the manifest content and that the more important latent content only emerges when, as expressed by Sheila Johnston, 'key elements are isolated from the body of the narrative and rearranged into a new (achronological) matrix of binary oppositions'.[7]

Wollen acknowledged these shortcomings in a subsequent article on the same film, where he pointed to the crucial structuring role played by 'the secret' in Hitchcock narratives.[8] The Hitchcockian hero is typically in pursuit not only of an object of desire but of the answer to an enigma. Now in so far as Propp allows for functions involving questions of knowlege he locates them either in the tale's preparatory section or towards its end, not, as in Hitchcock, in the main body of the narrative, where the lack of knowledge and the bid to liquidate that lack are essential to the plot dynamics. Wollen suggested that narratives dominated by a series of enigmas (in Barthes's terminology, by the hermeneutic code), such as Hitchcock's, are less susceptible to Proppian analysis than those in which the succession of events (Barthes's proairetic code) predominates.

Although Propp provided 'the most influential of all structural analyses of narrative', he was only briefly taken up by film theory.[9] Proppian analyses could play but a limited role in accounting for the political functioning of film, for while they explained something of the workings of signification they were silent on the all-important matter of the terms of the subject's implication in the text and the text's consequent relations to history and society. Significantly, the Propp who survived in film theory was not the Propp of *The Morphology* but the later Propp, who was concerned primarily to trace the material determinations on cultural production.[10]

At the micro level the most persuasive analyses of narrative have been those offered by Raymond Bellour. His global concept is that narrative consists of a play of sameness and difference. Although it might seem that difference is dominant, with continual changes of content through new events, characters, words spoken, and of form through framing, lighting, camera angle and most obviously the succession of shots, the lasting impression given by all successful narratives is one of cohesion and coherence. Alongside the tendency towards difference, therefore, there is a counter-tendency towards sameness: heterogeneity is countered by homogeneity; asymmetry by symmetry. Indeed the success of any narrative depends on the achievement of a balance between the two tendencies, which is what gives rise to the impression of unity. The question of how this balance is to be achieved, given the necessity of transformation and development, is answered in terms of the multiplicity of codes that every segment of every film, however apparently impoverished, necessarily involves. Within the plurality of codes some construct asymmetry, others symmetry.

Bellour gave an example of such codic functioning in an analysis of a brief scene (as defined by Metz in the *grande syntagmatique*) from *The Big Sleep* (1946).[11] A prime instance of 'relative poverty', it is sandwiched between two narrative climaxes and consists simply of two characters, Marlowe (Bogart) and Vivian (Bacall), declaring their mutual romantic attachment while seated in a car. What Bellour demonstrates is that the impression of unity given by the scene is achieved through a series of complex and subtle operations over the twelve shots by means of at least six codes (framing, camera movement, camera angle, presence or absence of character, presence or absence of dialogue, and duration of shot). The effect of these codes is to produce unity out of difference, specifically by balancing variation in some codes by repetition in others.

However, his study of the Bodega Bay sequence of *The Birds* affords a more extensive and penetrating analysis at the micro level.[12] The sequence begins with the arrival at Bodega Bay of Melanie Daniels, whose curiosity has been so aroused by an earlier conversation with Mitch Brenner in a San Francisco pet shop that she has driven the sixty miles to Bodega Bay with a pair of love birds as a birthday present for Cathy Brenner, Mitch's younger sister. Having hired a boat at the jetty to cross the bay to the Brenner house, and having set out in it, she sees Mitch's mother and Cathy leave in a truck and Mitch enter a barn. She is able to moor at his landing stage, take the love birds into the house with a note for Cathy and return to the boat without being seen. As she re-crosses the bay Mitch comes out of the barn and enters the house, where he discovers the love birds; he then re-emerges to look for whoever was responsible for their arrival. Melanie cuts her motor and crouches in the boat. But Mitch sees the boat, collects a pair of binoculars from the house, recognises Melanie and drives his car round to the jetty, where Mitch arrives at the same time as her. As their eyes meet a gull flies down and strikes Melanie, whom Mitch then helps from the boat. The whole sequence lasts just over six minutes and consists of eighty-two shots (though for reasons external to the analysis they are numbered 3-84).

From this synopsis it will be apparent that in terms of content there is both symmetry and asymmetry, with the latter outweighing the former. Though there is the symmetry of Melanie's outward and return journeys, there are also several asymmetrical features, namely, that on her return journey she is no longer unobserved, that a gift is offered, and that a gull attacks. As with the scene from *The Big Sleep*, more codes are at work than such a description of content reveals: codes that reintroduce symmetry through a series of formal homologies or rhymes. Where asymmetry enters at one level there is often a displacement into another code where the system of rhyming is once again taken up and compensates to an extent for the lost symmetry.

This idea can be best illustrated by the first half of the sequence, from shot 3 of Melanie arriving at the jetty to shot 56 of Mitch discovering her, a section that Bellour terms 'series A' and subdivides as follows: A1 – Melanie piloting the boat towards the landing stage, A2 – Melanie's progress towards the house, A3 – Melanie in the house, A4 – Melanie going back to the landing stage, and A5 – her departure in the boat and expectant wait for Mitch to find the love birds. In the section as a whole there is an obvious symmetry at the level of content, with the passage in both directions across the bay and the entry into and departure from the house. But at the level of formal organisation there is a more pronounced symmetrical pattern developed around the three oppositions of seeing/seen, close/distant and static/moving. In respect of seeing/seen, throughout A1 and A2 there is a strict alternation between shots of Melanie looking and shots of what she is looking at, an alternation that breaks down in A3, but is then taken up again with A4 directly echoing A2 and A5 echoing A1. This first opposition is then mapped onto the second, that of close/distant, with the framing such that Melanie looking is shown from medium shot to close-up and that what she is looking at is shown from medium to long shot. The final opposition is patterned so that A1 and A5 (Melanie in the boat) consist of static shots and A2 and A4 (Melanie approaching and leaving the house) of moving shots.

From the above it is evident that series A is composed of a pattern of rhymes and oppositions distributed symmetrically around its centre A3, creating an 'unbroken harmony' between A1/A2 and A4/A5. But it is equally evident that in certain respects these systems go awry in A3, when Melanie is in the house making the gift. The median position of A3 is marked by the degree of its disjunction from the rest of the section in terms of formal features. It comprises the only interior shots of the section; the alternation of seeing/seen is disrupted, with only one point-of-view shot, so that for the most part Melanie ceases to be the seer and becomes the seen; similarly, the alternation between close and distant breaks down; and, finally, A3 contains both static and moving shots, in contrast to the rest of the series which has either one or the other but not both. But symmetry is re-introduced at other levels. For example, the exterior shot of Melanie entering the house, followed by an interior shot of her completing her entry, is rhymed with the two shots of her leaving, as follows: 31 – Melanie from outside the door, medium shot; 32 – Melanie from inside the door, long shot; 36 as 32; 37 as 31. More significantly, the alternation of static/moving in the five shots of A3 (moving, static, moving, static, moving) echoes the alternation across the entire series (A1 static, A2 moving, A3 both, A4 moving, A5 static). The central subdivision A3, then, may be said to condense the whole series at a formal level. Bellour concludes 'Symmetry and asymmetry develop in a condensed series, in a dual movement of centring and decentring'.[13] That is, the asymmetry opened up by the progression of the plot is contained and offset by the system of formal symmetries in the narration.

Bellour's analyses powerfully demonstrated that fundamental to the working of narrative is the play of repetition and difference. But his work involved more than the identification and elaboration of formal codes, for it went beyond the limited structuralist project of Propp and his successors. In common with all the other major issues confronting film theory after 1968, the question of the subject was centrally on the agenda in the study of narrative, and Bellour's contribution here has been extensive. Before returning to it, however, we shall consider another immensely important contribution to the understanding of how the subject is implicated by narrative: that of Stephen Heath.

For Heath, it will be recalled, the subject is both constituting and constituted, a process engendered in the reading of the text. In the article 'Narrative Space' he undertook the task of establishing and elaborating this dialectic of the subject.[14]

The central idea informing Heath's often difficult writings, from which his position on narrative follows, is that the human subject is not first of all constructed and then placed within social and ideological formations, but that the constructing and the placing are one and the same process, which continues interminably. The system of narrative is just one of a number of subject-producing machines, albeit an important one. More specifically – and to express it in psychoanalytic terminology – the work of narrative is both an instance of the subject within the symbolic and is a return to and recapitulation of the subject's first entry into the symbolic, the moment of castration in which the subject becomes a subject by taking up a pre-given position. Because the subject always exceeds the position given by the symbolic, there is an experience of lack. This is fended off by the assumption of an imaginary wholeness, a set of images, in which the ego will once again achieve completion (a process already referred to as 'suture', the joining of imaginary and symbolic). The constant movement of alignment between the subjects of the enounced and the enunciation, between symbolic and imaginary, can be described as performance: the subject both performs the text and is performed by it. Since there is no Other of the Other, the subject can only occupy the place assigned by the symbolic, in this instance a place within the narrative. But if, in this respect, narrative resembles all other sites in which the subject is given an identity only to fade, it also differs from them. Suture within narrative has its own specificity, which resides in narrative's concern with the very process of the subject's constitution at the cost of division. That is, the experience of lack and the drive towards unity that characterise narrative (typically worked out in terms of Oedipal scenarios) exactly figure the experience of the subject within language. It is no accident that fiction moves across the lack instituted by the disruption of an initial equilibrium towards the imaginary wholeness of a concluding equilibrium, nor that its passage is so frequently concerned with the dynamics of desire. But it is a project destined to fail. Just as in the symbolic the subject exceeds its given representations, so too in narrative the sought-after unity is never finally achieved.

Compared with earlier theorists of the relation between subject and text, Heath placed a much greater emphasis on process: the continual emergence and fading of the subject. Whereas for his predecessors process derives from the movement of the text itself, thereby threatening the subject position constructed by the text, Heath's subject is always already in process. Far from being fixed in position by the text and subsequently maintained in position against threats of disruption, it can only be contained, its energies regulated by the narrative's organisation of images and representations. The subject is caught up by the text and bound not into positon but into the process of narrativisation. Rather then arresting the process of the subject the text performs it – something that is attested to by the etymology of the word 'entertainment', which is at once 'a holding in and a containment'. The text moves the subject, not as a disruption of a fixity, but in a constantly shifting regulation and containment. 'What moves in film, finally, is the spectator, immobile in front of the screen. Film is the regulation of that movement, the individual as subject held in a shifting and placing of desire, energy, contradiction, in a perpetual retotalisation of the imaginary (the set scene of image and subject).'[15]

Central to this process is the organisation of space, which, as we have already seen, only became conventionalised in classic cinema after evolving through a variety of forms in the very early years of cinema. The question then was: how does the organisation of space in classic narrative cinema implicate the spectator? In broad terms, Heath's answer was that narrative constantly constructs and reconstructs space in the interests of a sustained coherence, thereby achieving a match of film and world. By shifting the centre of spatial organisation and the system of perspective, the subject of vision can be constantly 'phased in' to the particular succession of images within a secure, all-embracing view. In thus annulling the threat posed by movement, the narrativisation pulls both the represented world and the spectator into place. On the one hand it centres the vision of the master-spectator and on the other its binds what Barthes called the text's 'festival of affects' into an economy.

To consider the argument in rather more detail, Heath first addressed the difficulties posed by movement within the frame. Whereas in classical painting composition is organised according to the lines of force that cross the picture space, with the principal figures placed at the strong points within the frame, in cinema such a solution is unavailable because of movement, whether of characters and objects within the frame or of the camera itself. Instead, the centring of the frame is based on action, the logic of the narrative. The continual relocation and realisation of a compositional centre accords with the centre of interest as defined by the narrative. In this way, 'the seen' is converted into 'a scene', space becomes place, and the spectator is situated by a constant renewal of perspective. Thus organised, the frame imposes a coherence and continuity, forestalling the risk of textual and subjective chaos. Indeed, 'the narrative is the very triumph of framing'.[16]

Next, Heath considered the way in which space is organised from shot to shot, where there is again the problem of achieving a coherence of space and unity of vision in the face of the potentially disruptive shifts of time and place engendered by cutting. Once more the threat is annulled by the superordinate movement of narrative, which, with its rhythms and climaxes, gives direction to the shifting action and the spectator's vision at one and the same time. As with Bellour, it is precisely film's fragmentation into shots that is the condition for its impression of unity – the life, you might say, of the thousand cuts. Segmentation and recomposition is a more effective means of binding the subject in place than the intolerable fixity of a series of tableaux. For example, the point about the shot/reverse shot system emphasised by the theorists of suture is not simply that it should transform off-screen space into on-screen space, but that it should appropriate the space posed as absent by the narrative and restore it as the answer to a demand. It is indeed part of the suturing process – though only in so far as the system is part of that larger process of narrativisation that constructs a space offering the spectator a stable, objective view. And it is this 'view for the viewer' that acts as the ground on which to construct the varying perspectives of characters' points of view.[17] Shot/reverse shot, then, should be conceived as but one component of the powerful apparatus of 'looks' on which narrative cinema is based: the look of the camera at the profilmic event, the look of the spectator at the screen, the intradiegetic looks of characters at one another and objects in their field of vision. This series of looks is both embedded (the spectator sees what characters see by looking at what the camera looks at) and to an extent reversible (the look of the camera is revealed by looking at the film at the same time as the former is a condition of the latter). The series engenders the relay of identifications essential for binding the spectator into the film. For instance, it is the exchange between first and second looks that establishes identification with the camera. Then the look at the film involves a relay of identifications from image, to human figures within the image, to the narrative, which in turn orders the flow of images. The looks of characters allow for the various point-of-view identifications of looking with a character or as a character (through subjective shots). The overall effect of the apparatus, despite a certain mobility, is one of control, of holding the spectator within a coherence of vision. It is the apparatus of look and identification that constitutes the cinematic machine, at once providing an object and a subject of vision. Out of a seeming fragmentation and dispersal of vision there comes a unifying, unified mastery that is given, says Heath, by that most crucial of looks, the look of oneself looking, giving 'the totalising security of "looking at"'.[18]

An important sub-system of the apparatus of look and identification is the spectator's identification with the camera. While this is 'rigorously constructed', the rules for doing so have been assimilated to the dominant conventions of filmmaking to such an extent that they appear natural and inevitable.[19] Among these unquestioned assumptions are the following:

1) the provision of a master or establishing shot, enabling the spectator to orientate himself or herself with respect to each new shot in the sequence

2) the 180° rule, ensuring that the spectator always finds the same characters in the same part of the screen, i.e., matching 'screen space and narrative space'[20]

3) the 30° rule, which prevents the spectator experiencing a jump in space and permits a smooth continuity between shots

4) the orchestration of actors' movements so that reframing and camera movement do not draw attention to themselves.

The function of these taken-for-granted procedures is to achieve a coherent narrative space and the maintenance of perspective; their apparent innocence masks their conventionality, and hence their ideological complicity and effectivity.

It might, on the strength of the above, be supposed that the work of narrative cinema is primarily directed to the effacement of all signs of its production. Indeed, formalists have argued exactly that, saying that mainstream cinema seeks to present itself as merely the transparent rendering of a pre-given reality and that the various formal devices are employed to achieve that end. As a consequence, the use of divergent formal strategies – say, shots taken from a place no observer could possibly occupy or apparently unmotivated camera movements disclosing a space that plays no part in the narrative – would subvert this process. Heath, on the contrary, took issue with such formalism, maintaining that it rested on a misconception. The fundamental point is that classical cinema does not efface the signs of its production, it contains them. Film 'as a series of relations with the spectator it imagines, plays and sets as subject in its movement' is 'perfectly available to certain terms of excess'.[21] An obvious example of controlled excess would be directorial style, which may well include elements such as impossible shots and autonomous camera movements and yet pose no threat whatever to successful narrativisation. As a consequence, the large claims made about the supposedly subversive effect of, say, Ozu's modernism – his inclusion of places and spaces between scenes that answer no narrative demand, for example – were, said Heath, unwarranted. Rather, such elements should be conceived as stylistic ornamentation, not as unassimilable contradictions. In other words, classical cinema is considerably more resistant to disruption than formalists imagine. What formalist strategies fail to make visible is that other scene of the construction of meaning and subjectivity within a specific signifying practice; that is, a political aesthetic of transgression effects no change in the relation of subject and film. What is needed instead is an aesthetic of transformation, making explicit the operation of narrativisation and the film's address to its spectator. Such a work of transformation is to be located in the films of Straub/Huillet and Oshima (to which we will return in chapter 7.)

Heath's thinking on narrative has been far-reaching, particularly as his central thesis that space is organised by the logic of the narrative has received authoritative support from the work of Bordwell, Staiger and Thompson. Taking up Jakobson's concept of 'the dominant', the element that in any text or tradition subordinates all others, they showed that in Hollywood the dominant was a form of narrative causality reliant on temporal and spatial systems. This can be contrasted with the quite different operation of narrative causality in primitive cinema, where space was organised in blocks in which action was seen to take place by spectators excluded from that space. In classical cinema, space becomes subordinated to the requirements of narration, which entails that the spectator is always placed in the optimum viewing position in each shot. A number of devices such as staging, set design, deep focus, lighting and camera movement combine 'to tailor space moment by moment to the demands of the narration'.[22] The spectator's attention is constantly centred on those aspects of the scene most relevant to the plot by the various spatial sub-systems (point of view, shot/reverse shot, etc.) and continuity rules (establishing shots, eyeline match, etc.). Space in classical narrative is in a constant process of being at once defined and moulded.

But Heath's thesis also provoked dissent, some of which may be attributed to certain misunderstandings of his position. In his concern to emphasise the materiality of specific signifying practice, he did appear to suggest, in some of his formulations, that the text was the sole determinant at work in the process of reception. As a consequence he came to be arraigned for the very formalism from which he had taken care to distance himself through the concept of the dialectic of the subject.

Thus, for instance, Dana B. Polan has characterised Heath's strategy as both essentialist and formalist: essentialist in claiming that there is a fixed identity to the cinematic apparatus and formalist in that the implied reader is the effect solely of the invariant structures of the text. It is, therefore, a version of the 'manipulation theory', with 'manipulating texts on one side tied to an order of representation; manipulated spectators on the other side, tied to the text'.[23]

Instead, cinema should be conceived as a practice and process, in which on the one hand spectators 'engender' the film and on the other the film 'engenders' them, in which both film and spectators are 'constituting contributors' to meaning. The irony is that Polan's position, established in opposition to his reading of Heath, reiterates its central emphases, of which none is more important than the constituting-constituted subject. The major discernible divergence between the two positions is that Polan allows the moment of reception a greater constitutive force than Heath, whose stress is on that of the text. But this is a matter of empirical degree not of theoretical principle: each is committed to a dialectic in which meaning and subject come into being together.

Much more hostile to Heath was Noël Carroll's lengthy review article on *Questions of Cinema*, in which he attempted to bring down the whole enterprise of film theory operating under the sign of Althusser and Lacan.[24] Since the implications of the disagreement are extensive, we shall examine his critique, Heath's reply and some of the ramifications of the debate in detail.

In the first place, Carroll charged that in so far as Heath was working within an Althusserian perspective his position was untenable. The line imputed to Heath on such grounds was that the spectator was reduced to an effect of the text and that any given text would interpellate all spectators in exactly the same way – typically, in a way that would cause spectators to misrecognise themselves as transcendental egos. According to Carroll, such 'discourse determinism' was inadequate in its failure to account in any way for the undeniable fact of spectator resistance, for example, that of a spectator of *Birth of a Nation* refusing to accept the Ku Klux Klan as Aryan heroes. As an alternative to what he understood as the insuperable problem of the Althusserian theory of the subject, Carroll proposed turning to empirical cognitive psychology. Film theory, he suggested, would be better served by a notion of the 'stable' subject rather than by what he termed the 'occurrent' subject, constituted from one moment to the next by the interpellating discourse. Stable subjects are agents engaging in a process of perception and cognition, and possess 'personality profiles that remain relatively intact over long periods of time'.[25] A model conceiving of the subject as an agent rather than as an effect of a structure could satisfactorily account for the fact of resistance. Heath's acceptance of the propositions of 'an arcane branch of psychoanalysis' as 'so many philosopher's stones' had blinded him to the superior explanations within cognitive psychology of how subjects respond to stimuli.[26] In the second place, Carroll maintained, in so far as Heath advanced on Althusser, he did so at the cost of even greater abstraction that bordered on vacuity. The concept of suture was so generally applicable as to explain nothing, its universality precluding it from contributing in any way to an explanation of what occurs in any given exchange between spectator and text. In brief, Heath's use of the concept was reductionist.

A comparable challenge to the early *Screen* position, though this was not specifically identified with Heath, was offered by David Bordwell. While accepting that films possess their own effectivity (as an example he cited those American films of Fritz Lang that, through their narration, impose a 'paranoid' point of view on the spectator), he disputed that they unilaterally determine readings. Such a view requires that the spectator be passive, a mere receptacle, which is incompatible with recent discoveries in perceptual psychology that show that in watching a film spectators exercise a number of skills. These include discriminating between significant information and 'noise', making inferences and drawing conclusions, formulating and testing hypotheses: spectators are engaged in 'a game of controlled expectation and likely confirmation', without which there can be no reading of the text at all.[27]

In reply to Carroll, Heath called his article 'a solid block of error': nothing in its seventy pages could teach anyone anything about recent theoretical enquiry into the political practice of film.[28] This is overstating the case, for whatever Heath's own position, there were aspects of an ambient film-theoretical culture to which the charges were applicable. For example, many Althusserians did invest the notion of the transcendental subject with undue importance, referring to it as the ideological lynchpin of bourgeois society. But as Carroll pointed out, alternative conceptions had been accommodated, even, he might have pointed out, the formulae of psychoanalysis. Conversely, the conception of the autonomous, self-directing subject is in all probability to be encountered not only in the capitalist mode of production but in all societies where technical practices and the division of labour require a degree of individual control. Again, the fact of resistance is a real problem for Althusser, and one Heath might have cited himself in his own critique of Althusser. And there was, undeniably, a tendency in much 1970s film theory to impute a solely determining force to the text itself.

But as far as Heath's own work is concerned, Carroll's objections and Bordwell's implicit criticisms were wide of the mark. While there may be traces of Heath's brief adoption of Althusserianism in *Questions of Cinema*, the major influence in it is unquestionably Lacan, albeit in a qualified fashion. The dialectic of the subject, not interpellation, is its guiding notion, and Heath's appropriation of Lacan makes him not so much opposed to the conception of the subject demanded by Carroll as concerned to go beyond it. Psychoanalysis does not deny the existence of perception and cognition (how could it?), but says that in a divided subject these processes are more complex than empirical psychology allows. 'Knowledge and belief can go in many ways and at one and the same time.'[29] They are bound up with the unconscious as much as with the conscious mind; if there is recognition there is also misrecognition. It is for this reason that Heath cannot set aside, as Bordwell does in his own study of cinematic narrative, 'the affective features of film meaning' in favour of a 'perceptual cognitive account'.[30] Any analysis, such as Heath's, of the political functioning of film ignores the affective at its peril, for that is an inescapable dimension of film's effectivity. Heath's commitment to such an analysis was equally a commitment to take on the formidable theoretical task of theorising the unconscious in its historical specificity.

In thus committing himself, Heath was certainly alive to the differences among spectators and their responses to the same text (Carroll's assertion that Heath denied this was simply wrong) but at the same time he needed to avoid the assertion of endless difference in order to prevent the text being denied any effectivity whatsoever. Texts for Heath are neither absolutely open and therefore able to mean anything at all, nor absolutely closed, containing a single inscribed meaning. Rather, the readings available are determined historically, 'and that historicality includes the determinations of the institution cinema, the conditions of the production of meanings, of specific terms of address. . .'[31] Against this, Carroll could only offer the common sense view that what spectators make of a film depends on the beliefs they bring to it. Such assertions as a film may make about reality are checked against these beliefs, irrespective of any textual strategy it may have adopted. Heath's response was scathing. Carroll's rhetoric amounted to saying that films have no effect at all, since the degree of assent accorded to any given film depends solely on its conformity to existing beliefs: 'spectators already think what they think and will continue to think it regardless of what they see'.[32] In any case, it may be asked: where do people get their beliefs from? And if the answer is anything more specific than 'society', involving, say, a notion of systems of representation, then it must be admitted that film might be one such system of representation; in which case it will have to be admitted that films do have effects and that such effects will depend in part on their textual strategy, 'including whether or not they are shown out of focus' – (a reference to Carroll's assertion that spectators would make judgements as to the truthfulness or otherwise of a film to life even if it were shown out of focus).[33]

While it is hard to fault Heath's insistence that not all films are the same film, that films, through their varying form, content and mode of address, do make a difference, it is still reasonable to ask, with Carroll, *what* difference they make. In other words, how is the difference to be specified?

Consider at this juncture, Brecht's account of his experience in watching the film *Gunga Din*, based on the Kipling short story. He relates how the film represented the Indians as primitive and either comic, when loyal to the British, or wicked, when hostile to them. The British on the other hand were honest and good-humoured, and when they used their fists to 'knock some sense' into a mob the cinema audience laughed. When an Indian sacrificed his life in order that his compatriots be defeated, the audience applauded. Brecht points out that he too felt like applauding, and that he laughed in the right places. At the same time he recognised that the representation of Indians and their culture was quite false, and that it would be easy to represent Gunga Din in a very different light, as a traitor to his people. But Brecht was amused and touched 'because this utterly distorted account was an artistic success'.[34] The conclusions he draws from this experience directly endorse Heath's arguments. Brecht writes:

Obviously artistic appreciation of this sort is not without effects. It weakens the good instincts and strengthens the bad, it contradicts true experience and spreads misconceptions, in short it perverts our picture of the world. There is no play and no theatrical performance which does not in some way or other affect the dispositions and conceptions of the audience. Art is never without consequences.[35]

Exactly; but equally art's consequences are not necessarily far-reaching. There is nothing in Brecht's account to suggest that his political outlook was affected for more than the duration of the screening. There remains, then, the problem of how the effects are to be assessed. On Heath's account, as we have already seen, the text not only constitutes the spectator as subject but is in turn constituted by the subject, who brings to the exchange the various historical determinations of his or her construction. It is at this point, Carroll contended, that Heath reached the impasse of the overly abstract notion of suture, an impasse that is not breached by a rhetorical call for concrete analyses of specific historical conjunctures, since that possibility had been foreclosed by the deployment of Lacanian generalities.

At this point a not altogether speculative reading of Heath's project, and particularly his use of psychoanalysis, will enable a rerouting of the argument past the 'passage barred' notice put up by Carroll. The assumption was that Heath had been concerned to lay the foundations for a purely theoretical understanding of cinema – and Heath has himself on occasion written in such terms, as indeed has Heath's mentor Barthes with regard to literature. But if Heath's reading of Barthes's project, and latterly Barthes's of his own, is taken as a precedent, then a very different perception of Heath's own work is possible. According to Heath, Barthes set out to investigate the limits of human thought and the grounds of intelligibility not in order to achieve a complete understanding of them (that being impossible), but to go beyond them, in Nietzschean fashion, by producing new perspectives. Through such 'strategies of displacement' (as Heath put it) new objects for study and new positions from which to study them would be produced. Breaking with the past in this manner necessarily entailed as much of a transformation of the subject as it did of the object. The same point was made by Foucault when he asked: 'What would the relentless pursuit of knowledge be worth if it had only to secure the acquisition of information and not. . . the displacement of he who knows?'[36] For Foucault, as for Barthes and, we are suggesting, for Heath, the point was not to interpret the world but to change oneself and, by implication, others. And for Barthes and Heath the vehicle for change was Lacanian psychoanalysis, and its justification was political: you change the world by altering the modes of being within it. All of which – whatever epistemological or even political assessment one may wish to make of it – undoubtedly shifts the domain of the debate away from the purely academic. This said, however, the thorny problem of specifying the effectivity of a particular text in a particular historical moment remained unsolved. 'Narrative Space' did appear to mark the limits of what could be said, and those who tried to advance from it tended to fall back towards formalism. As a consequence, attention shifted to other ways in which psychoanalysis might inform the study of narrative.

The idea of *the return of the repressed* is basic to Freud's thought; he maintained that what has been repressed is not destroyed but survives in the unconscious and will find its way back into consciousness in the guise of slips, jokes and symptoms. If, as has been suggested, narrative involves an act of containment, then, according to Freud, it can never be entirely successful since the repressed is always liable to return to trouble the sought-for unity and homogeneity of the text. Such a conception of the text as potentially fissured and con-tradictory was notably prevalent during the late 1960s, when, for example, Althusser's collaborator Pierre Macherey constructed a theory of the literary text along exactly these lines. Perhaps the out-standing example of its application in film theory was in *Cahiers'* analysis of *Young Mr Lincoln* (already discussed in chapter 4).

A second concept is that of *repetition compulsion*, as elaborated in Freud's *Beyond the Pleasure Principle*. What Freud found was that certain phenomena were incompatible with his fundamental doctrine that mental functioning is dominated by the pleasure principle, with its maximisation of pleasure and avoidance of unpleasure. Among these was the *fort-da* game, in which, it will be recalled, the child enacts the comings and goings of its mother in symbolic terms by throwing away, then retrieving, an object. Freud hypothesised that this repeated action was a bid for mastery by moving from a passive to an active role in relation to the unpleasurable experience of the mother's absence. A number of commentators have seen aspects of narrative that place it in a comparable category. The suggestion is that texts are characteristically economies of repetition and variation, involving symmetry and asymmetry, aimed at establishing mastery over a lack.

These two processes, moreover, are not unrelated, both in Freud's thought, in which the return of the repressed is also the repetition of a past conflict, and in a conception of narrative as a process of containment in constant difficulties. That is, narrative is troubled both by elements it fails to repress and elements if fails to master.

As an operation to achieve cohesion, balance, resolution – in sum to reintegrate the multiple elements put into play by its opening within a definitive equilibrium – it is destined to fail. The excess that narrative cannot figure is the impetus for yet another version of the same, which, as Barthes and others have shown, typically involves an Oedipal trajectory.

As well as the now unremarkable knowledge that 'every narrative . . . is a staging of the (absent, hidden or hypostatised) father', there is also the fact that in classic cinematic narrative the image of woman functions as the prime signifier of male fears, fantasies and obsessions.[37] The woman is both the problem and the solution: problem in that she figures as a centre of disruption and trouble, failing to fit into the male order, destabilising male identity, in the last analysis posing the threat of castration; solution, in the recurrent image of woman as *the* woman, the one who will make good the lack. In this sense, Heath has proposed, narrative is fetishistic: constantly returning to the moment of castration, it offers up the image of the woman as that which will restore the unity and mastery lost forever in that moment. Narrative is 'the discovery [of lack] perpetually remade with safe fictions'.[38] Clearly, there are narratives in which this does not apply: those in which women do not figure or do not do so in this way and those in which questions of desire and identity are posed differently. But equally clearly, much of Hollywood is susceptible to analysis in terms of narrative seeking to contain 'violence and dispersion' around the figure of a woman.[39] *Touch of Evil* is one such film.

By way of a preamble to his reading of *Touch of Evil*, Heath was careful to stress that his was by no means the only reading possible, and by no means exhaustive of its meaning.[40] Rather, he set out to trace some of the patterns of exchange among the various elements in play – in other words, to expose aspects of the logic of the narrative.

The pertinence of the *fort-da* scenario is evident from the outset, with the narrative inaugurated by an act of violence, rupturing a prior homogeneity whose restoration becomes the goal of the film. Its action, plot and movement converge on this end of producing a homogeneity that is at once the return of the same and its transformation into a new equilibrium. There is consequently a certain symmetry to the progression of the narrative; but once again this tendency is counterbalanced by the presence of the heterogeneous, the asymmetrical. In the very process of achieving its goal of containment it reinstates disorder, an excess that remains irrepressible and resists containment. With classical Oedipal precision the action opens with the killing of the father, one Rudy Linneker, along with his girlfriend, a stripper called Zita, in a bomb explosion as they drive across the Mexican–US border. The project of the narrative is twofold. It is, first of all, to restore the law that has been overthrown, which is figured by the struggle between Vargas, the honest Mexican UN narcotics agent, and Quinlan (played by Welles, who directed the film), the corrupt American police chief. The victory of Vargas, the embodiment of just law, over Quinlan, its corrupter, who appears following the father's death and dies before the end of the film, is the condition for narrative resolution. Furthermore, the narrative must restore the social order, sanctioned by law and disrupted by the murder, by returning the characters to their assigned places in that order. This is figured metaphorically by the motif of the border, which is crossed and recrossed throughout the film, with characters often finding themselves on the wrong side of it; and through the associated question of nationality, which articulates considerations of identity and position. But most decisively the restoration of social order is centred on Vargas and his American wife Susan (Janet Leigh), who are on their honeymoon and are separated as an immediate effect of the bomb explosion. The whole drive of the narrative is to bring them back together again, and with their resumption of the kiss interrupted by the explosion, it apparently achieves a satisfactory resolution. But while (the restoration of) Susan is the solution, she is also the problem.

The implication of Susan with desire and death is established from the beginning, by way of a metonymy between her and Zita, who represents the illicit sexuality whose outcome, literally and metaphorically, is an explosion – the kiss is interrupted; later in the film, there is a cut from Susan to a close-up of a hand plunging a detonator at a blasting site. While on the one hand the narrative's objective is to restitute Susan as the good object, as *the* woman who will convey the illusion of wholeness, it can on the other hand only do so through a narration marking her as a bad object threatening castration. At one point quite early in the film Susan goes to a motel where the nightclerk is utterly panicked by her sexuality. A comparable panic, Heath claims, organises the film's attempts to contain Susan. It does so in the classic manner of Hollywood as described by Mulvey, through aggression and fetishisation. In Oedipal terms, the corollary of the murder of the father is the desire for the mother, but this must be blocked; a way of doing so is to punish the woman who is the object of transgressive desire. Thus, variously, Zita is blown up, a poster depicting her is subsequently burned by acid, effacing her image, and most obviously there are a series of attacks throughout the film on Zita's stand-in, Susan. 'The narrative turns ceaselessly into the punishment of Susan as the image of its own desire, as the image of its own repression'.[41] For most of the film Susan is excluded, furthermore, from the main sites of action, being confined to another realm where violence reigns absolutely. Alternatively, the threat may be warded off by fetishisation, as when Susan, taking on Zita's role of stripper, undresses before a curtainless window and is then exposed in a flashlight beam shone from across the street. The two solutions, illumination or extinction, are combined in the scene in which Quinlan strangles the small-time crook who has abducted Susan, while her near-naked and unconscious body lies on the bed.

The role of Vargas in relation to Susan compounds the confusion. He is at once the father whom Susan is forbidden to desire and the husband she is required to desire. As father, he is the father of pure prohibition, the ideal father fixing the law in an image of himself, and hence is unable to fulfill the function of the real father of reconciling law and desire. It is for this reason, Heath proposed, that Vargas spends the greater part of the narrative away from Susan. He is apart from her in order to investigate the crime; but 'she is the crime';[42] therefore he can only be the law when he is not husband – 'Susan is an uncontrollable demand from which Vargas must separate himself in order to maintain his position'.[43] The resolution of the film is thus deeply troubled. Although everything comes right in the sense that the murder is solved and Susan is restored to Vargas, there is nevertheless an excess that defies the order imposed by the narrative. As with the subject's constantly failing the attempt to achieve an imaginary unity, so the text's drive towards homogeneity is disturbed by the insistence of the heterogeneity – scenes, for instance, that 'resist unification into any clear position of reading'.[44] One example of this is when Quinlan visits Tanya, the madame of *une maison close*, and the narrative 'slips, drifts'.[45] In relation to another film, *Letter from an Unknown Woman*, but equally applicable to these 'redundant' scenes with Tanya, Heath has written: '[The] image mirrors a structure that is in excess of its effect of containment, that bears the traces of the heterogeneity – the trouble – it is produced to contain: sexuality here is also the "more" that the look elides, that is elided from the look, and that returns, constantly, in the figure of its absence.'[46]

In both Heath's reading of *Touch of Evil* and Bellour's of *The Birds* there is a sustained avoidance on the one hand of speaking of content irrespective of form, and on the other of examining form independently from its content. As with Freud's insistence that the meaning of a dream resides in the dreamwork, that there is no meaning prior to its formalisation, so here form and content are seen to be inseparable. Our return to Bodega Bay, promised earlier as the exercise of subjectivity in and through narrative, will take as given this indissociability. Though no summary can do justice to the complexity and subtlety of Bellour's analysis, we shall in what follows attempt to indicate something of the productivity of psychoanalysis combined with close textual reading for purposes of understanding how subjectivity is implicated in narrative.

In his analysis of the text's codic and pluri-codic levels Bellour broke the segment in question down into two principal series of shots. The centre of series A, which we examined previously, is the depositing of the gift of lovebirds in the Brenner house. Series B has as its centre the moment when Mitch sees Melanie, that is, when the opposition seeing/seen is replaced by the opposition seeing/seeing as they look at each other. The two centres are linked in a number of formal ways. For example, both are situated within a series of shots organised around a principle of alternation that breaks down at the median point: shot 32 in series A of Melanie inside the house is followed by a close-up shot of her hand as she places the note beside the lovebirds; shot 56 in series B of Mitch looking towards Melanie is followed by a close-up of him as he raises the binoculars. In this and other ways associated with their occurrence at the centre of the two series, 'the moment of provocation and the moment of discovery' are linked to each other.[47] A system of condensations and displacements establishes centre B as a recurrence of centre A. The two centres, gift and exchange of looks, are in turn related to the gull's attack. So, as Melanie carries the lovebirds to the boat, birds can be heard on the soundtrack; as Mitch sees her through the binoculars birds appear in the foreground; then, as Melanie approaches the jetty, inclining her head in response to Mitch's gaze, a gull attacks. Further, the alternating pattern of shots of Melanie's return across the bay establishes a correspondence between Mitch's gaze and the gull's attack, in that if the alternation had continued, shot 77 would have contained Mitch and not the gull swooping down – in a movement, as it happens, that recalls Mitch's earlier movement. By this means the gull's attack becomes a metaphor for Mitch's look, linked as it is with centre B, when Mitch sees Melanie through the binoculars. But the attack also rhymes with centre A, in that the shot following that of the gull swooping down is a close-up of Melanie's glove with the index finger spotted with blood. The close-up here recalls the close-up of Melanie's hand in the house, which in turn is linked to the close-up of Mitch looking. In each case there is a detail offered from the preceding shot, and with the final close-up the identification of gull with gift and gaze is secured. Aggression is linked with desire and the look in a signifying chain, so that when Melanie and Mitch gaze at each other 'the bird of the gift appears in its baleful double'.[48]

In all this Bellour did much more than reiterate what has become a cliché of Hitchcock studies, namely, that his narratives play out an Oedipal scenario in which the desire embodied or aroused by the woman is experienced as transgressive and punished by an act of aggression – all deriving, of course, from Hitchcock's unresolved Oedipal problems. For a start Melanie is both the subject of the look, as much of the sequence attests through its persistent point-of-view shots, and the object of the look beginning with the look of the fisherman who helps her into the boat and relayed via the look of Mitch who will help her from the boat after the attack. And just as she is the subject and object of the look, so is she the subject and object of the birds. The good birds, indicating, with their invitation, Melanie as the subject of desire, become the bad birds, with Melanie as the object of aggression. The principle of reversibility thus organising the sequence ensures that 'the symbolic punishment which strikes her in Mitch's look in the metaphorical form of the killer birds, has from the beginning spoken in her own look'.[49] But matters are more complex still. Mitch is also both subject and object of the look. Through a series of formal homologies an identification is established between them. For instance, there is the equivalence of their two entries into the house; the framing and their movements within the frame on the outward and return journeys add further emphasis to this identification; and, most importantly, the structure of the final succession of shots around the gull 'obliges Mitch and Melanie to act in one another's places', so that, according to the expectations generated by the alternation of shots, it would be Mitch not Melanie who is attacked.[50] This final substitution refers back in its turn to series A, which, on the basis of the alternation Mitch/not-Mitch, should have had him in shot 33, not Melanie, leaving the lovebirds. A further refinement occurs after the attack when Melanie, while still the objet of Mitch's look, becomes the object of her own look as she gazes at her bloodstained glove.

Now it is easy enough to spot psychoanalytic motifs operative in the sequence on the strength of such an analysis. Most obviously there is that of aggression as the corollary of narcissism, a theme that fascinated Lacan, whose case studies of the Papin sisters' murder of the wife and daughter of their employer and of Aimée's assault on a well known actress in the street both involved attacks on an idealised figure with whom the attacker(s) had identified and who had come to be experienced as persecutory. There is also the theme of castration, one of the consequences of which is that one can never be seen from where one would wish to be seen. Again, there is the Sartrian motif, applauded by Lacan for its insightfulness, that the subject of the look is always in danger of becoming its object. But it is interesting that Bellour resisted the temptation to reduce the sequence to any one psychoanalytic formulation or a combination of them. Rather than illustrate a truth given elsewhere in the metalanguage of psychoanalysis, the sequence demonstrates in its irreducibility the absence of any such metalanguage. Bellour does not reveal 'the secret' of the text for the good reason that there is no such secret to reveal. For what Bellour terms 'the ultimate contradiction between symmetrical constraint and asymmetrical openness' figures another contradiction that cannot otherwise be figured.[51] Here too there is no Other of the Other: the sequence enacts the mise-en-scène of a desire that can appear in no other scene.

But where in all of this, it may be asked, is the spectator? Once again there is no easy answer. Something of its complexity may be gauged from Bellour's comments on the role of Hitchcock. Thus: 'There is no doubt that Hitchcock identifies with Mitch, who interrogates Melanie's look and allows himself to be bewitched by it, but there is even less doubt that Hitchcock identifies with Melanie, whose eyes bear the phantasm whose effects Hitchcock narrates.'[52] As in the fantasy 'A child is being beaten', the spectator is distributed across a number of positions: Melanie, who for much of the sequence possesses the initiative and the gaze; Mitch, who at certain important narrative junctures dispossesses her of the initiative and whose look comes to be dominant; and an omniscient observer, whom Bellour designates Hitchcock, able to fragment and fetishise Melanie's body as in the close-up of her hand and the gift in shot 33. What is certain is that there is no unitary position for the spectator to occupy. Rather, the subject is dispersed within a particular economy that the work of the text, and only the work of the text, makes possible.

As conceived by Bellour, the sequence is Hitchcock's way of articulating Freud's question 'What does a woman want?' Posed by men, it is not a question about women's sexuality; rather the woman is the pretext to represent a problem about the nature of desire. Given that 'the unconscious is the discourse of the Other' and 'man's desire is the desire of the Other' then the question becomes 'What does the Other want?'[53] A woman's want, Melanie's want, is a means of recasting that unanswerable question. As with Heidegger's question, 'What is being?', what matters is not the answer, for there can be none, but the various modalities of being in relation to it. The irreducibility of texts to single or even multiple meanings implies that meaning is always the achievement of an economy and not the representation of what has been or could be enunciated elsewhere. Existing representations are taken up and used by texts in a constant circulation between text and society, but meaning as an economy, meaning as a way of being is available in the text and nowhere else. It is less the result of an action than the action itself.

By way of conclusion, if not closure, we refer to a passage of Lévi-Strauss: 'Myth coded in sounds in place of words, the musical work affords a table of decodings, a matrix of relationships that filter and organise lived experience, substitutes itself for that experience and procures the beneficent illusion that contradictions can be surmounted and difficulties resolved.'[54] So too film, with its narrative economies, its figurations of desire (for Hollywood, male desire), its progressions from equilibrium to equilibrium, has its own unique specificity. Beneficent or not, narrative cinema offers the illusion of contradiction resolved when in reality it yields nothing of the sort.

CHAPTER 6

Realism

Questions of realism have been inscribed in the history of cinema since its beginnings, when the audience at the Lumière brothers' film *L'Arrivée d'un Train en Gare de la Ciotat* rose in terror at the train's approach, fearful they were in mortal danger. Although since then few spectators have mistaken the image for reality itself, film's extraordinary power to imitate reality has made realism a central feature of cinema aesthetics. Prejudices in favour of or against the new medium frequently centred on its unique capacity for mimetic representation, with some people maintaining that its mechanical reproduction of what was in front of the camera permitted little, if any, scope for creativity or self-expression, while others held with equal fervour that the disclosure of reality was at once the privilege and vocation of cinema.

In common with all other aspects of thinking about cinema, the debate around realism took a political turn after 1968. Moreover, questions of realism were to acquire a centrality in this politicised aesthetics for the overwhelming reason that the realist text – in whatever of the many modes of realism it exists – has a distinctive, even unique, epistemic status: it represents things as they are, it claims to tell the truth. The importance of realism is a direct consequence of its epistemic status, as Brecht recognised when he called it a major political, philosophical and practical issue. For all political positions and programmes are premised on a conception of social reality, which is why, of course, governments and other political agencies are so concerned to promote their version of reality, so concerned to present certain propositions as true and others as false. Any realist work, therefore, and none more so than films, with their remarkable power to effect belief in their constructions, has political ramifications. Cinema provides a sustained assertion, or a variety of assertions, as to the way things are – socially, politically, economically, internationally, and so on.

Post-1968 film theorists, then, were alert to the politics of representation, having recourse on the one hand to Althusser's theory of ideology and on the other to Foucault's conception of the imbrication of power and discourse, and they saw as one of their principal tasks an examination of the practices of realism. With a Saussurean theory of signification seemingly able to show that much supposed realism was illusionist, as well as explain how this effect was produced, they approached the task with confidence. But it soon became apparent that the task was more complex than had been appreciated, for doubt arose as to the adequacy for this purpose of a Saussure-influenced theory of textual functioning when the extent of the problem's entanglement with profound political and philosophical issues became evident. The fundamental difficulty was the problem of truth. Since the realist text advances a truth claim in saying how things really stand, and since truth claims cannot be established by the text that makes them but can only be true in relation to something else, then an analysis of realism entails making reference to a beyond-the-text. Thus any complete account of the functioning of realism would have to consider not just its textual practices but the social practices within which these are situated. A theory of the text alone was insufficient: what was needed was a more general theory of how truths and notions of reality are established in society. As thinking about realism proceeded this supplementary need became more evident and its absence became more keenly felt.

In what follows we shall have cause to elaborate in somewhat greater detail this necessarily schematic overview. In the interests of clarity we shall distinguish three principal approaches adopted in relation to realism, it being understood that in practice the three were by no means so clearly separated. They are the mediation thesis, Marxism, and structuralism.

The first of the three approaches seems in certain respects to entail little more than common sense. Cinema, it maintains, is but the mediation between reality and the spectator. As a practical illustration of the thesis, consider one of the arguments advanced against televising the House of Commons, namely, that to do so would necessarily give a false impression of the reality of its proceedings. Suppose a debate is to be televised. A whole series of questions then arises as to how. Is, for example, existing lighting to be used, at the risk of having some members in shadow and others not, with all the connotations thereby involved? What should the mix of background to foreground sound be – since any mix will have its different implications – when a member is speaking to the House? Should the editing be such that only the member speaking is shown, or should there be cuts to elsewhere in the chamber? If so, to what? An outraged opposition? Colleagues listening respectfully? A sleeping member? Should Mrs Thatcher be shot with a standard lens or in a glamorising soft focus? Should Tony Benn always be photographed with something other that the wide-angle lens he reputedly detests? Whatever answers might be given to these and other questions will necessarily condition the meaning of what is seen and heard. Choices have to be made and different pictures of the reality of the House of Commons are the result. For the opponent of televising parliament the point is that to do so would be to betray its innate reality, its essence. So it was too for the post-1968 generation of critics, who voiced a strikingly similar complaint, as the following passage of Jean-Louis Comolli makes apparent.

The basic deception of direct cinema is really its claim to transcribe truly the truth of life, to begin the position of witness in relation to that truth so that the film simply records objects and events mechanically. In reality the very fact of filming is of course already a productive intervention which modifies and transforms the material recorded. From the moment the camera intervenes a form of manipulation begins.[1]

Although an impression of reality is engendered, the argument ran, it is not the transparent rendering it sets itself up to be, but is rather a construction, and a disavowed one at that. With these critics, then, the mediation thesis came to be reinforced by a new emphasis on the conventionality of realism. Far from being the faithful depiction of reality it is assumed to be, realism, through the various forms it has taken throughout its history, shows itself to be neither window nor mirror but a set of conventions. There is, in other words, 'no realism but there are realisms'.[2] Their historical variation has been such that the term has been applied, as Andrew Tudor has noted, to a wide diversity of films including *Birth of a Nation, Nosferatu,*

Nanook of the North, Citizen Kane, La Règle du Jeu and *Paisa*. The many realisms derive from the differing historical moments that set them in opposition to other realisms, that mark this out as plausible and that as implausible, this as believably transparent and that as comically opaque.

The implications of understanding realism as a construction according to historically specific conditions were various. One of the first was a confrontation with the existing orthodoxy, associated above all with André Bazin, which, it was suggested, far from exposing the myth of the transparency of realism actually propagated it. But more was involved than the correction of the errors of Bazin and his followers, for the idea that film was a transparent medium was a commonly held one. A large-scale programme of demystification was therefore needed, to be conducted through education and through the development of a new self-reflexive cinema that did not efface the signs of its production.

Matters were not quite as simple, however, as they first appeared. For a start the Bazin of post-1968 revolutionary fervour was something of a straw man. Although Bazin's thought was non-systematic and at times confused, it was unfair to characterise him as a believer in the transparency of film. Rather, as Terry Lovell pointed out, his concern for the reality to be portrayed and the need to subordinate form and technique to any portrayal did not entail his believing in what she calls 'the reproductive fallacy' – namely, that the only realism is that which reproduced an exact copy of reality or the illusion of such a copy.[3] The reason Bazin was misunderstood, Polan and Hess have suggested, was that there was insufficient awareness on the part of his critics of the intellectual background to his work, notably the 1930s movement known as personalism, with its central figure of Emmanuel Mounier.[4] An amalgam of Catholicism and existentialism, personalism maintained that only through the exercise of choice could individual salvation be achieved. The world, Mounier said, expressed the Logos, but this could only be perceived by the individual who freely made an act of faith. Just as no one could make that leap for anyone else, so too the recognition of the Divine Will in the world was a personal matter. Bazin's film aesthetics derived from this belief. His condemnation of montage, with its fragmentation of the world, was on the grounds that any such reconstruction of reality imposes a directorial interpretation on it, thus manipulating the spectator and thereby rendering the presence of God in the world invisible.

Conversely, Bazin's advocacy of a form of cinematic realism that effaced itself before reality was on the grounds that it left the spectator as free as he or she was before reality itself to make or not to make the act of faith that could reveal the face of God. As Polan put it, personalism was a democratic theology without any need for the intercession of priests; Bazin's antagonism to directorial intervention and his distancing himself from *la politique des auteurs* was an attempt to deny a priesthood of film.[5] All in all, then, Bazin was revealed to be not the proponent of an intolerable orthodoxy, but in some respects the precursor of the post-1968 generation of critics who equally advocated a non-manipulative cinema. If politically Bazin and his critics were poles apart, theoretically they had more in common than many of the latter appreciated.

It also became evident that a concern with conventionality, while useful in specifying the various modes of realism, contributed little to the project of demystification. The fact that a representation calls on a historically specific convention does not affect its epistemic status. After all, if convention were the badge of falsity, then any proposition would be false in that language itself depends on a set of conventions. Such a notion is patently absurd: it is in, and only in, language and other systems of representation that truths can be stated; as equally, of course, can falsehoods. It is a point made by Foucault in rather different terms when he argues that power is productive in that discourses not only repress certain truths but produce others.

A third source of difficulty was that the concept of mediation proved to be more problematic than had been supposed. It seemed simple enough: mediation was the process whereby a pre-given reality was transformed by the act of filming into a filmed representation of that reality, which would at best offer a perspective and at worst a distortion. The problem was, however, locating the pre-given reality. Where, or what, is the reality – to return to our earlier example – of the House of Commons? Is it the Tory backwoods vision of the genius of the English constitution under constant threat from those it was designed to keep in their proper place? Is it not rather an outmoded institutional form of some provisional utility for the pursuance of class war? Or perhaps it is a theatre in which men and women depraved by Original Sin act out their individual dramas of damnation and salvation? Might not the Member for South Down prefer to conceive it as a manifestation of the will to power and the precipitous refuge of the last man? In short, one might propose that there are as many Houses of Commons as there are discourses to articulate its reality. Agreed, such a proposal requires that there are no facts, only interpretations, and might encounter the objection that surely there is a bedrock of certainty against which interpretation can be tested; but the tenor of much recent philosophy would run counter to the objection. Indeed one dominant strand in such philosophy has been to challenge what is often termed the myth of the given, the notion that one can locate a self-authenticating presence uncontaminated by interpretation.[6] This rejection of an uninterpreted, unconceptualised reality to which representations can correspond is paralleled within the philosophy of science by the arguments of Kuhn and Feyerabend that there are no facts prior to their articulation within one or another conceptual framework or paradigm. Now all of this is undeniably contentious and has encountered formidable opposition, including, within film theory, a sustained defence of philosophical realism by Terry Lovell. But our point would be that whatever position is taken *is* contentious, including that presupposed by the seemingly straightforward mediation thesis. Although filmic representation may differ in certain important respects from linguistic representation, it has nowhere been established that film is incapable of stating truths, least of all by the mediation thesis.

Before these difficulties with the mediation thesis could be explored, let alone resolved, the entire problem was recast in structuralist terms. Prompted primarily by the radical Lacanian rereading of Saussure that held that the world of words creates the world of things, this recasting was also in response to the problem of the subject, specifically the problem of explaining how spectators were deceived by realist texts. The favoured line of argument went as follows: spectators took films as transparent renderings of the real when in fact they simply produced a reality effect; films were able to do this by virtue of effacing all signs of their production; the only way, therefore, of breaking this ideological hold was through films organised so as to foreground their work of production, i.e. self-reflexive texts. However, if the subject was endowed with powers of judgement – albeit here giving rise to a misjudgement – then it was hard to see how the text alone could be responsible for the deception. Any judgement, whether correct or incorrect, must be by virtue of something other than the text, and it could only be on the basis of one of two things. Judgement is passed either on the basis of a correspondence of the text's representations to a directly knowable external reality, or, in the absence of an accessible reality, on the basis of coherence or otherwise with the spectator's existing beliefs about reality. In neither case was it clear how the form of the text could in itself give rise to an illusion when the spectator, either through correspondence or coherence, could establish whether its truth claim was valid or not. Of course on either model the spectator could be wrong about reality, in other words, subject to an illusion, but that did not secure the argument that the form of the text in itself had the power to deceive and that only self-reflexive texts did not. If it was allowed that the spectator was an agent passing judgement, whether on the basis of correspondence or coherence, then the text alone could not deceive. That is, its status derived not from an effacement of its work of production but from correspondence or non-correspondence, coherence or non-coherence, with what the spectator took to be reality. Nothing of any epistemic consequence could be established by self-reflexivity, *unless the spectator was not outside the text passing judgement on it but was constituted by it*. This, in essence, was the structuralist rescue of the notion that the form of the text could in itself create a reality effect. We shall defer consideration of its effectiveness until after we have looked at the Marxist approach to realism.

As Terry Lovell has made clear, all realisms rely on a conception of how things really are (an ontology) and a procedure for disclosing or representing them (an epistemology). The Marxist critique challenged existing realisms on both counts: their conceptions of reality were wrong, and they were bound to be so, given their means of representation. The critique took as its starting point Marx's propositions that if knowledge could be gained by simply looking around then there would be no need for science, and, more specifically, through the notion of commodity fetishism, that under capitalism social relations assume the misleading appearance of relations between things. Consequently the reality of the social process is quite different from its appearance, and the only way to discern what it is is through the science of historical materialism, which reveals the underlying structures and forces determining the dynamics of society. Such, broadly speaking, was the position shared by the two principal theorists of realism within the Marxist tradition, Györg Lukács and Bertolt Brecht.

Art's role, for Lukács and for Brecht, was to go beyond the misleading surface of things so as to show reality. Naturalism failed, according to Lukács, by taking the immediately apparent, but reified forms of social relations at face value, thereby revealing nothing of real social structures or historical process. An authentic realism, by contrast, although focused on the particular and therefore unable to produce the abstractions of science, could nevertheless yield a kind of knowledge, could still furnish an understanding of social and historical reality. Its means of doing so was by narratives organised around a hero whose life reflected the historical currents of his time. Neither an abstract personification nor a statistical average, the hero was a representative figure rooted in a specific historical moment, with its class conflicts and other contradictions. The individual life, caught up in and responsive to such forces, thus demonstrated how the particular is always mediated by the whole. Models for such an authentic realism were the novels of Scott, Stendhal and Balzac, produced while the bourgeoisie was still a progressive force and had an interest in revealing rather than masking the exploitation and oppression of society. Lukács urged writers in the service of the proletariat to model their own work upon these writings in order to develop a progressive realism that would penetrate 'the veil of reification'.[7]

Brecht, too, wanted an art that would show reality, and was therefore suspicious of any art that confined itself to appearances. Photography, for instance, earned this comment:

Less than at any time does a simple reproduction of reality tell us anything about reality. A photograph of the Krupp works or GEC yields almost nothing about these institutions. Reality proper has slipped into the functional. The reification of human relationships, the factory, let's say, no longer reveals these relationships. Therefore something has actually to be constructed, something artificial, something set up.[8]

More generally Brecht's criticism of the existing forms of realism were couched in terms redolent of Lukács's objections to naturalism, that is, that they described the observable surface of things rather than explained their hidden and contradictory reality.

While Lukács and Brecht, as Lovell has once again pointed out, had more in common than is sometimes allowed, there are still important differences between them. In particular Brecht questioned the adequacy of the nineteenth century novel as a model for progressive realism. His modernist alternative was not, however, the result of simply supposing that changed historical circumstances called for changed artistic conventions; rather, Brecht's whole understanding of those changed circumstances differed from that of Lukács. Whereas Lukács's Marxism was essentially optimistic, with the proletariat destined to triumph and the function of art therefore being to chart and applaud its progress, Brecht on the other hand was inclined to pessimism. In the face of fascism, which he recognised as the prevailing danger and a threat to all progressive social forces, the need was for an art that would shake people out of their complacent contemplation of historical inevitability and would convince them of the necessity of political action. Where Lukács placed the emphasis on the processes of identification and catharsis, which he believed could in some measure restore the alienated subjects of capitalism to their full humanity, Brecht wished to provoke audiences into active responses that would be a prelude to intervention in politics beyond the theatre.

The debate was resumed within post-1968 film theory. In common with both Lukács and Brecht, film theory, indebted as it was to Althusser's science/ideology couple, was distrustful of appearances; but beyond this it came down firmly on the side of Brecht against Lukács. Three reasons may be put forward for this alignment.

For a start, under the influence of Althusser, Lukács was identified with a discredited Hegelian Marxism that conceived the social formation in terms of essence and totalities rather than in terms of relatively autonomous practices. Consequently the works preferred by Lukács, in which the life of the hero at the centre of social conflict expressed the totality, could only be inappropriate to any understanding of society. For Althusser, by contrast, there could be neither essence nor expressive totality: the subject was decentred, incapable of embodying the social whole, as indeed in Brecht's major plays, where 'no character consciously contains in himself the totality of the tragedy's conditions'.[9]

The next objection to Lukács concerned his belief that art could provide knowledge of society. Given the Althusserian distinction between science and ideology, and the conclusion that only within scientific problematics was knowledge produced, it was clear that art equalled ideology and had therefore no special claim to knowledge. Matters, however, were complicated by Althusser's own reservations about what he termed 'real art', which, while not providing 'knowledge in the strict sense', could nevertheless not be equated with ideo-logy.[10] What such art does is enable its audience or readers to 'feel' or 'perceive' – which is not the same as to know – the ideology from which it derives and to which it alludes. From the Lukácsian canon Althusser cited the works of Balzac and Tolstoy, works that allowed a perception of the ideology they came from and spoke of. On the other hand, they neither produced any understanding of the mechanisms generating it nor gave any guidance as to how to combat it. The work of Brecht, however, did just this, in that it introduced an internal distance into both subject and representation, producing, in Heath's words, 'not a totality, but a series of social, political and ideological disruptions'.[11] In the critical distance established, both the working of contradictions and the possibility of their transforma-tion could be articulated. At its best, then, 'art is a struggle in ideology by the distance it establishes in respect of the ideological homogeni-sation of reality.'[12]

The third and final reason that post-1968 film theorists sided with Brecht was that Lukács paid little attention to the specificity of signi-fying practice. His virtual silence on the question of language, which he regarded as unproblematic, was irreconcilable with a theoretical enterprise whose very core was that language had its own specificity and productivity. Brecht, by contrast, with his emphasis on the con-struction of meaning, could be seen as the precursor of their project and as pointing the way forward in their search for a progressive cinema. We shall return to the Lukács-Brecht debate in the next chap-ter.

Marxism's hegemonic moment in film theory was, as we have already indicated, short-lived: its epistemological confidence was ill-suited to the hesitations and doubts about the possibility of know-ledge characterising post-structuralism. Nevertheless its influence on thinking about realism (among other things) continued to be felt, reinforcing suspicions that existing forms of realism disguised more than they revealed, so making the discovery of new forms all the more urgent. Colin McArthur spoke for a generation of film theorists when, in calling for a stylised cinema that would provoke a critical stance on the part of its audience, he referred to 'the pernicious belief (inherent in the realist position) that the world can be understood by contemplating its image'.[13]

What is at stake here is which version of reality, which realism, is to be taken as true. Of necessity every person and every culture privileges certain statements and discourses at the expense of others. Marxism, with its theory of ideology, explains something of how this privileging comes about: it has both a metalanguage with which to criticise existing realisms and a theory of the social origins of truth. Post-structuralism has neither, but frequently functions as though it does, continuing to refer to what is independently known to be true in order to test the claims of realism. This, however, is not altogether surprising, for although post-structuralism denies the possibility of a metalanguage, in passing judgement on other discourses, in disallowing the epistemological claims and totalising theory of Marxism, it is inescapably engaging in metalinguistic activity. There is no discourse that does not assert its own truth and challenge that of others (at best by explaining how what is false comes to be believed as true). Since post-structuralism denies itself this last possibility, and since Marxism decisively does not, theorists were reluctant to surrender the epistemological advantages Marxism conferred, even when its influence declined.

As we have suggested earlier in this chapter, the structuralist moment completely recast the problem of realism. Whereas for the proponents of the mediation thesis any representation was a partial or inaccurate rendering of a pre-existing reality, for structuralists there was no such reality for it to correspond to. Rather, reality was constructed within language, not in the sense that there is no real world but that all thought about it occurs through signifying systems. This is the sense of Lacan's statement that the world of words creates the world of things and Benveniste's that 'for the speaker there is a complete equivalence between language and reality'.[14] The existence of pre-discursive reality is not thereby put in doubt, but our experience of reality can never be pre-discursive. Indeed, as Lacan maintains, any attempt to formulate or return to a pre-discursive reality is itself routed through discourse. Given this orientation, then, realism could only be a construction, never a reflection: in Barthes's terms, 'writing can no longer designate an operation of recording, notation, representation'.[15] The slogan 'no signifieds without signifiers' was as true of images as it was of words, contrary to cinema's appearance of somehow transmitting reality directly. For the structuralist this realism effect was only the end product of the way a particular system of representation positioned the subject.

Although this structuralist variant of anti-realism achieved a position of dominance in film studies during the 1970s, it did not go unchallenged. In the forefront of those prepared to defend a more commonsensical, intuitively acceptable, position was Terry Lovell. In her book *Pictures of Reality,* she questioned whether Marxism (still at the time a major presence within film theory) could be reconciled with the anti-realist notions derived from Saussurean linguistics. Marxism is a realism, she argued, in that while acknowledging that language is theory-laden it nonetheless presupposes a reality independent of and irreducible to language, which is at the same time accessible and knowable. The anti-realist position – which was, she said, a form of conventionalism – in denying that there can be non-discursive access to reality, rested on a refusal of 'the very category of a knowable external reality'.[16] The limited position towards which all conventionalisms tend is that there is only access to reality through mutually exclusive discourses or theories, with the result that the concept of reality ceases to have any significance. It is the equivalent to saying that language literally makes reality: ontology and epistemology are one and the same. In effect, there are as many realities as there are conceptions of it.

Despite these objections the anti-realist tide was not turned, which was partly attributable to the generally low standing of realist epistemology following the interventions of Hindess and Hirst, but also partly because of the misplaced importance Lovell attached to the notion of reference. She maintained that reference posed a major problem for Saussurean linguistics, in that meanings of terms were given within the system of language, yet at the same time these terms referred to the real world outside the system. Post-Saussureans evaded the problem 'by making language in effect the only reality, or making reality a function of language'.[17] In consequence of the conventionalists' failure to distinguish between meaning and reference on the one hand, and their insistence that the real world is unknowable and hence unreferrable to on the other, discourses can only be validated in one of two ways: either through their internal consistency or through coherence with other privileged discourses. And this, she maintained, was an absurdity. A history of the Third Reich, for example, that fails to mention the holocaust is inadequate not for reasons of inconsistency or incoherence, but because it doesn't correspond to what actually happened. Such absurdity stems from the absence of the concept of reference. While representations necessarily occur within some signifying system or other, their validity depends in large part on the properties of what they refer to.

Intuitively satisfying though this line of reasoning on Lovell's part may be, the recourse to the concept of reference unfortunately does not help very much. It certainly does not prove the existence of a knowable external world, in that it is possible to believe a real object is being referred to when in fact it does not exist. Indeed, as Putnam has indicated, one of the major problems facing contemporary philosophy is the very elusiveness of the supposed realm of what grounds reference. The history of science shows that what was presumed to refer fifty years ago now does not; similarly, in fifty years' time, our terms of reference will have been deemed inadequate. Not only are theories continually being revised and outmoded, but so too are the validating procedures by which theories are tested.[18] Discourse certainly refers, but its continual revisions make appeals to what is out there as world as unconvincing as the referential discourse is unstable. Even the knockdown holocaust argument could conceivably, as certain historiographical interventions have recently made clear, be turned on its head: an equally referential historiography could have it that the holocaust never 'really' happened. In other words, the existence of reference does not prove that discourses are validated by a correspondence to reality. Philosophers from traditions as different as Foucault on one side, and Putnam and Rorty on the other (with possibly Hindess and Hirst somewhere in between), have favoured a version of validation through social practices and procedures.

These various difficulties associated with Lovell's position regrettably obscured the importance of her comments on the appeal to a touchstone when pronouncing on realism, the appeal to what we know independently to be the case, to be set against the claims of the realist text that something else is the case. There was undoubtedly a problem here, and there was equally a need for theoretical innovation to resolve it, although Lovell's own insistence that such a theory already existed in the form of the correspondence thesis did nothing to pave the way for such a development. Structuralist thinking came up against the problem (without recognising its dimensions) in asking how, if signification produces rather than reflects, it creates an impression of reality. Alternatively, how was it that some texts or representations came to be judged as true and others as false? For structuralists there was naturally no question of this occurring on the basis of correspondence or non-correspondence to any reality given prior to signification. There were nevertheless two alternative answers available.

The first was relatively simple, almost commonsensical, and was a variant on the coherence thesis. A text was realistic, it was held, in so far as it conformed to spectators' existing ideology. The realist effect was produced or not according to whether the representations of the text matched or failed to match the beliefs of spectators. Thus Stephen Heath, writing in the early 1970s, claimed that a work is realistic when it offers 'the representation of reality which a particular society proposes and assumes as "Reality"'.[19] And John Ellis, ten years later, wrote that a work yields the impression of truth 'to the extent that the form of narration is able to return to the audience the audience's own assumptions about what life is like'.[20] Very similar views can be found in the early work of Barthes, in particular in his collection of essays *Mythologies*. There Barthes analysed a number of aspects of popular culture and demonstrated their contribution to the circulation of the dominant ideology, later termed the 'doxa', that body of taken-for-granted truths whose apparent obviousness masks social reality. A feature of the analysis was its demonstration that while images and texts may appear to transmit a pre-given reality via a neutral medium they in fact secrete ideology, because they are necessarily received and read in terms of the doxa. His best known example was a cover of *Paris Match* depicting a young black soldier in French uniform saluting the tricolor. Over and beyond this overt meaning of the image, there was, for readers of *Paris Match* at the time, the further meaning that 'France is a great empire, that all her sons, without any colour discrimination, faithfully serve under her flag, and that there is no better answer to the detractors of an alleged colonialism than the zeal shown by this negro in serving his so-called oppressors.' While Barthes's thinking here involves both a Nietzschean perspectivism and a Marxist conception of ideology as masking the truth of real oppression, its most important aspect for our purposes is that the ideological effect is produced by the conjunction of the image and the doxa. That is, the meaning of the image depends upon a coherence with existing beliefs; if these change so too will the meaning. Put slightly differently, the total context of reading, including the doxa of the reader, will determine the meaning of any given text.

The disadvantage of the coherence thesis was certainly not any lack of plausibility, but lay rather in its unwelcome practical consequences. It implied that the ideological success of realism would continue until there were changes in both cinema and society. Changing the form of cinema alone would not be enough, because the existing belief system of spectators would constrain their reception. In that the thesis attributed agency to the spectator as well as to the text, the ideological hold of existing realist practices could not be broken merely by altering those practices. Since this in effect blocked the road of changing spectators by changing texts – the very road that was on the political agenda – an alternative account of how certain texts were privileged as realist came to seem desirable. This alternative version was classic structuralism.

The central proposition of structuralism in this case was that instead of the spectator being the judge of the text's claim to tell the truth, he or she is the effect of the text, the formal structures of which at once produce meanings and constitute the spectator as subject. Typically, the central mechanism for this is the effacement of all signs of the text's production and the achievement of an invisibility of process. Through the denial of their textual status, the constructed meanings seem to occur naturally, to derive from elsewhere. *Histoire* rather than *discours,* such a text does not address the spectator in the form of any voice or agency, but presents a reality that is itself presumed to speak for itself, recounts events that seem to be occurring or have occurred independently. One of the consequences of this narrational mode is that spectators think (and speak) of events and characters without regard to their fictional status. The impersonal narration characteristic of cinema (by contrast with television and some forms of novel) 'is responsible for the particular effect of reality that the classic narrative film has'.[21]

As in all models of textual functioning indebted to Althusser's notion of interpellation there was a tension between, on the one hand, the desire to attribute a specifiable effectivity to textual structure in isolation from any specific conjuncture, and, on the other, the necessity of recognising that the subject was agent as well as effect, and was therefore sited within a particular historical situation. The problem centres on the recognition/misrecognition couple, each element of which entails that an agent pre-exist the textual structure of which he or she is required to be only an effect. This tension was particularly evident in the work of Colin MacCabe, the importance of which is such as to merit consideration at some length.

MacCabe's distinctive position was that realism should not be defined by its content or capacity to mirror reality but by a certain textual organisation whose effect was to position the reader. The *locus classicus* of such textual structuration was the nineteenth-century realist novel, but by virtue of a similarity of narrative forms it was to be found extensively in mainstream cinema. The so-called classic realist text, then, whether George Lucas or George Eliot, is defined by a structure in which the various discourses comprising the text form a hierarchy. Among these various discourses, each of which proposes a version of reality, one is privileged as the bearer of *the* truth, and therefore functions as a metalanguage by which to judge the truth or falsity of the other discourses (which have thereby acquired the status of object languages). For example, in the classic realist novel quotation marks are used to designate discourses with the status of object language, whose relation to the real is established by the surrounding metalanguage. Even though the various discourses may be contradictory – a feature most marked in the detective novel – the function of the narration, whether first person explicit or third person implicit, is to provide the unquestioned authority by which their various claims may be tested. The reader is thus constantly given a place from which to pass judgement as to what is really the case and really should be believed.

In cinema, too, numerous contradictory discourses are framed by a dominant discourse that functions as a metalanguage. In the case of documentaries this is usually a voice-over commentary, binding together the various versions of reality proposed by images and other voices. For fiction films the same hierarchical structure pertains, but its terms are reversed, with the image prioritised over words. Here, the image-track corresponds to the narrative discourse outside inverted commas, showing the spectator what really happens. By way of an example, MacCabe referred to *Klute,* a film that was praised for its realistic portrayal of the call girl Bree (Jane Fonda). While various characters within the fiction offer answers to the question of what Bree wants (to stay in New York or depart with Klute, the detective), the truth, said MacCabe, is established by the image-track: when, at the end of the film, Bree's voice-over to her analyst expresses doubt as to her staying with Klute, the image of her packing assures the spectator of the opposite.

In both literature and film the narrating discourse appears to provide the truth, to render the real transparently. While the materiality of the other discourses is acknowledged, that of the metalanguage is not. In other words its status as discourse – or in Derridean terms, as writing – is disavowed; 'it is dematerialised to achieve perfect representation – to let the identity of things shine through the window of words'.[22] It was on the basis of this apparent transparency of the metalanguage that MacCabe designated the classic realist text as reactionary. To understand the thinking behind this judgement it is necessary to recall the structuralist conception of representation. In contrast to traditional notions of representation as capturing some pre-existing reality, the structuralist version of it is as a system that determines both the place where the object appears and the point from which it is seen. Production rather than reflection, representation brings into existence a knower and a known. Hence any suggestion that it can be transparent is profoundly misleading. Any system of representation, such as classic realism, making such a claim is tainted by empiricism, MacCabe said, drawing on Althusser; that is, it supposes that knowledge is given through experience and that a pre-given subject can discern the essence of a pre-given reality in a moment of vision, instead of allowing that knowledge is always productive of both subject and object.[23] The coincidence of truth and vision in the metalanguage of the classic realist text puts the real 'beyond argument': through the metalanguage 'we can comfortably read the repetition of our "evident" selves and our "evident" reality'.[24] The spectator is thus fixed in a position of 'dominant specularity', in apparent possession of knowledge that calls for no further activity.[25] Unaware that this position has been produced by the particular system of representation, the spectator imagines him or herself to exist outside production and to be in possession of complete and final knowledge. It is because of these relations with the spectator and not because of any distorted or partial picture of reality that the classic realist text is to be judged as reactionary. The unified subject confronts the hypostatised object, each locked into a paralysing fixity, with no perspective for struggle or possibility of transformation. In dissolving all contradictions the metalanguage places the spectator outside production, outside conflict, outside history.

What, then, were the alternatives to this reactionary textual practice? Two alternatives existed, MacCabe said, in the progressive text and the subversive text. The first of these was a classic realist text in which the narrating discourse contradicted the dominant ideology, for example, a film about economic class struggle told from a trade union viewpoint. The second, the subversive text, so organised its discourses that it 'broke with any dominance and. . . remained essentially subversive of any ideological order'.[26] Such a film would be Rossellini's *Germany Year Zero,* where the narration is not privileged over the discourses of characters, and by thus not giving the knowledge with which to judge their truth leaves many elements unresolved and unintegrated. Yet neither strategy was without its limitations. The progressive text was still classic realism and open to all the objections levelled against it, including that of being unable to encompass contradiction and envisage change – an example being *O Lucky Man,* with its view of the implacable march of capitalism against which nothing can be done except 'note our superiority to it'.[27] And the 'deconstruction' performed by the subversive text remained largely negative.

There remained one further alternative to the classic realist text, and that was the revolutionary text (exemplified in literature by Joyce and in film by Godard), which was concerned equally with the process of representation and the problem of what was represented. Since we shall be looking at this in some detail in the next chapter, we shall do no more here than note its existence.

MacCabe subsequently acknowledged that the first of his two articles on realism (which forms the basis for the position attributed to him above) was 'contaminated by formalism; by a structuralism that it claimed to have left behind'.[28] Although it was widely read as holding that the subject is the effect of the text, this was in some ways a misreading, because even in this first article there was a more dialectical notion of the subject than would be consistent with a strict structuralism. In it MacCabe explicitly stressed that textual structure was not the unilateral determinant of reading, pointing also to the ideological and class configurations in which the spectator was situated. And implicitly, as in all accounts of the spectator's response based on interpellation, the spectator was necessarily as much agent as effect, being called on to judge firstly the extent to which the narrating discourse was discrepant with the subordinate discourses within the test, and secondly the extent to which it conformed to the dominant social discourse and was thereby realistic. In any case, whether he had been misread or not, MacCabe recast his thesis in terms more indebted to Lacan than to Althusser.

As before, realism was conceived in terms of a hierarchical organisation of discourses within the text, with the dominant discourse 'assured of its domination by the security and transparency of the image'.[29] The spectator is thereby placed in a position of knowledge with respect to what is transparently given as pre-existing reality. Such knowledge is not, of course, delivered all at once, and indeed narratives typically turn on an initial lack of knowledge in relation to questions that they will later answer; but 'knowledge is guaranteed at the end of the story'.[30] Such a guarantee is crucial to the positioning of the spectator: knowing in advance that you will know by the end ensures a dominating unity. The film *American Graffiti,* like many other classic realist texts, is preoccupied with the question of identity, in particular that of its central figure, Curt Henderson. Whether Curt will leave town, thereby revealing his character, is the enigma the whole movement of the film is set to answer. Yet at the same time it denies this process, so that once the suspense as to what he will decide is resolved, his decision seems obvious. His established identity is read back into the text, with the result that it appears to be pre-given, just waiting to be revealed all along. The resolution, therefore, of the question of Curt's identity is also the production of a spectator position, one of knowledge and outside of contradiction. The spectator is seemingly outside of process and therefore can imagine him or herself as completely grasping process. Once again it is because the metalanguage suppresses its own productivity that the spectator is placed in this position of illusory mastery. However, this later conceptualisation of MacCabe's advanced on his earlier formulation in a number of important respects.

It was, first of all, an attempt to overcome the objection of ahistoricity that Lovell had directed at existing theories of the subject by making explicit what had earlier been implicit, namely, that the spectator was located in a determinate historical moment influencing the way the text was received and read. This dialectical relation of spectator to text, in contrast to the formulation of classic realism in which the spectator is always convinced of the truth of the metalanguage, allowed a certain latitude of interpretation in that the discourses available to the spectator test and interrogate the text's claim to truth. The greater the complexity of the text, the more it is open to a multiplicity of readings.

Secondly, the new formulation recast the notion of dominant specularity in a form allowing more fully for the complexities of the situation. The subject's relation to the dominant visual discourse was now conceived as a bid to enter the would-be security of the imaginary, a plenitude denying all difference and lack. A problem for this bid was that the subject's look is structured by difference and lack, since in the mirror phase the verification by the mother – 'that's you' – of the child's self-image is purchased 'at the cost of introducing a look, a difference where there should only be similitude'.[32] Subsequently the subject's look is always organised by the symbolic, hence there is necessarily a lack in the scopic field (for the Other is always lacking), a lack that the imaginary offers only the false hope of filling. Further, the unified self-image is also threatened by the difference opened up by the gaze of the other, which renders the subject an object and thus robs the subject of the dream of mastery. In the case of the classic realist text this drama of the subject and the gaze is played out in the subject's attempts to achieve a point of view that is all-seeing and safely situated outside the realm of difference, attempts that are threatened when a character with whose look the spectator identifies becomes the object of another's gaze. Just such a moment occurs in *American Graffiti*, in MacCabe's account, when the girl in the white T-bird looks at Curt and mouths 'I love you', which, with its explicit sexuality and objec-tifying directness, imperils his position. The spectator's position, by virtue of identification with Curt, is similarly threatened. If the spec-tator is to have his or her position re-established, Curt must find someone to function as a guarantee of identity, and there is none better for this than a father, which the text provides in the figure of Wolfman Jack. At the end of the film, immune now to the threat of the girl's gaze, Curt looks down on the town from his departing plane, a metaphor both for his own knowledge and the spectator's.

Thus the most obvious advantage of this new formulation was that it offered a theory of the pleasure to be had in realism. Given that dominant specularity was evidently insufficient fully to account for pleasure, in that many films in which it operated were box office disasters, MacCabe proposed that, rather in the manner of the *fort-da* game, threats to the imaginary dominance needed to be introduced and then overcome in order to ensure a fully libidinal investment of the field of vision. The classic realist text will therefore introduce the threatening gaze of the other, only then to annul the threat by guaran-teeing the supremacy of what MacCabe termed the point of view. It is in this constant oscillation that pleasure is to be located.

Thirdly and finally, the new formulation advanced beyond the earlier structuralist position in acknowledging that classic realism never entirely achieves the coherence and smoothness to which it aspires: there is always a potential surplus spilling over from the forward movement of the narrative that is liable to throw the text into crisis. One such moment occurs in *American Graffiti* when John Milner and Carol attack a car whose occupants have provoked them by squirting it with foam and letting down its tyres. This, says MacCabe, disturbs the narrative in two ways: firstly, its excessive sexual symbolism hints beyond pleasure towards death, which Milner personifies in his unceasing, positionless repetition; and secondly, during the attack, irregularities of camera position (breaking the 180° rule, for instance) and the fact that the film lights appear in the frame threaten to dislodge the spectator from dominant specularity – 'the film looks back at us'.[32] However, such disturbances fail to radicalise the classic realist text. Whatever fissures may exist and however progressive the content, this form of textual practice is incapable of dealing with contradictions. Unable to 'introduce the spectator to his or her own constitutive contradictions' the classic realist text is condemned to 'the endless repetition of the imaginary'.[33]

MacCabe's work on realism, particularly his notion of the classic realist text, proved to be widely influential, but it was not without its critics, two of whom – David Bordwell and Colin McArthur – we will consider briefly.

Bordwell took issue with MacCabe's derivation of classic realism from the nineteenth-century novel, and contrasted his approach unfavourably with that of Bakhtin. Although both conceive of the novel as a set of discourses, for Bakhtin its form is typically dialogic, a site where no single discourse absolutely triumphs over the rest. Those novels picked out by MacCabe were therefore atypical of the bourgeois tradition, whose norm was better represented by the work of such as Tolstoy and Eliot, where the narrator's interventions, far from providing a secure metalanguage, rather constitute 'heterogeneous attacks upon various pre-defined conceptions of reality'.[34] Such novels are a site of struggle, of competing versions of the truth, rather than the assertion of one encompassing truth.

Colin McArthur's disagreement with MacCabe centred not on the concept of the classic realist text, but on MacCabe's evaluation of it as lacking in any progressive potential. McArthur's contention was that in certain conjunctures it had a considerable degree of political effectivity. More particularly, he disagreed that it was incapable of handling contradictions, and cited as evidence moments from *Days of Hope*, the series of television films. One such instance occurs when the gentlemanly coalmine owner lectures a group of miners on the peaceful gradualism of the British constitutional way while soldiers brought in to quell dissent in the coalfield are seen to be engaging in bayonet practice in the background. In response to McArthur, MacCabe maintained that this example actually confirmed his position, in that the contradiction is one between what the mineowner is saying and what the image is showing: 'this is exactly the classic realist form which privileges the image against the word to reveal what the mineowner says is false'.[35] That is, the contradiction is stated, only to be resolved straightaway. Instead of positioning the spectator where he or she has to engage in an active response to work on the contradiction, the text offers the security of final and guaranteed knowledge, constructs an unquestioned position for the spectator.

The most fundamental objection to MacCabe's position is that the hierarchy of discourses defining the classic realist text can be applied to texts held to be unrealistic. The mechanism can therefore explain neither how the distinction between unrealistic and realistic texts is made, nor how spectators come to uphold the claims to realism of some texts while denying those of others. The realism effect depends, obviously enough, on an act of judgement in which the text's claims are measured against what the spectator independently believes to be the case; that is, it depends not on the text alone, but on a correspondence between the text's metadiscourse and that of the spectator. From this it follows that a text's realism is a historical variable. As beliefs about reality have changed, so too have the forms of realism. Any theory of realism, then, must provide an account both of the hierarchisation of discourses within the test and how the spectator comes to privilege, at a particular historical moment, certain discourses over others. The difficulty of this undertaking is increased by the dialectic of the subject, in which meaning and being occur together. It is not simply a matter of pre-existing beliefs encountering the truth claims of the text, but rather that the text's own effectivity determines in part what the spectator believes to be true. One way of avoiding this difficulty had been to make, as the structuralists did, the spectator an effect of the text through interpellation – a solution that was invalidated by the post-structuralist attribution of agency to the subject. But post-structuralism did not bring a theory of realism any closer.

A fundamental emphasis of post-structuralism is that if language organises reality, then truth is established not by correspondence to any reality given prior to language, but by social processes. In the words of Richard Rorty, a philosopher in the analytic tradition who has recently moved close to certain post-structuralist positions, '[the fact] that words take their meaning from other words rather than by virtue of their representative character [has as its] corollary the notion that vocabularies acquire their privileges from men and women who use them rather than from their transparency to the real'.[36] As a consequence there is always, as Foucault put it, 'a politics of truth', in that the process of privileging some discourses as true and others as false is inextricably caught up in power relations.[37] However, neither Rorty nor Foucault offer explanations as to how this designation of discourses as realistic or non-realistic comes about; there is, in other words, no post-structuralist social theory of truth. Indeed, the whole tenor of post-structuralist thinking has been to deny the possibility of any such theory, involving as it does an account of the historical construction of the subject, since there is nowhere outside of social process from which to mount it. In the case of realism, neither the subject nor the reality effect pre-exist the exchange between text and reader; each defines the other in an endless process. Hence, post-structuralists argue, the spectator's stake in the process cannot finally be theorised.

Despite this impasse, it may nevertheless be possible to elucidate some aspects of the problem of realism by means of psychoanalysis. As was importantly pointed out by MacCabe, the pleasure of the realist text depends in large part on its delivery of the anticipated verisimilitude and plausibility. Psychoanalysis would suggest that the pleasures thus provided are, firstly, that of being (associated with identification), and secondly, that of having (associated with desire). MacCabe's emphasis was on identification, especially that in which the spectator misrecognised him or herself as transcendent, as occupying a position of imaginary dominance. But like the notion of the hierarchy of discourses, this form of identification could be found equally in films considered to be unrealistic and in box office failures. It therefore neither specified the pleasures peculiar to realism nor identified the crucial component in the provision of pleasure by a film. What is required, then, is a theory that can account for two differences: that in the response of different spectators to the same film and that in the response of the same spectator to different films.

Our suggestion would be that the spectator judging the text to be realistic identifies with the one who knows the truth. The powerful attraction of realism is thus twofold. Its character as self-evident truth legitimates the spectator's idealised self-image as the one who knows (in a manner similar to the mother's confirmation of the child's self-image in the mirror phase). Further, the identifications made with characters in the realist film may persist, in contrast to those made with characters in films judged to be unrealistic (nobody identifying with Superman believes they can fly after the film ends). Rather as members of religious or political sects assume idealised identities that sustain them in other activities, so spectators of realist films can carry over their identifications in order to fend off lack in subsequent social exchanges. If this latter form of identification is instantiated by realism, it would explain why different spectators with their own specific histories find pleasure in different films.

There is also, we would suggest, something beyond identification involved in the pleasure of the realist text, namely fantasy. By no means all texts deemed realistic are experienced as pleasurable: some are in the 'worthy but dull' category, others offer even less pleasure. Being the one who knows is therefore insufficient; not any reality will do. Only those where an absent object of desire is figured will suffice to bring pleasure, or more precisely, where a particular fantasy bringing pleasure to the spectator can be designated as true by the film's textual economy. If this is the case, then evidently there is a more complex pattern of identifications at work than MacCabe allows for. The question then arises as to what the implications are for any politics of the text.

Questions of realism extend beyond aesthetic and academic debate into the public sphere, as is evidenced by the often heated discussion as to the truthfulness, the realism, of this or that text – *The Deerhunter* in relation to its allegations of Vietcong sadism, *Scum* in respect of Borstal life, television news concerning the effect of US bombing raids on Libya, and most narrative cinema as regards the representation of women. The tendency in the male-dominated film theory of the 1970s was to stand aside from these specific issues, partly out of a lack of competence to judge and partly from a suspicion of questions of correspondence to any pre-given real, and to favour instead the formulation of a general theory of the working of realist texts. Hopes for such a knowledge-providing metalanguage were never to be fully realised, as we have indicated above. At the same time a more heterodox attitude to theory and practice was gaining credence, one not of refusing theory altogether but of using it locally in relation to specific issues of representation and to particular, purportedly realist, texts. The paradigm for this alternative has been within women's struggles: engagement with the politics of truth has for women been too urgent a matter to await the final settlement of grand theory.

CHAPTER 7

The avant-garde

Indissociable from the condemnation of the old cinema, along with its systems of production and distribution, was a call for a new kind of cinema, announced by the formation of the Estates General in 1968. Indeed, one motive behind the subsequent analyses of the now despised Hollywood was to ascertain how far such a call might be realisable. As to the question of what form this new cinema might take, of the various answers given none was more influential than that, based on the assumption of the power of the dominant ideology over signifying practices, which demanded a complete break with mainstream cinema, with what had been characterised by Godard as Hollywood-Mosfilm. Whereas before there had been a privileging of realism over escapism, or of European art cinema over American commercial cinema, or of auteurs over metteurs-en-scène, there was now an overwhelming tendency to privilege the avant-garde over all other forms of cinema.

The association of the Left with the avant-garde was by no means unprecedented, with the Soviet cinema of the 1920s and the surrealist movement both prefiguring the post-1968 alignment. In thinking through the implications of their position, the new generation of film theorists returned to earlier discussions of the relations between the avant-garde and politics, focusing their attention chiefly on the debates of the inter-war period, when Marxists were concerned to mobilise art in the struggle against fascism. Four figures dominated these debates: Lukács, Brecht, Benjamin, and Adorno.

The least sympathetic to the avant-garde was Lukács, who saw modernism as a retreat into an art that dealt only with appearance and immediate experience. While its subjectivist tendency testified to the disintegration of bourgeois society it did nothing to explain it, breeding only fatalism and despair with its vision of life as 'opaque, fragmentary, chaotic and uncomprehended'.[1] What was needed, said Lukács, was a new realism that would do for the twentieth-century proletariat what the novels of Balzac and Stendhal had done for the nineteenth-century bourgeoisie, namely, promote a knowledge of society and the understanding that it can be changed by purposive action. Lukács's position found little favour with Brecht, who considered his advocacy of realism to be a deluded and timeless formalism. It was impossible, Brecht agued, to deduce the aesthetic forms appropriate to the advancement of socialism from the cultural needs of the bourgeoisie a century before. New social realities called for new modes of representation; and modernism, suitably transformed, could serve a progressive purpose.

Brecht conceived his own artistic role as that of 'educator, politician, organiser'. His aim was to develop a form of theatre that would engage the audience both emotionally and intellectually: it would evoke anger at prevailing injustices and inspire people to change the society that tolerated them; at the same time it would provide knowledge of the society that produced them. Such theatre would expose the exploitative and oppressive reality of social relations, something that existing theatre signally failed to do, being no more than an opiate paralysing the reason, inducing 'hypnosis, undignified intoxification and befuddling of the senses'.[2] Committed to a view of the world as intrinsically unchanging, with suffering depicted as unavoidable, traditional theatre encouraged unconscious participation in the progression of the narrative and relied on audience identification with characters, processes by which all social contradictions could be annulled or universalised. Brecht's epic theatre would do none of this. Characters would no longer be subjected to the inescapable dictates of fate – 'humanity must not be smeared with tragedy' – and audiences would no longer be held in thrall by manipulative techniques.[3] In epic theatre the spectator would not be 'a simple consumer, he must also produce'.[4]

At the centre of Brecht's aesthetics was the well-known concept of *Verfremdung*, defamiliarisation or distanciation (to be distinguished from the formalist concept of *ostranenie*, making strange, by its goals of cognition and social change rather than a solely aesthetic renewal of perception). A series of devices ensured that audiences retained a critical detachment, and hence a capacity to perceive, learn, decide and act when confronted by the dramatic performance. Above all there was an insistence on artifice: elements of staging convention- ally hidden, like lighting sources, were exposed; actors might address the audience directly; and there was a consistent separation between actors and their roles, making it plain they were quoting lines rather than speaking from the supposed subjectivity of the character. The purpose of the acting style was to oppose mimesis, the naturalistic copying of individual psychology, and instead, by drawing attention to the typicality of actions, to show characters as the product of his- torically specific forms of social organisation. The action or gesture encapsulating a character's social situation and determinations Brecht termed a *gest*. In addition, interruptions (such as songs or discontinu- ous scenes) were used to punctuate the dramatic flow and prevent audience involvement in the action. Similarly, forms of literarisation (such as projected titles, commentaries and quotation) enabled him to introduce ideas that would bear on the the drama and encourage audiences to think about it. Through these various means Brecht's epic theatre challenged the dominant naturalism; confronted by it, 'the spectator, instead of being enabled to have an experience, is forced, as it were, to cast his vote'.[5] By denaturalising theatre Brecht hoped to denaturalise society, showing that it is made and not ordained, and is therefore capable of being changed. His theatre required that audiences take up a position in relation to the historical possibility of change: they would ideally be maintaining an intellec- tual detachment above the drama whilst simultaneously engaging in an impassioned critique of social reality.

The conventional forms of manipulation available to theatre directors were, Brecht believed, intensified in the cinema. Indeed, the attitude of the mainstream director could be summed up by Abel Gance's comment, 'For me a spectator who maintains his critical sense is not a spectator. I wanted the audience to come out of the theatre amazed victims.'[6] More generally, cinema displayed a number of fea- tures that gave Brecht profound misgivings. The fact that the camera imposes its vision on the spectator, yielding only a fixed viewpoint, was one such feature. Worse still was what he termed the 'fundamental reproach' towards cinema: the fact of mechanical reproduction con- ferring an unalterability on film, which deprives the audience of any possibility of influencing the production.

Brecht's pessimism about cinema contrasted with the optimism of Walter Benjamin, who welcomed it for its destruction of what he

termed the 'aura' surrounding traditional art forms. Deriving originally from art's association with religious ritual, and surviving in
secularised form in the cult of *l'art pour l'art,* the aura is that air of
magical authority or authenticity attaching to high art. By inculcating
submissive attitudes towards the art work, and by extension towards
the existing social order, auratic art served the cause of political reaction. Cinema, by contrast, with its new technology of mechanical
reproduction, potentially inaugurated an era of mass appropriation
of art. It was, for Benjamin, the vehicle for the emergence of a new
proletarian consciousness; freed from the intrusiveness of the artist's
subjectivity, cinema could objectively register the historical presence
of the masses and give form to their reality and aspirations. While
in practice there were difficulties – the star system in particular constituted an obstacle to mass self-representation – the potential was
there. The form cinema assumed under capitalism was by no means
fixed; the directive use of montage was, for example, a possible way
of inhibiting audiences' tendency to identify with actors. Most importantly, cinema required no specialised skills for its appreciation, and
therefore encouraged the critical, active, undeferential attitudes spectators displayed at sports events. It heralded the eclipse of distance
in the production and reception of art, which instead of being an
agent of domination becomes a means of collective self-expression
and emancipation. Contemporary industrial workers and city
dwellers, whose perception of the world was so fragmented and accel-
erated by their conditions of life, could find in film the formal resolution and organisation of their experience. Film was the medium
such transformed modes of perception required to act as a guide in
the modern world.

Such a valorisation of cinema was strongly criticised by Adorno,
who maintained that technological developments, far from becoming
the means of human liberation, constituted a new form of political
control. Cinema and other aspects of mass culture such as jazz and
popular music Adorno termed 'the culture industry', an integral part
of a repressive, administered society dominated by exchange values
and by instrumental rationality in which every life was 'a damaged
life'. Benjamin's idea that film was the one truly revolutionary art
form was at best 'enchantingly wrong-headed' and at worst 'identification with the aggressor'.[7] Far from being the spontaneous self-
expression of the masses, however much the culture industry might
present them as such, film and other popular art forms were in reality

imposed on the masses and functioned to manipulate, regiment and mystify. Any appearance of inventiveness and creativity masked the reality of standardised commodification, a sameness serving to convince that the only possible social order was the existing one. The pleasures afforded were mere palliatives, dreams of fulfilment impossible to achieve under the exisiting social order: 'The culture industry perpetually cheats its consumers of what it perpetually promises.'[8] Cinema in particular permitted no room for reflection on the part of the audience, imposing itself irresistibly as reality. It might have destroyed the aura, but only at the cost of liquidating truth. Although towards the end of his life Adorno was to revise his estimate of popular culture, and even to rehabilitate cinema to an extent, he consistently located resistance to and criticism of the administered society in modernism (but not in its every manifestation). Modernism was simultaneously part of the world of reification and alienation, and a repository of authenticity and protest against it. All art, whether avant-garde or popular, bore the imprint of the administered society, but some forms of modernism, notably expressionism, were able to articulate what ideology sought to conceal, were 'a pre-figurative cypher of redemption'.[9]

In reviving these debates the post-1968 film theorists quickly made it known where their sympathies lay. Least favoured was Lukács, whose advocacy of realism in no way appealed to a generation committed to finding new cinematic forms to challenge the prevailing realism of the mainstream. If Lukács was rejected, Adorno was largely ignored, his 'strategy of hibernation' hardly commending itself to the spirit of activism. Consequently, as has been pointed out by Lovell, film theory missed an opportunity to take advantage of a line of thinking which, in its condemnation of mass culture and its advocacy of the avant-garde, paralleled its own. Attitudes towards Benjamin were ambivalent, though on the whole favourable. In Britain his estimate of cinema's progressive potential was particularly valued as a useful counter to the prevailing Leavisite antipathy towards all cinema as a component of mass culture. Although he had been, as Heath put it, 'totally mistaken as to the actual development of cinema under the hegemony of Hollywood', he could also be seen as having affirmed the potential for a different kind of cinema.[10]

Of the four, it was Brecht whose influence was unreservedly dominant, his name being invoked by those of quite different persuasions to authorise the most diverse of practices. Activists inspired by the events of 1968 adopted him because of the political urgency of his work, and because of his conception of art as intervention. For Althusserian Marxists, he was the exemplar of materialist practice in art, aiming to 'produce a critique of the spontaneous ideology in which men live'.[11] The reflecting, but always distorting, mirror through which a society recognises itself was effectively shattered by the decentred, dissociated structure of his plays, producing instead a new active and critical relation between audience and performance. He appealed to post-Saussureans because his ideas of self-reflexivity and of the exposure of the means of dramatic production squared with their own about the productivity of language. Finally, for Lacanians, the suggestion by Althusser that Brecht's practice produced a new spectator could be supported and explicated by the theory of the subject as produced within language. Heath, for example, reread the notion of distanciation from a psychoanalytic perspective drawn partly from Barthes.

In his essay 'Diderot, Brecht, Eisenstein' Barthes had proposed a conception of representation not in terms of the imitation of reality but of a structure setting in place a spectacle that in turn sets in place the spectator. Because the spectator is literally at a distance and in a place from which the representation may be securely appropriated, the structure, Barthes said, is therefore fetishistic. In taking up this proposal, Heath suggested, paradoxically, that Brechtian distanciation undermined the distance that is the condition of classic representation, whether in the theatre or cinema. Just as the fetish, in its disavowal of lack, installs the subject in a position where identity is assured, so too does the technology and scopic regime of cinema place the spectator in a position of stable unity in relation to a fixed 'reality', precisely what Brechtian practice puts in question. Distanciation pulls the spectator out of fixity by an endless displacement of identification and representation, so producing an understanding both of the construction of representation and of the spectatorial position as contradictory. That is, distanciation 'disinterpellates'.[12]

A very similar case was made by MacCabe on behalf of Brechtian techniques, arguing that the supposedly unalterable identity conferred on the spectator by classic cinema is thereby destabilised, largely because no point of identification is offered within the Brechtian text.[13] Just as the identities of character are produced by social and historical forces, so too is that of the spectator; this knowledge, however, brings with it a renewed experience of the lack that the plenitude of representation had been designed to ward off. Now though, the lack inaugurates desire; hence knowledge and desire come to replace belief and pleasure.

There was in these articles an evident tension between Brecht and Lacan: the one, with his conception of theatre as education and his respect for science, was very much the upholder of the rationalist belief in the knowability and controllability of history; the other, for whom the Other always had its say, was less sanguine by far about either of these latter possibilities. No Lacanian could subscribe to Althusser's expectation of Brechtian techniques producing 'a new true and active consciousness in spectators',[14] any more than they could to Heath's claim for distanciation, that 'the spectaror is himself included in the movement from ideology to real, from illusion to objective truth'.[15] The implication in much Brechtian writing on cinema that it was possible for the spectator to stand outside and perceive himself or herself seeing was ultimately incompatible with the Lacanian pronouncement that there was no Other of the Other, no place beyond language of metalinguistic refuge. It was therefore a matter of choosing Brecht or Lacan, but not both, in thinking through the relationship between spectator and film, between subject and signifying practice. Many theorists, Heath included, followed the Lacanian course (his Brecht paper was not subsequently included in his collection of film essays), one that was charted by those associated with the journal *Tel Quel,* along with Brecht the greatest influence on thinking about the avant-garde after 1968.

Although founded in 1960 by Philippe Sollers, it was only towards the end of that decade, when it was championing particular forms of the avant-garde, that *Tel Quel* came to exert its influence on film theory. Its characteristic mix of Marxism, semiotics and psychoanalysis was the inspiration for many of the theoretical endeavours of the 1970s. Politically, at this time, it was moving towards a Maoism that emphasised cultural revolution and, concomitantly, the creation of a new subjectivity. Given their adherence to the Lacanian conception of the subject as constructed within language, it was a short step for the *Tel Quel* writers, most notably Julia Kristeva, to conclude that this changed subjectivity could best be achieved by changing language. Text and subject, Kristeva said, are inextricably bonded, and in certain instances, 'the text is a practice that could be compared to political revolution: the one brings about in the subject what the other introduces into society'.[16] The only genuine social change would depend on the coincidence of a revolution in the relations of power and a revolution in language, because, as Sollers bluntly aphorised the imbrication of language with social control, 'grammar is already a question of the police'.[17]

In coming to such conclusions Kristeva developed a theory of language and subjectivity that diverged in certain important respects from that of Lacan. While her conception of the symbolic as 'the functioning of language and everything which, in translinguistic practices, is assimilable to the language system proper' was close to Lacan's, she departed from Lacan in conceptualising the way in which the subject's identity was challenged by the unconscious.[18] Counterposed to the symbolic was not the imaginary and the real, but what Kristeva called the semiotic, which here meant something very different from its conventional usage. The semiotic for Kristeva refers both to the child's organisation of bodily drives prior to the accession to the symbolic and to the way these return to language in the forms of rhythms, intonations and other paralinguistic features. The regulation and articulation of these drives in the infant takes place not in accordance with the symbolic, but through the mother's body. Preceding identity and unity, a place of heterogeneity and maternally related pulsions, the semiotic must inevitably give way to the symbolic in a process of transition that Kristeva designated the thetic phase, when the child enunciates 'I'. In the thetic moment there is both a separation from and identification with what is other, a process that corresponds in this respect to the mirror phase and to castration, where in each case there is an assumption of an identity that is other, whether the image of the unified being or an idealised parental figure. But equally the being of the subject is irreducible to its representations. Every enunciation recapitulates the thetic moment, and since there is always an excess of being over identity the semiotic always returns to contest the apparent unity of the subject within ideology. There is, therefore, 'a contradiction between symbolic and semiotic inherent in any speaking being from the moment it speaks to another by means of signs'.[19]

Although the semiotic, as the repressed, returns, it does so differently according to the linguistic practice through which it is articulated. The dominant linguistic forms sanctioned by capitalism systematically efface the working of bodily drives, but there are others, 'aligned with political experiences and social movements that contest existing relations of production', that allow the revolutionary potential of the semiotic to be realised.[20] Foremost among these is the avant-garde poetic language of the nineteenth and twentieth centuries, which puts into play a very different relation between the symbolic system and the semiotic. Through it the subject is set in process, new modes of subjectivity are made available, and the existing symbolic structures of family and state are called into question. The work of Mallarmé, Joyce and Artaud 'contests the identity of the sign, associating itself with music and working in a rhythmic and acoustic register directly based on the drives.'[21] Not only are ideological systems thereby assailed but the very structures of power and domination are threatened.

Tel Quel's influence on 1970s film theory, though not always made explicit, was nonetheless far-reaching, and was most evident in the emphasis laid on the revolutionary role of avant-garde art. In this sense, at least, *Tel Quel* could be aligned with Brecht, since both maintained that the moment of the text's reception was of central importance for aesthetics, and that its formal structure was a major determination in that moment. However, it was a considerable step from agreeing in principle that avant-garde cinema was the way forward, to bringing together theory and practice by mapping and exploring the diversity of the existing avant-gardes. Here the key figure was Peter Wollen, whose 1975 polemical article 'The two avant-gardes' was the first large-scale reconnaissance of the field and initiated the task of rethinking the relationship of cinematic modernism and politics.

As is indicated by the title of the piece, Wollen's central proposition was that there were two distinct avant-gardes that differed sharply in 'aesthetic assumptions, institutional frameworks, type of financial support, type of critical backing, historical and cultural origin'.[22]

One tradition centred on the North American co-op movement and was represented by what P. Adams Sitney called 'structural film'. Based in New York, the capital of the American art world, it was closely associated with the visual arts, especially the modernist movement, with its roots in the likes of Léger, Picabia, Eggeling, Richter, Man Ray and Moholy-Nagy, who had in various ways tried to extend the scope of their art beyond the two-dimensional framed colour-field of traditional painting. Cubism, Wollen proposed, was the first break with a traditional concern with signifieds and reference in favour of a concern with the relation between signifier and signified within the painterly sign; but this in turn gave rise to a more radical abandonment of signifieds altogether. Various options were thereby opened up. One was abstraction, with its various attendant transcendental meanings; another was an art concentrating on the pure presence and objecthood of things, freed from any requirement to represent. But what soon emerged as the dominant strand was that theorised by Clement Greenberg as art's self-interrogation of its own practices and materials, as calling attention to itself. This feature of self-reflexivity was particularly pronounced in the movements such as minimalism and conceptualism most associated with Greenberg's reading of modernism. The cinematic avant-garde linked with modernism in the visual arts developed along similar lines. There was originally a cinema of abstraction, where narrative and verbal language were absent; but this came increasingly to be replaced by a cinema self-reflexively concerned with its own filmic materiality, foregrounding only those codes specific to cinema (like camera movement, depth of field, focus, projection, framing) and excluding the rest (like music, verbal language, gesture, facial expression, narrative). What such a cinema at its limit does is to forbid 'any semantic dimension other that reference back to the material of the signifier itself, which becomes it own unique field of signification'.[23]

The other tradition identified by Wollen was predominantly European and was centred, if anywhere, on Paris; it included Godard, Straub/Huillet, Jancsó and Oshima. By contrast with the co-op avant-garde, which it saw as complicit with bourgeois art, it was avowedly political. It, too, was indebted to modernism, though a modernism concerned primarily with literature, drama and film rather than painting, with such figures as Brecht and Eisenstein among the main influences. As a consequence, narrative and verbal language continued to play an essential part, and there was nothing like the shift completely away from signifieds towards an investigation of signifiers. The literary avant-garde had been less concerned with interrogating its own materiality than with developing new techniques adequate to the expanded subject matter of modernity. In Brecht – for Wollen as for others a key figure – there was no question of abandoning the realm of reference beyond the play, nor of equating anti-illusionism with the suppression of all meaning. Similarly with the Soviet filmmakers, the task was to construct a new set of signifieds through a radical transformation of the means of expression, not to free signifiers from signifieds altogether. 'This', comments Wollen, 'was not so far wrong'.[24]

Various objections to Wollen's argument can be and were raised. One problem was his distinct separation of signifiers and signifieds, and the suggestion that they could be worked on in isolation, something that runs counter to the requirement of post-Saussurean linguistics that they cannot exist independently of each other. There was also the problem that so decisive a categorisation as Wollen proposed, with all the heterogeneity of modernism neatly dichotomised into two opposing trends, was liable to fall foul of recalcitrant empirical reality. Given the diversity and contradictoriness of modernism, this was indeed the case for at least two of the figures Wollen referred to. Peter Gidal, for example, whose explicit and recurrent concentration on the processes of film itself placed him squarely within the co-op tradition, was nonetheless avowedly political, as his interventionist writings firmly establish. Again Godard, whom Wollen put into the European avant-garde, displays a concern for the processes of generating meaning that is in some ways closer to the abstractionism of the North Americans, and it would perhaps be better to say that his work is in a category of its own.

Wollen himself acknowledged the force of the various objections raised when he later characterised his article as 'naive or at least ill-starred'.[25] By way of amendment, he proposed a rather different reading of the avant-garde in the visual arts, distinguishing what he now termed 'modernism' from 'the avant-garde'. Modernism is 'concerned with reflexiveness (film as film, film about film) and semiotic reduction (foregrounding one category or signifier, or, more radically, of the material substrate; movement towards suppression or suspension of the signified)'.[26] The avant-garde 'is not purist [and] rejects ontological presuppositions or investigations and is concerned with semiotic expansion (mixed media, montage of different codes, signs and semiotic registers, heterogeneity of signifiers and signifieds)'; it seeks to develop 'new types of relations between signifier and signified through the montage of heterogeneous elements'.[27] This new dichotomy clearly cuts differently across the diversity of practices within the visual arts and film, with only a residual alignment between the first avant-garde and modernisn, and the second avant-garde and the avant-garde as newly defined. Moreover the basis for the taxonomy has shifted from fairly general historical and geographical determinations to ones contained largely within the art practices themselves.

One of the impulses behind the original article was, Wollen explained, to bring together the modernism of New York with the theory of post-1968 Paris, both in respect of filmmaking – something he tried to do in his work with Laura Mulvey, most notably in *The Riddles of the Sphinx* – and of film theory, which he wanted to make less Paris-centred and more cosmopolitan. In practice, however, it was the second avant-garde that received the greater emphasis, one that was reiterated in the later articles, where it was noted as having 'much greater potential'.[28] Such a judgement was consistent with Wollen's high estimation of the work of Godard, whose film *Vent d'Est* had been the starting point for an article on the filmic avant-garde (i.e. the second avant-garde), termed in this instance 'counter-cinema'.[29]

Defining counter-cinema in terms of its opposition to mainstream cinema, Wollen identified some seven binaries articulating their difference. These are as follows.

Narrative transitivity versus narrative intransivity: in mainstream cinema, narrative follows a clear developmental pattern, with the disturbed initial equilibrium being finally succeeded by a new equilibrium, a progression to which each move in the narrative, including characters' psychological motivations and physical actions, causally contributes; in Godard, by contrast, in order to break the emotional hold of the narrative, the flow is disrupted by interruptions, digressions and the absence of immediately apparent connections.

Identification versus estrangement: among the devices used by Godard to thwart the process of identification at work in mainstream cinema are absence of match between voice and image, introducing actors as themselves and as characters, and having the actors directly address the audience, so raising the question 'What is this film for?' instead of the conventional 'Why did that happen?' or 'What is going to happen next?'

Transparency versus foregrounding: whereas mainstream cinema effaces its own work, Godard draws attention to the process of meaning-construction, for example, by scratching the celluloid to show that film is production not reflection or by providing a commentary on the adequacy of the images shown.

Simple versus multiple diegesis: the world of the Hollywood narrative displays a consistent order of time and space that can easily accommodate devices like flashbacks and films within the film;

Godard, by contrast breaks with a single integrated diegesis, as for example in *Weekend,* in which characters from different historical periods and different fictions are interpolated into the main narrative, so that the text become a composite, even contradictory, plurality.

Closure versus aperture: instead of the self-contained, closed text organised under the sign of the filmmaker's unifying vision that characterises the mainstream, counter-cinema opens out onto an intertextual field where different discourses and voices encounter each other and conflict, with the result that it can no longer be read as expressive of the author's intention.

Pleasure versus unpleasure: while Hollywood doles out entertainment for an addicted consumer society, counter-cinema produces 'a collective working relationship between filmmaker and audience, in which the spectator can collaborate in the production/consumption of meaning'.[30] In discussing this opposition Wollen was more critical of counter-cinema's practices than anywhere else, arguing that it tends to devalue pleasure and fantasy, both of which, as Brecht knew, have an important role in revolutionary art. 'Unless a revolution is desired (which means nothing less than coinciding with and embodying collective fantasies) it will never take place'.[31]

Lastly, fiction versus reality: unlike traditional cinema, which is fiction above all else, counter-cinema tends to distrust it as mystification and ideology, seeing representation as illusion and acting as lying, and seeks to put truth in its place (although some forms of counter-cinema, in recognising that there is no outside to ideology, counterpose their own ideology and fantasy against the dominant ones).

As well as Godard, the work of Straub/Huillet and Oshima was held up (and not only by Wollen) as exemplary for a truly radical cinema. These four were in effect, despite all the talk of breaking with the pantheons of auteurism, constituted as the new canon. The tendency was for them to be read in terms of the positions and aesthetics of Brecht and *Tel Quel,* which in the case of Godard and Straub/Huillet was relatively straightforward given their explicit Brechtian debt. Thus in addressing the problem identified by Godard – 'not to make political films but to make films politically' – both filmmakers frequently cited Brecht's ideas and example in their work, and more importantly mobilised classic Brechtian devices like distanciation, literarisation, and the separation of elements.[32]

The most obvious effect of these devices is a denaturalisation of cinema, a project to which both Godard and Straub/Huillet had stated their commitment. Godard writes, 'Unfortunately cinema is a language but I try to destroy that language, to make films that do not take any account of that language.'[33] Similarly Straub claims, 'At every moment a film must destroy what it was saying the moment before; we are stifling in stereotypes and it is important to help people destroy them.'[34] Such denaturalisation typically involved foregrounding what the mainstream effaced, the process of meaning-production itself, so rendering visible what was commonly invisible. In this way they showed that the language of dominant cinema was not the only language available. By problematising cinematic discourse they challenged the assumption peddled by the mainstream that reality itself spoke in its images – witness the statement in *Vent d'Est*, 'This is not a just image, just an image.'[35] And by putting in question the ideology of the visible and refusing the supposed transparency of the image, they in effect built on Brecht's point about the photographic image, which appears to yield knowledge but actually does no such thing. As Godard phrased it, 'The photograph is not the reflection of reality but the reality of the reflection.'[36] His and Straub's films do not provide images of reality, then, but rather draw images from reality that allow an analytic distance on the part of the spectator, a distance at which the objective and contradictory script of social reality may be read. Vision and knowledge, as the theorists never tired of repeating, were two very different things.

But the process of questioning the transparency of cinematic discourse involved more than simply revealing the conventions of dominant cinema. The larger strategy of which this was a part was that of instantiating a new mode of subjectivity, of transforming – in Barthes's much quoted phrase – the spectator from a consumer of the text into a producer of the text, and so putting into question the very institution of cinema. It was this concern to change the spectator, rather than some supposed fidelity to Brechtian techniques, that, in the view of the principal proponents of the avant-garde such as Heath, MacCabe, Wollen and Martin Walsh, marked out the work of Godard and Straub/Huillet as Brechtian. Although these filmmakers experimented with cinematic form, their project was far removed from the formalism of Wollen's first avant-garde. In foregrounding and interrogating the materiality of film they were interested not in its essence but in the implication of the subject in the material processes of the text. In other words, their questions were not questions of aesthetics but of politics – 'questions which render action possible'.[37]

How this spectatorial dispensation was interpreted varied according to the theoretical standpoint: as Althusserians, the theorists understood it as a putting-into-process of a spectator fixed in position by dominant cinema; as Lacanians, it was a matter of displacing the subject. In discussing it, MacCabe and Heath each drew on their earlier work on narrative space and the classic realist text, contrasting the practices of Godard and Straub/Huillet with those of the mainstream.

It will be recalled that in the classic realist text typical of mainstream cinema the image track functions as a metalanguage, providing the spectator with the truth. In Godard, by contrast, no such metalanguage is offered. Instead there is a separation of the constitutive elements of the film, so that image, sound, music and writing are not hierarchised but constantly jostling with each other in relations of shifting discrepancy. The image itself, the source of imaginary plenitude for Hollywood, is here disrupted by montage within and between frames, and by various forms of literarisation where the 'action' is interrupted by captions, slogans, book covers and puns, all of them juxtaposing the image with language and so punctuating representation with discourse. The resulting relation between film and spectator in Godard is therefore quite different from the self-contained unity and secure positionality established by the classic realist text. Confronted by the contradictions of the Godardian text the spectator is constantly required to work on its meanings, required to produce meaning. Its 'fissures and differences', MacCabe wrote, '. . . demand an activity of articulation from the subject – which articulation in its constant changes and contradictions makes known – shows – the contradictions of the reader's position within and without the cinema'.[38]

As with Godard, so too with Straub/Huillet. In his analysis of *History Lessons,* Martin Walsh proposed that it was another example of a film in which no one discourse predominated, so that the spectator was not fixed in position, but was 'given room to construct his own reading, to work at a plurality of possible meanings'.[39] Because of the absence of illusionism and the pre-packaged message, through this work of meaning-production, the spectator comes to realise that his reading is itself a form of writing, by contrast with the reading of that which presents itself as already written – the classic realist text.

In a rather more Lacanian vein, Heath similarly contrasted the organisation of space in Godard (at least during his 'Dziga Vertov' period) and Straub/Huillet with that of mainstream narrative. In neither case does the films' heterogeneity allow the conversion of 'the seen' to 'a scene'. For instance, the separation and discrepancy in Godard between sound and image, and in Straub/Huillet the refusal to assign the voice either a dominant or a subordinate role and the use of direct sound rendering off-screen space present, all constitute space 'not as coherence but as contradiction'.[40] As with sound, so too their use of the image track subverts the conventions of narrativisation and identification: Godard uses multiple images, divided images, images with the disturbing 'noise' of the television screen, images written on; Straub uses black leader to interrupt the image flow, images extended to excessive duration, images overburdened by movement within the frame. The effect of all these strategies is to make the illusion of direct vision impossible, and so to change the relation of the subject to representations.

In order to flesh out the preceding generalities with some specifics, and in order to give an instance of what was held in many quarters to be exemplary avant-garde practice, we shall follow through Martin Walsh's reading of Straub/Huillet's *Introduction to Arnold Schoenberg's Accompaniment for a Cinematographic Score*.

The film was made as an intervention in a specific institutional conjuncture, namely, for a late-night, twice-monthly television programme about experimental film and music on the Federal Republic of Germany's third channel. Its address was therefore to an audience primarily concerned with aesthetics, people (Straub said) for whom politics didn't exist. They would probably have expected from such a film, Walsh suggested, an account either of Schoenberg the man (his anguish at his wife's infidelity expressed through atonal music, etc.) or of Schoenberg the revolutionary artist (the technical and formal problems attendant on serialism). In either case, the expectation would have been that the music would be presented as high art beyond politics and history; indeed, as a sanctuary from the stress of political conflict. Its role would not be seen as one of challenging the status quo. Such a conception of the relationship of art and politics was exactly what Straub/Huillet were to dispute.

During much of the film a voice is heard reading from two letters Schoenberg wrote to Kandinsky in response to his invitation to come to Weimar and help found the Bauhaus. In these letters Schoenberg stressed his Jewishness, refusing to be set apart by virtue of his artistic genius from the social and historical situation.

I am not a German, not a European, indeed perhaps scarcely a human being (at least the Europeans prefer the worst of their race to me) but that I am a Jew.

When I walk in the street and all men look to see if I am a Jew or a Christian, I cannot tell everyone that I am the one whom Kandinsky and some others make an exception of, while doubtless Hitler is not of this opinion.[41]

Such sentiments, like the musical 'accompaniment' headed 'Threatening Danger, Fear, Catastrophe', that begins during the reading, are, Walsh pointed out, open to a 'universalist, expressionist' interpretation, but Straub/Huillet circumvent this by contextualising the letters historically.[42] In succession, there is newsreel footage of American bombs being manufactured, loaded and dropped over Vietnam; a photograph of the communards massacred by Thiers; a newspaper report about the acquittal of concentration camp architects; quotations from Brecht's address to the 1935 Paris Congress of Intellectuals Against Fascism stating that fascism could be confronted only if its link with capitalism was acknowledged. The context, Walsh argued, makes explicit the traces of political oppression inscribed in the music, it forcibly expresses Benjamin's assertion that 'there is no document of civilisation which is not at the same time a document of barbarism'.[43]

The film, furthermore, is exemplary in the way it develops a genuinely Brechtian practice, not as a mere contextualising element, but in its novel articulation and reformulation of Brechtian notions. Eschewing the traditional documentary approach, which in providing pre-established knowledge of Schoenberg would simply fix the spectator in a position of passive consumption, the film offers a series of different discourses, none of which is given as the unifying and authoritative metalanguage. The role of the narrator is dispersed among various voices – Straub himself, the man reading Schoenberg's letters, Huillet quoting Brecht, etc. Even more striking is the Brechtian separation of elements, with the image track and soundtrack (and in particular the music) non-hierarchised. Literarisation occurs through the persistent use of quotation, both written and spoken, thus conforming to Brecht's call to acknowledge that acting is indeed quotation and not origination. Black leader is used to make the montage construction and discontinuous structure of the film explicit. The camera is set diagonally in relation to the performers, so preventing any sense of inclusion in the action or identification with the actors. All these elements function to distanciate, to make the spectator reflect and analyse, to give room for the active construction of meanings.

But over and beyond distanciation there are less easily analysable textual processes at work, which are best approached from a *Tel Quel* perspective. Various elements challenge what Walsh terms 'the solidification of signifier and signified into an identity', and hence act to transform the spectator's subjectivity.[44] One of these is the flat delivery of the quotations, which reasserts the musical and rhythmical cadences of spoken language. Most importantly there is the music itself, unsubordinated to the narrative, unsynchronised with the spoken, which thereby enjoys an aesthetic independence, a 'transcendent existence outside the realm of persecution'.[45] Here Walsh drew on Adorno to suggest that whatever Schoenberg may have said about the absence of political intent in his work it was in reality revolutionary. Adorno considered that 'against his will that which crystallised in his work embodied immanent musical opposition to [his] socially naive conceptions'.[46] By renewing musical form, Adorno believed, Schoenberg's work offered a challenge to a solidified culture industry. This idea was developed by Walsh, who compared Schoenberg's output with what Barthes had demanded of art: that it should 'unexpress the expressible', where 'the expressible' stands for the whole realm of socially sanctioned and regularised meaning.[47] It is the combination of Schoenberg's music, with its capacity for estrangement (*Verfremdung*), and the other textual elements used with the film that gives the *Introduction* its peculiar force – a text, Walsh concluded, not so much of pleasure (*plaisir* in Barthes's distinction) as of bliss (*jouissance*). Though it leaves culture and language 'in pieces', the loss of security 'is not experienced by us as loss, but as the reopening of barred paths, as the reformulation of aesthetic activity'.[48]

Matters were not so straightforward in the case of Oshima. Martin Walsh, for one, was of the opinion that Oshima's work could not be situated within a Brechtian aesthetic, being insufficiently distancing to break with conventional modes of spectating. Heath and MacCabe, on the other hand, disagreed, while conceding that in certain respects, notably his provision of figures for identification, Oshima was closer to mainstream cinema. However, the fundamentals of his practice were as radical as anything in Godard and Straub/Huillet and not dissimilar. There was, for example, a comparable denaturalisation of cinematic discourse, as in the 'hybrid text' *Dear Summer Sister,* where the 'multiple heterogeneity' functioned to call into question the established language of conventional cinema.[49] Moreover, despite the absence of the more obvious Brechtian devices his work was close to Brecht in spirit. For Heath, it amounted to a cinematic exploration of 'the political relations of the subject and the subjective relations of the political in a double and simultaneous movement'.[50] MacCabe understood it as being organised around a strategy of interruption, where, variously, narrative homogeneity is disturbed by the introduction of heterogeneous elements, identifications are established only to be broken, and the conventions of realism are transgressed – as in *Death by Hanging,* with its documentary-style beginning, followed by realist fiction and finally fantasy.

In this film the character R's body refuses execution. Having been hanged he fails to die, and instead develops a form of amnesia, which causes considerable trouble for his executioners since they cannot proceed further until he is conscious of his identity and his guilt. They therefore have to embark on an 'education programme'. The action of the film thus turns on a 'disturbance of the habitual (of the "realistic") on which Brecht insists in his accounts is a theatre of distanciation'.[51] In their somewhat different formulations both Heath and MacCabe emphasise this distancing aspect of the film. Heath's conception is of a relay of contradiction from social processes to the image to the spectator. For MacCabe the distanciation occurs through a disruption of identification with the character on the screen, resulting in an awareness both of the constitution of that character as an identity and our own as spectators. Essential to this conception of MacCabe's is the absence of a metalanguage in *Death by Hanging;* hence, of any secure knowledge by which to judge the epistemological status of events in the film as fact, fiction or fantasy. Just as the film puts the identity if R into question, so it does with the spectator, alerted 'to his or her own constitutive contradictions'.[52] Like R in the narrative, the spectator is enabled to leave fantasy behind and begin an 'engagement with the real'.[53] As R 'learns to take up his position sexually and socially so that he can understand why he, a Korean sub-proletarian, raped and murdered a Japanese girl, so we too are learning what it is to sit in the cinema'.[54]

These large, though perfectly respectable, Brechtian claims for

Oshima were, however, at odds with the Lacanian formulations that MacCabe was equally committed to. Indeed the tension between the two, Brecht and Lacan, is latent within much of the writing about the avant-garde at this period. Specifically, as Heath carefully pointed out, the real that Brecht urges artists to concern themselves with is not the same as the real of Lacan, which is neither given in any text nor in the relation of the spectator to particular textual forms. Lacan's real is present wherever there is subjectivity, already there as a constitutive lack beyond symbolisation and experienced only as resistance. It must therefore be distinguished within the imaginary and the symbolic 'to contain the real lack, the lack of the real'.[55] The real exists, then, in every exchange between spectator and text as an unsymbolisable absence around which the dialectical production of the subject and meaning occurs. Thus, apropos of the pattern of multiple identifications spectators commonly engage in (with characters, with the camera, with the act of looking), 'the real can be nowhere in the pattern but its outside, is only to be grasped as what breaks the series of looks, as what falls from film and screen'.[56]

Heath's own reading of *Death by Hanging* is consequently more circumspect and less confidently utopian than MacCabe's, while remaining broadly along the same lines. The spectator of the film is, for Heath, not so much confronted with the truth of his or her own contradictory historicity as discomforted, deprived of the fiction of unity, dispersed into otherness and difference. Through the various strategies of the constant displacement of images, the multiple levels of discourse and the fragmentation of address, the film, although still a narrative, 'resolves nothing, it dissolves'.[57] Instead of being held in place, occupied, as in narrative realism, with the film turning on the fiction of the unified subject and its own fictive unity, the spectator of *Death by Hanging* finds that this double economy is unavailable.

Similarly with Oshima's most celebrated film, *Empire of the Senses*, in which the heroine strangles and subsequently castrates the hero, Heath discovered a similar engagement with politics in the problematisation of the apparatus of representation and ideological formation. The film does this by first articulating, then exposing, the organisation of looks and the terms of cinematic vision as precisely a construction, and not natural reproduction or simple reflection. By fracturing the look through a series of formal refusals or omissions – like violating the 180° rule and the shot/reverse shot system – there arises a 'disphasure of look and sight' that ensures that the apparatus is no longer able to guarantee the spectator's unity of vision.[58] The film confronts the spectator with a series of questions concerning his or her role in seeing it: Where are you in this film? What is this film for you to be there? What is it to be the viewer of a film? To have its view?

Across all the writing on the avant-garde there was a tendency to oscillate between two positions. At one pole was the Althusserian and Brechtian position, characterised by a confidence that theoretical issues relating beyond art to the social formation were in principle settled, with the outstanding question therefore being how art can best serve the cause of revolutionary change. At the other, there was the Lacanian and post-structuralist position, in which the question of progressive art was settled – it should displace subjectivity – but in which there was far less confidence in relation to the social formation, both in terms of what it was and of the desirability of revolution. In the course of a decade the question inspired by the Brecht/Althusser position came to be answered at the same time as the confidence about society and social change originating it evaporated. For Heath, MacCabe and others initially committed to an Althusserian position, the films of Godard, Straub/Huillet and Oshima were valued for their Brechtian potential for knowledge; only later, as they shifted towards post-structuralism, was this view tempered by the idea that the merit of these films lay primarily in their capacity to put the subject in process. To the critics of post-structuralism the displacement of subjectivity was but a leap in the dark: once the nature of society is again open (with the breakdown of Althusserianism), the fact of displacement cannot automatically be taken as beneficial. Questions as to where the subject was being displaced, and to what end, were therefore decisively back on the agenda.

In recent years the *Tel Quel/Screen* orthodoxy on the avant-garde has been strongly challenged. The fundamental objections have been that this orthodoxy, like the Frankfurt School it in many respects resembles, has tended to be elitist, politically pessimistic, and isolated from any mass political movement. In particular it has been criticised on two related counts, the first of which concerns its condemnation of mass culture as the manipulation of a passive audience. Terry Lovell, speaking for a non-Althusserian conception of ideology, has argued against the functionalist version of culture offered by Althusser, by

which popular cultural forms simply fulfill the ideological requirements of capitalism, in favour of the view that oppositional ideology
can by expressed in popular culture. Progressive art can assume a
popular form and only in so doing can it become politically effective,
since otherwise it remains the preserve of cognoscenti isolated from
oppressed groups in society. 'It is impossible', Lovell wrote, 'to produce a truly revolutionary text in a discourse in which only the dominant have any facility'.[59] In support of her position she cited Brecht's
commitment to accessibility and popularity, something which, she
claimed, *Tel Quel* and *Screen*'s appropriation of him had largely
ignored.

Another defender of popular culture has been Fredric Jameson,
whose stress has been on its utopian dimension. Along with what
he called the negative hermeneutic, that broadly functionalist critique
of culture as legitimating and reproducing an oppressive power structure, there has to be a positive hermeneutic that would recognise
that 'the effectively ideological is also, at the same time, necessarily
utopian'.[60] Elsewhere, Jameson writes:

The works of mass culture, even if their function lies in the legitimation of
the existing order – or some worse one – cannot do their job without deflect-
ing in the latter's service the deepest and most fundamental hopes and fantasies of the collectivity, to which they can therefore, no matter in how distorted a fashion, be found to have given voice.[61]

The second closely related criticism was that the orthodoxy failed
to take sufficient account of the moment of reception of the text.
The problem here had been that of an undue emphasis, stemming
from Althusser, on the subject as constituted, with insufficient weight
being given to the subject as constituting. Lovell pointed out that
little sense could be made of the class struggle unless the subject was
both, and Jameson considered that the concept of the subject as a
simple bearer of a position (*träger*) was 'negative'. The point was
that subjects, by virtue of being agents as well as effects, could resist
the positioning imposed by the text, could read texts critically. What
the *Tel Quel/Screen* position omitted was historical determination of
subjects; it allowed determination only by the text, whose effects
were always the same, irrespective of the conjuncture of reception.
These arguments were expressed most forcefully within film journals
by Tim Clark and Paul Willemen.

Although concerned with the medium of painting, Clark's work in *Screen* related directly to film theory in being a contribution to the debate between Willemen and the formalists (discussed above in chapter 2). Like Willemen, Clark did not accept that the spectator was positioned by the text alone and argued that once it was allowed that the text could be read unpredicatably there were important consequences for the conceptualisation of avant-garde practice. According to the formalists the avant-garde text was one that put established systems of signification into crisis and thereby displaced the spectator from any position of centrality. Clark, however, doubted the effectivity of such a 'disidentificatory' strategy and proceeded to substantiate his claim with a study of Manet's *Olympia*. While this painting of a naked prostitute undeniably subverted existing codes of representation and was therefore disidentificatory, Clark argued that this diminished rather than enhanced its political effectivity, because it left spectators at a loss to know how to read it. For the critics of 1865, *Olympia* in some measure failed to signify: it could not be pulled into the available discourses concerning women and aesthetics (although now it is clear how the painting contested those discourses). It neither offered the male spectator the distance deriving from the classical representation of the nude, by which the woman seems to become available to him, nor did it provide a realism with which to critique such representation, and thereby deny access to the woman. The result was a stalemate, 'a kind of baulked invitation', making the painting unintelligible and confusing.[62] All this led Clark to conclude that modernist practice as such was no guarantee of political effectivity: the work must relate to history and to class and be seen to do so. If, for example, Manet had depicted Olympia so as to bring out the terms of her subjection through gender and class, the painting would have been readable within the available discourse relating to prostitution. His failure to achieve this left *Olympia* caught up in 'the dance of ideology', uninterpretable.[63] In order to escape this dance of ideology, avant-garde practice must always root itself in the actually existing signs and meanings through which the dominated struggle to express their domination.

Clark's contentions did not pass unchallenged. Peter Wollen, in taking up the defence of the avant-garde, saw Clark's position as essentially an assault on modernism, whose outcome could only be a progressive realism of a Lukácsian stamp. Where Clark was mistaken, Wollen argued, was in supposing that contradictions within the art work made it merely an act of provocation rather than one of resistance. The essential point was that such contradictions were not confined to the system of representation, but were the derivatives of contradictions in social reality, and were therefore crucial to the work's political effectivity. The progressive realism proposed by Clark was, on the contrary, utopian, in that the alternative ideology it required was yet to be produced by class struggle. Indeed, without the disidentificatory practices of the avant-garde there would be nothing but the dance of ideology. Challenging the structures of ideology was, as Brecht had perceived and his artistic practice exemplified, 'a common task, to be finished together by artist and spectator'.[64]

In reply Clark maintained that Wollen had misrepresented him: he was not against modernism *in toto,* he was not in favour of closed or simplistic art, and he was in no way advocating a return to Lukács. What he was against were theorists and practitioners who failed to ask questions as to who the art work was for, what its mode of address was, and whether its address confirmed or challenged certain kinds of misunderstanding.

A more extensive re-evaluation of the avant-garde was offered by Paul Willemen, drawing on the work of Peter Burger and Andreas Huyssen.

Taking as his starting point the proposition that art can only be comprehended in relation to society, as an institution, Burger distinguished between modernism and the avant-garde, terms that are often conflated. Modernism, said Burger, was essentially a continuation of romanticism and aestheticism, maintaining the autonomy of art from society; whereas the avant-garde, in its manifestations as dada, surrealism and the post-revolutionary Russian avant-garde, sought to reintegrate artistic and social practices. However, with the failure of the avant-garde to achieve its avowed aims, there was a tendency for its techniques and procedures to be recuperated by a sterile aestheticism, self-reflexivity for its own sake. Burger's ideas were taken up and further developed by Huyssen, who saw the role of the avant-garde in the first three decades of this century as that of undermining the legitimising discourse of high art in European society.[65]

Paul Willemen concurred with Burger's distinction between modernism and the avant-garde, and with his assessment of their respective roles. Modernism in effect functioned to contain and limit the challenges posed by the avant-garde by adopting its techniques to concentrate on exploring the specificity of the medium, so turning the process of renewal into a preservation of the past. This is precisely what had happened to Brecht: the 'mechanical deployment of techniques of "distanciation"'.[66] In applying these ideas to the history of and possibilities for experimental film, Willemen argued for the replacement of Wollen's two avant-gardes with an opposition between modernism and the avant-garde (which, incidentally, despite the same terminology, was quite different from Wollen's own revision of his earlier conception, that being based solely on textual features). Such a perspective showed up the shortcomings of much supposedly avant-garde cinema in the post-1968 period. The assumption had been that there were only two options open to filmmakers: a realism whose transparency produced a passive audience or an avant-garde whose foregrounding of the specificity of cinematic signification produced an active audience. In fact many examples of the latter had been modernist rather than genuinely avant-garde. The distinction between the two could in no way be made on textual features alone, but must be made by reference to the historical conjuncture within which the work was sited. But the conjuncture was what film theory had tended to ignore, both in its structuralist phase, when aesthetic practice was defined in terms of strategies of signification, and in its Lacanian phase, when a concern with history was certainly part of the rhetoric of subject and meaning coming into being together, but remained, according to Willemen, largely gestural. Thus in both phases the dichotomy of realism versus avant-garde remained in place, and because of the absence of historical determination, the avant-garde so conceived tended towards modernist textual disruption alone. The questions 'Displacing fixity for what purpose?' and 'Shifting subject positions in which direction?' were therefore not posed. Any genuine avant-garde practice would be centred on these questions; it would be addressed to a particular audience and its concerns; it would seek to connect with the experience of particular classes and to place that experience within new explanatory models. As with Brecht, it would above all be concerned with the historical and political situation of its audience and have as its primary objective the explication of that situation. The textual production of subjectivity would be but 'one process within and overdetermined by the forces that shape social existence'.[67] These ends would be achieved not through the rejection of narrative, as much of the supposed avant-garde had demanded, but through its readoption, albeit in a very different form from that associated with classic realism, 'a narrative that neither instructs nor absorbs, but one which leaves a space between production and consumption'.[68] The spectator would engage in what Brecht had called 'complex seeing', a simultaneous awareness of dramatic action and commentary on it by means of written titles. Such films as *Maeve* and *So That You Can Live* achieved something comparable through their splitting of narrative and setting (which is conventionally assimilated to the plot and character), so that the setting can become another text, with its own dynamic and meanings. Hence history can be read through landscape itself, 'allowing narrative events to reverberate and to interact with or against an accompanying reading of history'.[69] In this way certain hierarchical power relations between discourses are problematised, prior to their transformation.

The various themes associated with the rethinking of the avant-garde – the upward estimation of popular culture, the questioning of the avant-garde's claim to be the sole form of oppositional practice, the emphasis on the moment of reception and the active role of audiences – recurred within the debate around postmodernism.

The term 'postmodernism' has existed for the last fifty years; and even within the last twenty or so it has been used to designate a variety of phenomena. It is therefore a remarkably slippery concept. However, three recent uses of the term can be relatively easily distinguished. The first of these uses refers to a movement in architecture and may be dealt with very briefly. Postmodernism in this context describes an architectural aesthetic that has renounced modernism, with its universalism and belief in progress, finding in it only elitism and dehumanising utopian pretention. In its place it offers a populist rhetoric allied to a conscious blurring of codes between past and present, high and popular culture, the functional and the decorative.

More generally, the term has been used to refer to various forms of experimentation during the last two decades in literature, music, dance and the visual arts. Its meaning here is particularly unstable, since there is consensus neither on what constitutes the postmodern canon, nor whether postmodernism is the heir to or the adversary of modernism, nor whether it is a term of praise of abuse. Even a commentator as astute as Andreas Huyssen has said of postmodernism both that it marks the end of the avant-garde as a genuinely adversary culture and that it has a critical potential.[70] The confusion has been compounded by the fact that discussion of postmodernism has often proceeded on the basis of highly selective histories of modernism, that have tended to omit work that did not conform to the developing thesis, and to read modernist works out of context, disregarding both the intentions of the artists producing them and their actual historical reception. Notably absent has been any concern to place work historically (as Clark did with Manet). For these reasons, then, this application of the term 'postmodernism' has been extremely muddled; but equally this is the most important use of it, since it represents an attempt to map the extraordinary diversity of contemporary artistic practice in relation to modernism, given the prevailing sense that existing explanatory frameworks are inadequate for the task.

A third sense of postmodernism refers to a mode of philosophy within post-structuralism particularly associated with Jean-François Lyotard. Like Foucault, Lyotard followed Nietzsche in denying the possibility of systematising, totalising theory. No one theory can hope to encompass the irreducible particularity of the real. Further, language for Lyotard (as for Nietzsche), does not reflect a pre-given reality but presents it through incommensurable practices. In his early, more influential thinking on the relation of language and society Lyotard adopted the terminology of the later Wittgenstein, speaking of language as a multiplicity of 'games' in which individual utterances were the equivalent of 'moves'. Each language-game is involved in specific activities and embodies its own perspective, a consequence of which is that no single language-game can be totalised as a meta-language. One Foucauldian corollary of this is that language-games are involved in competition and conflict; another is that no one is completely powerless, having at least some control over the moves in whatever language the game is being played. Subsequently, Lyotard came to abandon this terminology as too anthropomorphic, implying as it did speakers existing outside of and simply using language instead of their being situated within it and positioned by it, but in revising it (the term 'phrase' replacing 'language-game') he retained the emphasis on language as constitutive and on linguistic practices as events.

All this bears on postmodernism in that the status of certain discourses within our society is changing, an effect of the continual jostling for position among them. During what Lyotard terms the modern era, science was the discourse against which most others were judged and found wanting (most typically because they employed narrative modes, which science consigned to the status of the primitive). Science legitimated itself by invoking certain metadiscourses, or 'grand narratives', one of which was that it contributed to the cause of human emancipation, the other that it was the road to a full and final knowledge of reality. In the postmodern era – this is indeed its defining characteristic – grand narratives provoke incredulity; science can neither be legitimated by them, nor can it legitimate discourses other than itself, becoming merely one language-game among others. Although Lyotard's focus in *The Postmodern Condition* was science and its changing status, his comments on the impossibility of credible metadiscourses have been perceived as having far wider application, and have become the centre of the postmodernist debate. Failing confidence in the idea of progress, abandonment of the concept of truth in favour of utility, a loss of universal horizons, suspicion of science, all make their contribution to the *Zeitgeist*. But equally, according to Lyotard, there is little mourning for the lost metadiscourses; people instead are alive to the possibilities for invention and innovation offered by their absence. Against the techno-totalitarian nightmare of Auschwitz or the Gulag, the postmodern condition can embrace inventive pluralism and proliferate resistance to existing forms of oppression.

Given the confusion around the term 'postmodernism', one response would be to dismiss it as transient and without heuristic value – and so indeed it may prove. For the moment, however, it does provide a focus for thinking about the status of the avant-garde in the late 1980s. The issue is simply this: is the existing paradigm within which the avant-garde has been conceived still valid? For all its formal radicalism the avant-garde theory and practice of the post-1968 moment was in a direct line of descent from that of an earlier generation, which was in turn the product, as Huyssen has indicated, of a quite different conjuncture, 'the age of Hitler, Stalin and the Cold War'[71] The avant-garde of the 1970s was shaped by its own historical situation, above all by the non-occurrence of revolution in advanced industrial countries. The question now posed by postmodernism is whether that historical moment has passed, and whether in consequence the relations between art, society and history have to be reconceptualised. In contending that this is indeed the case, postmodernists have argued something as follows.

The first reason for supposing that the avant-garde no longer exists in the way it did is its institutionalisation, its transformation into official art within galleries, museums and the educational apparatus. A second reason is that the current pluralism testifies less to continuing innovation than to stylistic exhaustion, with the dominant mode being one of pastiche or parody, to which the ambitions of modernism are not immune. Thirdly, and more significantly, there has been the loss of a clear distinction between the avant-garde and other artistic practices. With the increasing diversity of forms, the distinctions between dominant art and the avant-garde, between mass culture and the avant-garde, have become eroded. Avant-garde techniques such as self-reflexivity, discontinuity, and montage have been taken up by the mass culture, notably in pop videos, advertisements and television, though without intending or achieving the distanciation held by the post-1968 theorists to be their consequence. Similarly, elements of popular culture have begun to be incorporated into high art: pulp fiction into serious literature, advertising images into painting, kitsch into architecture, and so on. As a result of such a breaking down of distinctions, the avant-garde finds itself with nothing to oppose, no other against which to define itself.

Such changes are only a problem, postmodernists contend, for those adhering to the old paradigm of culture conceived in terms of commodity production, mystification, manipulation and recuperation. Developments in popular culture, particularly popular music, have, they say, confounded the Marxist notion of the culture industry as manipulating the passive masses. Peter Wollen argued that such developments (including, by extension, certain forms of film and video) made it clear that popular culture 'was no longer pyramidal in structure with everything coming downwards from the top, if ever it had been.'[72] Under such a conception the masses were already not passive consumers but active producers. Though a problem for Marxism, the emergence of these changed relations around popular culture was quite compatible with, indeed all part of, postmodernism.

More generally, writers sympathetic to postmodernism have concurred in the impossibility both of containing the heterogeneity of contemporary artistic practice within a single paradigm – hence the failure to agree on an all-embracing definition of postmodernism – and of finding any single totalising theory of society. Instead of the latter, of which Marxism is the prime example, the particularism offered by Foucault and Lyotard seems more appropriate. Instead of two cultures, based on two opposed classes, there are many, reflecting a multiplicity of groupings and allegiances, all of them involved in different modalities of power and resistance. Thus the growing sense that existing theories of culture and of society are inadequate may be traced to developments within post-structuralist philosophy, above all to the Lacanian pronouncement on the impossibility of a metalanguage. None of the contending social, cultural, artistic or theoretical factions can lay claim to the single unifying truth any longer. And in the absence of metalanguage, particularly the grand narrative of progress, the role of the avant-garde can no longer be what the term implies, the advance guard entering territory that will soon be settled by the following mass. Once faith in a brave new world is lost, the *raison d'être* of the avant-garde goes with it. One could indeed argue that the avant-garde filmmaking of the late 1960s and early 1970s – work by Straub/Huillet, Godard, Oshima – is all but played out. The prospect of overthrowing the capitalist order that underlay and informed it is notably absent from currently fashionable non-mainstream filmmaking: slick exercises in style from a bevy of French directors, deep-seated pessimism with no hope for the future from Fassbinder and Wenders, resurgent humanism (we suspect) from Oshima. Even Godard, instructively, has forsaken revolutionary macro and micro politics for postmodern pastiche and meditations on art and religion. Only within the women's movement, where there remains some justifiable expectation for the future, does experimental filmmaking look like avant-garde work heralding progress rather than one style among others.

The political counterpart to a conception of the avant-garde in art is, it is fair to say, Leninism: the supposition that there is a privileged cadre elite that leads where history dictates others will follow. Hence any defence of a traditional conception of the avant-garde entails, as MacCabe has pointed out, 'attitudes and assumptions which are unacceptable to any kind of committed democratic politics.' MacCabe continues by saying that the ideas on which such Leninist politics are founded are 'at best outmoded, depending on a reduction of all practices to the political, and at worst lethal, insisting on such reduction.'[73] Thus the political colour of postmodernism has been a democratic liberalism far removed from the Althusserian Leninism of film theory in the aftermath of 1968.

There have, however, in the midst of all this haste to avoid the taint of totalitarianism, been some voices raised in defence of the theory and practice of the avant-garde. Foremost among them have been Jurgen Habermas, the intellectual heir to the Frankfurt School, and Fredric Jameson.

Habermas has characterised those associated with post-structuralism, principally Foucault, Derrida and Lyotard, as neo-conservatives who have effectively abandoned the possibility of social critique through their retreat from any epistemological distinction between various discourses.[74] He has equally castigated postmodernists for their hostility to the project of modernity, which was inaugurated with the Enlightenment and has since then held out the prospect of human emancipation. Both groups have failed to perceive the fundamental social processes of capitalist modernisation and their correlative cultural manifestations. In the broadest terms these have amounted to a one-sided scientific and administrative rationality that has hindered the development of human emancipation. Against this the project of modernity has attempted to reverse the resulting loss of meaning and freedom, without losing the cognitive advances associated with scientific rationality. Art, then, has a central role to play in combatting encroachments from the techno-administrative sphere into what he calls 'the life world'. Art, particularly avant-garde art, can, Habermas maintains, provide a critique of these new modes of reification and keep alive the utopian elements in our cultural tradition. At the same time he is conscious of the extent to which the institutionalisation of avant-garde art has hindered its potentially liberating role of exposing the way life has become deformed by the consumerism and bureaucracy of late capitalism. Nevertheless, with certain changes in the context of reception, especially when linked to political struggles, art can still contribute to the cause of human emancipation and fulfilment. Modernism is thus an incomplete project and far from being a lost cause.

Like Habermas, Jameson has maintained the continuing viability of Marxism in the face of post-structuralism and postmodernism. It is still possible, he has said, to avoid both the reductionism condemned by post-structuralism and the sheer heterogeneity characterising postmodernism. As an interpretive master code, Marxism *can* account for the emergence of modern popular culture: by reference, firstly, to the presence, within the social formation, of contradictory modes of production, including those only as yet foreshadowed, allowing for the emergence of a popular culture in which the masses are the active producers; and secondly, to the aforementioned revised conception of ideology in which utopian, oppositional impulses are expressed. Equally, it can explain postmodern practice as the cultural manifestation of commodity production within late capitalism. The outstanding feature of this cultural moment is that art no longer enjoys the relative autonomy it once had, and therefore cannot provide its audience with the means of grasping their relation to society and history. For example, those films known by the French as *la mode rétro,* which are either situated in the past (*Chinatown, American Graffiti*) or adopt a style from the past (*Body Heat),* destroy our sense of history by reducing history to a series of aesthetic modes and styles (in the case of the former) and by effacing anything that might speak of the specifically contemporary (*Body Heat* is set in 'some eternal Thirties').[75] Art such as this is symptomatic, claims Jameson, of the waning of our historicity in late capitalism and our decreasing capacity to represent our current experience.

Predictably, the arguments put forward by Habermas and Jameson have cut little ice with postmodernists and post-structuralists. Lyotard, for example, has characterised Habermas's project of modernity as issuing from the now discredited grand narrative of emancipation.[76] Huyssen has written of the unattractiveness of Enlightenment rationalism for many of those engaged with the new politics, largely because of its indifference to difference.[77] Contra Jameson, and often Althusser, postmodernism has harboured the suspicion that any attempt to spell out the links between late capitalism and contemporary culture is reductionist in principle and proves gestural in practice.

Finally, to complicate an already complicated picture, Lyotard may in certain respects be aligned with the critics of postmodernism. On the one hand he has condemned much so-called postmodern art, with its eclectic style, as pandering to consumerist sensibilities; and on the other hand he has retained an allegiance to a certain tendency within the avant-garde that questions existing ideas of reality and identity (that he terms 'postmodern' – confusingly, since it would usually be labelled modernist). In valorising this latter art, he draws on the Kantian distinction between the beautiful and the sublime: the beautiful, for Lyotard, being that which induces pleasure by harmonising a conception and its presentation, and the sublime that which evokes both pain and pleasure, by virtue of the conception exceeding the presentation. What the postmodern tendency within the avant-garde does is to show that there exists something unrepresentable, but (and in this it is to be distinguished from the modern) it offers no solace or nostalgia for this unrepresentability. As well as within the traditional art forms, Lyotard finds the postmodern within film.

In contrast to mainstream cinema, whose confirmation of existing ideas of reality and identity is achieved by the construction of a representational order based on the twin principles of exclusion and effacement, the avant-garde gives access to intensities barred by mainstream cinema's operation. For example, the mainstream is subject to the imperative of narrative unity, so that everything redundant to this becomes excluded. Thus the striking of a match can only be presented in so far as it contributes to the narrative; striking it for its own sake, as a child might do simply for the fun of it, is not permitted. But such narratively sterile moments are precisely what gives avant-garde films their charge, creating intensities of pleasure analogous to *jouissance*. Films characterised in particular by extremes of mobility or immobility succeed in escaping the recurrent sameness and suppression of diversity of the mainstream; they cease to be an ordering force, but release libidinal energy that has no purpose over and beyond its own enjoyment. Like the works of other postmodern artists, the effect of avant-garde cinema is 'not to supply reality but to invent allusions to the conceivable which cannot be presented'.[78]

Such thinking evidently has close affinities with the theories of the avant-garde described earlier in this chapter. It is consequently open to the postmodern critique, notably, that it relies more than it admits on the grand narrative of emancipation, and that its conception of the relation of art and society owes more to fantasy than to serious appraisal. Specific criticisms of Lyotard's call for an art of the sublime have been voiced by Richard Rorty: 'this quest is wildly irrelevant to the attempt at communicative consensus which is the vital force which drives [liberal democratic] culture'.[79] Imagining that such art can serve the interests of the oppressed is a delusory attempt to make social needs coincide with the special needs of Leftist intellectuals, stemming, says Rorty, from the Romantic tradition.

While this debate, like others touched on in this chapter, remains unresolved, it does however seem likely at this juncture that the next stage of the development of film theory will give due recognition to the questions posed in relation to postmodernism. We seem to be at a point in the narrative when some new departure is called for.

When, in 1969, *Cahiers de Cinéma* announced its change in direction, it was in terms of a new 'scientific criticism' that would completely break with 'the tradition of frivolous and evanescent writing in the cinema'.[1] Other journals made similar announcements in comparable terms. Since then the study of film has remained theoretical, but other than that the course of its development has been very different from that so confidently envisaged. Having once eaten 'the apple of theory' there was no going back to a pre-theoretical Eden.[2] But it has long abandoned what Roland Barthes termed 'a euphoric dream of scientificity'.[3] Theory is now thoroughly pragmatic, deploying particular theoretical modes for tactical ends, drawing on a multiplicity of paradigms. The difference between twenty years ago and now is that between a belief in the possibility of a metalanguage, a discourse that would describe and explain the workings of all other discourses, and the acceptance that there is no such metalanguage, only different perspectives dependent on whatever discourse is currently being used.

As was suggested in the foreword, post-1968 film theory had a knockdown argument: there was nowhere outside of theory, in that any thinking, however anti-theoretical, drew on a background of suppositions, beliefs and judgements. Given this, there were just two possibilities: either this background theory could be explicated and criticised, or it could not. There are, broadly speaking, two schools of thinking within modern philosophy on this issue, the one holding that all bids to create such a metalanguage must fail since theorisation necessarily proceeds within social practices and is limited by this context, the other holding that the context can be transcended, with theory proceeding uncontaminated by its social origins.

The first position can be associated with Wittgenstein and Heidegger. For them, there is no outside of theory in the sense that all thinking takes place through a set of background beliefs that are themselves grounded in social practice, but in such a way that they cannot be fully theorised. On Wittgenstein's account, understanding a language is possible only by participating in a form of life. One is either involved in a particular culture, able to play the appropriate language-game, or one is not. But neither involvement nor non-involvement place one in a position to critique a language-game in its totality.

From within the possibilities are merely those of modifying it, playing it differently; and from the outside one is simply incapable of understanding it, being engaged in some other language-game (cf. 'If a lion could talk, we could not understand him.') Along similar lines, Heidegger argued that the subject (*Dasein* – literally, being there) is already in a determinate world, engaged in practices that embody a particular mode of understanding the world. To be human is to exist within an interpretive horizon, a structure of pre-understanding, whose principle components are *Vorhabe* (fore-having), the circumambient culture defining what we are and what we find intelligible; and *Vorsicht* (fore-sight), the conceptual framework that unconsciously moulds our thinking in relation to any problem.

In both cases this notion of thought as inextricably bound up with social practices is perhaps given its clearest expression in respect of language. Though neither went as far as Nietzsche when he referred to language as a 'prison-house', each maintained that it was in some degree constitutive of social being and therefore limited what could be thought. Even in his later philosophy Wittgenstein remained close to his early view that 'the limits of. . . language mean the limits of [the] world'.[4] Heidegger wrote, in a Lacanian vein, 'Language speaks us'.[5] Elsewhere he elaborated, 'For words and language are not wrappings in which things are packed. . . [it] is in words and language that things first come into being and are.'[6]

The alternative position is that traditionally associated with Marxism and given renewed emphasis through Althusser. Here too it was held that reality was interpreted in terms of background belief (ideology), but differed in that it was possible to escape from this into the realm of knowledge (science). Thus a metalanguage was possible – a discourse free of determination by other social practices, which could explain how other discourses were produced and what their relation was to society and history.

Having set out on the second of these roads, film theory was to find itself travelling on the first. Having begun with a Marxist structuralist confidence in the possibility of knowledge it found itself increasingly inclined towards the Wittgensteinian and Heideggerian views of post-structuralism and postmodernism. As we have suggested earlier, the reasons for the shift were both external and internal to theory. Those external concerned the waning of a traditional conception of socialism and the rise of new political allegiances among those inclined to challenge the status quo. The proponents of the new politics were, however, clearer about the desirability of change than about what was actually to replace the old, which perhaps explains the attraction of the avant-garde, since its project of putting the subject in process was very much in tune with a reluctance simply to proffer political solutions. The internal reasons for the change were in part the collapse of Althusserianism and the science/ideology distinction (discussed in chapter 1), but more importantly the difficulties encountered by film theory in pursuit of its own project. Since this book has to a large extent been concerned with the unravelling of the attempted synthesis of historical materialism, semiotics and psychoanalysis, we shall here limit ourselves to a few concluding remarks.

Initially it seemed that Saussure's diacritical theory of meaning was a secure foundation for the theoretical edifice. In particular it appeared to mesh easily with historical materialism, offering the possibility of relating the materiality of linguistic practice to that of other social practices. However, the adoption of a Lacanian reading of Saussure, that language was constitutive, proved to be the crucial step that shifted film theory towards the tradition of Wittgenstein and Heidegger, culminating in post-structuralism. There were three specific consequences of this move that had not been foreseen by the Althusserians. The first of these was that signification became an autonomous practice effectively swallowing up society and history rather than explaining them. If meaning was produced only by a system of differences, there was no question of expressing or representing meanings anterior to language. Society and history were thus constructs of language instead of the reality beyond it. (See the CCCS/Coward debate in chapter 2). The second consequence was that the discourse of the theorist, by virtue of constructing a reality, was itself an intervention; or, according to Foucault, it was an engagement in a struggle for power ('A "theory" is the regional system of this struggle.')[7] Finally, if each discourse produced its own reality, then no discourse was reducible to any other. Each was, as Lyotard used Wittgenstein to argue, a unique language-game legitimated by nothing more than the fact that it was played. Therefore semiotics, introduced to break with impressionism, ended by legitimating it as one among other irreducible language-games serving a particular form of life. While questions of identity, recognition, pleasure, etc. continue to matter for spectators, the discourse of impressionism is likely to continue (as indeed the everyday – or late night – discussion of films among theorists well testifies).

Of these three outcomes only the first is not the problem it was taken to be. For the diacritical theory of meaning is a theory in name only, in that it does not even begin to explain how meaning occurs. The search for a satisfactory theory of meaning has been at the fore-front of analytic philosophy for over a century, to the extent that all other philosophical questions can be seen as waiting for its formula-tion or for agreement that there can be no such thing. This alternative in fact demarcates the disputants in the current controversy within analytic philosophy: on the one side the followers of Frege who believe that a theory can be developed, and on the other the followers of Wittgenstein who maintain it cannot. The participants in the debate are perfectly aware of the existence of Saussure's contribution to linguistics, but in contrast to film theorists appreciate that it has little to offer by way of a theory of meaning. If one considers the question Ernst Tugendhadt has identified as the most fundamental within contemporary philosophy – 'What is it to understand a sen-tence?' – it becomes plain that Saussure offered only a *condition* for the emergence of meaning, namely, the existence of a system of dif-ferences. One has only to substitute the word 'understanding' for the word 'meaning' in the sentence 'meaning is produced by a system of differences' to become aware of the limitations of Saussure's theory. A system of differences may be a condition of understanding but it can hardly be said to produce it. And if Dummett is right in saying that the philosophical question of meaning should be construed as a question about what it is to understand a meaning, then Saussure offers no answer to the problem, which evidently requires an account of the subject who interprets any utterance.[8]

Now as we have seen repeatedly, film theory encountered the need for a theory of the subject in order to explicate the exchange between spectator and text. By positioning a subject who was as much con-stituting as constituted, the route was opened from signification to society and history, for it is here that constituting subjects are pro-duced. But rather than take the direct route, film theory detoured via psychoanalysis on the presumption that it offered an account of the constitution of the subject in its historical specificity, as well as more immediately providing a way of thinking through the relation-ship between text and subject. The choice of psychoanalysis added, however, to the problems encountered by the project of achieving would-be scientific knowledge. For although Lacan may have been little influenced by Wittgenstein he was steeped in Heidegger, his dialectic of the subject being closely related to the Heideggerian notion of subject and world as co-determining. The impact of Lacanian psychoanalysis was to complete the realignment of film theory from the one metadiscursive position to the other.

We return here to the dimension of Lacan only hinted at in our earlier discussion: the core of his return to Freud, which was the recovery of the radical force of the unconscious. The fact of the unconscious means that each person is like 'the "messenger-slave" of ancient usage... who carries under his hair the codicil that condemns him to death know[ing] neither the meaning nor the text, nor in what language it is written, not even that it had been tattooed on his shaven scalp as he slept'.[9] Psychoanalysis, said Lacan, had retreated from the implications of Freud's discovery, all too often proceeding as if it had direct access to the unconscious. As Jeffrey Mehlman has put it, the fact of repression had itself been repressed.[10] Those who think they know the unconscious, however, are mistaken; '*les non-dupes errent*'.[11] The analysand presumes, mistakenly, that the analyst knows what he or she does not: 'they expect from him what they do not want to know (the secret of their "trouble")'; but all the analyst knows is that the unconscious speaks (*ça parle*), in slips and dreams and symptoms, and that it is structured like a language in transindividual forms.[12] About its meaning the analyst knows only that it is unique, being a function of the analysand's own history, which is different from any other, and of the ever-changing immediacy of the analytic situation. The only one who could know its meaning is the analysand, but he or she will never know, because the unconscious is 'knowledge that can't tolerate one's knowing that one knows'.[13] From this there follows profound consequences for discourse: since there is nowhere to speak except in the symbolic, the unconscious must speak everywhere, even, especially, through the discourse that would presume mastery. In the words of Julia Kristeva, 'interpretation necessarily represents appropriation, and thus an act of desire and murder.'[14]

Forced to relinquish the dream of mastery, the theorist is left occupying a position analogous to that of the analyst, whose role, as we have already indicated, is not that of imparting knowledge, but of punctuating the speech of the analysand. Whatever intervention the theorist may make, it is done in the awareness that its effectivity will be determined elsewhere. Having been introduced into film theory for the purpose of achieving knowledge, psychoanalysis has concluded by imposing limits on what can be known. This does not entail, however, that we are left simply with a postmodern ethos of anything goes, with each theorist making his or her own unique contribution to what Richard Rorty has called 'the conversation of mankind'. Film theory has little truck with any such cosy notion, perceiving intervention in terms rather of a power struggle in which certain discourses are privileged and enjoy a status as orthodoxy, and others are peripheral and fighting for validation. It is this hierarchy of discourses, with its concomitant relations of domination and subjection, that is at stake for film theory. Though the prime concern may now be that of gender rather than class, the political stakes remain as high as they were at the moment of the post-1968 departure from what had gone before. The grand theoretical hopes of that moment have foundered, but not its political commitment. The result is that the terrain of film studies, more so than any other area of cultural studies, has been won, and held, by the Left.

FILM THEORY: A RETROSPECT

Introduction

Let's not overthink this. (Clint Eastwood)
If things were simple word would have gotten around. (Jacques Derrida)

While never monolithic, Theory, as it came to be termed, was characterised by recurrent concerns and themes and by a fundamental political orientation. Its project was that of the Enlightenment: critique of the status quo through the analysis of existing cinematic practices, coupled with the prescription of an emancipatory alternative. Cinema was conceived as first and foremost a social institution; what was at stake was its political effectivity and valency. On the one hand Theory sought to ascertain the role of the cinematic machine in contributing to and maintaining an oppressive and unjust social order; on the other, it advocated an avant-garde cinematic practice that would question and combat the prevailing system.

Theory was indebted to its reading of certain recent Continental thinkers, most notably Althusser, Lacan and Saussure, crystallised into a number of structuring principles: everything is intrinsically political; there is nowhere outside history; language is constitutive; the subject is not originary. On the basis of these axioms it sought to create a metalanguage that would tell the truth about cinema, an approach which embodied the modernist move of revealing the reality behind appearances. Thus, everything is political: while it might seem that cinema is no more than harmless entertainment, in reality it is an ideological operation reproducing capitalism and patriarchy. There is no outside of history: while mainstream cinema presents the human condition as in essence unchanging, in reality all such conceptions are instances of historically specific ideologies. Language is constitutive: while it appears that realist cinema transparently renders a pre-given reality and auteurist cinema expresses a pre-given artistic vision, in reality the meaning of such texts was the effect of a system of differences and did not exist prior to the processes of signification. The subject is not originary: far from being a stable and already fixed entity, the subject is rather in process, endlessly constituted and reconstituted.

These propositions lay at the heart of Theory, and their elaboration was to give rise to a distinctive interpretative synthesis and, as a corollary, an equally distinctive programme for a counter-cinema. For the novelty of Theory lay in a renewed stress on the relationship between the spectator and the film. Although directors as varied as Lang, Hitchcock and Godard had spoken of the spectator as completing or co-creating the text, Theory made this explicit as never before. Its thesis was that the spectator's subjectivity is not a given and, crucially, that the terms of its constitution determine how reality is perceived. (Indeed this is a matter of everyday observation, as when in an episode of *Frasier* the sports jock Bulldog, having fallen in love for the first time, announces 'Now I understand all those songs on the radio!') In arriving at this position, Theory was firstly indebted to Lacan, from whom it took the notion that the subject, as constituted in the mirror phase, misrecognises itself and that this misrecognition then shapes its perception of reality. Hence Lacan's insistence that the question to ask in analysis is 'Who is speaking?', since who the subject imagines himself to be will determine how he misperceives the world. The meaning and significance of what is said is dependent on the speaker's subjective position and how the speaker misrecognises that self and position. Theory's other conceptual debt was to Althusser's notion of interpellation: in accepting an assigned social role and concomitant identity, the subject misrecognises both himself and social reality and is thereby subjected to the 'truth' of the dominant ideology.

On this basis Theory postulated that meaning is never isolable from the relationship of text and spectator. In seeking to explicate this imbrication of meaning and subjectivity, it elaborated a model of textual functioning: the text interpellates the spectator, reconstituting his identity in such a way that he is lost to ideological misrecognition. The model came in two contending forms. In the non-dialectical form the text is endowed with the power to position the spectator and thus dictate the terms of its reading; the spectator accepts the perspective inscribed in its structure. In the dialectical model text and spectator are co-constituting; in their exchange each transforms the other, making available meanings which would otherwise not emerge.

But in whatever form, the stress was on relationship. What mattered were the identifications and desires in play. Thus in Metz what mattered was less the content of the film than the spectator's identification and hence misperception of himself as occupying a transcendent position. In the positions developed by *Screen*, Lacan's 'Who is speaking?' became 'Who is spectating? Who is reading this text?', the answer to which was seen as the crucial determinant of the meanings produced and therefore as the key to understanding the ideological operation of cinema. Who the spectator takes himself to be, his mode of enunciation, determines how the film is read.

The work of Laura Mulvey[1] (to which we shall return in what follows), arguably the most influential of Theory's practitioners, well illustrates the *Screen* line. First, the (political) reality behind (pleasurable) appearance: Hollywood narrative might seem to be innocent enough entertainment but in reality it was an instrument of patriarchal ideology. Second, the relationship between spectator and film: here the concern was less with the content of the image, whether it was positive or negative, than with how the institution of cinema made possible for male spectators a voyeuristic and fetishistic 'relationship' with women. To the question, 'Who is spectating?' the answer was a (male) subject enunciating the (fetishistic) disavowal, 'I know perfectly well that women lack, but nevertheless...(in these images of perfection they lack nothing)', thereby giving rise to characteristic misrecognitions of himself and women. Faced with the power of mainstream cinema to so position the spectator, the only challenge to the specious security of the male spectator was a self-reflexive avant-garde that would, among other things, deny him the (voyeuristic) pleasures afforded by Hollywood.

Leibniz once remarked that the fate of thinkers is to believe themselves in port only to discover that they are still at sea – a fitting epitaph for the overly confident advocates of Theory. With its foundations challenged, its certainties eroded, Theory is today less in evidence than, say, the auteurism it sought to displace. Its supersession and marginalisation has been the result of so many readings, critiques and counter-approaches that no synoptic account of these is possible. We have chosen therefore to outline four general orientations in relation to Theory, which among the myriad competing and conflicting viewpoints seem to us the most compelling. For each of the four readings we have revisited some of the central topics of the foregoing text – psychoanalysis, realism, authorship, the avant-garde, etc. – together with one not previously covered, the institution of stardom; and to provide greater focus we have concentrated on a limited number of films for illustrating these themes.

Our account relies more on ideal types than specific writers on cinema and on constructed generalised positions rather than specific citations. The reasons for this are threefold. Firstly, most writers, whether in the same text or different texts, consistently or inconsistently, straddle more than one of the positions outlined here and there is simply not the space to do justice to the intricacies or indeed muddle of individual cases. Secondly, such detailed analyses would obscure the larger picture, which is complex enough as it is. Thirdly, some of the debates are internal; we are genuinely torn between aspects of the readings proposed. Our hope is simply that out of this internal aporia and debate we have created a preliminary and provisional map to enable readers of the earlier text to orientate themselves among more recent developments. As will be apparent from what follows, it is always possible to read differently.

Reading 1: contra Theory

This first of the four readings is a thorough-going indictment of Theory. Far from being the continuation of the Enlightenment project of emancipation it imagined itself to be, Theory was its betrayal: neither its politics nor its theoretical sources provided grounds for critique. Its politics, at least in its Althusserian Marxist phase, was gestural and, more importantly, misconceived, based as it was on a naïve misreading of 1968 (who now considers the events of May and June in France a failed October in the west or indeed wants an October in the west?). Paradoxically, 1968, which saw people take to the streets, was taken as evidence of the power of the 'dominant ideology' to immobilise the masses. Despite the manifest importance of agency, in that many people, far from being passive, were actively shaping history at the time, Theory interpreted the *événements*, or at least their failure, as proof of the efficacy of ideological structures, or more precisely that subjects constituted by structures and institutions were lost to ideological misrecognition.

A similar blindness to the importance of agency informed Theory's deployment of the three figures enlisted to provide an account of the misrecognitions produced by the institution of cinema: Lacan, Althusser and Saussure. Lacan's theory of the mirror phase assumes precisely what it sets out to explain, namely the constitution of the subject in a state of misrecognition: if the subject as agent does not yet exist who misrecognises himself in the mirror? Similarly Althusser's theory of ideological interpellation failed to explain why an individual accepts one form of interpellation but not others, why interpellation succeeds in some instances and fails in others. As for Saussure, whatever his achievements, his linguistics does not amount to a theory of meaning, for while a system of differences may be a condition for the production of meaning a full explanation requires some notion of agency, that is, of a subject with intentions, competences, beliefs and so on.

Failure to appreciate the importance of agency caused Theory problems in three crucial areas: spectatorship, realism and authorship. Undialectical Theory held that spectators passively accepted the meanings and derivative affects inscribed in the text. Quite the reverse, say these critics of Theory: understanding or indeed misunderstanding a text requires more than the text; knowledges and competences must be brought to bear; texts are always read intertextually and it is the spectator who performatively links any given text to this broader context.

Realism provides a signal example. Since meaning was held to be the effect of the system of differences, Theory argued that what is termed 'realism' was in practice a reality effect: texts did not reflect a pre-given reality but rather produced an impression of reality; or, more precisely, textual mechanisms had the power to so position the spectator as to convince him that the filmic images were a trans- parent rendering of reality itself. But this, say the Theory-sceptics, will not do. A text is not realistic in virtue of some textual structure or combination of devices; it is not self-validating. Rather it is realistic in virtue of something other than itself, realistic if, and only if, it corresponds to or coheres with what is taken to be reality. A text is realistic only if it is adjudged to be so, and the institution of realism requires a spectator capable of passing such judgments, in other words a subject acting as an agent. A film may propose itself as realistic but it is the spectator who decides whether it is or not; hence it may convince one spectator with a particular history and body of knowledge but fail with another.

A similar line of argument applies to authorship, where Theory's concern to distance itself from auteurism blinded it to the impor- tance of agency. In fact the concept of intentionality is indispensable to the human sciences and indeed much social interaction. Once agency is given its due, the notion of authorship not only ceases to be problematic but becomes unavoidable, as has been fully recognised in the twenty-five years from the heyday of Theory, with auteurist studies now rightly thriving as never before.

When feminism displaced Marxism – those favouring this reading maintain – Theory moved on to surer ground both politically and intellectually. Few would deny that much of Hollywood is masculinist fantasy and that many men do gaze voyeuristically at images of women on the screen. Mulvey was a much better guide than *Cahiers du Cinema* in its historical materialist moment, but problems stemming from an over-reliance on certain *maîtres à penser*, notably Freud, remained. However persuasive Mulvey's account of the male spectator, her analysis snagged on its Freudian dogmatism, for it was unable to explain why women enjoy cinema. If Hollywood is essentially a cinema of sadistic male voyeurs, it can offer neither place nor pleasures to women except through identification with either a masculinised position or a masochistic position, neither of which are likely to be very satisfying. The problem here is that many women patently do enjoy such films. Amongst the many pieces of ethnographic research attesting to women's enjoyment of cinema, Jackie Stacey's admirable *Star Gazing*[2] may serve as an example.

Dissatisfied with the easy generalisations and universalist assumptions of psychoanalysis, Stacey decided to study a historically specific female audience. Through advertisements in two women's magazines she contacted women who had been cinema-goers in the 1940s and 1950s and asked them about their experience of and attitude to Hollywood's female stars. Their responses in questionnaires and letters made plain the delight that these women took in film and in particular female stars. Each respondent had her favourite(s), often modelling her clothes, shoes, hats, hairstyles and demeanour on the star's style. It is apparent that Hollywood was more than mere masculinist fantasy. Far from being subjugated to masculinist ideals of femininity, Stacey's respondents experienced stars as catalysts in bringing about a fuller, more exciting life. Here are some examples:

'My favourite star of all time, even now, is Doris Day. To me she was my idol. I loved every film she ever did, and watched most of them several times.' (Veronica Millen)[3]

'The effect she [Deanna Durbin] had on me can only be described as electrifying.' (Patricia Robinson)[4]

'Rita Hayworth was a joy to watch dancing. She had a lovely square face and beautiful hair. I grew my hair as long as hers and put it up and made it bounce when I walked as hers did.' (Doreen Gibson)[5]

Contrary to the implications of Mulvey's thesis, women did not experience discomfort watching Hollywood's supposedly patriarchal output (indeed the production studios' own research showed that women enjoyed cinema more than men and preferred female to male stars). Hence these were no isolated examples. Rather they pointed to a fundamental problem with Theory, namely that in its quest for abstract generalities (often imported from French *maîtres*) it over-simplified and refused to acknowledge that cinema and the experience of cinema were always more complex than it allowed. Even when Theory was at its apogee, evidence of this tension was not hard to find – as the present writers can personally attest – for a salient feature of conferences at the time was the disjunction between what was said in the seminar room and what was said in the bar afterwards, which far from the discourse of subject position or the imaginary signifier tended to be about what films one had enjoyed and which stars one liked – 'guilty pleasures' that were then perceived as ethical shortcomings or political frivolity.

According to this reading, attention to the true complexity of film culture and, more particularly, of the viewing experience indicates the direction writing on cinema should have taken. In place of Theory's global ambition for a theory of everything cinematic, the study of cinema should seek to do justice to its innumerable specific forms and, in place of Theory's almost mediaeval reliance on certain dogmas, researchers should return to cinema itself. Although Theory often spoke of the need for studies of specific historical and cultural moments, it was too attached to 'high level' theorisation about the cinematic institution to analyse film in all its diversity and hetero-geneity – a task that is now rightly being undertaken. Likewise, instead of abstract analyses of 'the institution of cinema', the focus should be on particular institutions in their specificity. For example, in relation to the institution of stardom, such research would mean an avoidance of glib generalisations and instead involve attention to its myriad heterogeneous forms. Not only has stardom functioned very differently in different countries at different historical moments – Hollywood is not Hindi cinema (Bollywood) – but famously Hollywood itself operated differently in the studio system than it does today when stars have their own production companies.

Again, rather than discussing 'the spectator' in the abstract the emphasis should be on particular audiences. Stacey, for instance, stresses the historical and social specificity of her research group (white British women recollecting their cinema-going experience of the 1940s and 1950s), pointing out that women from different backgrounds may well have responded very differently. She also emphasises the differentiated nature of the group. For example, she reveals how their capacity to emulate their favourite stars varied over time as rationing was first relaxed and then abolished, and that even after the ending of rationing, although some of them could afford to buy hats, shoes and clothes in the desired style, others could not. Similarly there were differences in the nature of the emotional ties to the stars: some formed homo-erotic attachments, some did not.

If writing upon the cinema is to have any validity, it must do justice to these particularities. Whereas Theory was always the same old story, the dominant ideology controlling everything other than a few pockets of avant-garde resistance, responsible writing and research should investigate the diverse institutions and innumerable stories that constitute the history of cinema. 'Who', asked Theory, 'is speaking?'; yet, argues this reading, it was deaf to all but the voices theorised by its conceptual schemas. It is the duty of scholarship to rescue those many voices from silence.

Reading 2: continuing critique

A second possible reading provides an altogether more positive evaluation of the legacy of Theory. Sharing Theory's commitment to justice and emancipation, writers working in the tradition of critique hold that in social orders scarred by injustice and inequity there is no more important task for writing on film than to continue Theory's work of critique and its associated political imperatives.

Even in the welter of uncertainty that is postmodernity – long gone the days of high modernism's serene confidence in the power of grand explanatory schema – there are many sites of struggle where grounds for critique clearly obtain, most prominently in relation to persisting discrimination on the basis of gender, race, social class, sexual orientation and age, and to the grotesque inequalities between the industrialised world and the countries of the South. And given that these evils are inextricably caught up in the politics of ideological representation the business of responsible writing on the cinema is equally clear: the contestation of hegemonic media images which demean, marginalise, subordinate and oppress.

In this perspective Laura Mulvey constitutes an exemplary figure.

Whatever the intellectual problems with some aspects of her work that have been raised by this reading (of which more in a moment), politically she made a difference. Her theories had an impact far beyond academia. In conjunction with other feminists, she rendered visible what had been invisible: the violence within representation and, more particularly, the reproduction of patriarchy within mainstream cinema. She revealed and confronted the self-interested and misogynistic nature of representations of women by white middle-class heterosexual males and thereby contributed to the transformation of gender-based relations of domination.

Nevertheless, though seeking to continue Theory's work of critique, this orientation has a very different take on politics, theory, film-making practice, and the relations among them. Crucially it distances itself from Theory on two counts: it insists both on the differentiated nature of cinema and on the agency of spectators.

(1) Difference. Theory tended to elide many forms of difference. While concerned with class and gender differences, it was, at least initially, blind to many other forms of difference, notably in relation to struggles around race, ethnicity and most markedly, an index of its Eurocentrism, the politics of post-colonialism. Indeed, lack of attention to difference was the basis for much of the criticism levelled at Mulvey in the 1980s and 1990s: femininity is not a monolithic homogeneous category. What of lesbian spectators? What of female spectators from oppressed ethnic groups and other cultures? Today differences are even more evident: there is much discussion in the press (yet again) of the 'death of feminism', and no less an authority than Judith Butler reports that many of her female students just want to be 'babes'[6]. But if feminism seems passé or is of little relevance to certain social strata in developed societies, it remains of inestimable importance for countless women engaged in a variety of gender-related struggles around the globe.

(2) Agency. In its Althusserian moment Theory conceived of spectators as passively accepting the dominant ideology; interpellated by the address of the text they necessarily assented to its ideological representations. But, this reading insists, spectators are active: interpellation can be and is resisted, with audiences contesting, resisting and negotiating within antagonistic power relations.

Consider, for example audience reception of stars. Analyses of the star system in the tradition of Theory saw the institution of stardom as complicit with the dominant ideology, in that stars, by embodying particular ideals of masculinity and femininity, naturalised and reinforced existing stereotypes in which spectators passively acquiesced. But spectators are more active than this suggests, appropriating the images and personae of stars for their own purposes. For example, Richard Dyer has shown how sections of the gay subculture appropriated the image of Judy Garland as figuring a resolve to go on performing despite her travails.[7] Again, to return to Jacky Stacey's study, it would appear that the majority of her correspondents were engaged in 'the active negotiation and trans-formation of identities'.[8] Far from being the passive, constructed spectators called for by interpellation, they selected, converted and used the personae of stars to negotiate their identities in a culture where women were both subjects and objects of commodity exchange.[9] In appropriating the style of their favourites they were not engaged in objectification and self-commodification, but rather were exploring new forms of expression for female subjectivity. Inspired by the power and confidence of star personae, such as those of Katherine Hepburn or Bette Davis, they resisted the straitened and confining roles on offer.

It is evident that in many respects this emphasis on difference and agency aligns writers in this orientation with those of the previous reading. However, while opponents of Theory tend to see the heterogeneity of cinema and the active nature of spectatorship as an argument for scholarly research into specific cinematic modes, for those continuing the tradition of critique the principal lesson is political. While they have no objection to empirical research, their concern is to examine the implications of cinema's diversity and the agency of spectators for the politics of writing about cinema.

Their most obvious conclusion is that no one theoretical strategy or film-making practice is appropriate in all circumstances. Against Theory's tendency to argue that the ideological operation of main-stream cinema was everywhere the same and that only one opposi-tional strategy could succeed, that of avant-garde film-making, the proponents of Reading 2, like those of Reading 1, consider what they perceive as Theory's overvaluation of the avant-garde to be a corollary of its overestimation of the power of the text in inducing misrecognition. If audiences can contest and resist texts, there is no need of self-reflexive distanciation techniques to liberate them.

More generally, there is a need for a greater awareness of the differences between socio-political contexts and the concomitant need to rethink theory. Put simply, there are many conjunctures where it is possible to engage effectively in emancipatory struggles without being overly concerned with the finer points of Theory. This is most evidently the case with thinking about language and subjectivity. In the case of language and, by implication, all signifying systems including cinema, the argument is that, although Theory may be right in claiming that language is constitutive and does not transparently render a pre-existing reality, this does not proscribe realism as an effective oppositional practice. Even if ultimately there may be a violence inherent in all representation, nonetheless the mobilisation of existing forms of representation can constitute an effective form of intervention for the purposes of immediate and urgent political tasks. By challenging false and pejorative representations and by reconfiguring modes of understanding, realism can function as an emancipatory force for those whose oppression has been masked or elided by prevailing modes of representation. Similarly in the case of subjectivity, Theory may be right to stress that the subject is not originary, and more recent theories (see Reading 3 below) may be correct in describing identity as unstable and mutable, but in many contexts what matters politically are actually existing, relatively stable modes of subjectivity. In such contexts, for immediate political purposes, identities, subjects, needs and interests can be taken as pre-given. Thus the call might be for an authorial cinema expressing, say, the rejection of interpellation, the desire to articulate minority experience, and the aspiration to achieve both self-definition and recognition.

In broad outline, three forms of context can be discerned. In the first of these, the nature of the political problem is clear. Because injustice and the suffering it causes are self-evident, there is no prior requirement to unmask existing appearances. Hence theoretical abstractions can be dispensed with and terms in common currency suffice both to articulate the situation and to frame a political programme for transforming it. Writing on cinema should therefore promote film-making practices countering the dominant regime of representation. In most instances this entails the advocacy of progressive forms of realist and or authorial cinema.

In relation to realism, the question then becomes: realism for whom and to what end? Given prevailing misrepresentation, distortion and prejudice in relation to whatever group, ethnicity or social fraction, the need is for a cinema that confronts ideology with accurate, truthful representation. For example, in certain societies, the call might be for texts depicting women other than through the deformation of stereotypes and masculinist fantasies and combating their actual situation under oppressive ideological and power configurations. *A Time for Drunken Horses* (Bahman Ghobadi, 2000) and *The Circle* (Jafar Panahi, 2000) would be exemplary texts here.

Similarly in relation to authorship, in situations where social groups who through discrimination lack the authority to speak, the need is for such groups to have the opportunity to discover and represent themselves. Such a need has become all the more pronounced in the post-colonial world of migration, diaspora and hybridity, in which the expression of identities can secure at least their temporary and provisional recognition. The role of theory here is to increase awareness of and clarify the issues around the ideological weight of texts' representations. The question would be less 'Who is speaking?' than 'Who is speaking of whom and in what terms?' For example, in relation to *The Piano* (Jane Campion, 1993), a film that speaks of and celebrates modes of experience unavailable to circumscribed male subjectivities, there are contexts where the representation of the Maoris might be the priority for analysis. Similarly there are contexts where the issue in relation to *Beau Travail* (Claire Denis, 1998) is whether it exoticises and hence dehumanises the African women depicted in the film.

In the second of the three types of context referred to above, there is a greater need to break with the self-evident, to distanciate and question, and hence a greater role for theory. Because misrecognition and delusion still predominate, the task, as in Mulvey, is to unmask the reality of the situation and analyse the mechanisms producing misrecognition and mystification. For example, feminists unconvinced by Stacey's arguments might contend that stardom naturalises certain notions of femininity and seek to make explicit the ideology shaping gender roles.

Consequently certain aspects of theory continue to be relevant. An obvious example would be the Freudian model of repression and the return of the repressed, as mobilised by Mulvey. *Eyes Wide Shut* (Stanley Kubrick, 1999), for instance, is open to a reading in such terms along the following, necessarily schematic, lines. The film begins with Alice (Nicole Kidman) as fetishistic spectacle taking off her dress. What happens thereafter can then be analysed as an attempt to resolve the problem identified by Mulvey, namely how to integrate such frozen images into the dynamics of narrative. Having repressed female desire in the fetishised image, the film has the problem of maintaining that repression in a narrative where the repressed will inevitably return – a clear instance of a text troubled by a female desire it cannot contain. The strategy of containment is precisely that described by Mulvey, namely aggression, which begins in the next shot of Alice, where she is depicted in all her human ordinariness seated on the toilet, and continues with a series of attacks displaced on to the other women Harford (Tom Cruise) encounters on his quest, culminating in the death of Mandy.

From this standpoint the most valuable films are those which engage in culturally disruptive forms of resistance by questioning assumptions by means of denaturalisation and problematisation. For example, in the 'intercultural cinema' analysed by Laura Marks,[10] various films she describes combat commodity fetishism through film-makers excavating and disclosing the labour that went into their production. Thus *Ananas* (Amos Gitai, 1983) 'de-alienates' the labour that went into the production of a can of pineapples; while *Love Women and Flowers* (Marta Rodriguez and Jorge Silva, 1988) exposes the production history of carnations grown with the aid of fungicides that cause workers to sicken and die.[11]

In the third type of context – the only one of the three where there is a role for self-reflexive avant-garde practices which put the subject in process – the problem addressed is less easily categorisable, and impossible to define precisely. It is rather a case of the subject embarking on a voyage of exploration in order to seek out new forms of subjectivity and as yet undiscovered, hopefully happier economies. Mona Hatoum's *Measure of Distance* (1988) can serve as an example. In a style redolent of one of Theory's canonic texts, Chantal Akerman's *News from Home* (1977), there is a disjunction of the picture track and the soundtrack. As in Akerman much of the soundtrack is given over to the film-maker reading letters from a mother who has remained at home while the daughter has travelled abroad. Hatoum combines these extracts with visual images of her mother's naked body in the shower, on which she has superimposed the handwritten letters in their original Arabic and punctuates the readings with recorded conversations with her mother. The result, as in Godard and Straub/Huillet, is an open-ended text in which the relationship of the two women to the father is explored in the interests of an, as yet, unformulated mode of freedom. Such work is no longer critique in the same sense as in the earlier contexts, since the subject can no longer be treated as a given and hence the grounds of critique are less secure. As such this approach prefigures the next reading, to which we now turn.

Reading 3: postmodern amendments

In their very different ways writers within this orientation seek to think cinema otherwise, exploring and experimenting in order to create a space in which something new can emerge. While not abandoning Theory's commitment to 'tell it like it is', they are suspicious of its more totalising ambitions. Similarly, while sympathetic to the project of critique they are concerned about the absence of grounds. In consequence the various thinkers we have selected as emblematic of such postmodern amendments are inclined to distance themselves both from Theory and the two readings already outlined.

Lyotard

A key reference for any such departure from Theory is Jean-Francois Lyotard. Three of the ideas developed in his work are of relevance here.

(1) As explained in Chapter 7 above, Lyotard defined postmodernism as an incredulity towards metanarrative. Just as there came a moment when for many people it was no longer possible to believe in God, so today it is no longer possible to believe in the grand narrative of, for example, progress and emancipation. Hence the legitimation provided by such grand narratives – for example, that of emancipation, upon which Theory relied so extensively – no longer obtains, and critique is robbed of its authority.

(2) In *The Postmodern Condition*[12] Lyotard claims that the social consists of a multiplicity of language games, each with its own set of rules and criteria determining which moves are legitimate and which not. As these rules are instituted by human communities, they can be changed, displaced and reinvented; language-games can form and change in unforeseeable ways. This suggests – to avoid a self-refuting relativism, it can be no more than a suggestion – that Theory's ambitions to construct a metalanguage which would both tell the truth about and displace existing discourses was unlikely to succeed. Language games are so heterogeneous and disparate that no explanatory overview seems possible and their displacement and replacement

by Theory appears even less possible. As our earlier example of the post-seminar conversation in the bar illustrates, films can feature in very different language games. For Lyotard these problems are not the occasion for despair. On the contrary, he welcomes the demise of the authority of metanarratives and metalanguages since this removes constraints on developments within language games and enables those currently silenced to speak. When he later recast the notion of language games in terms of 'phrases' or, more accurately, 'phrase regimens', he pointed out that phrases can be linked in innumerable ways and urged that metanarratives should not be allowed to inhibit their linkages.

(3) Lyotard gives a further reason why Theory's ambition to construct a metalanguage was always going to be in difficulties, namely that the event of art eludes theoretical capture; there is in it what cannot be phrased. The event of art, the 'it happens' of art, is always in excess of any determination, the 'what happens' of art. An example, from *Beau Travail*, would be the choreographed scenes in the desert of soldiers engaging in something between drill and dance, irreducible to theoretical comprehension.

This resistance of art to conceptualisation is particularly evident, for Lyotard, in postmodern art. Whereas realist art chimes with existing notions of reality, thereby generating a recognition effect that confirms prevailing beliefs, postmodern art by contrast calls into question received notions of reality and points to what lies beyond them. Against the demand for simplicity, unity and communicability met by realism, against its suppression of doubt and its reinforcement of the authority of dominant regimes of representation, postmodernism indicates that there is something that goes unpresented in existing representations. Though not presenting the unpresentable itself – that would be a contradiction in terms – it points to the existence of that which is unpresentable.

It does so by means of the sublime, the concept Kant deployed to denote an experience where cognition fails, and which for Lyotard characterises all art which challenges the existing consensus. Hence there is a continuing role for the avant-garde insofar as it disrupts dominant modes of understanding and opens up the possibility of new ways of seeing and feeling. In contrast to realist works which stabilise the referent and package the world in easily decipherable forms, avant-garde works in their difficulty and resistance to easy intelligibility testify to the presence of what is not presented in realism's pre-established forms. By finding an idiom to voice what cannot be phrased in existing phrase regimens they point to the eventualities of as yet unimaginable futures.

Lyotard cites as an example Claude Lanzmann's nine-hour film *Shoah* (1985). Rather than attempt to represent what happened at Auschwitz, Lanzmann instead relies on a distillation of hundreds of hours of testimony by survivors, delivered direct to camera. In contrast to a realist text like *Schindler's List* (Steven Spielberg,1993) which seeks to represent the horror of the Holocaust through images, words, music – a means, Lyotard claims, of making us forget, and all the more so because of the severity and exactness of its images – *Shoah* testifies to the existence of an unpresentable. Lyotard writes, '[Lanzmann] hardly offers a single testimony where the unrepresentable character of the extermination is not indicated, even momentarily, by an alteration of voice, a tightening of throat, a tear, a sob, the disappearance of a witness out of frame, an upset in the tone of the narrative, some uncontrolled gesture. So that we know that the witnesses are surely lying, or "playing a role" or hiding something, however impassive they may appear.'[13]

All of this suggests a reconceptualisation of the role of theory as experiment and invention, an emphasis that is distinctively different from that of the two previous readings.

In relation to the Theory-sceptic position, it would be argued that, while there is nothing objectionable about scholarly research, such research is necessarily conducted in terms of certain concepts, which are neither fixed nor given. For example, as we have seen in our discussion of Mulvey, any analysis of the political dimension of cinema has recourse to the concept of 'woman' but, as the development of feminism makes clear, the meaning of the term 'woman' has never been and is never likely to be fixed once and for all. Thus alongside, say, historical analyses of particular periods of cinema, Theory has a role in exploring and developing the possibilities for change afforded by new concepts, new idioms and vocabularies.

The phenomenon of stardom provides a further example. While stars can be, and have been, theorised in terms of commodification, mystification and illusion, demonstrated by the manufacture of their images and personae through promotions and publicity machines etc., it is equally possible to provide alternative accounts – for example, by adopting (and adapting) the vocabulary of Georges Bataille. Thus stars can be described in the terms suggested by their appellation: suns, generating energy and making their energy available to their audiences. So conceived, stars can articulate trans-formational power. Recall that many of Stacey's respondents were inspired by stars to live more fully. Insofar as they embody a more passionate and intense form of existence, and one that can instil emulation, stars are to be celebrated, not denounced as complicit with misrecognitions.

In relation, very briefly, to those still engaged in political critique, the argument would be that it is not a matter of doing justice to existing groups and individuals but to people still to come. The task is not to contest the dominant regime of representations, meanings and identities in the name of the truth, but rather to explore other possibilities in the name of what as yet does not exist, but which in some unforeseeable future could exist.

In addition to Lyotard, the work of three thinkers – Richard Rorty, Michel Foucault and Gilles Deleuze – is important for this direction in theory. All three can be mobilised within the plurality that is postmodernism to alert us to new possibilities. Although very different, their thinking has certain strands in common, which are relevant in the present context: a distrust of supposed metalanguages and a consequent insistence that there are only strategies and interventions; an emphasis on historical contingency and the heterogeneity and multiplicity of the social field; and their anti-foundationalist, anti-essentialist stances. All follow Nietzsche in seeking to 'shatter the idols', so new possibilities can emerge, and in claiming 'the way does not exist.'[14]

Rorty

Because the world is known only within specific discourses, vocabularies and practices, Rorty maintains, there can be no question of ever having immediate access to things. What is known, what something is, always depends on what it is related to in particular contexts; and in different contexts things assume different identities and meanings. There are no intrinsic, non-relational properties.

By way of illustration of this proposition, consider once again the phenomenon of stardom. Contrary to the cliché that whatever the role, the star is always the same, stars, within a Rortian perspective, have no value in themselves: their valency varies from role to role, their identity is relational. For example, despite the enormous success of the series, none of the stars of *Friends* has been able to successfully translate to the context of a movie; George Clooney had many television roles before that of Doug Ross in *ER* propelled him to international stardom. Indeed, as the Hollywood money-men well know, no star, however bankable to date, guarantees a sure-fire hit for his or her next movie. Equally, extra-cinematic developments can alter perceptions of a star. Cultural change can quickly make a star look passé; a scandal can irreparably tarnish a star's image (for example, the divorce of Cruise and Kidman led many people to takes sides in the conflict to the detriment of the other party). Thus the identity of a star is never established once and for all. There is no Cruise or Kidman in themselves, only different figures in particular roles and contexts.

What can be said of stars applies equally to texts. They too have only relational properties: their meaning and identity varies according to the context. Within this perspective, Theory, at least in its non-dialectical variant, emerges as an instance of what Rorty terms metaphysics: the attempt to go behind appearances, in this case an evening's entertainment, to the underlying reality, namely the reproduction of the dominant ideology. Non-dialectical theory makes this move on the basis of an analysis of textual structure alone; but if there are no non-relational properties, if texts assume different identities in different contexts, then such metaphysical unmasking is impossible. Since texts do not determine the contexts of their reception, they can always be construed differently. Deprived of a final vocabulary and an ultimate context, the totalising ambition of Theory to describe the functioning of mainstream cinema is doomed.

In place of metaphysics Rorty urges a pragmatist strategy. If things are known only under the aspect of a particular description, then redescription is always possible. The task of theory becomes the provision of redescriptions better suited to particular interests and needs. Consider the following dilemma arising from Mulvey's use of a Freudian problematic. Mulvey assumes that woman is castrated and hence must be fetishised by masculinist cinema, with narrative as the attempt, through fetishisation, to evade the threat of castration inherent in the female body. Operating a telling example of the repression/containment model, she argues that narrative seeks to stage woman as spectacle but is always threatened by the disruption implicit in woman as the embodiment of castration. Hence women, most obviously in the films of Hitchcock, are alternately fetishised and attacked. Now on the one hand, this is far from convincing. If woman as such embodied the threat of castration, then all women would menace, which is self-evidently not the case. In Hollywood most women on screen (like most men), are treated largely with disregard, being presented as of minor importance or as a means of making the stars look good by comparison. As such they are neither threatening nor alluring; the absence of the penis as phallus is of no consequence. On the other hand, the pattern described by Mulvey is discernible in many Hollywood films in relation to female stars presented as objects of desire. After fetishising Alice in its opening sequence, *Eyes Wide Shut* may be seen as continuing with a succession of displaced attacks upon her – every surrogate woman encountered on Harford's quest comes to grief.

Faced with this dilemma, it is possible to redescribe the narratives analysed by Mulvey in a historicised and non-gender-specific variant on Lacanian psychoanalysis (although it is doubtful if Rorty himself would approve of this particular choice of vocabulary). Recall that for Lacan desire is always for an irreparably lost object. It is impossible to have it all: in *The Piano* Ada can have either the piano or Baines but not both. Desire never attains complete satisfaction; something is always missing. Consequently, when a subject demands that the other makes good his lack the other necessarily disappoints and, conversely, when the other addresses a similar demand to the subject, the subject disappoints the other.

In this perspective lack is on the side of the subject as much as the Other, and castration can be redescribed as this twofold experience of lack. If the consequence of the lack in the Other is that every subject is a desiring subject, then the subject in its dealings with other subjects encounters lack both without and within. It confronts the lack in the other subject when it discovers that the other is not the lost object of desire and it confronts its own lack when it discovers that it does not embody the other's object of desire. These twin discoveries, namely that it cannot meet the other's demands and the other cannot meet its demands, constitute 'castration'. For a heterosexual male, woman is castrated in that she lacks what would make good his own lack and she is castrating in that she brings home to him his inability to make good her lack. For example, in *Eyes Wide Shut* Harford discovers the lack in the Other when he discovers that Alice also desires and fantasises about another. Castration occurs not when he glimpses female genitalia (with which as husband and doctor he is presumably familiar), but when he discerns that his wife's desires go elsewhere (a repeated motif of the film and the posters is of Alice's looking off-screen beyond Harford and whatever he has to offer). As a result of this blow to his (somewhat excessive) narcissism, he perceives Alice as at once castrating (she has exposed his lack) and castrated (she is no longer the woman of his fantasy). Here lack is not some inherent deficiency peculiar to women (as in certain of Freud's formulations of castration), but a relational property ascribed to them by certain men. Women are seen as lacking only from the point of view of men making impossible demands upon them and are seen as 'castrating' only from the point of view of men who fear or discover they are unequal to the demands women may make of them. It is because his wife matters to him that her lack affects Harford, while that of, say, the woman down the hall, to whom he has never given a thought, does not.

This immediately raises the question of why, if both men and women are lacking, the lack in women is seen as the problem. The advantage of this form of redescription would be that the question as to why women have been stigmatised in this way can be answered in historico-political terms without reference to Freud's theory of anatomy-centred fantasy. Put simply, woman as lacking is a heterosexual male perspective in a world ordered by a historically specific asymmetry of power between the sexes. In patriarchal culture it is, generally speaking, men who are empowered to make demands and women who are assigned the impossible task of meeting them. As the recipients of impossible male demands, women are perceived by heterosexual men, and only by such men, as lacking.

Under such a redescription, rather than conceiving of female sexuality as disruptive in itself and resistant to containment within the narrative, what is figured as explosive is simply the discordance of desire in a culture ordered by historically specific forms of heterosexual male desire. Women are seen as a disruptive force by men who demand of them something that does not exist. When such a man makes his demand of a woman he discovers both that she does not possess what he desires and that her own desire is at variance with his own, the fact it goes elsewhere and aims at something other than what he can give. Ada's attachment to her piano does not seem to be a problem for her but only for the men who desire her desire. Again, in *film noir*, the femme fatale constitutes a problem for the man who desires her, not because of her sexuality per se, but because her desire is directed towards something other than himself, usually, given the conventions of this genre, the sum of money that drives the plot (e.g. *Double Indemnity* (Billy Wilder, 1944), *Body Heat* (Lawrence Kasdan, 1981), *Romeo is Bleeding* (Peter Medak, 1992) or *The Last Seduction* (John Dahl, 1993)).

If women are no more and no less intrinsically castrated than men, since men too are necessarily in receipt of impossible demands and inevitably must be found wanting, then a structure of disavowal should also operate in relation to men. And this is precisely what occurs. Within the never wholly latent fascism of classic Hollywood, where some human beings, usually played by stars, are deemed intrinsically superior to others, men can be situated on a spectrum running from the *Untermenschen* to the *Ubermenschen*. In the former category the lack gapes. Played by such male actors as Norman Wisdom, Woody Allen, Danny Kaye, Jerry Lewis, Bob Hope, Jack Lemmon and more recently by the likes of Hugh Grant and Ben Stiller, they are plainly lacking something – and for Hollywood, especially as figured in the romantic comedy genre, the supposition is that the lack will be made good by the idealised female who is the object of their desire. Indeed the degree of lack such male characters embody precisely correlates with the degree to which they need the woman. By contrast, the *Ubermenschen* characters typically played by the likes of John Wayne, Clint Eastwood, Sylvester Stallone and Arnold Schwarzenegger are defined by an improbable self-sufficiency and invulnerability. Here there is little if any sign of lack: they are complete without, and hence neither need nor desire, the woman.

Historically the primary demand placed upon men has been the demand by other men that they correspond to the current male definition of what a man should be. As men no more than women can embody an ideal, this is an impossible task. Anatomy alone does not provide the answer: even the most self-sufficient males seem to need something extra, a supplement, if they are to signify masculinity. This supplement can be a skill, an expertise, a form of knowledge, a form of prowess or a form of remarkable power, for example, high office. It can be over-developed muscles, a magic mask, the capacity to turn into a green hulk, an ability to dance, a way with maths problems, or knowing how to whisper to horses. Usually, however, it's a gun. As far as we know, nobody has ever calculated the proportion of men in classic Hollywood who carried a gun. Whatever it may be, it is certainly a much higher percentage than in the population at large. The gun is the classic indicator that a man is a 'real', that is, imaginary man. Thus contra Freud the male anatomy too seems to be lacking. Generally speaking, the invulnerable male hero is therefore concentrated in films addressed primarily to male audiences (thrillers, crime films, action movies, westerns, war films, etc.).

This redescription would have the further advantage of explaining another problem with Freud and with Mulvey's account of fetishistic disavowal, namely that fetishistic disavowal is not confined to the male fetishist's relation to the supposedly lacking female body. The formula 'I know perfectly well but...' is to be found in many other contexts. For example, many of Stacey's respondents were perfectly aware that their favourite stars did not really match up to their screen image. Similarly, the knowledge that Steve McQueen was a drunk who abused women does not necessarily (though it may well) detract from the appeal of his screen persona in *Bullitt* (Peter Yates, 1968), any more than that of Sinatra's unsavoury association with the mob prevents him from coming across as the attractive romantic of *Songs for Swinging Lovers*. Or more generally with cinema itself. Thus I know perfectly well that this is a film but nevertheless I find myself worried on behalf of the protagonist. Will Harford be unmasked? Will Stewart discover Ada's relationship with Baines?

If Nietzschean elements are implicit in Rorty, they are explicit in Foucault and Deleuze. Nietzsche is the philosopher of the notion that everything is created. For Nietzsche the world is an open-ended dynamic process, a field of forces in endless flux, out of which forms emerge and irreversible processes of individuation occur. Forces combine and collide to constitute organisations such as those which are the focus of Theory: texts, authors, spectators, meanings, subjectivities, sexualities, and so on. What a Nietzschean perspective brings to their interpretation is a twofold insistence: firstly, that each is the effect of differential power relations and secondly that, as such, none assumes a final form. As the play of forces continues everything is both open to and liable to change. Thus what counts in the exchange between spectator and film is less the textual structure than the forces in play – those constituting the spectator, those constituting the text and those produced by their encounter. In this perspective, contrary to non-dialectical Theory, no text has an intrinsic nature or essence, for depending on the forces at work texts can be taken in innumerable directions. Thus *Eyes Wide Shut* is not inherently misogynist and *The Piano* is not inherently feminist. Each can be read very differently, for example, as a transgressive exploration of the existing limits of sexual conduct. Different aspects of such a Nietzschean perspective are explored by Michel Foucault and Gilles Deleuze.

Foucault

In this section we ignore the greater part of Foucault's work (valuable though much of it is as a resource for proponents of Reading 2), and concentrate only on two of its more Nietzschean moments. In the earlier of these, he explicitly adopted the view that everything is produced, that everything is the effect of the interplay between forces. Foucault's term for these forces, whose interactions produce every determinate individual being, is power. Hence power is not what represses, but what produces, an ever-changing force field where the inequalities between conflicting forces generate texts, subjectivities, sexualities and the rest.

Language on this account does not exist in itself; instead specific forms of discourse emerge at particular historical moments. Such discourses are at once constituted – like everything else they are produced by the differential play of forces – and constituting, for they, in turn, act upon the force field. Produced by power relations, they then exercise power, most obviously through the constitution of objects. Hence the objects of knowledge are not pre-given, awaiting discovery, but are constituted within discourse. Power produces knowledge.

The purpose of critique is through genealogical analyses to trace the constitution of domains of objects within discourse in order to demonstrate that they are historically constituted and that reality could have been constituted otherwise. Seeking to explore what becomes possible with the transgression of existing limits, critique becomes a form of experiment. No longer does it proceed in the name of what already exists, but in the name of what could exist. While the commitment to emancipation continues, its aim is an as yet undefined form of freedom.

Sexuality is a pertinent example.[15] Far from being a pre-given desire that is discovered and/or repressed by discourse, it is constructed by the power relations immanent to particular discursive practices. The truths of sexuality supposedly uncovered by psychoanalysis and the like are rather constituted within discourse; not an essence waiting to be revealed, but existing only by virtue of historically specific forms created by historically specific discourses. From this perspective Mulvey's thesis is open to significant criticisms. By adopting Freudian notions she assumes castration is *the* truth of female sexuality. Hence her mobilisation of the repression hypothesis: when she writes of women's desire returning to trouble and disrupt the text she is claiming that female sexuality exists as a given prior to its repression. She thus accepts and perpetuates a particular regime of sexuality and thereby inhibits the exploration of other forms. If for Foucault the purpose of critique is to explore the limits the dominant discourses place upon our existence, then the charge against Mulvey would be that she stayed within existing limits, a heterosexist presumption foreclosing the exploration of other forms of sexuality.

Foucauldian genealogical analyses show that there is nothing natural or inevitable about existing forms of sexuality; desire and pleasure could have been thought otherwise. The business of critique is to explore the possibilities of transgressing existing, contingent limits, of passing beyond the limitations currently imposed on relationships and identities by a poverty-stricken culture in order to invent, to think, love and live differently. Such is the task addressed by Queer theory. Following Foucault, Queer theory argues that because there is no essential truth of human sexuality, it is not a matter of contesting existing sexual norms in the name of a pre-existent sexual identity or of liberating repressed or silenced sexualities. Rather in the name of sexual identities yet to be created it urges an ethic of exploration that mobilises the heterogeneity of forces present in every individual. On this basis *Eyes Wide Shut* could be read as the quest of a sexually ambiguous figure (Harford) for an as yet undefined form of sexual satisfaction.

The later phase of Foucault's Nietzschean thinking, in which he developed his notion of technologies of the self,[16] is of particular interest to Queer theory. As the self is not pre-given but rather a task to be accomplished, there is the possibility of creating it differently. The fluidity and mutability of ever-changing power relations permits practices of freedom. For example, an author, in creating, may engage in the kind of unpredictable metamorphosis that Foucault held to be the aim of his own work – a process of self-transformation rather than one of simply providing knowledge of the world. Similarly a spectator in encountering a text can experiment, making something new of it and thereby of herself. Reading as a mode of technology of the self can transform both text and spectator, promoting new forms of each. In the interests of becoming something other, Foucault urged an ethics of self-fashioning, of seizing the opportunity through self-restraint and self-regulation to develop new modalities of subjectivity and new forms of sexual relationship. Like Nietzsche, he argued for an aesthetics of existence: people should endeavour to become living works of art.

Such an approach provides yet another way of thinking about stars and their audiences. On the one hand the institution of stardom can be seen as an aspect of bio-politics, in which stars contribute to the reinforcement of the dominant discourse's codes of normality by being constrained by the system to remain within existing definitions of masculinity and femininity. Think, for example, of how few film stars (in contrast to musicians, say) have felt able to 'come out', and how even fewer have been able to engage in queer experimentation. Equally spectators can be seen as constituted by discourses around stars. In his work on the prison system Foucault described the Panopticon where the prisoners under constant surveillance internalise a set of norms and develop their own form of self-surveillance until they become self-disciplined docile bodies.[17] Some feminists have argued that women under patriarchy have similarly internalised fashionable ideals of feminine beauty and have instituted a similar mode of self-surveillance where they critically scrutinise their hair, make-up, figure, clothing, etc. in pursuit of an impossible perfection. Insofar as the glamour of female stars is complicit with these ideals, it functions as part of a system turning women into conformist, self-policing bodies.

On the other hand, in the light of Foucault's later work,[18] some (by no means all) stars could be viewed as instances not of media invention but of self-invention. They are products not (solely) of publicity and marketing but of pre-personal forces: far from replicating existing norms and definitions they have redefined what it is to be a man or a woman, having engaged in a work of freedom that turns them, at least intermittently, into works of art. Such stars transcend what is in the script or the PR handout; they are not merely written, they write. A distinction may be made here between actors (including PR-generated or the more self-effacing stars) and stars having this special quality. While bringing something distinctive to a role, actors – one thinks, for example, of De Niro or Hoffman – do not embody a style of being or a stance towards existence. By contrast, certain stars, e.g. James Dean or Madonna, have forged a new subjectivity, a new relation to self. Over and beyond the immediate role they speak of an art of living: there is a gap between the input to which they are subject and the outcome they produce. Or as Foucault would say, they have introduced an interval, a fold into the flow of experience. It is there in the restraint of a gesture which speaks of self-mastery or the quality of a smile whose affirmation is tinged by sadness and courage. Catherine Deneuve's or Charlotte Rampling's faces in their more recent work, or Gary Cooper's style and manner in his later westerns, reveal what they have made of their life.

On this Foucauldian account, stars who are unhappy with their star status and crave recognition for their acting abilities, often in unglamorous roles that demonstrate their 'range', fail to see that their greatest artistic achievement is the persona that they have created, however fugitively, beyond any scripted role. Although for many of Stacey's respondents their love of the stars was avowedly escapist, at best a compensatory strategy of resistance to the mundane monotony of their lives, for others it was an encouragement to engage themselves in self-fashioning and self-transformation. Many were evidently inspired by the star persona to try and live differently and more fully. Thus stars can contribute to the emergence of new modes of self-formation, new economies of bodies and pleasure.

Deleuze

Like Foucault, Deleuze was a philosopher not of things but of events. The world is a world of endless variation, an open-ended dynamic process of energies and forces, out of which organisations, forms and structures, among them individual human beings, are produced, and nothing is produced in a final form. We thus exist only as the outcome of becoming, inhabiting an acentric cosmos of unformed and unstructured flows where everything reacts on everything else.

Two features of these organisations are significant for what follows. Firstly, though emerging from the flux of energies, the organisations generated can turn against these energies; they can function actively or reactively. Secondly, organisations never fully capture the energies in play, never completely seal off the forces either inside or outside. No stabilisation or unification is permanent and the boundaries of any structure remain permeable. Territorialisation is always accompanied by a deterritorialisation which in turn gives rise to a reterritorialisation.

The task of theory is to explore what is possible in such an ever-changing world. Some of the implications of such a position in relation to the four recurrent themes of this retrospect – authorship, realism, spectatorship, and Mulvey's thesis – are signalled in what follows.

(1) Authorship. Deleuze's approach recasts the question of authorship. If the subject is constituted by and composed of the play of active and reactive forces, then an author is similarly the product of imperceptible, pre-individual forces. On this account the author is less constitutive than constituted in that he is the product of forces of which he is in large part unaware. His work is a symptom of the forces in play so the business of analysis is to diagnose the health or otherwise of the mode of existence his work implies. When we ask of an author, 'Who is speaking?', we are asking of his films what pre-personal forces find expression there. Are they active or reactive? Is life freed or imprisoned? For example, to the question as to what forces speak in Kubrick's texts, one might point to a certain fear, suspicion and hatred of life that frustrate all hopes of control.

(2) Realism. Similar questions arise in relation to realism. If reality is in a state of becoming it can never be completely captured in a text. Realist texts do not mirror reality, rather they act upon it. Instead of reflecting reality they produce a reality effect. The question is the same as that posed by Theory: Whose reality? But whereas Theory, in asking this question, was concerned to determine what ideologies were being articulated, a Deleuzian, for whom each person's world-view is a symptom of their mode of being, would be concerned to determine whether the forces are active or reactive. The question, 'Whose reality is this?' becomes, 'What type of person defines our condition in such terms?' For example, the question to ask of supposedly realist texts like *American Beauty* (Sam Mendes, 1999), *Happiness* (Todd Solondz, 1998), *Your Friends and Neighbours* (Neil Labute, 1998), *Amores Perros* (Alejandro González Iñárritu, 2000) or *L'Humanité* (Bruno Dumont, 1999) is who takes such a soured view of life? Who takes this to be the essence of our condition?

The question matters in that realist texts enjoy a particular authority. If we are convinced by the truth claims of a particular text, that inhibits further thought. Realist texts often operate according to a model of recognition; they seek to reduce the open-ended processes of the real to the already known. This reproduction of hegemonic, taken-for-granted, pre-determined conceptions of reality hampers our ability to think otherwise. Deleuze is fond of citing Godard's 'not a just image, just an image'.[19] For Deleuze this means that attempts to find and present the 'just image', 'the right image', in realist texts always end up reproducing already accepted notions of reality. At best they secure a recognition effect that indicates that they belong to the already known. Therefore we should abandon the search for the just image and produce images which are just images, thus calling in question existing regimes of representation. In place of representation, Deleuze advocates invention, for, in a cinema of experiment, there is the possibility of a break with the order of the same. Consequently his admiration for the work of Duras, Godard and Straub/Huillet rivals that of Theory.

(3) Spectatorship. What holds for authors similarly holds for spectators, who are equally constituted by pre-individual forces. Whom the spectator takes to be speaking in a text is an interpretation, an interpretation that is an outcome of the forces in play. Thus for Deleuze the encounter between spectator and text is an experiment, an exploration of possibilities. It is also a test that reveals something of the nature of the forces in play in both the text and the spectator.

While such a conception of the reading process may seem remote, it actually chimes with the way people tend to discuss films. To return to the post-seminar conversation posited earlier, each participant, in listening to the other, is engaged in assaying what of life he or she is expressing. For example, in speaking of stars and performances they like or dislike they are saying as much about the forces within themselves as of those perceived to be embodied on screen. On this account, in contrast to our Foucauldian rethinking of stardom as self-fashioning, a star is not given in him or herself. Rather an estimate or reading of a star, like the estimate or reading of a text, is a symptom of the spectator's mode of being. What Stacey's respondents made of the stars whom they admired said as much about the forces at work in them as about the forces in the stars. In some instances their connection to the screen was reactive, an identification enabling them to hide from life, but in other cases they opened themselves to the new, to become other, to become 'Katherine Hepburn', 'Bette Davis' or whoever. Indeed it is arguable that active forces triumph in every major star: unlike those broken or cowed by the burdens of existence, they affirm life (although this may not be visible to every spectator, since spectators get the stars, and indeed the texts, merited by their way of life).

Because neither text nor spectator possesses an essence, there are as many readings of a text as there are configurations of forces acting on it. Readings are temporary and provisional stabilisations that emerge from the interplay of forces, each the effect of a territorialisation which is accompanied by a deterritorialisation. Hence the structures of both texts and spectators are finally open; their 'identities' are never fixed. The encounter of spectator and text is always a unique event, in which each acts upon and transforms the other. Like Lyotard, Deleuze is a philosopher of singularities that can never be captured, territorialised, by any theoretical structure.

With this shift in focus from meaning to effect, the question becomes not what a text signifies but what it does. And the answer to this question is intrinsically open, since just as Deleuze, following Spinoza, claims we do not know what a body can do, i.e. how it can affect and be affected in future encounters, neither can we be certain what a text can do. Contrary to undialectical theory, with its claim to know the effectivity of texts, Deleuze argues that what a text may become is indeterminate and undecidable (if nonetheless open to discussion).

(4) Mulvey. Nowhere is the need to think otherwise more apparent than in matters sexual. If everything is produced, if structures of subjectivity are the effect of pre-personal forces, and if no structure is finally closed, then sexual identity is never fixed once and for all. Deleuze insists that the Freudian model of binary opposition, adopted by Mulvey, is a historically specific organisation and like every organisation it is not closed upon itself. Insofar as sexual identities exist they are the effect of a territorialisation that is constantly being undone by processes of deterritorialisation. There are not two sexes, there are a myriad, each in a state of becoming. Instead of accepting, as Mulvey does, the reactive form of binary sexual difference associated with Oedipalisation, we should explore what it would be to be sexually otherwise. What a body is or can do depends on what it is connected to. In *The Piano* Ada's connection to her instrument should not be reduced to a crude Freudian notion of a pre-Oedipal attachment, but rather is to be seen as an invention of a new form of sexuality, a 'becoming-piano'. For Deleuze, as for Foucault, critique is the exploration of the limits of existing conceptions and the

creation of new forms of thought, proceeding in the name not of actually existing subjects but of peoples yet to be invented. Theory is invention and experiment.

What would theory as experiment look like? Deleuze offers us a marvellous example in his two-volume work *Cinema 1: The Movement-Image* and *Cinema 2: The Time-Image*.[20]

As elsewhere Deleuze's thinking is informed by the model of self-organising processes emerging from the flux of unstructured flows. Here this model draws upon two theses of Bergson, both of which have strong affinities with the Nietzschean views outlined above. The first thesis is that time is invention. This combines the Nietzschean notion that time as becoming is a crucial component of ever-changing, open-ended cosmic processes with the further notion that out of this flux organisations emerge, that is there is a constant elaboration of the new. Time is part of an open-ended, ceaselessly changing process, termed the 'Open' by Bergson, out of which novelty arises. Original works of art provide the best example: breaking with pre-established forms, these appear unpredictably in ways that could not have been anticipated. Who could have foreseen the unique event that is *Beau Travail*?

The second thesis, deriving from Bergson's *Matter and Memory*,[21] is the apparently baffling claim that the universe is composed of images. Things, argues Bergson, are themselves images, because images are not in our brain, which is just one image among others. Although not an easy notion to grasp, in this context it amounts to little more than a restatement of the idea that we inhabit an acentred universe where each item is constantly acting on and reacting to every other item. Thus everything is an image insofar as it is at once receiver and transmitter, everything registers and is registered by everything else.

Here again the theme of self-organisation recurs. For among this flux of images, gaps emerge between actions and reactions. These intervals, termed 'living images' or 'centres of indetermination'[22] by Deleuze, which can for present purposes (if at the cost of considerable simplification) be called subjects, select what images they react to and how they themselves then act on other images. In other words a centre (or subject) regulates its relations with the forces acting upon it. On this account perception involves subtraction. Whereas an atom, for example, relates to all the forces at work in the universe and thus could be said to perceive the whole universe, the subject selects. The subject isolates certain images from among all the competing and interacting images, selecting only those that concern it. This is most apparent in sensori-motor situations. When we engage in such acts, for example when driving a car, we subtract from our reception all that does not interest us. Our responses become, in a measure, habitual and automatic. Hence we no longer encounter the full force of what Deleuze terms the Outside. As such we are not impelled to think differently.

Following this line of thought Deleuze distinguishes two modes of cinema. The first, the cinema of the movement-image, provides only an indirect image of time. Time is subordinated to movement in that time appears as the measure of movement. Time as invention and becoming is thereby occluded. The best example within the cinema of the movement-image is the cinema of the action-image, organised in terms of sensori-motor situations where the protagonist perceives a situation, has an emotional reaction to it and then responds by an action seeking to modify or adapt the original situation. Typically the protagonist, after confronting and sizing up a challenge, acts upon his emotional and psychological response and seeks to surmount the obstacle to his project. For example, in *Eyes Wide Shut*, Dr Harford is summoned by his friend to a young woman suffering from a drugs overdose, to whom he is able to provide emergency medical aid. That is, he reacts to the initial situation with an action that transforms it. And just as in extra-cinematic sensori-motor situations this pattern of reaction/action occludes time as becoming and invention, the powers of thought are in consequence inhibited. By implication the spectator is himself caught up in a sensori-motor situation and is not impelled to think differently. In such films the spectator is concerned above all with what will happen next, and time is experienced only in relation to the narrative.

This narrative organisation is sustained at the level of the organisation of the shots. As each shot constitutes a relatively closed set – recall that for Deleuze no structure can be wholly closed – it possesses a measure of unity and stability. This is threatened by the arrival of the subsequent shot and the introduction of difference. But as the new shot is immediately subordinated to the logic of the narrative, the threat of difference is immediately contained. The cut between the two shots becomes a rational link forging a further sequence of the unfolding narrative chain; the discontinuity is succeeded by a (provisional) continuity. Thus there is differentiation in that something new is always happening, but this differentiation is immediately succeeded by integration into the expanding organic whole of the narrative. The pattern is yet again that of deterritorialisation and reterritorialisation. Something happens – a woman overdoses – that disturbs an apparent equilibrium (deterritorialisation); Harford then saves her, restoring an apparent equilibrium (territorialisation). The new development, the crisis of the overdose, is integrated into a larger narrative. Similarly at the level of formal organisation something happens, a different shot appears, (deterritorialisation), only to be reterritorialised into the overall narrative structure.

It is only in the cinema of the time-image (Cinema 2) that there is a direct image of time. Here time as becoming impels us to think beyond habitual response. At first glance this is redolent of Theory, in that there is a distinction between the cinema of the movement-image (Cinema 1), where the spectator, caught up in sensori-motor situations, cannot think beyond their horizons and another form of cinema, that of the time-image (Cinema 2), exemplified by such figures from the *Screen* canon as Godard, Straub/Huillet, Duras or Syberberg which gives rise to new forms of thought. But Deleuze is not Theory come again. Indeed, in contrast to Theory, he explicitly denies privileging the avant-garde over the mainstream. The reason is simple. As always in Deleuze, emergent organisations never capture all the forces in play. Although in the indirect images of time, time is subordinated to the representation of movement, time as becoming necessarily overflows the structure, the organisation of the cinema of the movement image necessarily remains open. While the tendency of the cinema of the movement-image may be to integrate becoming in an organic whole, it never entirely succeeds. Any reterritorialisation is incomplete and is always accompanied by deterritorialisation. As ultimately the cinema of the movement-image opens on to a cosmos of universal variation beyond the sensori–motor situation, a Bergsonian Open that is neither given nor giveable, it does not stand condemned, for it can prompt spectators to think otherwise. And although the hold of the more clichéd forms of the cinema of the action-image may militate against this, even their grip is far from total. Nevertheless, Deleuze argues that the release of these powers of thought ultimately requires the abandonment of the bond between movement and image characteristic of the cinema of the movement-image and the creation of a cinema of the time-image.

In the cinema of the time-image sensori-motor situations no longer obtain. Typically the protagonist confronts situations where he is uncertain how to react. Whereas in the party scene from *Eyes Wide Shut* Harford takes in the situation at a glance and does what has to be done, later when confronted by Alice's admission of a desire for another man he is at a loss how to respond and act. Similarly in *Beau Travail* Galoup is at first uncertain how to react to his discharge from the legion. At these moments there is a crisis of the action-image, out of which something new may emerge. Perceiving the problems of the character, the spectator asks 'What is there to see in the image?' (instead of 'What are we going to see in the next image?'). No longer locked into a pattern of habitual responses, the spectator by implication has gained the ability to see something of what was lost in the pattern of action or reaction constitutive of the sensori-motor situation.

Deleuze's favoured example of the cinema of the time-image is the work of Godard. Rather than an organic narrative where there is a rational link between each shot, there is a serial form where the intervals are irrational and it is impossible to predict what the next shot will bring. Whereas the cinema of the movement-image seeks to determine what 'x' is, Godard explores what 'x' can become. Godard's cinema is one of 'this and then that', a cinema inquiring what happens when 'x' is brought together with 'y', when shots and other filmic elements are linked in new ways.

The end of *Beau Travail* offers another example of the cinema of the time-image. Exiled in his hotel room in Marseilles, Galoup contemplates suicide. There is then an irrational cut to Galoup on the dance-floor dancing to 'The Rhythm of the Night'. The status of this shot is unclear. Is it fantasy, memory or the rejection of suicide and a new beginning? What is certain is that it arrives as a surprise. It is unanticipated; it breaks with the cinema of the sensori-motor situation. It can be read as an encounter with the outside and more an affirmation of the possibilities such an encounter brings. It is an affirmation, a Yes! to the possibilities of existence. As such it is in the spirit of Deleuze's books on cinema.

The encounter with the outside confounds our ready-made schemas and impels us to think differently. This is the key to his project and the index of his distance from Theory. Unlike Theory Deleuze has no desire to arrive at the final truth about cinema. The cinema books, in their celebration of difference, are not an attempt at the creation of a new paradigm within which more detailed analyses can proceed; rather they are examples of experiment and invention. They are critique only insofar as critique is 'the active expression of an active mode of existence'.[23] Their message is, 'This is what I made of cinema. What can you make of it?'

Reading 4: the call of the impossible

Thinking in this vein assumes many disparate forms but common to all of them is the notion that we are always already in the world and that the world sets us impossible tasks. Like the previous approach it would stress the need for invention but, in contrast to it, this would be invention in response to demands which are ultimately impossible to meet. In what follows we shall address just one aspect of this line of thinking, namely the fact that being in the world is being with others. The wager would be that, for at least some spectators from the more comfortable strata of western society, what matters above all are the impossibilities attendant on our relations with others, and that the institution of cinema is first and foremost a site of their negotiation.

Levinas

Paradoxically, although Levinas distances himself from Heidegger, the simplest approach to Levinas's thinking is through Heidegger. For Heidegger, Dasein (approximately, the human subject) finds itself always already in the world. Hence questions about whether or not the world exists are pseudo-problems, and the philosophical scandal is not that we have failed to prove the existence of the external world but that the question should ever have been raised in the first place. Similarly for Levinas, the subject is always already under an infinite ethical obligation to the other; obligation befalls it. Again the philosophical scandal is not that we have failed to locate the grounds of this obligation, failed, for example to derive an ought from an is, but that philosophy has sought such grounds when we are necessarily and inherently obligated. Evidently the emphasis here is different: where for Heidegger being in the world is being with others, for Levinas it is being for the other. This relationship to the other is so problematic that Levinas terms it a non-relation, in that the subject finds itself infinitely indebted to that which is primordially unknowable.

A first approach to understanding Levinas's thinking would be through his Jewish background. Although he insisted on distinguishing his theological from his philosophical work, the echoes are unmistakable: just as in Judaism the believer is confronted with an unknowable God, so for Levinas the subject is confronted with an enigmatic other in every encounter. And, just as in Judaism the believer has an infinite obligation to God, so each person is infinitely obligated, indebted, to every other person. Again, just as the relationship of a believer to God is asymmetric and non-reversible – there can be no reciprocity with a transcendental God – so too is the relationship of the subject to the other. Unable to redeem its debt of obligation, the subject is forever hostage to the other. Since the relationship to the other is the condition of all that appears and anterior to all representation it cannot itself appear or be represented. Eluding thematisation or theorisation, the other is, as the title of one Levinas's key works has it, 'otherwise than being'. The other resists subordination to the limits of conceptual understanding.

While Levinas did not write specifically on film, his work could have profound implications for thinking about cinema. Firstly, it suggests an ethics of cinema, an undeniable responsibility on the part of writers on cinema. What is not and can never be clear is the nature of this obligation, in that the ethical demands of the other are not determinable – to do justice to the other is not necessarily to do what the other consciously wills. Confronted by various others making conflicting demands upon him, to whom is the theorist to respond? Is his obligation to the author, to spectators, or to his immediate readership?

Secondly, in recognising that film-goers may seek to evade these ethical demands Levinas's work suggests a pathology of cinema, whose analysis would require at once the rehabilitation and rethinking of the notion of the cinematic institution. In Theory's conception of that institution the subject is first of all the subject of the enunciation, the subject whose mode of subjectivity determines the meaning and political valency of the text. It operated to so constitute the subject that he saw the world in a particular ideological light. For Levinas on the other hand the subject is spoken to before he speaks to the other; rather than the subject of the enunciation he is the addressee (of an impossible enigmatic demand), and as such he is seen rather than seeing. However, cinema offers the illusion of turning the tables on the other, enabling the spectator to imagine he sees without being seen. As Metz demonstrated, at the cinema the spectator can imagine himself transcendent (the very reverse of the Levinasian position that it is the other who occupies the transcendent position). Thus the cinematic spectator can imagine he has eluded the irreversible, asymmetric relationship with the other, has circumvented the uncircumventable alterity of the other. Hence on this account cinema is used by spectators to escape not from themselves but from the other; they take refuge in the cinema not temporarily to escape mundane day-to-day existence but to evade the demands of the other.

Such an approach has implications for rethinking stardom. We have already called attention to the faces of stars, an emphasis which takes on new force through Levinas's conception of the 'face' of the other.[24] In an at first sight confusing use of language, the term is used to designate, not a visible phenomenon, but the invisible and non-phenomenal nature of the other. Like the face of God it is hidden; above me, not in front of me. For Levinas, because it resists appropriation, the face interrupts the circuits of narcissism. Contrast this with what can happen at the cinema, where the faces of the stars appear in all their lustre and the spectator can appropriate them either through identification or by annexing them to fantasy scenarios of desire. The other is no longer what interrupts the subject's narcissism but what subtends it. The subject is both the fantasy figure on the screen and the apparently transcendent spectator of the scene, able to imagine that the other is transparent to one's gaze. Through publicity material – tabloids, celebrity magazines, talk shows, film posters – the faces of the stars are fetishised in order to mask and evade the alterity of the other. Within this perspective the structure of spectatorship set out by Mulvey becomes one instance among many of the spectator's appropriation of the other for his own purposes – like Harford who wants the Alice of his fantasies, not Alice in her alterity.

Of course, cinema does not of necessity function like this. It is perfectly possible for the spectator not to employ a film as a means of evading ethical responsibilities but instead to heed the call of the other. Levinas talks of modernist works where the impossibility of saying it all becomes apparent[25] and in that moment the reader appreciates that the other is intractably enigmatic, that he can never know who is speaking. Insofar as the reader realises that something of the author resists appropriation by his ready-made schemas of comprehension, he becomes aware of the infinity of the other and his ethical debt to her. Indeed, much of the intercultural cinema analysed by Laura Marks (cited above) could be redescribed in just these terms: in it, the imaginary of the spectator is ruptured.

On this basis, in a manner redolent of Theory, two forms of cinema could be distinguished. In the first the spectator may, while surrendering to the spell-binding, mesmerising quality of the images and allowing himself to be carried along by the flow, imagine himself safely in occupation of a self-sufficient, transcendent position. In the second form, on the other hand, he escapes the mirror-play of the fetishising images and confronts the trace of the other. Levinas himself gives an example of such an image: that of a dying Columbian girl buried up to her neck in mud after an avalanche in 1986. Although some viewers might respond voyeuristically, he claims that at least some might register the face behind the image crying out in its helpless, hopeless destitution.[26]

Derrida

Although there are good grounds for including Derrida in Reading 3, since many of his texts, particularly the earlier ones, have marked affinities with Nietzschean postmodernist thinking, we have placed him here because of his increasing self-alignment with Levinas. Before coming to this aspect of Derrida's thought, we must however first consider his writings on identity and meaning.

If identity exists, what are its conditions of possibility? How, for example, is it possible for us to speak of 'this film' or 'that director'? As a first approach, Derrida's answer is that 'here' is 'here' because it is not 'there'. 'This film' is 'this film' because it is not 'that film'. Thus identity depends on what Derrida terms 'différance', a neologism designating a process of differentiation that is at once spatial and temporal. But if différance is the condition of identity's possibility it is also the condition of its impossibility. Put at its simplest, if identity depends on what is other, then identity is divided. Since identity is always inscribed within 'a mobile system of relations',[27] it is never finally established and self-identity therefore is impossible.

What is true of identity is equally true of meaning. Meaning like identity depends on difference. No signifier has a meaning in itself; rather its meaning depends on its relationship to and difference from other signifiers, and that relationship is unstable. Context is again crucial: if a sign is to signify, it must be intelligible i.e. recognisable.

And if it is recognisable it must be repeatable; there can be no identity without the possibility of repetition. Signs and texts are iterable; they can be cited in or grafted on to different contexts. But iteration alters. In a different context, – and every context is different – the identity and meaning of the text will be in some measure transformed. Proper names provide a useful example. At first sight it might seem that a proper name, say 'Tom Cruise', always has the same meaning irrespective of context; but in fact it is always different. Thus Tom Cruise has a different meaning for those who have seen more of his oeuvre than the present authors. It has a different meaning for those who identify him by differentiating him from Charlie Sheen, Rob Lowe and Nicholas Cage than those who differentiate him from Humphrey Bogart, James Stewart and John Wayne. It almost certainly has a very different meaning for Nicole Kidman than for Penelope Cruz.

In stressing context and contingency by arguing that texts assume different meanings and identities in different contexts, Derrida is close to Rorty. On the other hand the implications of the absence of self-identity explored by Derrida move in a different direction from Rorty. Two are relevant for a reading of Theory.

(1) If identity is given by the other and no text is self-identical, then meaning is unstable. With signifiers constantly entering into new relations with other signifiers, their identities are in flux and chaos threatens. For meaning to emerge a measure of stability must be introduced. Some force or forces beyond the flow of signifiers must fix, at least temporarily, the relationship between the signifiers, something other than the text must stabilise it for meaning to emerge. Contrary to the impression given by Derrida's most famous dictum, 'there is nothing outside the text',[28] something outside the text has to operate for meaning to be produced. At its simplest this is the spectator. Since texts do not contextualise themselves, any text calls for a decision on the part of the spectator as to which context to read it through and within.

All of which puts Derrida at odds with Theory. For Theory, such decisions are occasioned by avant-garde texts but are foreclosed by the operation of mainstream cinema. Theory would accept that the production of meaning requires a stabilisation, indeed it would claim to be an account of those very mechanisms of stabilisation, but it would argue, contra Derrida, that in mainstream cinema stabilisation occurs in forms other than a decision. Identification is the principal

mechanism of stabilisation and identification is involuntary. For
Theory in its non-dialectical mode the textual structure is such as to
invite a form of identification. If identification – typically with a star
– occurs, then certain meanings emerge. For Theory in its dialectical
mode the process of stabilisation is more complex in that text and
subject are co-constituting but again meaning happens rather than is
decided. On both accounts meaning befalls the spectator.

Both modes of Theory are concerned to emphasise how textual
form matters. Texts are structured in a particular way, focussing on
this rather than that, imparting information in a particular sequence.
In *Eyes Wide Shut* it matters that there is a measure of uncertainty as
to what has happened. In *Beau Travail* it matters that past and
present are intercut in relations which are not wholly determinate.
We have all had the experience of being carried along by a film even
though we find it implausible and are at odds with its politics.
Brecht's response to *Gunga Din*[29] would be one instance of this; and
Edward Said gives a similar example, recalling as a boy how he
watched colonialist adventure films and sided with the white hero
against the native population.[30] Of course the text may not 'take',
but if it does the spectator's subjectivity is reconstituted.

Although theorists following Derrida would contest the determinism implicit in such subject positioning, they would agree that
Theory was not entirely wrong and that texts do, to some extent,
programme their own reading. Textual structure cannot be discoun-
ted, and it does impose an inherent bias towards a particular reading
and a corresponding affective response (a degree of puzzlement,
perhaps, as to what actually took place during and after the masked
orgy sequence in *Eyes Wide Shut* or a certain exhilaration tinged by
anxiety when reflecting on the questions of choice and contingency
raised by *Beau Travail*). Moreover, the cultural context also exercises a programming force. This much conceded, they would nonetheless maintain that textual structures are never so closed upon
themselves as to preclude contingent readings. Programming is
never complete; there is always a gap. The institution of cinema does
not exist. There are only institutions – every reading is an institution
– and they are established by the decisions of spectators, decisions
that are ultimately ethico-political. Now for a decision to be a decision
there must be uncertainty and undecidability – if the outcome were
clear-cut it would not be a decision, merely the application of a rule
or formula. A decision calls for invention or it is no decision. If no

more than the implementation of an existing programme it would never give rise to anything new, and texts would be denied their chance. This brings us to the second point.

(2) It is this possibility of something new emerging through reading texts differently that Derrida wishes to affirm and safeguard. Deconstruction is opposed to sedimented interpretations and dedicated to the dissolution of the institutions which harbour them – hence Derrida's uneasiness about any programmed readings which find in a text only what they seek to find there and reduce the alterity of the text to the order of the same. Psychoanalysis is the obvious target here. For Derrida, psychoanalytic readings are instances of logocentrism, in that they assume that texts are the expression of meanings given prior to the text; they consequently 'discover' only what they imagine is already there. More precisely such analyses are phallogocentric: whatever the text, it always turns out to be about the phallus and the woman as lacking. Although psychoanalysis stresses the singularity of the analysand and the need to approach him or her in a unique fashion, in applied psychoanalysis the singularity of each text is reduced to the familiar repertoire of motifs. As such they foreclose other possibilities, all the more so in that logocentric and phallogocentric readings often claim to be exhaustive – an enclosure of texts within particular institutions of reading.

In this perspective Derrideans would be critical of Mulvey insofar as she remains within a Freudian problematic. As we have seen, the problem for many feminists was that however persuasive her account of male spectatorship she left the nature of female spectatorship unclear. As a result there was much subsequent discussion of the position or the place of the female spectator. A Derridean contribution to this debate would not advance a 'solution' in the form of a new concept of woman or a specification of her place as, for example, spectator. On the contrary, it would resist any such closure. While plainly believing that castration is not the truth of woman, Derrida does not counter with an alternative, preferring instead to keep the question open. Because the signifier 'woman', like any other signifier, is not self-identical, any meaning attributable to it can be reinterpreted, any determination respecified. Therefore instead of suggesting what the place of woman and, by implication, that of the female spectator is, he questions whether such a place exists. By asking 'Why must there be a place for woman? And why only one, a single, completely essentialist place?',[31] he keeps open as yet unknown future possibilities for women beyond consignment once and for all to existing categories. He thereby seeks to do justice not only to existing women but to those to come.

It will be immediately and rightly objected that politics demands determinations – the condition, for example, of Mulvey's intervention – and Derrida would wholeheartedly agree. He would only argue that the notion of woman and her place could have been determined differently. While strategically intervening in the present, it is vital simultaneously to keep the situation open for the emergence of something new. As identity is never finally achieved, it is possible to become sexually otherwise.[32] Instead of the sexual binaries posited by psychoanalysis we should think of the possibility of non-binarised 'sexual differences in the plural',[33] of a 'sexuality without number'.[34]

Consider the implications of such an approach for the Freudian notion of fetishism. On the one hand, fetishism, functioning as a means for men of assuaging their hermeneutic anxiety before the alterity of women, obviously stands condemned insofar as it suggests that the fetish/veil conceals the truth of woman, namely castration. Thus conceived, it inhibits the invention of other ways of thinking and forecloses other possibilities. On the other hand, insofar as fetishism oscillates between positions – woman is and is not castrated – it hints at an acknowledgement that there can be no final determination of the truth of woman. Thus, while hardly the best starting point, even fetishism indicates the existence of a space for the invention of the other: the possibility for both men and women of becoming sexual otherwise. In place of a single inherent sexual difference between men and woman Derrida's dream is of 'irreducible particularities unheard of and incalculable sexual differences' in which 'there would be no more sexes' but rather 'there would be one sex for each time'.[35] Indeed, rather like the ontological argument for the existence of God, the very fact of this dream of innumerable sexualities points to its reality, a desire for that whose substance is nothing other than desire. 'But where would the 'dream' of the innumerable come from, if it is indeed a dream? Does the dream itself not prove that what is dreamt of must be there in order for it to provide the dream?'[36]

(3) Identity. While accepting that the notion of the subject may be indispensable in certain contexts, Derrida is reluctant to use the term in that it implies the existence of a being who is self-present and

self-collected. Since each of us depends on language for our identity, we can never be self-identical. And that is our chance. Just as the meaning of a text is not fixed once and for all, so too the identity of human beings is never established once and for all: in a different context it can become different.

Once again Stacey's respondents instantiate this idea. Frequently they would model their style of dress on their favourite stars, for example, choosing a hat like Rita Hayworth's or Doris Day's. Seeking to repeat the stylishness of their idol in their own situation they were citing a signifier – the hat – in another context. But iteration alters: in the new context the meaning of the hat changed, as, arguably, so too did the identity of its wearer. Each transformed the other. Because Stacey's respondents never coincided with their ideal, there was always a gap between them and the stars they admired, a gap that afforded a space for transmutation and invention. In the difference between themselves and the images on the screen, in the endless deferral of desire, there was the opportunity to create something new.

Read in these terms Derrida appears as a Nietzschean philosopher of the play of the signifier, who thinks of textual readings as stabilisations within an ever-changing force field and whose concern is to explore the possibilities opened up by the inherent instability of identity and meaning – in short, a postmodernist.

While certain of Derrida's texts support this reading, it is doubtful if Derrida himself would approve, in that he is no voluntarist. He rarely uses the term freedom; instead, following Levinas, he prefers to emphasise responsibility. Far from being an advocate of readers and spectators exploiting the free play of the signifiers to decide what to make of the text, in his later work, he insists, like Levinas, that we are always already infinitely indebted to the other. Any decision we make relating to a text must start from this irreducible given.

Our relationship to the other can be summed up in a single word: justice. In Reading 3 we encountered Deleuze's citation of Godard's 'not a true image, just an image' in support of his argument that if we try to present a true image we will inevitably present one which conforms to pre-established meanings when what we should do is experiment, creating images which confound rather than confirm accepted notions of truth and reality. In a sense Derrida would subscribe to this way of thinking. He is similarly opposed to ready-made answers. But at the same time he would insist that since the relation to the other entails a demand for justice that we are consequently obligated by our (non-)relation to the other to undertake the task of rendering the other his or her true image. Although this task may be impossible, the obligation nonetheless remains.

Famously in 'Violence and Metaphysics'[37] Derrida, while accepting that the other in its irreducible alterity defies comprehension, criticised Levinas's condemnation of attempts at comprehension as acts of violent appropriation. Derrida pointed out that in order to have any kind of relationship with the other, there has to be an attempt at comprehension; the imperative to understand is as inescapable as the concomitant violence. Obviously this is not to condone violent appropriation; Derrida's work is not a licence to fetishise. Rather it confronts us with an aporia: we must at one and the same time respect the alterity of the other and relate to the other even if that relationship necessarily entails violent appropriation. As always for Derrida, such aporias exist as a call to invent. Derrida's hope is that in confronting the contradictory imperatives we will create a happier form of relationship. If our relationship to others is always 'cannibalistic', if it always involves appropriation, then we must learn to 'eat well',[38] that is, we must find less violent forms of appropriation. If, as Mulvey suggests, many men relate to women only through an act of appropriation, the challenge for such men is to find a mode of engagement that respects women in their alterity. In negotiating this impossibility, the hope is that they will invent a less instrumental form of relationship.

Lacan

The conjunction of Lacan with Levinas and Derrida may seem odd. After all, Levinas mistrusted psychoanalysis, suspecting it was little better than a form of pornography, and Derrida's condemnation of Lacan's phallogocentrism damaged Lacan's standing more than any other criticism. But there are profound affinities. All three are concerned with the experience of impossibility that is our uncircumventable relationship to the other. Although they conceive of this experience very differently, each insists that a radically enigmatic other's exacting demands set us tasks that are as impossible as they are ineluctable. Two moments in Lacan's thinking are pertinent for the theorising of cinema as a response to the call to impossible tasks.

The intersubjective Lacan

Theory was, first and foremost, a theory of ideological misrecognition. As indicated in the Introduction, a theory of misrecognition already existed in Lacan's notion that the subject in the mirror stage is constituted by an identification with an idealised image. When, in less apparently ideological times, Theory's concern to elaborate an analogous account of the cinematic spectator as similarly constituted within a structure of misrecognition came to be seen as misplaced, the concept of misrecognition was largely abandoned and with it all interest in the mirror stage. But this is to ignore resources made available by the concept. The impossibility of the subject coinciding with its self-image, the fact that there is always a gap, opens up perspectives on a number of issues. Three can serve as examples.

(1) The gap between the subject and the idealised image opens a space for the subject's transformation. If the subject does not coincide with the specular image, if, to use the philosopher Philippe Lacoue-Labarthe's term, the subject 'desists',[39] then its identity is never fixed. Such mutability of the subject is of course the founding premise and ultimate purpose of psychoanalysis. Subjects can and do change in analysis. Equally it is uncontentious that subjects are transformed through other means too – for example, by encounters with other subjects and with structures and organisations like works of art, among them films. In this perspective, rather than being locked into prisons of misrecognition, film spectators are freed to become otherwise. Cinema is not necessarily an ideological trap; it can be the springing of the trap.

(2) The non-coincidence of subject and idealised image offers a possible explanation for the aggression often associated with the institution of stardom, in that aggression is the corollary of narcissism. The child, in a bid to escape its sense of helplessness, identifies with the ideal figure it assumes will command the mother's love. It thereby obtains a sense of security but only at the price of a concomitant sense of persecution, for in attempting to coincide with the ideal it faces an impossible task. In consequence the child oscillates between elation when it imagines it does coincide with the ideal and depression when it becomes aware of its failure to match up to the ideal. One outcome of this situation, as Lacan's early case studies illustrate, is aggression directed against figures presumed to embody the ideal and with whom the subject has identified.

One of the most striking features of stardom is that the initial phase of idealisation is invariably followed by attacks on the star's persona. As stars so often complain, they are built up only to be knocked down. One moment they are the most perfect of beings, the next they are being savaged by tabloids magnifying their every flaw, weakness, lapse and indiscretion, raking up their past misdeeds and exposing current scandals. Adulation turns to vilification and resentment. Although no evidence is cited in her text, it would be surprising if many of Stacey's respondents, after the exhilaration of identifying with a star, were not at other times unhappily aware of the gap between themselves and their ideal. For Lacan as for Deleuze the response to this gap would be symptomatic of the spectator's mode of being: for some it would the occasion for disabling despair, for others the opportunity for creative invention.

(3) The apparent disappearance of the gap between subject and the ideal can explain the power of certain cinematic moments. Typically when the child looks in the mirror and says 'That's me', the (m)other assents. Part of the jubilation the infant experiences derives from that validation. Similar moments occur in analysis. There is a well-known analytic phenomenon in which the analysand imagines he has discovered a magic phrase which finally and fully makes sense of his identity, desire and situation and resolves all outstanding issues. Clear as to who he is and what he wants, the jubilant analysand hurries to impart the important news to his confidantes, only to find them curiously unimpressed by the supposed profundity of the phrase. To them it is neither new nor profound; they can't see why their friend is so excited, for there is nothing in it he has not discussed before. But more puzzling still for the analysand is the fact that in a day or two the phrase's significance drains away and he is left wondering what he ever saw in it. A Lacanian explanation of this phenomenon would be that, as Theory rightly perceived, the meaning of the phrase did not reside in some putative intrinsic meaning but in the relationship between the signifiers and the subject. That is, it depended on the context of the analysis and more precisely on the identifications in play at a particular moment. The impact of the phrase was a function of who, at that moment, the analysand took himself to be and who he imagined the analyst was.

The interest of this phenomenon is that something similar can occur in cinema, especially art cinema. There too the spectator can experience moments when she feels both that she has understood the essence of things and that she has been validated. For example, at the end of *The Piano* it could appear that the human condition has been summed up: despite the ordeals (the assaults by Stewart) and irreparable losses (the finger and the piano), satisfactions are still available (marriage and playing her new piano with her prosthetic finger), albeit that these satisfactions are haunted by the spectre of something far richer (that might have been).

The parallels with the analytic example extend further, for just as the all-encompassing phrase comes to seem a banality so too does the conclusion of the film come to seem no answer at all. Equally evanescent, the meaning produced was the effect of the identifications in play: who the spectator took the auteur to be and who he took himself to be. Typically the spectator of the art movie, reading the text as realistic and truthful, at once identifies with an idealised image of the auteur as a figure of uncompromising authenticity and imagines that insofar as he concurs in the director's vision he is validated by the auteur. The imaginarised auteur in all his supposed authenticity and integrity is at once the spectator's ideal and the other as guarantor, the object of the spectator's identification and the validation of that identification. Thus the force of what is said depends not on the text alone but on the relationships to others cinema makes possible. The institution of cinema allows a distribution of identifications enabling the spectator to imagine he has overcome the impossibility of coinciding with his idealised image.

The intrasubjective Lacan

In this phase of Lacan's thinking the fundamental axiom is the proposition that the Other of language is lacking. The crucial signifier, which would express the subject's identity, is missing. Lacan's exploration of the implications of this thesis provides resources for thinking about cinema and, in particular, stardom at every turn. Here we shall consider only the most salient.

The lack in the Other has two effects on the subject: alienation and separation.

(1) Alienation. The subject is constituted by an interpellation; he is summoned to assume an identity assigned by the Other. As the signifier to express the subject does not exist the subject has to identify with a signifier with which he will never coincide. Without the assumption of this identity the subject cannot function, for there is no subject other than the subject of the signifier; nevertheless, it

gives rise to a sense of alienation. In *The Piano* Ada is mute, for any speech would be an act of self-betrayal, and much of her attraction for the spectator is that she has no truck with compromised contaminated speech. The subject's division, at once included in and excluded from the signifying chain, is dramatised in *Beau Travail* where Galoup is at home neither in the Legion nor in Marseilles after his discharge – as he himself remarks, he is fitted for neither military nor civilian life. Although he experiences Marseilles as a state of exile, the film makes clear that he never really belonged in the Legion, and his sense of it as his true home is a retroactive construct.

Paradoxically, while there is no self prior to the identification with the signifier, the subject feels that a true self has been betrayed. The dream of an authentic self is, of course, one of the attractions of certain stars. They seem to possess the missing integrity; to retain their authenticity whatever the role. Self-collected, each seems the master of his or her identity, each seems his or her own person. Notice the contrast with politicians (at least those who are answerable to their electorates). In interview situations, though they too can appear self-collected they fail to be points of identification because they are so obviously trying to be what the other wants. They do not seem to be the masters of their identity; they lack integrity.

But there is more to it than that. As we have seen, the infant faced by its condition of helplessness and dependence takes refuge in a narcissistic identification with a fictive ideal. This pattern is repeated in later life. Confronted by the vicissitudes of existence the subject finds solace in narcissistic misrecognition, in the notion of a 'real me' different from the interpellated roles he plays so badly. It is most obvious in the analytic situation where the patient, after outlining his senseless, shaming, neurotic anxieties, demands that the analyst return him to his 'true self', a carefree, fun-loving being untroubled by the slightest worry. However, this tendency to believe in a true self that is more than society takes the subject to be is apparent elsewhere. Think of the student who is academically not very successful but who imagines that in reality he is an unacknowledged genius; or the young woman who is far from conventionally attractive but who imagines that she is really rather beautiful, and certainly better looking than her passport photograph suggests. Beliefs such as these are sustained by the star system, for as well as physical beauty stars seem to possess an inner self to match. Richard Dyer writes of stars as possessing charisma, a term he defines as 'a certain quality of an individual personality by virtue of which he is set apart from ordinary men and treated as if endowed with supernatural, super-human or at least superficially exceptional qualities.'[40] Whatever the role or circumstances, they possess an aura reflecting a hidden treasure, what Lacan termed the agalma – which is precisely what accounts for their lustre. This true self, the impression that there is more to stars than could ever be captured in words or pictures, does not precede their performance; it is a retroactive construct, but for their fans it appears to be their intrinsic nature.

(2) Separation. The second effect of the lack in the Other is separation. In entering the social order, in accepting an identity which is not her own, the subject is separated from something of life, something of being, and becomes 'a want to be' (*manque à être*). Thus after Ada is forced to leave her piano on the beach by the representative of the symbolic order, her husband, she seeks to retrieve it and the life to which it gave access. And later when she settles down to domesticity with Baines, without her original piano, there is a sense that something of her being is missing; she is haunted by a lost *jouissance*. Similarly at the end of *Eyes Wide Shut* when Bill and Alice are reconstituted as a couple, it is evident that something of life is absent: her suggestion that they 'fuck' offers little hope that this will make good their sense of loss.

Lacan terms what is lost 'the object a' (*l'objet a*), two features of which are relevant here. Firstly, although the object a impels the metonymic movement of desire, it cannot be put into words; there is an impossible to say. Secondly, although lost, it never existed. Like the true self experienced as lost in alienation, the object a is a retro-active construct (exemplified by the retroactive construction by Galoup in exile of the Legion as a lost paradise). Thus the subject is set two impossible tasks: to say what cannot be said and to find an object which cannot be found. To be human is to be subjected to unfulfillable imperatives. Not only is Harford unable to say what it is he is looking for in his nocturnal quest, but it is equally apparent that it will elude him.

Even if irremediably lost the object a nevertheless continues to function as the cause of desire. Rather than accepting its absence, the subject imagines it exists elsewhere, the supposed incarnation of absolute *jouissance*. Herein lies another of the investments in stars, for if they can know such *jouissance* then despite the evidence to the contrary the object a can be imagined to exist. This accounts for the form of the countless stories devoted to stars in magazines like *Hello*, which typically stress two apparently contradictory features. First their happiness: whatever their past troubles (drugs, health problems, marital break-ups, etc.) the star is now happy again or well on the way to attaining that state. Secondly their ordinariness: although remarkable (accomplished, beautiful, successful, etc.) the stars have surprisingly similar concerns, tastes, foibles and so on to those of the readership. The star, as presented, is at once ordinary (like us) and extraordinary (he or she has access to a *jouissance* we can only fantasise about). Thus the message of *Hello* takes the form of a syllogism: stars are in many respects very similar to you; stars can be perfectly happy; therefore you could be perfectly happy.

Thus in both cases – alienation and separation – stars function to sustain the belief that the Other is not lacking and as such offer what Slavoj Žižek terms 'a support in the Other'.[41]

The impossibility of the sexual relation

This desire to believe in the existence of the object a is most evident in sexual relationships. Given the innumerable forms of sexual relationship, it is nice to imagine that somewhere among all of them there exists one that will constitute a perfect union, a closure to desire as consummate as any Hollywood romantic ending. But the reality is otherwise, for each partner seeks in the other not the other as such but the object a, the irreparably lost and ever elusive object of desire. Whatever the relationship, whether homosexual or heterosexual, each demands of the other what the other cannot provide, and each brings to the other, not what the other lacks, but lack itself. The desires of the participants are discordant not complementary. Hence Lacan's epigram: loving is giving what one does not have. In *Eyes Wide Shut* it is no accident that Harford is saved from the consequences of his pursuing his desires to the end only by the sacrifice of a woman: Mandy has to die that he may live. In that sense Mandy could be read as everywoman, a possibility that is supported by the fact she is played by two different actors.

Rather than accept the impossibility of the sexual relation, there is a tendency to cling to the belief not only that the object a exists but that it is incarnated in a potential sexual partner. Both men and women seek the ideal being who is their lost complement. Heterosexual men seek 'the Woman' i.e. the woman who will make good their lack, while heterosexual women, for their part, aim at a spectral man beyond their flesh and blood partner. But nobody coincides with either ideal; such a being does not exist. To avoid confronting this truth men and women fantasise, appropriating the other to their fantasies – indeed ultimately every fantasy is the fantasy that the sexual relation exists. Fetishism in this perspective is just such an appropriation of the other: heterosexual men do so by privileging part of the female anatomy or a displacement from it (clothing or shoes, for example), heterosexual women by attributing to their choice of male an unwarranted aura.

In the absence of a sexual relation subjects must seek to foster misrecognitions in the other. Each partner must play along with the other's fantasy and appear to embody the other's object of desire; each must pretend to be something he or she is not. Men, as indicated in the section inspired by Rorty, must engage in the comedy of virility, and pretend to have 'that something extra'. Women must engage in the feminine masquerade, enter their chosen male's fantasy frame and pretend to embody his supposed object a. In practice, as the illusions evanesce, this procedure is rarely successful for long. While we might prefer to forget the real as impossible, it does not forget us. At some point the alterity of the Other has its say.

In response to the absence of the sexual relation, cinema can function as a site of evasion, both at the level of fantasies within particular narratives and at the level of the institution. The spectator can escape the impasse of desire by fantasising that the object a is embodied in this or that star. Similarly narratives can supply an alibi, most obviously through the romantic ending where the couple finally get together after overcoming the various obstacles and misunderstandings that have kept them apart – at which point the film has to close in order not to expose the hollowness of its pretensions. But even, and especially, in those films – call them romantic tragedies – where the protagonists are denied their final union, the narrative is able to secure the belief in the possibility of sexual rapport precisely through the contingent circumstances that prevent it occurring. *The Piano* may be read as offering such an 'if only' scenario, for the spectator can imagine that if only it were not for patriarchy Ada could have had it all. Similarly male spectators of film noir can believe that if only it were not for the heartless character of the femme fatale the duped hero would have found happiness.

Typically in relating to these fantasies the spectator moves between identifications. Indeed the simplest way for the subject to overcome the impossibility of a sexual relation is to identify with both the male and female figures and imagine a rapport between them. In this sense the spectator is like the hysteric, who through a double identification with both man and woman in fantasy seeks to install harmony in place of discord: each is cut to the cloth of the other's desire; each appears to be the complement of the other. The distribution of identifications, made available by the institution of cinema, renders just such fantasies possible but with an important difference. Whereas the real as impossible disrupts such fantasies when the hysteric seeks to actualise them, the institution of cinema largely removes the threat of any such crisis, at least for the duration of the film.

As in the Levinasian model discussed above, the alterity of the other does not emerge and does not disrupt. But whereas from that perspective the cinema is a means of evading the infinite ethical demands of the other, here, in this Lacanian model, cinema functions as a place where subjects of every sexual orientation can evade the infinite sexual demands of the other, i.e. the demand the subject give what he does not have. Cinema is a one-way system in which the desires of the spectator can proceed safe in the knowledge that he will, in the majority of instances, not encounter the discordant desire of the other coming in the opposite direction.

The gaze

Within the institution of cinema the gaze is the most salient form assumed by the call of the impossible. Contrary to received wisdom and Mulvey's account, for Lacan the subject is less a being that looks than a being that is looked at; the gaze is not on the side of the subject but that of the object. As in Levinas the subject is looked at before it looks. If the gaze precedes the subject and the gaze is unmasterable then contra Mulvey it is too simple to claim that men look and women are looked at. Nobody whether male or female, homosexual or heterosexual, can be a subject without being subject to the other's gaze. Further, because desire is inscribed in every gaze and, as we have seen, desire cannot be spoken, every subject is confronted with the unanswerable question, 'What does the other want?' and has to negotiate the concomitant impossibilities.

Once again the institution of cinema functions as a means of evading the alterity of the other. In the two examples that follow, a Lacan-inspired reading converges, in significant respects, with the Levinas-inspired reading outlined earlier.

(1) To escape the troubling, anxiety-inducing gaze of the radically enigmatic other the subject may seek to capture the gaze by being what the other wants. But because this is the object a, which cannot be spoken, the subject can never be finally certain that he has succeeded. Hence one of the attractions of stars, for they seem to have succeeded in capturing and taming the gaze of the other. Thus by identifying with the idealised figure of a star, the subject can imagine that he too has accomplished this impossible feat, thereby shielding himself from the uncertainties inscribed in the other's gaze. Again the distribution of identifications made possible by the institution of cinema enables the subject to short-circuit its relationship to the other.

(2) The male voyeuristic spectator is drawn to fetishised images not in order to see women but in order not to see them. He fetishises so that he can deny the alterity of the other and evade the emergence of the real of her desire, the fact that it is always ultimately unknowable, unfulfillable and discordant. As Metz emphasises, the voyeur is very careful to maintain a gulf, an empty space, between the object and the eye.[42] On the one hand he does not want to know that the woman is not the embodiment of the object a and that she cannot satisfy his desire. (Since the phallus is the pretence the object a exists, insofar as fetishisation is phallicisation, it is an attempt to mask the absence of the object a). On the other hand he wishes to know nothing of her desire, for he can no more satisfy her desire than she can his. In short he wishes to evade the impossibility of a sexual relation. Crucial to this process is that the gaze is not returned, for it is precisely because the male voyeur is not subject to the gaze of the woman he has objectified that he can cling to the illusion of mastery: as Mulvey rightly emphasised, fetishisation is an attempt to silence and repress women's desires.

Since there is nowhere outside the gaze, not being looked at is not an option. Hence, in pursuit of the happiest possible economy, subjects seek to be looked at as they would wish to be seen and, above all, to be looked at by the other whose gaze/desire they wish to capture/appropriate. Being the object of the gaze is not of itself oppressive for we all want to be looked at by a particular other in a particular way. Just as in analysis what matters is who is speaking and to whom, so in both cinema and life what matters is who is looking and at whom. In the first sequence of *Eyes Wide Shut* Alice complains to Harford that he does not look at her as she wishes to be looked at.

In *The Piano* Ada is aroused by the gaze of Baines and repelled by that of Stewart. The experience of being looked at all depends on the identifications in play.

As touched on in our use of Lacan in the 'Rortian' redescription the problems for men and women in relation to the gaze have differed historically. Men were appraised by other men and many women in terms of their correspondence to prevailing ideals of masculinity. Women were similarly appraised in terms of dominant notions of femininity but in addition, given the asymmetries of power, also found themselves summoned by male suitors to embody the alto- gether less explicit ideal of their singular object of desire – in other words called upon to undertake the doubly impossible task of embodying both the cultural, collective ideal and the always singular object a. Thus the problem for women, insofar as they wished to be desired by men and wished to be looked at in a particular way, was twofold: to find a man whose gaze was experienced as pleasurable and to be what would attract him.

Here too the institution of cinema offers a form of imaginary rescue. Multiple identifications – for the spectator can identify both with the subject and the object of the gaze – can circumvent the problems posed by the impossibilities associated with the gaze: the spectator can occupy the positions of both the idealised subject and the idealised object of the gaze. Not only is the gaze welcome, but because the spectator occupies both positions its troublingly enigmatic quality disappears and opacity gives way to transparency.

The transference

In response to the lack in the Other, to the experiences of alienation and separation, subjects engage in fantasy and imaginary identifica- tions. Everyone does this and the cost is usually no higher than the incidence of the common or garden miseries described by Freud. However, there are instances where the choice of fantasy and identi- fication is particularly unhappy, causing disturbing and painful symptoms to emerge. In such cases the subject may well seek analysis.

The purpose of analysis is to give the analysand the opportunity to find another, less troubled way of relating to the lack in the Other. The good news for the analysand is that he can change, the bad that he must first confront the lack in the Other. A last defence against confronting this lack – which at its simplest means that desire never attains its object (a truth from which the neurotic is in flight) – occurs through transference. Here the subject imaginarises the analyst as the master of identity and desire, as the one who knows both his true identity and how to attain the object of his desire. In identifying with this ideal the analysand delegates the task of confronting the lack in the Other to the analyst. The role of the analyst is then to make manifest his lack so that the analysand can disidentify and traverse his existing fantasy frame. In so doing he discovers that although the object of desire remains necessarily unattainable, the other side of the coin is that desire is inseparable from life itself, indeed the best of life occurs when the risk of desire, and the risk of change entailed by its pursuit, is undertaken. At this point the status of the analyst changes. Ceasing to be the ideal, he becomes at best an example, an individual whose style may suggest a way forward on the road the subject and the subject alone must travel.

This concluding moment has two immediate implications for cinema.

(1) Just as the analysand can delegate the business of living to the analyst, so spectators can have the star confront life's vicissitudes in their stead and live on their behalf. But, as in analysis, there is no necessity that this will be the case. For psychoanalysis indicates that how stars function is not pre-determined, but depends on the stance adopted by the spectator: rather than delegates, stars can equally function as a stimulus to live more fully and imaginatively.

(2) If there is a lack in the Other, if the crucial signifier which would express what we want to say is missing, then we have to invent. And here, as in Derrida, impossibility becomes the condition of possibility. The fact of alienation, that there are no identities only identifications, implies it is possible to desist from a particular identification and to make new identifications – and one site where this may be done is in the making and reading of films (as seems to have occurred, for example, among at least some of Stacey's correspondents). Similarly the fact of separation, the unattainability of the object of desire, can act as an impetus to discover new ways of formulating and negotiating desire. Again, the absence of sexual relation suggests that whatever a couple has managed to construct their relationship around is both creative and mysterious.

The message of psychoanalysis as well as of deconstruction is that confronted by certain inescapable impossibilities it is up to each individual to create and invent their own way. Just as we can choose whether to be reactive or affirmative in the face of these constitutive limits in terms of our lives, so too can cinema and writing on cinema choose the path of inventiveness and untried possibilities. It's all a question of style. If the Other is lacking, *the* way does not exist and nor does *the* style. And that is our opportunity. Lacanian analysis does not enable the analysand to pronounce the final word – given the lack in the Other, that is impossible – but it can help the analysand to think and speak differently. The analysand discovers that if he cannot say everything he can at least speak well. There is, as Lacan puts it, the possibility of the '*bien-dire*'. Equally analysis does not enable the analysand to access absolute *jouissance* – again this is precluded by the lack in the Other – but it can help him to enjoy differently. This is Lacan's ultimate lesson, the lesson embodied in his style. However apparently dispiriting the subject matter – the absence of the sexual relation, the impossibility of conclusive self-knowledge, the inevitability of division and alienation, etc. – the style of Lacan's seminars and writings is far from gloomy. Indeed, reading his work can be an exhilarating, even joyful experience. That, more than any specific theoretical content (about, say, the gaze), is the import of his teaching for theory. If Theory's ambition of pronouncing the final word on cinema is doomed, it is still possible for individual theories to 'speak well' of cinema, that is, to speak of cinema in ways that open both film-makers and spectators to new possibilities, new knowledges and new modes of pleasure. While cinema can certainly be a means of evasion, this, as deconstruction and psychoanalysis demonstrate, is by no means inevitable. In contrast to Theory in its non-dialectical form, the experience of cinema, rather than being pre-programmed, can be transformed into adventure and invention.

Debates and Rejoinders

It will be apparent that the readings and critical directions sketched above have no claim to being a synoptic overview. Plainly at odds with each other, they offer a variety of approaches to and evaluations of Theory and the particular topics we have focussed on – authorship, realism, the avant-garde, Mulvey's thesis and the institution of stardom. In conclusion we would like to indicate briefly how each reading might view the others.

Proponents of Reading 1, contra Theory, would have no difficulty with the general orientation of Reading 2, continuing critique, but they would wish to take each struggle on a case by case basis. Their watchword would be specificity. In relation to both Readings 3 and 4, they would have little time for the positions advanced, considering them to be as unfounded and unwarranted as Theory itself.

Proponents of Reading 2 would have no quarrel with contra Theory's emphasis on scholarly research but they would question its political value. Their exemplar would be Mulvey – an academic who made a difference. They might find sections of Reading 3, postmodern amendments, interesting, but again would question its relevance to the urgent business of politics. Reading 4, the call of the impossible, especially its psychoanalytic component, would arouse their suspicion and antipathy. In their view much of psychoanalysis is shot through with patriarchal ideology, and in the majority of instances is part of the problem, not part of the solution.

Proponents of Reading 3 would be broadly supportive of the first two readings but would insist that as all thinking, whether about the cinema or anything else, is irreducibly conceptual, there is a continuing role for theory in exploring the possibilities opened up by alternative vocabularies. Their ire would be reserved for Reading 4, insofar as it suggests there are cultural and historical invariants. Acceptance of such invariants can only foreclose on other possibilities

Proponents of Reading 4, more precisely the defenders of psychoanalysis, would find themselves on the back foot. Against their critics' denunciation of psychoanalysis as unfounded and damaging dogmatism they would counter with the psychoanalytic adage that whereof one cannot speak thereof one must not be silent. In brief, their argument would be twofold. Firstly, that, because every analysand is singular and every analysand unique, psychoanalysis is not and can never be a finished body of doctrine: as Lacan stressed, it must be reinvented in every session. Consequently psychoanalysis is, to adopt a phrase of Derrida's, always 'to come'. Secondly, in that we are of necessity addressed by desiring others and have to respond, we have to try to understand what psychoanalysis seeks to understand. Of necessity, we have to address the issues and problems addressed by psychoanalysis. In that sense there is no outside of psychoanalysis. Flaws in a particular form of psychoanalysis are not grounds for its wholesale abandonment, only for its reinvention. In response, their critics might rejoin that this hardly constitutes a defence of psychoanalysis per se. Utterly different vocabularies might be more to the purpose.

For no reason other than personal preference we would like to give the last word to Deleuze and Guattari. In *Anti-Oedipus* they write, 'We always make love with worlds and our love addresses itself to this libidinal property of our lover, to either close himself or herself off or open up to more spacious worlds'.[43] Cinema, too, enables its lovers to enter and participate in the worlds it creates, and as such opens the way to new and different modes of being. If this retrospect has likewise contributed to the reader's understanding of the diversity of ways of thinking about cinema, thereby opening up new conceptual horizons, it will more than have served its purpose.

NOTES

Foreword

1 Alan Parker, *British Cinema: A Personal View*, 12 March 1986, Thames Television.

2 Frank Lentricchia, *Criticism and Social Change* (Chicago: University of Chicago Press, 1985), p. 192.

1 Politics

1 Karl Marx, *A Contribution to the Critique of Political Economy*, in K. Marx and F. Engels, *Selected Works*, I (Moscow: Progress Publishers, 1969), p. 503.

2 Karl Marx, *The German Ideology* (London: Lawrence and Wishart, 1974), p. 64.

3 Louis Althusser, *Reading Capital*, trans. Ben Brewster (London: New Left Books), p. 59.

4 Vincent Descombes, *Modern French Philosophy*, trans. L. Scott-Fox and J. M. Harding (Cambridge: Cambridge University Press, 1980), p. 128.

5 Louis Althusser, 'Ideology and ideological state apparatuses', in *Lenin and Philosophy*, trans. Ben Brewster (London: New Left Books, 1971), p. 130.

6 Louis Althusser, *For Marx*, trans. Ben Brewster (Harmondsworth: Penguin Books, 1969), p. 111.

7 *Ibid.*, p. 113.

8 Sheelagh Strawbridge, 'From overdetermination to structural casuality', *Radical Philosophy*, August 1984, p. 38.

9 Karl Marx, *Capital*, I, trans. Ben Fowkes (Harmondsworth: Penguin Books, 1976), p. 92.

10 Karl Marx, quoted in D. N. Rodowick, 'The difficulty of difference', *Wide Angle* 5, 1, p. 6.

11 Althusser, *Lenin and Philosophy*, p. 153.

12 *Ibid.*, p. 151.

13 Althusser, *For Marx*, p. 232.

14 Althusser, *Lenin and Philosophy*, p. 162.

15 Jean-Louis Comolli and Jean Narboni, 'Cinema/ideology/criticism', *Screen Reader* 1 (London: Society for Education in Film and Television, 1977), p. 5.

16 *Ibid.*, p. 5.

17 *Ibid.*, p. 7.

18 *Ibid.*, p. 7.

19 Gerald Leblanc, quoted in Thomas Elsaesser, 'French film culture and critical theory: *Cinéthique*', *Monogram* 2, 1971, p. 34.

20 Anthony Easthope, 'The trajectory of *Screen*', in *The Politics of Theory*, ed. Francis Barker (Colchester: University of Essex, 1983), p. 121.

21 Jacques Lacan, *The Four Fundamental Concepts of Psychoanalysis*, trans. Alan Sheridan (London: The Hogarth Press, 1977), p. viii.

22 Louis Althusser, *Essays in Self-criticism*, trans. Grahame Lock (London: New Left Books, 1976), p. 125.

23 Useful discussions can be found in Barry Smart, *Foucault, Marxism and Critique* (London: Methuen, 1983), and Alex Callinicos, *Is There a Future for Marxism?* (London: Macmillan, 1982).

24 See, for example, Descombes, *Modern French Philosophy*, pp. 123-4; Andrew Levine, 'Althusser's Marxism', *Economy and Society* 10, 3, August 1981, p. 263; and Terry Lovell, *Pictures of Reality* (London: British Film Institute, 1980), p. 33.

25 Levine, 'Althusser's Marxism', p. 278.

26 Antony Cutler, Barry Hindess, Paul Hirst and Athar Hussain, *Marx's 'Capital' and Capitalism Today*, I (London: Routledge and Kegan Paul, 1977), p. 169.

27 *Ibid.*, p. 210.

28 See Lawrence Harris, 'The science of the economy', *Economy and Society* 7, 3, August 1978.

29 Paul Hirst, *On Law and Ideology* (London: Macmillan, 1979), pp. 40-74.

30 Althusser, *Essays in Self-criticism*, p. 173.

31 For a useful discussion of these issues see William Connolly, *Appearance and Reality in Politics* (Cambridge: Cambridge University Press, 1981), especially chapter 2, and Susan James, 'Louis Althusser', in *The Return of Grand Theory*, ed. Quentin Skinner (Cambridge: Cambridge University Press, 1985).

32 Diane Macdonnell, *Theories of Discourse* (Oxford: Basil Blackwell, 1986), pp. 24-42.

33 Barry Hindess and Paul Hirst, *Mode of Production and Social Formation* (London: Routledge and Kegan Paul, 1977), p. 22.

34 Hirst, *On Law and Ideology*, p. 18.

35 Paul Abbott, 'Authority', *Screen* 20, 2, summer 1979, p. 62.

36 Perry Anderson, *In the Tracks of Historical Materialism* (London: Verso, 1983), p. 32.

37 Friedrich Nietzsche, quoted in Nicholas Davey, 'Nietzsche's doctrine of perspectivism', *Journal of the British Society for Phenomenology* 14, 3, October 1983, p. 249.

38 Friedrich Nietzsche, quoted in Arthur C. Danto, *Nietzsche as Philosopher* (London: Collier Macmillan Ltd, 1970), pp. 38-9.

39 Michel Foucault, *The History of Sexuality*, I: an introduction, trans. Robert Hurley (London: Allen Lane, 1979), p. 102.

40 Michel Foucault, *The Order of Things: An Archaeology of the Human Sciences* (London: Tavistock Publications, 1970), p. 386.

41 Michel Foucault, 'The order of discourse', *Untying the Text,* ed. Robert Young, (London: Routledge and Kegan Paul, 1981), p. 53.

42 Michel Foucault, quoted in Alex Callinicos, 'Postmodernism, post-structuralism and post-Marxism', *Theory, Culture and Society* 2, 3, winter 1985.

43 Abbott, 'Authority', p. 47.

44 Teresa de Lauretis, *Alice Doesn't: Feminism, Semiotics, Cinema* (London: Macmillan, 1984), p. 84.

45 Abbott, 'Authority', p. 14.

46 de Lauretis, *Alice Doesn't.* While speaking of the possibility of this particular use of Foucault, de Lauretis was not herself subscribing to it.

47 Michel Foucault, *Language, Counter-memory, Practice: Selected Essays and Interviews* (Ithaca, N.Y.: Cornell Universaity Press, 1977), p. 207.

48 Michel Foucault, 'The history of sexuality: interview', trans. Geoff Bennington, *Oxford Literary Review* 4, 2, 1980, p. 13.

49 Camera Obscura Collective, *Camera Obscura* 1, fall 1976, p. 3.

50 Claire Johnston, *Notes of Women's Cinema,* Screen pamphlet 2, (London: Society for Education in Film and Television, 1973), p. 2.

51 Molly Haskell, *From Reverence to Rape: The Treatment of Women in the Movies* (Harmondsworth: Penguin Books, 1974); Marjorie Rosen, *Popcorn Venus* (New York: Avon Books, 1973).

52 Johnston, *Notes of Women's Cinema,* p. 26.

53 Sharon Smith, 'The image of woman in film: some suggestions for future research', *Women and Film* 1, 1972, p. 13.

54 Laura Mulvey, 'Feminism, film and the avant-garde', *Framework* 10, spring 1979, p. 4.

55 E. Ann Kaplan, *Women and Film* (London: Methuen, 1983), p. 2.

56 Johnston, *Notes of Women's Cinema,* p. 4.

57 Joan Mellen, quoted in Marsha McCreadie, *Women on Film: The Critical Eye* (New York: Praeger Publishers, 1983), p. 58.

58 For an early account of this, see Haskell, *From Reverence to Rape,* p. 155.

59 Mary Ann Doane, Patricia Mellencamp and Linda Williams, 'Feminist film criticism: an introduction', in *Re-vision: Essays in Feminist Film Criticism,* eds. Doane, Mellencamp and Williams (Los Angeles: American Film Institute, 1984), p. 12.

60 Pam Cook, 'Approaching the work of Dorothy Arzner' in *The Work of Dorothy Arzner: Towards a Feminist Criticism,* ed. Claire Johnston (London: British Film Institute, 1975), p. 9.

61 Annette Kuhn, *Women's Pictures: Feminism and Cinema* (London: Routledge and Kegan Paul, 1982), p. 44.

62 Elizabeth Cowie, 'The popular film as a progressive text – a discussion of *Coma',* Part 1, *M/F* 3, 1979; Part 2 *M/F* 4, 1980.

63 Johnston, *Notes of Women's Cinema,* p. 30.

64 Cook, 'Approaching the work of Dorothy Arzner', p. 11.

65 Sylvia Harvey 'Women's place: the absent family of film noir', in

Women and Film Noir, ed. E. Ann Kaplan (London: British Film Institute, 1978), p. 33.

66 Janet Bergstrom, 'Rereading the work of Claire Johnston', *Camera Obscura* 3/4.

67 Judith Mayne 'Feminist film theory and criticism', *Signs* 11, 1, autumn 1985.

68 Laura Mulvey, 'Notes on Sirk and melodrama', *Movie* 25.

69 Mulvey, 'Feminism, film and the avant-garde', p. 6.

70 Laura Mulvey, 'Textual riddles: interview with Laura Mulvey', *Discourse* 1, p. 92.

71 Kaplan, *Women and Film,* p. 18.

72 Doane, Mellencamp and Williams, 'Feminist film criticism', p. 12.

73 *Ibid.,* p. 11.

74 Christine Gledhill, 'Developments in feminist film criticism', in *Revision,* p. 42.

75 Aimee Rankin, 'Difference and deference', *Screen* 28, 1, winter 1987, p. 92.

76 Stephen Heath, 'Difference', *Screen* 19, 3, autumn 1978, p. 99.

2 Semiotics

1 These phrases appeared in the polemics of Kevin Brownlow, John Coleman, Nigel Andrews, and Clive James.

2 Ferdinand de Saussure, *Course in General Linguistics,* trans. Wade Baskin (Glasgow: Fontana/Collins, 1974), p. 16.

3 Colin McArthur, 'Analysing cinematic sign language', in *Dialectic!* (London: Key Texts, 1982), p. 38.

4 Christian Metz, quoted by Jim Hillier, *Movie* 20, spring 1975, p. 25.

5 Geoffrey Sampson, *Schools of Linguistics: Competition and Evolution* (London: Hutchinson, 1980), p. 48.

6 Saussure, *Course in General Linguistics,* p. 120.

7 Kaja Silverman, *The Subject of Semiotics* (New York: Oxford University Press, 1983), pp. 16-17.

8 C. S. Peirce, quoted in Silverman, *The Subject of Semiotics,* p. 18.

9 C. S. Peirce, quoted in Robert Almeder, *The Philosophy of Charles S. Peirce: A Critical Introduction* (Oxford: Basil Blackwell, 1980), p. 24.

10 Almeder, *The Philosophy of Charles S. Peirce,* p. 25.

11 *Ibid.,* p. 25.

12 Silverman, *The Subject of Semiotics,* p. 22.

13 Doane, Mellencamp and Williams, *Re-vision,* p. 6.

14 Gilles Deleuze, *Cinema 1: The Movement-image,* trans. Hugh Tomlinson and Barbara Habberjam (London: Althone Press, 1986); de Lauretis, *Alice Doesn't.*

15 Jacques Lacan, *Ecrits: A Selection,* trans. Alan Sheridan (London: Tavistock Publications, 1977), p. 65.

16 Jacques Lacan, quoted in Juliet Flower MacCannell, *Figuring Lacan:*

Criticism and the Cultural Unconscious (London: Croom Helm, 1986), p. 46.

17 The graph is reproduced from Lacan, *Ecrits*, p. 303.

18 Christian Metz, quoted in Stephen Heath, 'Film/cinetext/text', *Screen Reader* 2 (London: Society for Education in Film and Television, 1981), p. 104.

19 Christian Metz, quoted in Heath, 'Film/cinetext/text', p. 106.

20 Christian Metz, *Film Language* (New York: Oxford University Press, 1974), p. 116.

21 *Ibid.*, p. 105.

22 See Metz, *Film Language*, chapter 5.

23 The analysis can be found in Metz, *Film Language*.

24 David Bordwell, *Narration in the Fiction Film* (London: Methuen, 1985), p. xii.

25 See Christian Metz, *Language and Cinema*, trans. D. J. Umiker-Sebeok (The Hague: Mouton, 1974).

26 Oswald Stack, *Pasolini on Pasolini* (London: Thames and Hudson in association with the British Film Institute, 1969), p. 29.

27 Pasolini, quoted in de Lauretis, *Alice Doesn't*, p. 42.

28 Umberto Eco, *A Theory of Semiotics* (London: Macmillan, 1977), p. 200.

29 *Ibid.*, p. 3.

30 Umberto Eco, 'Articulations of the cinematic code', in *Movies and Methods: An Anthology*, ed. Bill Nichols (Berkeley: University of California Press, 1976), p. 604.

31 Eco, *A Theory of Semiotics*, p. 49.

32 *Ibid.*, p. 235.

33 de Lauretis, *Alice Doesn't*, p. 47.

34 Eco, *A Theory of Semiotics*, p. 49.

35 Heath, 'Film/cinetext/text', p. 100.

36 *Ibid.*, p. 103.

37 See Julia Kristeva, 'The system and the speaking subject', *The Times Literary Supplement*, 12 October 1973, p. 1249.

38 Rosalind Coward and John Ellis, *Language and Materialism: Developments in Semiology and the Theory of the Signifier* (London: Routledge and Kegan Paul, 1975), p. 68.

39 Emile Benveniste, quoted in Antony Easthope, *Poetry as Discourse* (London: Methuen, 1983), p. 43.

40 Emile Benveniste, *ibid.*, p. 41.

41 Emile Benveniste, *ibid.*, p. 43.

42 Christian Metz, 'History/discourse: note on two voyeurisms', trans. Susan Bennett, *Edinburgh Magazine 1976*, p. 24.

43 Stephen Heath, 'The turn of the subject', *Cine-tracts* 7/8, summer/fall 1979, p. 33.

44 *Ibid.*, p. 43.

45 Stephen Heath, 'Screen images, film memory', *Edinburgh Magazine*

1976 p. 40.

46 Stephen Heath, 'Anato Mo', *Screen* 16, 4, winter 1975/76, p. 50.

47 Heath, 'The turn of the subject', p. 41.

48 *Ibid.*, p. 43.

49 *Ibid.*, p. 43.

50 Stephen Heath, *Questions of Cinema* (London: Macmillan, 1981), p. 88.

51 Heath, 'The turn of the subject', p. 44.

52 Stephen Heath, '"Jaws", ideology and film theory', *Film Reader* 2, 1977, p. 167.

53 Heath, *Questions of Cinema*, p. 62.

54 de Lauretis, *Alice Doesn't*, p. 37.

55 The principle articles in the former debate were Rosalind Coward, 'Class, "culture" and the social formation', *Screen* 18, 1, spring 1977; Iain Chambers *et al.*, 'Marxism and culture', *Screen* 18, 4, winter 1977/78; Rosalind Coward, 'Response', *Screen* 18, 4.

56 Paul Willemen, 'Notes on subjectivity – on reading "Subjectivity under siege"', *Screen* 19, 1, spring 1978, p. 45.

57 *Ibid.*, p. 44.

58 *Ibid.*, p. 43.

59 *Ibid.*, p. 69.

60 Colin MacCabe, 'The discursive and the ideological in film – notes on the conditions of political intervention', *Screen* 19, 4, winter 1978/79, p. 35.

61 *Ibid.*, p. 35.

62 *Ibid.*, p. 38.

63 *Ibid.*, p. 38.

64 Colin MacCabe, *Theoretical Essays* (Manchester: Manchester University Press, 1985), p. 24.

65 *Ibid.*, p. 24.

66 Jacques Derrida, 'Living on: borderlines', in Harold Bloom, Paul de Man, Jacques Derrida, Geoffrey H. Hartman and J. Hillis Miller, *Deconstruction and Criticism* (London: Routledge and Kegan Paul, 1979), p. 81.

67 *Ibid.*, p. 84.

68 Jacques Derrida, 'White mythology', in *Margins of Philosophy,* trans. Alan Bass (Brighton: Harvester, 1982), p. 248.

69 Jacques Lacan, 'Seminar on "The Purloined Letter"', *Yale French Studies* 48, 1972, p. 72.

70 Jacques Derrida, 'The purveyor of truth', *Yale French Studies* 52, 1975, p. 65.

71 Lentricchia, *Criticism and Social Change,* p. 105.

3 Psychoanalysis

1 Jacques Lacan; quoted in Jacqueline Rose, 'The Imaginary', in *The Talking Cure: Essays in Psychoanalysis and Language,* ed. Colin MacCabe (London:

Macmillan, 1981), p. 135.

2 Juliet Mitchell, Introduction I to Jacques Lacan, *Feminine Sexuality: Jacques Lacan and the École Freudienne*, eds. Juliet Mitchell and Jacqueline Rose (London: Macmillan, 1982), p. 5.

3 Lacan, *The Four Fundamental Concepts of Pschoanalysis*, p. 158.

4 *Ibid.*, p. 206.

5 Heath, *Questions of Cinema*, p. 81.

6 Jacques Lacan, *Ecrits: A Selection* (London: Tavistock Publications, 1977), p. 298.

7 Lacan, *The Four Fundamental Concepts of Psychoanalysis*, p. 218.

8 Jacques Lacan, quoted in Heath, *Questions of Cinema*, p. 82.

9 Juliet Mitchell, review of Jane Gallop, *Feminism and Psychoanalysis: The Daughter's Seduction* in *The Times Literary Supplement*, 14 January 1983, p. 39.

10 Jacqueline Rose, Introduction II to Jacques Lacan, *Feminine Sexuality*, p. 40.

11 Jane Gallop, *Reading Lacan* (Ithaca, N.Y.: Cornell University Press, 1985), p. 142.

12 Catherine Millot, 'The feminine super-ego', *M/F* 10, 1985, p. 26.

13 *Ibid.*, p. 38.

14 Juliet Mitchell, review of Jane Gallop, *Feminism and Psychoanalysis*, p. 39.

15 Ann Rosalind Jones, 'Inscribing femininity: French theories of the feminine', in *Making a Difference: Feminist Literary Criticism*, eds. Gayle Greene and Coppelia Kahn (London: Methuen, 1985), p. 83.

16 The graph is reproduced from Lacan, *Ecrits*, p. 315.

17 Lacan, *Ecrits*, p. 304.

18 *Ibid.*, p. 86.

19 Laura Mulvey, 'Visual pleasure and narrative cinema', *Screen* 16, 3, autumn 1975, p. 8.

20 Jean-Louis Baudry, 'Ideological effects of the basic cinematographic apparatus', *Film Quarterly*, winter 1974/75, p. 43.

21 *Ibid.*, p. 43.

22 Jean-Louis Baudry, 'The apparatus', *Camera Obscura* 1, fall 1976, p. 113.

23 Christian Metz, 'The imaginary signifier', *Screen* 16, 2, summer 1975, p. 62.

24 *Ibid.*, p. 48.

25 *Ibid.*, p. 49.

26 Christian Metz, 'The cinematic apparatus as social institution – an interview with Christian Metz', *Discourse* 1, p. 20.

27 Here and in the pages immediately following we have retained Metz's use of masculine pronouns, both for reasons of consistency with the quotation and because of analysis may well be more appropriate to the male spectator.

28 Metz, 'The imaginary signifier', p. 51.

29 *Ibid.*, p. 51.

30 Heath, *Questions of Cinema*, p. 120.

31 John Ellis, *Visible Fictions: Cinema, Television, Video* (London: Routledge and Kegan Paul, 1982), p. 44.

32 Metz, 'The imaginary signifier', p. 54.

33 *Ibid.*, p. 63.

34 *Ibid.*, p. 63.

35 *Ibid.*, p. 64.

36 Metz, 'The cinematic apparatus as social institution', p. 14.

37 Metz, 'The imaginary signifier', p. 72.

38 Metz, 'The cinematic apparatus as social institution', p. 11.

39 *Ibid.*, p. 12.

40 Jean-Pierre Oudart, 'Cinema and suture', *Screen* 18, 1, winter 1977/78, p. 41.

41 Daniel Dayan, 'The tutor code of classical cinema', *Movies and Methods*.

42 *Ibid.*, p. 449.

43 Barry Salt, 'Film style and technology in the Forties', *Film Quarterly*, fall 1977, p. 52.

44 William Rothman, 'Against "The system of the suture"', *Movies and Methods*.

45 Heath, *Questions of Cinema*, p. 98.

46 *Ibid.*, p. 118.

47 Metz, 'The imaginary signifier', p. 19.

48 D. N. Rodowick, 'The difficulty of difference', *Wide Angle* 5, 1, p. 10.

49 Constance Penley, 'Feminism, film theory and the bachelor machines', *M/F* 10, 1985, p. 42.

50 Ellis, *Visible Fictions*, p. 42.

51 J. Laplanche and J.-B. Pontalis, *The Language of Psychoanalysis* (London: The Hogarth Press, 1973), p. 318.

52 *Ibid.*, p. 314.

53 Elizabeth Cowie, 'Fantasia', *M/F* 9, 1984, p. 91.

54 Sigmund Freud, 'A child is being beaten: a contribution to the study of sexual perversions', *On Psychopathology*, The Pelican Freud Library, X, p. 186.

55 *Ibid.*, p. 187.

56 Laura Mulvey, 'Afterthoughts. . . inspired by *Duel in the Sun*', *Framework*, summer 1981, p. 14.

57 *Ibid.*, p. 14.

58 Lacan, *The Four Fundamental Concepts of Psychoanalysis*, p. 185.

59 Cowie, 'Fantasia', p. 79.

60 *Ibid.*, pp. 93-102.

61 Elisabeth Lyon, 'The cinema of Lol V. Stein', *Camera Obscura* 6, p. 29.

62 J. Laplanche and J.-B. Pontalis, 'Fantasy and the origins of sexuality', *International Journal of Psychoanalysis*, 1968, p. 17.

63 Penley, 'Feminism, film theory and the bachelor machines', p. 44.

64 Lacan, *The Four Fundamental Concepts of Psychoanalysis*, p. 106.

65 Metz, 'The cinematic apparatus as social institution', p. 8.

66 Lovell, *Pictures of Reality*, p. 46.

67 Mary Ann Doane, 'Woman's stake: filming the female body', *October* 17, summer 1981, p. 26.

68 Stephen Heath, 'Difference', *Screen* 19, 3, autumn 1978, pp. 65-6.

69 Penley, 'Feminism, film theory and the bachelor machines', p. 52.

70 Jane Gallop, 'Phallus/penis: same difference', in *Men by Women, Women and Literature* II, ed. Janet Todd (New York and London: Holmes and Meier, 1981), p. 247.

71 Mary Ann Doane, 'Film and the masquerade – theorising the female spectator', *Screen* 23, 3/4, Sept./Oct. 1982, p. 76.

72 Doane, 'Woman's stake', p. 23.

73 Doane, 'Film and the masquerade', p. 79.

74 Doane, 'The "woman's film": possession and address', *Re-vision*, p. 74.

75 Rodowick, 'The difficulty of difference', pp. 8-9.

76 Williams, 'When the woman looks', *Re-vision*, p. 83.

77 Mulvey, 'Afterthoughts. . . inspired by *Duel in the Sun*', p. 13.

78 Doane, 'The "woman's film": possession and address', p. 79.

79 *Ibid.*, p. 72.

80 Doane, 'Film and the masquerade', p. 79.

81 Doane, 'Woman's stake', p. 23.

82 Penley, 'Feminism, film theory and the bachelor machines', p. 40.

83 Doane, 'Film and the masquerade', p. 81.

84 *Ibid.*, p. 87.

85 Joan Copjec, 'The anxiety of the influencing machines', *October* 23, winter 1982, p. 58.

86 Doane, 'Woman's stake', p. 33.

87 Joan Copjec, 'India Song/Son nom de Venise dans Calcutta désert: the compulsion to repeat', *October* 17 summer 1981, p. 49.

88 Luce Irigaray, 'Women's exile: interview with Luce Irigaray', *Ideology and Consciousness* 1, May 1977, p. 64.

89 Doane, 'Woman's stake', p. 33.

90 Penley, 'Feminism, film theory and the bachelor machines', p. 52.

91 *Ibid.*, p. 54.

4 Authorship

. 1 John Hess, 'World view as aesthetic', *Jump Cut* 1, May/June 1974.

2 Victor Perkins, 'The British cinema', *Movie Reader,* ed. Ian Cameron (London: November Books, 1972).

3 Sam Rohdie, Review: 'Movie Reader, film as film', *Screen* 13, 4, winter 1972/73, p. 135.

4 Althusser, *Lenin and Philosophy*, p. 209.

5 Claude Lévi-Strauss, *The Raw and the Cooked*, trans. John and Doreen Weightman (London: Jonathan Cape, 1970), p. 12.

6 Geoffrey Nowell-Smith, *Luchino Visconti* (London: Secker and

Warburg, in association with the British Film Institute, 1967), p. 10.

7 *Ibid.*, p. 10.

8 Geoffrey Nowell-Smith, 'Cinema and structuralism', *Twentieth Century Studies* 3, May 1970, p. 133.

9 Peter Wollen, *Signs and Meaning in the Cinema* (London: Secker and Warburg in association with the British Film Institute, third edition, 1972), p. 96.

10 Brian Henderson, *A Critique of Film Theory* (New York: E. P. Dutton, 1980).

11 Wollen, *Signs and Meaning in the Cinema*, p. 102.

12 *Ibid.*, pp. 167-8.

13 *Ibid.*, p. 168.

14 See Alan Jenkins, *The Social Theory of Claude Lévi-Strauss* (London: Macmillan, 1979), p. 20.

15 Paul Ricoeur and Claude Lévi-Strauss, 'A confrontation', *New Left Review* 62, July/August 1970.

16 James Boon, 'Claude Lévi-Strauss', in *The Return of Grand Theory*, p. 162.

17 André Bazin, 'La politique des auteurs', in *The New Wave,* ed. Peter Graham (London: Secker and Warburg in association with the British Film Institute, 1968), p. 142.

18 Andrew Sarris, *The American Cinema: Directors and Directions 1929-1968* (New York: E. P. Dutton, 1968), p. 36.

19 Edward Buscombe, 'Walsh and Warner Brothers', in *Raoul Walsh,* ed. Phil Hardy (Edinburgh: Edinburgh Film Festival, 1974), p. 54.

20 *Ibid.*, p. 59.

21 Colin MacCabe, 'Film culture', *Screen* 16, 1, spring 1975, p. 129.

22 John Ellis, 'Made in Ealing', *Screen* 16, 1, spring 1975, p. 91.

23 'John Ford's *Young Mr Lincoln*', a collective text by the editors of *Cahiers du Cinéma,* trans. Helen Lackner and Diana Matias, *Screen* 13, 3, autumn 1972, p. 7.

24 *Ibid.*, p. 17.

25 Janet Staiger, 'The Hollywood mode of production to 1930', in David Bordwell, Janet Staiger and Kristin Thompson, *The Classical Hollywood Cinema: Film Style and Mode of Production to 1960* (London: Routledge and Kegan Paul, 1985), p. 87.

26 *Ibid.*, p. xiv.

27 Sarris, *The American Cinema*, p. 20.

28 Pam Cook, *The Cinema Book* (London: British Film Institute, 1985), p. 173.

29 Paul Willemen, 'Towards an analysis of the Sirkian system', *Screen* 13, 4, winter 1972/73, p. 128.

30 Bernard Dort, *Lecture de Brecht* (Paris: Editions du Seuil, 1960), quoted in Willemen, *Screen* 13, 4, p. 129 (see also p. 296).

31 Willemen, 'Towards an analysis of the Sirkian system', p. 129.

32 Paul Willemen, 'Distanciation and Douglas Sirk', *Screen* 12, 2, summer 1971, p. 65.

33 Willemen, 'Towards an analysis of the Sirkian system', p. 130.

34 See Pam Cook, 'Authorship', in *The Cinema Book*, p. 175.

35 *Ibid.*, p. 175.

36 'Young Mr Lincoln', p. 13.

37 *Ibid.*, p. 8.

38 *Ibid.*, p. 15.

39 Ben Brewster, 'Notes on the text "Young Mr Lincoln" by the editors of *Cahiers du Cinéma*', *Screen* 14, 3, autumn 1973, p. 37.

40 'Young Mr Lincoln', pp. 40-1.

41 *Ibid.*, p. 40.

42 *Ibid.*, p. 41.

43 *Ibid.*, p. 37.

44 *Ibid.*, p. 39.

45 *Ibid.*, p. 37.

46 Roland Barthes, *Image-Music-Text*, essays selected and translated by Stephen Heath (London: Fontana, 1977), p. 143.

47 *Ibid.*, p. 146.

48 Stephen Heath, 'Comment on "The idea of authorship"', *Screen* 14, 3, p. 87.

49 *Ibid.*, p. 91.

50 Barthes, *Image-Music-Text*, p. 145.

51 *Ibid.*, p. 148.

52 Stephen Heath, 'Film and system, terms of analysis' Pt II, *Screen* 16, 2, summer 1975, p. 107.

53 Barthes, *Image-Music-Text*, p. 148.

54 *Ibid.*, p. 142.

55 *Ibid.*, pp. 146-7.

56 *Ibid.*, p. 147.

57 Michel Foucault, 'What is an author?', trans. Donald F. Bouchard, *Screen* 20, 1, spring 1979, p. 28.

58 *Ibid.*, p. 19.

59 *Ibid.*, p. 21.

5 *Narrative*

1 Roland Barthes, 'Introduction to the structural analysis of narratives', *New Literary History* VI, 2, winter 1975, p. 238.

2 Jean Mitry, *Esthétique* II, p. 354, quoted in Dudley Andrew, *Concepts in Film Theory* (Oxford: Oxford University Press, 1984), p. 76.

3 Noël Burch, 'How we get into pictures: notes accompanying *Correction Please*', *Afterimage* 8/9, winter 1980/1.

4 Bordwell, Staiger and Thompson, *The Classical Hollywood Cinema*.

5 Vladimir Propp, *The Morphology of the Folktale* (Austin and London: University of Texas Press, 1973), p. 30.

6 Peter Wollen, 'North by Northwest: a morphological analysis', in *Readings and Writings* (London: Verso, 1982), p. 29.

7 Sheila Johnston, 'Film narrative and the structuralist controversy', in *The Cinema Book,* p. 236.

8 Peter Wollen, 'The hermeneutic code', in *Readings and Writings.*

9 Dudley Andrew, *Concepts in Film Theory* (Oxford: Oxford University Press, 1984), p. 83.

10 de Lauretis, *Alice Doesn't,* chapter 5, especially pp. 131-2.

11 Raymond Bellour, 'The obvious and the code', *Screen* 15, 4, winter 1974/75.

12 Raymond Bellour, '*The Birds* – analysis of a sequence' (London: British Film Institute Education Department, 1972, reprinted 1981).

13 *Ibid.,* p. 19 (1981 edition).

14 Stephen Heath, 'Narrative space', in *Question of Cinema.*

15 *Ibid.,* p. 53.

16 Heath, 'Film, system, narrative', in *Question of Cinema.*

17 Heath, 'The question Oshima', in *Questions of Cinema,* p. 150.

18 Heath, 'Film performance', in *Questions of Cinema,* p. 120.

19 Heath, 'The question Oshima', p. 147.

20 Heath, 'Narrative space', p. 41.

21 *Ibid.,* p. 52.

22 Kristin Thompson, 'The formulation of the classical style 1909-28', in Bordwell, Staiger and Thompson, *The Classical Hollywood Cinema,* p. 230.

23 Dana B. Polan, *Image-Making and Image-Breaking* (Stanford University Ph.D. 1981, University Microfilms International 1981), p. 39.

24 Noël Carroll, 'Address to the Heathen', *October* 23, winter 1982.

25 *Ibid.,* p. 97.

26 *Ibid.,* p. 131.

27 David Bordwell, 'The classical Hollywood style 1917-60', in Bordwell, Staiger and Thompson, *The Classical Hollywood Cinema,* p. 39.

28 Stephen Heath, 'Le père Noël', *October* 26, fall 1983, p. 65.

29 *Ibid.,* p. 96.

30 David Bordwell, *Narration in the Fiction Film* (London: Methuen, 1985), p. 30.

31 Heath, 'Contexts', in *Questions of Cinema,* p. 243.

32 Heath, 'Le père Noël', p. 98.

33 *Ibid.,* p. 99.

34 Bertolt Brecht, 'Two essays on unprofessional acting', in *Brecht On Theatre,* ed. and trans. by John Willett (New York: Hill and Wang, 1964), p. 151.

35 *Ibid.,* p. 151.

36 Michel Foucault, quoted in Pasquale Pasquino, 'Michel Foucault: the will to knowledge', *Economy and Society* 15, 1, 1986, p. 108.

37 Roland Barthes, *The Pleasure of the Text* (London: Jonathan Cape, 1976), p. 47.

38 Heath, *Questions of Cinema*, p. 154.

39 *Ibid.*, p. 154.

40 Heath, 'Film and system' Pts I and II, *Screen* 16, 1, spring 1975; *Screen* 16, 2, summer 1975.

41 *Ibid.*, Pt I, p. 96.

42 *Ibid.*, Pt I, p. 94.

43 *Ibid.*, Pt II, p. 37.

44 Heath, *Questions of Cinema*, p. 182.

45 Heath, 'Film and system' Pt I, p. 98.

46 Heath, *Questions of Cinema*, p. 146.

47 Bellour, 'The Birds', p. 23.

48 *Ibid.*, p. 27.

49 *Ibid.*, p. 29.

50 *Ibid.*, p. 28.

51 *Ibid.*, p. 37.

52 *Ibid.*, p. 38.

53 Lacan, *The Four Fundamental Concepts of Psychoanalysis*, p. 131, p. 235.

54 Claude Lévi-Strauss, *L'Homme Nu*, pp. 590-1, quoted and trans. James Boon in *The Return of Grand Theory*, p. 171.

6 Realism

1 Jean-Louis Comolli, *Cahiers de Cinéma* 209, 1969, quoted in *Realism and the Cinema*, ed. Christopher Williams (London: Routledge and Kegan Paul, 1980), p. 226.

2 Ellis, *Visible Fictions*, p. 8.

3 Lovell, *Pictures and Reality*, p. 81.

4 Polan, *Image-Making and Image-Breaking*; John Hess, 'La politique des auteurs: part one, world view as aesthetic', *Jump Cut* 1, May-June 1974, pp. 19-22.

5 Polan, *Image-Making and Image-Breaking*, p. 125.

6 See Richard Rorty, *Philosophy and the Mirror of Nature* (Oxford: Basil Blackwell, 1980), chapter 4.

7 Györg Lukács, quoted in Eugene Lunn, *Marxism and Modernism* (London: Verso, 1985), p. 98.

8 Bertolt Brecht, quoted in Walter Benjamin, 'A short history of photography', *Screen* 13, 1, spring 1972, p. 24.

9 Althusser, *For Marx*, p. 144.

10 Althusser, *Lenin and Philosophy*, p. 204.

11 Stephen Heath, 'Lessons from Brecht', *Screen* 15, 2, summer 1974, p. 110.

12 Stephen Heath, 'From Brecht to film: theses, problems', *Screen* 16, 4, winter 1975/76, p. 35.

13 McArthur, *Dialectic!*, p. 51.

14 Emile Benveniste, *Problems in General Linguistics* (Miami: University of Miami Press, 1971), p. 47.

15 Barthes, *Image-Music-Text,* p. 145.

16 Lovell, *Pictures of Reality,* p. 82.

17 *Ibid.,* p. 16.

18 Hilary Putnam, 'Reference and truth', in *Philosophical Papers* III, Realism and Reason (Cambridge: Cambridge University Press, 1983), pp. 85-6.

19 Stephen Heath, *The Nouveau Roman* (London: Elek Books, 1972), p. 20.

20 Ellis, *Visible Fictions,* p. 63.

21 *Ibid.,* p. 75.

22 Colin MacCabe, 'Realism and the cinema: notes on some Brechtian theses', *Screen* 15, 2, summer 1974, p. 8. The two articles 'Realism and the cinema' and 'Principles of realism and pleasure', originally published in *Screen,* are reprinted in *Theoretical Essays.*

23 Colin MacCabe 'Memory, fantasy, identity: *Days of Hope* and the politics of the past', *Edinburgh Magazine* 1977, p. 15.

24 Colin MacCabe, *James Joyce and the Revolution of the Word* (London: Macmillan, 1978), p. 31.

25 MacCabe, 'Realism and the cinema', p. 12.

26 MacCabe, *Theoretical Essays,* p. 77.

27 MacCabe, 'Realism and the cinema, p. 26.

28 MacCabe, *Theoretical Essays,* p. 77.

29 *Ibid.,* p. 63.

30 Colin MacCabe, '*Days of Hope* – a response to Colin McArthur', *Screen* 17, 1, spring 1976, p. 99.

31 MacCabe, *Theoretical Essays,* p. 66.

32 *Ibid.,* p. 72.

33 *Ibid.,* p. 80.

34 Bordwell, *Narration in the Fiction Film,* p. 19.

35 MacCabe, '*Days of Hope*', p. 100.

36 Rorty, *Philosophy and the Mirror of Nature,* p. 368.

37 Michel Foucault, 'The political function of the intellectual', *Radical Philosophy* 17, summer 1977, p. 14.

7 The avant-garde

1 Györg Lukács, 'Realism in the balance' in *Aesthetics and Politics* (London: Verso, 1980), p. 39.

2 K. A. Dickson, *Towards Utopia: a study of Brecht* (Oxford: Clarendon Press, 1978), p. 233.

3 Bertolt Brecht, quoted in Stephen Heath, 'Lessons from Brecht', *Screen* 15, 2, summer 1974, p. 109.

4 *Ibid.,* p. 112.

5 Bertolt Brecht, quoted in Richard Wolin, *Walter Benjamin: An Aesthetic of Redemption* (New York: Columbia University Press, 1982), p. 151.

6 Abel Gance, quoted in Richard Philpott, 'Whose Napoleon?',

Framework 20, p. 10.

7 Theodor Adorno, quoted in Susan Buck Morss, 'Walter Benjamin – revolutionary writer' II, *New Left Review* 129, September/October 1981, p. 91; and in J. G. Merquior, *Western Marxism* (London: Paladin, 1986), p. 131.

8 Theodor Adorno, quoted in Martin Jay, *Adorno* (London: Fontana, 1984), p. 121.

9 Theodor Adorno, quoted in Richard Bernstein, introduction to *Habermas and Modernity,* pp. 6-7.

10 Heath, 'Lessons from Brecht', p. 125.

11 Althusser, *For Marx,* p. 144.

12 Heath, 'Lessons from Brecht', p. 104.

13 Colin MacCabe, 'The politics of separation', *Screen* 16, 4, winter 1975/ 76.

14 Althusser, *For Marx,* p. 143.

15 Heath, 'Lessons from Brecht', p. 116.

16 Julia Kristeva, *Revolution in Poetic Language* (New York: Columbia University Press, 1982), p. 17.

17 Philippe Sollers, quoted in Mary Ann Caws, 'Text and revolution', *Diacritics,* spring 1975, p. 2.

18 Julia Kristeva, 'Signifying practice and mode of production', trans. Geoffrey Nowell-Smith, *Edinburgh Magazine 1976, p. 68.*

19 Ibid., p. 68.

20 *Ibid.,* p. 69.

21 Julia Kristeva, 'Revolutionary semiotics', *Diacritics,* fall 1974, p. 31.

22 Wollen, *Readings and Writings,* p. 92.

23 *Ibid.,* p. 197.

24 *Ibid.,* p. 99.

25 Peter Wollen, 'The avant-gardes: Europe and America', *Framework* 14, 1981, p. 9,

26 *Ibid.,* p, 9.

27 *Ibid.,* pp. 9-10.

28 *Ibid.,* p. 10.

29 Peter Wollen, 'Godard and counter-cinema: *Vent d'Est'*, in *Readings and Writings.*

30 *Ibid.,* p. 89.

31 *Ibid.,* p. 88.

32 Jean-Luc Godard, quoted in Colin MacCabe, *Godard: Images, Sounds, Politics* (London: Macmillan in association with the British Film Institute, 1980), p. 19.

33 Jean-Luc Godard, quoted in Stephen Heath, 'Lessons from Brecht', p. 120.

34 Jean-Marie Straub, quoted in Stephen Heath, 'Lessons from Brecht', p. 120.

35 Jean-Luc Godard, quoted in Stephen Heath, *Questions of Cinema,* p. 242.

36 Jean-Luc Godard, quoted in Stephen Heath, 'From Brecht to film', p. 37.

37 Bertolt Brecht, quoted in Stephen Heath, *ibid.*, p. 35.

38 MacCabe, 'The politics of separation', p. 48.

39 Martin Walsh, *The Brechtian Aspect of Radical Cinema*, ed. Keith M. Griffiths (London: British Film Institute, 1981), p. 77.

40 Heath, *Questions of Cinema*, p. 56.

41 Arnold Schoenberg, quoted in Jean-Marie Straub and Danièle Huillet, 'Scenario of *Introduction to Arnold Schoenberg's Accompaniment to a Cinematographic Score*', *Screen* 17, 1, spring 1976, p. 78.

42 Walsh, *The Brechtian Aspect of Radical Cinema*, p. 80.

43 Walter Benjamin, quoted in Walsh, *ibid.*, p. 84.

44 *Ibid.*, p. 86.

45 *Ibid.*, p. 87.

46 Theodor Adorno, quoted in Walsh, *ibid.*, p. 81.

47 Roland Barthes, quoted in Walsh, *ibid.*, p. 82.

48 *Ibid.*, p. 90.

49 Heath, 'From Brecht to film', p. 43.

50 Heath, 'Anato mo', p. 59.

51 *Ibid.*, p. 57.

52 Colin MacCabe, 'Principles of realism and pleasure', *Screen* Vol 17, 3, autumn 1976, p. 27.

53 *Ibid.*, p. 27.

54 *Ibid.*, p. 26.

55 Heath, 'Anato mo', p. 53.

56 *Ibid.*, p. 64.

57 *Ibid.*, p. 58.

58 Heath, *Questions of Cinema*, p. 153.

59 Lovell, *Pictures of Reality*, p. 87.

60 Fredric Jameson, *The Political Unconscious: Narratives as a Socially Symbolic Act* (London: Methuen, 1981), p. 286.

61 Fredric Jameson, 'Reification and Utopia in mass culture', *Social Text* 1, winter 1979, p. 144.

62 Timothy J. Clark, 'Preliminaries to a possible treatment of *Olympia* in 1865', *Screen* 21, 1, spring 1980, p. 34.

63 *Ibid.*, p. 39.

64 Peter Wollen, 'Manet – modernism and avant-garde', *Screen* 21, 2, summer 1980, p. 23.

65 Andreas Huyssen, 'The search for tradition: avant-garde and postmodernism in the 1970s', *New German Critique* 22, winter 1981.

66 Paul Willemen, 'An avant-garde for the 80s', *Framework* 24, spring 1984, p. 56.

67 *Ibid.*, p. 68.

68 *Ibid.*, p. 68.

69 *Ibid.*, p. 70.

70 Huyssen, 'The search for tradition: avant-garde and postmodernism in the 1970s', pp. 31-4.

71 Andreas Huyssen, 'Mapping the postmodern', *New German Critique* 33, fall 1984, p. 26.

72 Wollen, *Readings and Writings,* p. 213.

73 Colin MacCabe, 'Defining popular culture', in *High Theory/Low Culture* (Manchester: Manchester University Press, 1986), p. 7.

74 Jurgen Habermas, 'Modernity: an incomplete project', in *The Anti-Aesthetic,* ed. Hal Foster (Washington: Bay Press, 1984).

75 Fredric Jameson, 'Postmodernism, or the cultural logic of late capitalism', *New Left Review* 146, July/August 1984, p. 68.

76 Jean-François Lyotard, *The Postmodern Condition: A Report on Knowledge,* trans. Geoff Bennington and Brian Massumi (Manchester: Manchester University Press, 1984), p. 66.

77 Huyssen, 'The search for tradition', pp. 38-49.

78 Jean-François Lyotard, 'What is postmodernism?', trans. Regis Durand, in *The Postmodern Condition,* p. 81.

79 Richart Rorty, 'Habermas and Lyotard on postmodernity', in *Habermas and Modernity,* ed. Richard Bernstein (Cambridge, Mass.: The MIT Press, 1985), p. 174.

Afterword

1 Comolli and Narboni, 'Cinema/ideology/criticism' 1, p. 2, p. 9.

2 The phrase is Geoffrey Strickland's.

3 Roland Barthes, quoted in Rosalind Coward and John Ellis, *Language and Materialism* (London: Routledge and Kegan Paul, 1977), p. 25.

4 Ludwig Wittgenstein, *Tractatus Logico-Philosophicus,* trans. Pears and McGuiness (London: Routledge and Kegan Paul, 1961), 5.6.

5 Martin Heidegger, quoted in Charles Guignon, *Heidegger and the Problem of Knowledge* (New York: Hackett and Co., 1982), p. 125.

6 Martin Heidegger, *An Introduction to Metaphysics,* trans. Ralph Mannheim (New Haven: Yale University Press, 1959), p. 13.

7 Michel Foucault, 'Intellectuals and power', in *Language, Counter-memory, Practice,* trans. Donald F. Bouchard and Sherry Simon (New York: Cornell University Press, 1977), p. 208.

8 See Michael Dummett, 'What is a theory of meaning?' II, in *Truth and Meaning,* ed. G. Evans and J. McDowell (Oxford: Oxford University Press, 1976), especially p. 69.

9 Lacan, *Ecrits,* p. 302.

10 Jeffrey Mehlman, 'The "Floating Signifier" from Lévi-Strauss to Lacan', *Yale French Studies* 48, 1973.

11 This is the title of Lacan's Seminar 21, forthcoming publication, Editions de Seuil.

12 Michel de Certeau, 'Lacan: an ethics of speech', *Representation* 3, summer 1983, p. 28.

13 Jacques Lacan, quoted in Shoshana Felman, 'Psychoanalysis and education: teaching terminable and interminable', *Yale French Studies* 63, p. 26

14 Julia Kristeva, 'Within the microcosm of "The Talking Cure"', in *Interpreting Lacan*, eds. Joseph H. Smith and William Kerrigan (New Haven: Yale University Press, 1983, p. 33.

Film theory: a retrospect

1 Laura Mulvey, 'Visual pleasure and narrative cinema', *Screen* 16, 3, autumn 1975, in particular.

2 Jackie Stacey, *Star Gazing: Hollywood Cinema and Female Spectatorship* (London: Routledge, 1994).

3 *Ibid.*, p. 81.

4 *Ibid.*, p. 139.

5 *Ibid.*, p. 206.

6 Discussion at the IAPL Conference 'Writing Aesthetics', Leeds, May 2003.

7 Richard Dyer, *Heavenly Bodies: Film Stars and Society* (Basingstoke: Macmillan, 1987), especially the chapter 'Judy Garland and gay men' pp. 141-94.

8 Stacey, *Star Gazing*, p. 208.

9 *Ibid.*, p. 9.

10 Laura U. Marks, *The Skin of the Film: Intercultural Cinema, Embodiment and the Senses* (Durham NC: Duke University Press, 2000).

11 *Ibid.*, p. 97.

12 Jean-Francois Lyotard, *The Postmodern Condition: A Report on Knowledge*, trans. Geoff Bennington and Brian Massumi (Manchester: Manchester University Press, 1984).

13 Jean-Francois Lyotard, *Heidegger and 'the jews'*, trans. Andreas Michel and Mark S. Roberts (Minneapolis: University of Minnesota Press, 1990) p. 26.

14 Friedrich Nietzsche, *Also Sprach Zarathustra*, trans. R. J. Hollingdale (London: Penguin, 1961) p. 213.

15 Michel Foucault, *The History of Sexuality* (Harmondsworth: Penguin, 1990).

16 Michel Foucault, *Technologies of the Self: A Seminar with Michel Foucault*, eds. Luther H. Martin, Huck Gutman and Patrick H. Hutton (London: Tavistock, 1988).

17 Michel Foucault, *Discipline and Punish* (London: Penguin, 1991).

18 Michel Foucault, *The History of Sexuality*, Volume 2, *The Uses of Pleasure*, trans. Robert Hurley (London: Penguin, 1987) and Volume 3, *The Care of the Self* trans. Robert Hurley (London: Penguin, 1990).

19 Gilles Deleuze, *Negotiations*, trans. Martin Joughin (New York: Columbia University Press, 1995) p. 38.

20 Gilles Deleuze, *Cinema 1: The Movement-Image*, trans. Hugh Tomlinson and Barbara Habberjam (London: Athlone Press, 1992). *Cinema 2:*

The Time-Image, trans. Hugh Tomlinson and Robert Galeta (London: Athlone Press, 1989).

21 Henri Bergson, *Matter and Memory* trans. Nancy Margaret Paul and W. Scott Palmer (London: George Allen & Unwin, 1911).

22 Gilles Deleuze, *Cinema 1*, p. 62.

23 Gilles Deleuze, *Nietzsche and Philosophy*, trans. Hugh Tomlinson (London: Athlone Press, 1983), p. 3.

24 Emmanuel Levinas, *Totality and Infinity*, trans. Alphonso Lingis (Pittsburgh: Duquesne University Press, 1969), especially section 3 'Exteriority and the Face', pp. 187-219.

25 For a useful discussion, see Richard Kearney, *The Poetics of Modernism: Toward a Hermeneutic Imagination* (Atlantic Highlands, NJ: Humanities Press, 1995), pp. 111-15.

26 Kearney, *The Poetics of Modernism*, p. 116.

27 Jacques Derrida, *Edmund Husserl's Origin of Geometry: An Introduction* (Lincoln: University of Nebraska Press, 1989), p. 104.

28 Jacques Derrida, *Of Grammatology*, trans. Gayatri Chakravorty Spivak (Baltimore: Johns Hopkins University Press, 1976), p. 58.

29 Bertolt Brecht, 'Two essays on unprofessional acting', in *Brecht on Theatre*, ed. and trans. John Willet (New York: Hill and Wang, 1964), p. 151.

30 'Profile of Edward Said', BBC 4, 12 June 2003.

31 Jacques Derrida, *Points: Interviews 1974-94*, ed. Elisabeth Weber, trans. Peggy Kamuf *et al.*,(Stanford, CA: Stanford University Press, 1995), p. 93.

32 'Choreographies: an interview with Jacques Derrida', in Jacques Derrida, *The Ear of the Other: Otobiography, Transference, Translation*, ed. Christie McDonald (Lincoln, Nebraska: University of Nebraska Press, 1988), p. 184.

33 Derrida, *Points*, p. 163.

34 Derrida, 'Choreographies', p. 194.

35 'Women in the Beehive', in *Men in Feminism*, eds. Alice Jardine and Paul Smith, (London, New York: Methuen 1987), p. 199.

36 Derrida, *Points*, p. 108.

37 Jacques Derrida, 'Violence and metaphysics', in Jacques Derrida, *Writing and Difference*, trans. Alan Bass (London: Routledge & Kegan Paul, 1978).

38 Derrida, *Points*, p. 282

39 Philippe Lacoue-Labarthe, *Typography* (Stanford CA: Stanford University Press, 1989), pp. 174-5.

40 Richard Dyer, 'Charisma', in *Stardom: industry of desire*, ed. Christine Gledhill (London: Routldege, 1991), pp. 57-9.

41 Slavoj Žižek, *For They Know Not What They Do: Enjoyment as a Political Factor* (London: Verso, 1991), p. 171.

42 Christian Metz, *Psychoanalysis and Cinema: the imaginary signifier* trans. Celia Britton (London: Macmillan, 1982), p. 60.

43 Gilles Deleuze and Felix Guattari, *Anti-Oedipus: Capitalism and Schizophrenia*, Volume 1, trans. Robert Hurley, Mark Seem and Helen R. Lane (Minneapolis: University of Minnesota Press, 1983), p. 294.

Select Bibliography

Parveen Adams, *The Emptiness of the Image: psychoanalysis and sexual difference*, London: Routledge, 1996.

Parveen Adams (ed.), *Art: sublimation or symptom*, London: Karnac, 2003.

Ian Aitkin, *European Film Theory and Cinema: a critical introduction*, Edinburgh: Edinburgh University Press, 2001.

Richard Allen and Murray Smith (eds.), *Film Theory and Philosophy*, Oxford: Clarendon Press, 1997.

Louis Althusser, *For Marx*, translated by Ben Brewster, Harmondsworth: Penguin, 1969.

Louis Althusser, *Reading Capital*, translated by Ben Brewster, London: New Left Books, 1970.

Louis Althusser, *Lenin and Philosophy*, translated by Ben Brewster, London: New Left Books, 1971.

Manuel Alvarado and John O. Thompson (eds.), *The Media Reader*, London: The British Film Institute, 1990.

Dudley Andrew, *Concepts in Film Theory*, Oxford: Oxford University Press, 1984.

Ien Ang, *Watching 'Dallas': soap opera and the melodramatic imagination*, London: Methuen, 1985.

Bad Object-Choices (eds.), *How Do I Look?: queer film and video*, Seattle: Bay Press, 1991.

Roland Barthes, *Image-Music-Text*, translated by Stephen Heath, Glasgow: Fontana/Collins, 1977.

Roland Barthes, *The Pleasure of the Text*, translated by Richard Miller, London: Jonathan Cape, 1975.

Roland Barthes, *S/Z*, translated by Richard Miller, London: Blackwell, 1993.

Raymond Bellour, *The Analysis of Film*, edited by Constance Penley, Bloomington: Indiana University Press, 2000.

Catherine Belsey, *Critical Practice*, London: Methuen, 1980.

Walter Benjamin, *Illuminations*, translated by H. Zohn, London: Fontana/Collins, 1973.

Harry Benshoff and Sean Griffin (eds.), *Queer Cinema, the Film Reader*, London: Routledge, 2004.

Emile Benveniste, *Problems in General Linguistics*, translated by Mary Elizabeth Meek, Miama: University of Miami Press, 1971.

Janet Bergstrom (ed.), *Endless Night: cinema and psychoanalysis, parallel histories*, Berkeley: University of California Press, 1999.

Homi Bhabha, *The Location of Culture*, London: Routledge, 1994.

David Bordwell, *Narration in the Fiction Film*, London: Methuen, 1985.

David Bordwell, *Making Meaning: inference and rhetoric in the interpretation of cinema*, Cambridge, Massachusetts: Harvard University Press, 1989.

David Bordwell, Janet Staiger and Kristin Thompson, *The Classical Hollywood Cinema*, London: Routledge and Kegan Paul, 1985.

David Bordwell and Noel Carroll, *Post-Theory: reconstructing film studies*, Wisconsin: University of Wisconsin Press, 1996.

Edward Branigan, *Narrative Comprehension and Film*, London: Routledge, 1992.

Bertolt Brecht, *Brecht on Theatre*, edited and translated by John Willett, New York: Hill and Wang, 1964.

Peter Brunette and David Wills, *Screen/Play: Derrida and film theory*, Princeton NJ: Princeton University Press, 1989.

Stella Bruzzi: *Undressing Cinema: clothing and identity in the movies*, London: Routledge, 1997.

Paul Burston, *What Are You Looking At?: queer sex, style and cinema*, London: Cassell, 1995.

Alison Butler, *Women's Cinema: the contested screen*, London: Wallflower, 2002.

Judith Butler, *Gender Trouble: feminism and the subversion of identity*, London: Routledge, 1990.

Judith Butler, *Bodies That Matter*, London: Routledge, 1993.

Cahiers du Cinéma, Vol 1: the 1950s, edited by Jim Hillier, London: Routledge, 1996.

Cahiers du Cinéma, Vol 2: 1960-8, edited by Jim Hillier, Cambridge, Massachusetts: Harvard University Press, 1986.

Cahiers du Cinéma, Vol 3: 1969-72, edited by Nick Browne, London: Routledge in association with The British Film Institute, 1990.

Cahiers du Cinéma, Vol 4: 1973-8, edited by David Wilson, London: Routledge, 2000.

Camera Obscura, passim.

Ian Cameron (ed.), *Movie Reader*, London: November Books, 1972.

Noel Carroll, *Mystifying Movies: fads and fallacies in contemporary film theory*, New York: Columbia University Press, 1988.

Noel Carroll, *Philosophical Problems of Classical Film Theory*, Princeton NJ: Princeton University Press, 1988.

Noel Carroll, *Interpreting the Moving Image*, Cambridge: Cambridge University Press, 1998.

John Caughie (ed.), *Theories of Authorship*, London: Routledge and Kegan Paul, 1981.

Stanley Cavell, *Pursuits of Happiness*, Cambridge, MA: Harvard University Press, 1982.

Rey Chow, *Primitive Passions: visuality, sexuality, ethnography and contemporary Chinese cinema*, New York: Columbia University Press, 1995.

Carol Clover, *Men, Women and Chain Saws: gender in the modern horror film*, Princeton NJ: Princeton University Press, 1992.

Steven Cohan and Ina Rae Hark, *Screening the Male: exploring masculinities in Hollywood cinema*, London: Routledge, 1993.

Pam Cook (ed.), *The Cinema Book* (2nd edition), London: British Film
Institute, 1999.

Joan Copjec (ed.) *Shades of Noir: a reader*, London: Verso, 1993.

Rosalind Coward and John Ellis, *Language and Materialism*, London:
Routledge and Kegan Paul, 1977.

Elizabeth Cowie, *Representing the Woman: cinema and psychoanalysis*,
Basingstoke: Macmillan, 1997.

Barbara Creed, *The Monstrous Feminine: film, feminism, psychoanalysis*,
London: Routledge, 1993.

Gregory Currie, *Image and Mind: film, philosophy and cognitive science*,
Cambridge: Cambridge University Press, 1995.

Anthony Cutler, Barry Hindess, Paul Hirst and Athar Hussein, *Marx's
'Capital' and Capitalism Today*, I and II, London: Routledge and
Kegan Paul, 1977, 1978.

Gilles Deleuze, *Nietzsche and Philosophy*, translated by Hugh Tomlinson,
London: Athlone, 1983.

Gilles Deleuze, *Cinema 1: the movement-image*, translated by Hugh
Tomlinson, London: Athlone, 1986.

Gilles Deleuze, *Cinema 2: the time-image*, translated by Hugh Tomlinson
and Robert Galeta, London: Athlone, 1989.

Gilles Deleuze, *Negotiations*, translated by Martin Joughin, New York:
Columbia University Press, 1995.

Gilles Deleuze, *Essays Critical and Clinical*, translated by Daniel W. Smith
and Michael A. Greco, London: Verso, 1998.

Gilles Deleuze and Felix Guattari, *Anti-Oedipus: capitalism and schizophrenia*, Vol. 1, translated by Robert Hurley, Mark Seem and Helen R
Lane, London: Athlone, 1984.

Gilles Deleuze and Felix Guattari, *A Thousand Plateaus: capitalism and
schizophrenia*, translated by Brian Massumi, London: Athlone,
1988.

Gilles Deleuze and Felix Guattari, *What is Philosophy?* translated by Graham
Burchill and Hugh Tomlinson, London: Verso, 1994.

Jacques Derrida, *Of Grammatology*, translated by Gayatri Spivak, Baltimore:
Johns Hopkins University Press, 1976.

Jacques Derrida, *Writing and Difference*, translated by Alan Bass, London:
Routledge Kegan and Paul, 1978.

Jacques Derrida, *Margins of Philosophy*, translated by Alan Bass, Chicago:
University of Chicago Press, 1982.

Jacques Derrida, *Specters of Marx: the state of the debt, the work of mourning
and the new international*, translated by Peggy Kamuf, London:
Routledge, 1994.

Jacques Derrida, *Points: interviews 1974-94*, edited by Elisabeth Weber,
translated by Peggy Kamuf and others, Stanford, CA: Stanford
University Press, 1995.

Jacques Derrida, *Resistances of Psychoanalysis*, translated by Peggy Kamuf,

Pascale-Anne Brault and Michael Naas, Stanford, California: Stanford University Press, 1998.

Vincent Descombes, *Modern French Philosophy*, Cambridge: Cambridge University Press, 1980.

Manthia Diawara, *African Cinema*, London: Routledge, 1992.

Mary Ann Doane, *The Desire to Desire: the woman's film of the 1940s*, Bloomington: Indiana University Press, 1987.

Mary Ann Doane, *Femmes Fatales: feminism, film theory, psychoanalysis*, London: Routledge, 1991.

Mary Ann Doane, Patricia Mellencamp and Linda Williams, *Re-vision*, Los Angeles: American Film Institute, 1984.

James Donald, *Fantasy and the Cinema*, London: British Film Institute, 1989.

Richard Dyer, *Stars*, London: British Film Institute, 1979.

Richard Dyer, *Heavenly Bodies: film stars and society*, Basingstoke: Macmillan 1986.

Richard Dyer, *White*, London: Routledge, 1997.

Terry Eagleton, *Literary Theory*, Oxford: Basil Blackwell, 1983.

Antony Easthope, *What a Man's Gotta Do: the masculine myth in popular culture*, London: Paladin, 1986.

Antony Easthope, *British Post-Structuralism*, London: Routledge, 1988.

Antony Easthope, *Literary into Cultural Studies*, London: Routledge, 1991.

Antony Easthope, *Privileging Difference*, Basingstoke: Palgrave, 2002.

Umberto Eco, *A Theory of Semiotics*, London: Methuen, 1983.

John Ellis, *Visible Fictions*, London: Routledge and Kegan Paul, 1982.

Lucy Fischer, *Shot/Countershot: film tradition and women's cinema*, Princeton NJ: Princeton University Press, 1989.

Gregory Flaxman, *The Brain is the Screen*, Minneapolis: University of Minnesota Press, 2000.

Hal Foster (ed.), *The Anti-Aesthetic*, Washington: Bay Press, 1984.

Michel Foucault, *The Order of Things: an archaeology of the human sciences*, London: Tavistock Publications, 1970.

Michel Foucault, *Language, Counter-Memory, Practice*, New York: Cornell University Press, 1977.

Michel Foucault, *The History of Sexuality*, I, translated by Robert Hurley, London: Allen Lane, 1979.

Michel Foucault, *Power/Knowledge: selected interviews and other writings 1972-1977*, edited by Colin Gordon, Brighton: Harvester, 1980.

Michel Foucault, *Technologies of the Self: a seminar with Michel Foucault*, edited by Luther H Martin, Huck Gutman and Patrick H. Hutton, London: Tavistock, 1988.

Michel Foucault *Discipline and Punish: the birth of the prison*, translated by Alan Sheridan, London: Penguin, 1991.

Patrick Fuery, *New Developments in Film Theory*, Basingstoke: Macmillan, 2000.

Jane Gallop, *Feminism and Psychoanalysis*, London: Macmillan, 1982.

Christine Gledhill, *Home is Where the Heart Is: studies in melodrama and the woman's film*, London: British Film Institute, 1987.

Christine Gledhill, *Stardom: industry of desire*, London: Routledge, 1991.

Molly Haskell, *From Reverence to Rape: the treatment of women in the movies*, Chicago: University of Chicago Press, 1974.

Susan Hayward, *Cinema Studies: the key concepts*, London: Routledge, 2000.

Stephen Heath, *Questions of Cinema*, London: Macmillan, 1981.

Stephen Heath and Teresa de Lauretis (eds.), *The Cinematic Apparatus*, London: Macmillan, 1980.

Martin Heidegger, *Poetry, Language, Thought*, New York: Harper and Row, 1975.

John Hill and Pamela Church (eds.), *The Oxford Guide to Film Studies*, Oxford: Oxford University Press, 1998.

Jim Hillier, *The New Hollywood*, London: Studio Vista, 1993.

Barry Hindess and Paul Hirst, *Mode of Production and Social Formation*, London: Routledge and Kegan Paul, 1977.

Paul Hirst, *On Law and Ideology*, London: Macmillan, 1979.

Joanne Hollows and Mark Jancovich (eds.), *Approaches to Popular Film*, Manchester: Manchester University Press, 1995.

Chris Holmlund, *Impossible Bodies: femininity and masculinity at the movies*, London: Routledge, 2002.

bell hooks, *Yearning: race, gender and cultural politics*, Boston: South End Press, 1990.

bell hooks, *Reel to Real: race, sex and class at the movies*, London: Routledge, 1996.

Maggie Humm, *Feminism and Film*, Edinburgh: Edinburgh University Press, 1997.

Fredric Jameson, *Marxism and Form*, Princeton, NJ: Princeton Univerity Press, 1971.

Fredric Jameson, *The Political Unconscious*, London: Methuen, 1981.

Fredric Jameson, *Signatures of the Visible*, London: Routledge, 1990.

Fredric Jameson, *Postmodernism: the cultural logic of late capitalism*, London: Verso, 1991.

Fredric Jameson, *The Geopolitical Aesthetic: cinema and space in the world system*, London: British Film Institute, 1993.

Claire Johnston (ed.), *Notes on Women's Cinema*, London: Society for Education in Film and Television, 1973.

John J. Joughin and Simon Malpas (eds.), *The New Aestheticism*, Manchester: Manchester University Press, 2003.

E. Ann Kaplan, *Women in Film Noir*, London: British Film Instute, 1980.

E. Ann Kaplan, *Women and Film*, London: Methuen, 1983.

E. Ann Kaplan, *Looking for the Other*, London: Routledge, 1997.

E. Ann Kaplan (ed.), *Psychoanalysis and Cinema*, London: Routledge, 1990.

Barbara M. Kennedy, *Deleuze and Cinema: the aesthetics of sensation*, Edinburgh: Edinburgh University Press, 2000.

Julia Kristeva, *Desire in Language: a semiotic approach to literature and art*, translated by Thomas Gora, Alice Jardine and Leon S. Roudiez, Oxford: Basil Blackwell, 1980.

Julia Kristeva, *The Revolution in Poetic Language*, translated by Margaret Waller, New York: Columbia University Press, 1982.

Frank Krutnik, *In a Lonely Street: film noir, genre, masculinity*, London: Routledge, 1991.

Annette Kuhn (ed.), *Alien Zone: cultural theory and contemporary science fiction*, Cinema, London: Verso, 1990.

Annette Kuhn (ed.), *Alien Zone II: the spaces of science-fiction cinema*, London: Verso, 1999.

Jacques Lacan, *Ecrits*, translated by Alan Sheridan, London: Tavistock Publications, 1977.

Jacques Lacan, *The Four Fundamental Concepts of Psychoanalysis*, edited by Jacques-Alain Miller, translated by Alan Sheridan, London: Hogarth Press, 1977.

Jacques Lacan, *Feminine Sexuality*, edited by Juliet Mitchell and Jacqueline Rose, translated by Jacqueline Rose, London: Macmillan, 1982.

Jacques Lacan: *Encore: on feminine sexuality and the limits of love and knowledge, the seminar of Jacques Lacan: Book XX*, edited by Jacques-Alain Miller, translated with notes by Bruce Fink, London: W. W. Norton, 1998.

Teresa de Lauretis, *Alice Doesn't*, London: Macmillan, 1984.

Teresa de Lauretis, *Technologies of Gender: essays on theory, film and fiction*, Bloomington: Indiana University Press, 1987.

Vicky Lebeau, *Psychoanalysis and Cinema*, London: Wallflower, 2001.

Peter Lehman (ed.), *Masculinity: bodies, movies, culture*, London: Routledge, 2001.

Emmanuel Levinas, *Totality and Infinity*, translated by Alphonso Lingis, Pittsburgh: Duquesne University Press, 1969.

Emmanuel Levinas, *Otherwise than Being or Beyond Essence*, translated by Alphonso Lingis, The Hague: Nijhoff, 1981.

Emmanuel Levinas, *Time and the Other*, translated by Richard A. Cohen, Pittsburgh: Duquesne University Press, 1987.

Claude Lévi-Strauss, *Structural Anthropology*, translated by Claire Jacobson and Brookes Grundfest Schoepf, London: Allen Lane, 1968.

Claude Lévi-Strauss, *The Raw and the Cooked*, translated by John and Doreen Weightman, London: Jonathan Cape, 1970.

Terry Lovell, *Pictures of Reality*, London: British Film Institute, 1980.

Jean-Francois Lyotard, *The Postmodern Condition*, translated by Geoff Bennington and Brian Massumi, Manchester: Manchester University Press, 1984.

Jean-Francois Lyotard, *The Differend: phrases in dispute*, translated by Georges Van Den Abbeele, Minneapolis: University of Minnesota Press, 1988.

Jean-Francois Lyotard, *Heidegger and 'the jews'*, translated by Andreas Michel and Mark S. Roberts, Minneapolis: University of Minnesota Press, 1990.

Jean-Francois Lyotard, *The Inhuman: reflections on time*, translated by Geoffrey Bennington and Rachel Bowlby, Stanford, California: Stanford University Press, 1991.

Colin MacCabe, *James Joyce and the Revolution of the Word*, London: Macmillan, 1978.

Colin MacCabe, *Godard: images, sounds, politics*, London: Macmillan, 1980.

Colin MacCabe, *Theoretical Essays*, Manchester: Manchester University Press, 1985.

Colin MacCabe (ed.), *The Talking Cure*, London: Macmillan, 1981.

Janet McCabe, *Feminist Film Studies: writing the woman into cinema*, London: Wallflower, 2004.

Paul McDonald, *The Star System: Hollywood's production of popular identities*, London: Wallflower, 2000.

Simon Malpas (ed.), *Postmodern Debates*, Basingstoke: Palgrave, 2001.

Richard Maltby, *Hollywood Cinema: an introduction*, Oxford: Blackwell, 1995.

Laura U. Marks, *The Skin of the Film: intercultural cinema, embodiment and the senses*, Durham NC: Duke University Press, 2000.

Judith Mayne, *The Woman at the Keyhole: feminism and women's cinema*, Bloomington: Indiana University Press, 1990.

Judith Mayne, *Cinema and Spectatorship*, London: Routledge, 1993.

Christian Metz, *Film Language*, translated by Michael Taylor, New York: Oxford University Press, 1974.

Christian Metz, *Language and Cinema*, translated by Donna Jean Umiker-Seboek, The Hague: Mouton, 1974.

Christian Metz, *Psychoanalysis and Cinema*, translated by Celia Britton, London: Macmillan, 1983.

Toby Miller and Robert Stam, *A Companion to Film Theory*, Oxford: Blackwell, 1999.

Juliet Mitchell, *Psychoanalysis and Feminism*, London: Allen Lane, 1974.

Tania Modleski, *The Women Who Knew Too Much: Hitchcock and feminist theory*, London: Methuen, 1988.

David Morley, *Television, Audiences and Cultural Studies*, London: Routledge, 1992.

Laura Mulvey, *Visual and Other Pleasures*, Bloomington: Indiana University Press, 1989.

Laura Mulvey, *Fetishism and Curiosity*, London: British Film Institute, 1996.

Hamid Naficy, *An Accented Cinema: exilic and diasporic film-making*, Princeton NJ: Princeton University Press, 2001.

Steve Neale, *Genre*, London: British Film Institute, 1980.

Steve Neale, *Cinema and Technology: image, sound, colour*, London: British Film Institute, 1985.

Steve Neale and Murray Smith (eds.) *Contemporary Hollywood Cinema*, London: Routledge, 1998.

Bill Nichols (ed.), *Movies and Methods*, I and II, Berkeley: University of California Press, 1976, 1985.

Friedrich Nietzsche, *The Will to Power*, edited by Walter Kaufman, New York: Random House, 1967.

Constance Penley, *The Future of an Illusion: film, feminism and psychoanalysis*, London: Routledge, 1989.

Constance Penley (ed.), *Feminism and Film Theory*, London: British Film Institute, 1988.

Constance Penley and Sharon Willis (eds.), *Male Trouble*, Minneapolis: University of Minnesota Press, 1993.

Jim Pines and Paul Willemen (eds.), *Questions of Third Cinema*, London: British Film Institute, 1989.

Dana Polan, *Power and Paranoia*, New York: Columbia University Press, 1986.

Deirdre Pribram (ed.), *Female Spectators: looking at film and television*, London: Verso, 1988.

Vladimir Propp, *The Morphology of the Folktale*, Austin: University of Texas Press, 1973.

Robert B. Ray, *A Certain Tendency of the Hollywood Cinema 1930-80*, Princeton NJ: Princeton University Press, 1985.

D. N. Rodowick, *The Crisis of Political Modernism: criticism and ideology in contemporary film theory*, Berkeley: University of California Press, 1988.

D. N. Rodowick, *The Difficulty of Difference: psychoanalysis, sexual difference and film theory*, London: Routledge, 1991.

D. N. Rodowick, *Gilles Deleuze's Time Machine*, Durham NC: Duke University Press, 1997.

D. N. Rodowick, *Reading the Figural, or, Philosophy After the New Media*, Durham NC: Duke University Press, 2001.

Richard Rorty, *Philosophy and the Mirror of Nature*, Oxford: Basil Blackwell, 1980.

Richard Rorty, *Contingency, Irony, and Solidarity*, Cambridge: Cambridge University Press, 1989.

Richard Rorty, *Objectivity, Relativism, and Truth: philosophical papers*, I, II and III, Cambridge: Cambridge University Press 1991, 1998.

Jacqueline Rose, *Sexuality in the Field of Vision*, London: Verso, 1986.

Edward Said, *Orientalism*, London: Routledge, 1978.

Ferdinand de Saussure, *Course in General Linguistics*, Glasgow: Fontana/Collins, 1974.

Screen, passim.

Screen Reader, 1 and 2, London: Society for Education in Film and Television, 1977, 1981.

Steven Shaviro, *The Cinematic Body*, Minneapolis: University of Minnesota Press, 1993.

Ella Shohat and Roberta Stam, *Unthinking Eurocentrism: multiculturalism and the media*, London: Routledge, 1994.

Kaja Silverman, *The Subject of Semiotics*, New York: Oxford University Press, 1983.

Kaja Silverman, *The Acoustic Mirror: the female voice in psychoanalysis and cinema*, Bloomington: Indiana University Press, 1988.

Kaja Silverman, *Male Subjectivity at the Margins*, London: Routledge, 1992.

Anneke Smelik, *And the Mirror Cracked: feminist cinema and film theory*, Basingstoke: Palgrave, 2001.

Joseph H. Smith and William Kerrigan, *Images in our Souls: Cavell, psychoanalysis and cinema*, Baltimore: Johns Hopkins University Press, 1987.

Vivian Sobchak, *The Address of the Eye: a phenomenology of film experience*, Princeton NJ: Princeton University Press, 1992.

Jackie Stacey, *Star Gazing: Hollywood cinema and female spectatorship*, London: Routledge, 1994.

Janet Staiger, *Interpreting Films: studies in the historical reception of American cinema*, Princeton NJ: Princeton University Press, 1992.

Robert Stam, *Subversive Pleasures: Bakhtin, Cultural Criticism and Film*, Baltimore: Johns Hopkins University Press, 1989.

Robert Stam, *Film Theory: an introduction*, Oxford: Blackwell, 2000.

Robert Stam, Robert Burgoyne and Sandy Flitterman-Lewis, *New Vocabularies in Film Semiotics: structuralism, post-structuralism and beyond*, London: Routledge, 1992.

Robert Stam and Toby Miller (eds.), *Film and Theory: an anthology*, Oxford: Blackwell, 2000.

Melvyn Stokes and Richard Maltby (eds.), *Hollywood Spectatorship: changing perceptions of cinema audiences*, London: The British Film Institute, 2001.

Gaylyn Studlar, *In the Realm of Pleasure: Von Sternberg, Dietrich and the masochistic aesthetic*, Urbana: University of Illinois Press, 1988.

Kristin Thompson, *Breaking the Glass Armor: neoformalist film analysis*, Princeton NJ: Princeton University Press, 1988.

Sue Thornham (ed.), *Feminist Film Theory*, New York: New York University Press, 1999.

Graeme Turner, *British Cultural Studies: an introduction*, London: Unwin Hyam, 1990.

Graeme Turner, *Film as Social Practice*, London: Routledge, 1993.

Ginette Vincendeau, *Stars and Stardom in French Cinema*, London: Continuum, 2000.

Martin Walsh, *The Brechtian Aspect of Radical Cinema*, London: British Film Institute, 1981.

Claire Whatling, *Screen Dreams: fantasising lesbians in film*, Manchester: Manchester University Press, 1997.

Paul Willemen, *Looks and Frictions*, London: British Film Institute, 1994.

Christopher Williams (ed.), Realism and the Cinema, London: Routledge and Kegan Paul, 1980.

Ludwig Wittgenstein, Philosophical Investigations, Oxford: Basil Blackwell, 1972.

Peter Wollen, Signs and Meaning in the Cinema, London: Secker and Warburg, 1972.

Peter Wollen, Readings and Writings, London: Verso, 1982.

Robin Wood, Hitchcock's Films Revisited, New York: Columbia University Press, 1989.

Lola Young, Fear of the Dark: 'race', gender and sexuality in the cinema, London: Routledge, 1996.

Robert Young (ed.), Untying the Text, London: Routledge and Kegan Paul, 1981.

Slavoj Žižek, The Sublime Object of Ideology, London: Verso, 1989.

Slavoj Žižek, Enjoy Your Symptom!: Jacques Lacan in Hollywood and outside, London: Routledge, 1992.

Slavoj Žižek (ed.), Everything You Always Wanted to Know About Lacan But Were Afraid to Ask Hitchcock, London: Verso, 1992.

Slavoj Žižek, Looking Awry, Cambridge MA: The MIT Press, 1993.

Slavoj Žižek, The Ticklish Subject: the absent centre of political ontology, London: Verso, 1999.

Slavoj Žižek, The Fright of Real Tears: Krzysztof Kieslowski between theory and post-theory, London: British Film Institute 2001.

Index